D1070727

The Public Stake in Union Power

Edited by Philip D. Bradley

Edward H. Chamberlin
Frank H. Knight
F. A. Hayek
Gottfried Haberler
James W. McKie
David McCord Wright
Albert Rees
Philip D. Bradley
H. Gregg Lewis
Gary S. Becker
William Fellner
John R. Meyer
G. Warren Nutter
J. M. Clark
P. T. Bauer
Armen A. Alchian

UNIVERSITY OF VIRGINIA PRESS

Charlottesville : 1959

Library of Congress Catalog Card No. 59-11490

Preface

THROUGHOUT THE HISTORY of any country a series of major economic problems passes continuously across the political stage. In the case of the United States the disposal of public lands, tariffs, improper and unfair business practices, the reform of the financial system—to name but a few—has each at some time been the focus of public attention. In all these situations the public has had an important stake. Currently the power of trade unions is a subject of controversy, and in this instance, too, the public has a stake.

In matters of such scope and complexity there is great temptation to rely on the specialist. As regards these problems, which are commonly termed "practical," a predisposition exists to assume that they should be dealt with only by persons deemed expert by those who have a direct knowledge of and an immediate interest in the subject.

This has been the approach employed in a variety of organizations, including numerous university economics departments and business schools, in approaching the issues inherent in the powers of unions. Reliance has been placed either on persons versed in the skills of labor arbitration or on persons who follow the adaptive approach and emphasize psychological and other techniques that are helpful when adjusting to difficult situations. Both points of view have a useful place in an imperfect world. Yet it is observable that most academic experts in this field have largely ignored two of the major public issues in the contemporary scene: the consequences of union monopoly power; and corruption, with its twin "thug unionism."

Similarly, in the history of broad national economic issues it is observable that specialists in one or another individual aspect of a problem have not always been able to provide solutions. Significant as have been the opinions of experts who had direct business involvement in particular situations, their composite view has not always been synonymous with the public interest, nor has it necessarily provided a sound basis for public policy.

By contrast, the generalist, the man who cuts across established modes of thought, who has some comprehension of society in all its dimensions, has been peculiarly well qualified to point to the moral and other principles on which the issues must ultimately be determined. And this has necessarily been the case. For only the generalist's breadth of view has sufficient scope to accommodate the many facets that are always inherent in problems affected with a great public interest. "War is too serious a business to be left to the soldiers," as Talleyrand is alleged to have said and Briand to have repeated.

The humanistic view that looks at society in the round is the counterpoise to the compromise that emerges when vested business interests sit down with vested labor interests—to the outcome Adam Smith foresaw when he wrote, "People of the same trade seldom meet together, even for merriment and diversion, but the conversation ends in a conspiracy against the public, or in some contrivance to raise prices." Objective and dispassionate scholarship is, or can be, the counterpart to practical know-how. Pure research, if not the parent, is at least the partner of applied research—and there has been little of either in the field of union power.

By bringing together in this volume the wide-ranging views of distinguished economists who collectively may best be described as theorists, or generalists, Philip Bradley has initiated a new approach to assessing the consequences of union power. Indirectly if not directly he has indicated that the issues inherent in the problem of a state-within-a-state extend very far and are not the exclusive province of the technician or the special pleader. And in doing these things he has done a signal public service.

For these reasons I am particularly happy that this volume has been developed under the auspices of the Graduate School of Business Administration of the University of Virginia.

Charles C. Abbott, *Dean*
Graduate School of Business Administration

Charlottesville

Introduction

WHEN CHARLES C. ABBOTT asked me to give a course in labor relations I agreed to do so, subject to one condition. The condition grew out of the fact that my home in the Washington area lies some 120 miles distant from the University of Virginia classrooms in Charlottesville. Neither love of teaching, which could have been satisfied in my own neighborhood, nor the financial remuneration which universities offer, would have compensated for making a weekly trip of that length. My counter proposal to the Dean was designed to extract the kind of compensation that would induce me to undertake commuting on the Charlottesville scale.

Labor experts have often said that the individual employee is utterly helpless in bargaining with the corporate employer on wages and working conditions. The agreement reached with Mr. Abbott suggests that this is not always the case. Our agreement provided for the participation of additional lecturers in the course. Each Monday during the spring term a different lecturer was to take over the class. Each Tuesday the session was to be mine. Given the quality of those invited to participate, this arrangement made it possible for me as the moderator on Mondays to take far more out of the course than I put into it as lecturer on Tuesdays.

Invitations to guest lecturers did not specify the topic each participant was to develop. Rather, we indicated the range of subject matter in which we were interested and then left it to each participant to choose a topic within the indicated range. The field, as it developed, extended from wage theory, at one extreme, through collective bargaining practices and institutions to the extra economic aspects of the labor field at the other extreme.

The effect of this arrangement was to assign considerably more importance to the role of the lecturer than to the detailed coverage of every topic within the range of subject matter. The possibility that two or more lecturers would provide identical or almost identical analyses of the same topic caused little concern. Nor did the possibility that conflicting analyses would be made of a given topic justify abandonment of the approach described. Realization of the first possibility would constitute an interesting note on the development of economics as a science, while the occurrence of the second would tend to confirm the suspicion that economists do not always agree. In any case these unimportant risks were preferred to the certainty that insistence upon complete coverage of subject matter would produce more than one uninspired performance. Stimulation of the student and the opening up of vistas in the field were the primary objectives.

Thanks are owed to the faculty members in other universities who responded to our request for the names of scholars who excel in economic analysis. Their suggestions were numerous. Our principal regret is that the fifteen lecture dates were too few to accommodate all those nominated. In issuing invitations we did our best to see that all age groups would be represented.

Having organized the course in this way, if indeed the word "organization" can be used when individual choice is allowed so large a part, we looked forward with considerable curiosity to see how the several parts would fit together. To a remarkable degree order did emerge among the uncoordinated lectures. Thirteen of the fifteen lectures developed one aspect or another of a common theme—the theme caught, it is hoped, by the title of the present volume.

The division of this volume into two parts was suggested by a number of people who read the original manuscript. They thought that the general reader would be helped if the chapters employing techniques of analysis not generally familiar were placed in a separate section. In accordance with this suggestion the more technical chapters have been placed in Part II. The two concluding chapters constitute exceptions to the rule followed in making this division. Mr. Alchian does not write about union power, while Mr. Bauer does not write about union power in the United States. Here subject matter, not technical complexity, governed the location of the chapters.

The weekly visits to the University at Charlottesville during the spring term of 1958 provided me with pleasure and satisfaction. Gratitude is felt to those who had the vision and resourcefulness to create the splendid way of life which is the University of Virginia today, and to the freedom and the responsibility which it places on the individual, whether student or faculty member. My feeling of appreciation to the many individuals who offered assistance and friendship cannot be reduced to a few words. My principal debt is owed to Mr. Abbott. Anyone who has taught in his school learns that the justification of administration is the opportunity it affords for developing the potentialities of individual men and thus, in an academic institution, the contribution it can make to the advancement of scholarship and of learning. To the faculty of the Graduate School of Business Administration I want to express my feeling of indebtedness for their unfailing kindness and helpfulness.

Much of whatever success the course in labor relations enjoyed is due to the several members of the Department of Economics who participated in the discussion periods which followed the lectures. In this connection I want to express appreciation to James M. Buchanan, H. Warren Nutter and to Frank H. Knight, who was a visiting lecturer in the Department during the spring term. Without their help and the help of other members of the economics faculty the course would have lost much of its flavor. In the complete cooperation he offered throughout the term the chairman of the department, Mr. Buchanan, surely established a new, high standard by which to judge the relationships between departments of economics and schools of business in American universities. To acknowledge my indebtedness to him is a very real pleasure.

To the students in the Graduate Business School I want to say again how very much I enjoyed our weekly meetings and to wish them success in their chosen careers.

For an expert and detailed commentary on Chapter 8 the author owes a very substantial debt to Harold C. Passer. From this it should not be inferred that the views expressed therein are necessarily shared by Mr. Passer.

For the assistance he provided in preparing this volume for publication I am greatly indebted to J. D. Forbes. Thanks are also owed to

Charles E. Moran, Director of the University of Virginia Press, for the highly efficient way in which he expedited the publication process. Appreciation is also expressed to Miss Ruth Crandall, Miss Althea MacDonald and Sam Shelsky for the assistance they provided.

PHILIP D. BRADLEY

Charlottesville
June 20, 1958

Table of Contents

PART II

Part I

1

Labor Union Power and the Public Interest

Edward H. Chamberlin

I START from the proposition that labor unions do have monopoly power. Of course, some have more than others, and no doubt some have very little. In this and in other ways labor monopoly power is no different from monopoly power anywhere else in the economy. Although economists may vary in their estimate of how considerable and of how threatening on the whole this power is, I believe there would be wide agreement as to its existence.

The term monopoly has normally been associated with business and the profit income, not with labor and the wage income. Laborers are numerous, and the individual laborer a tiny part of the aggregate. Even under organization, this part of the economy appears *superficially* to be so highly "atomized" compared with big industrial enterprises as to be by its very nature competitive.

Indeed, it is this very helplessness of the individual laborer which has given rise since the Industrial Revolution to one movement after another—political, philosophical, social and economic—aiming to strengthen his position in the social system. Socialism and Communism, in their many varieties, are of course leading examples of such movements, with the objectives of either overturning the system by revolutionary means or leading it through peaceful and gradual evolution to some kind of social and economic "democracy" in which "social justice" would prevail.

As is well known, the labor movement in Continental Europe has been, with variations in different countries, strongly socialist (or Communist) in its underlying philosophy. In Europe the idea of class was natural—and still is—for historical reasons, and the Marxian analysis of a class struggle had real meaning. (Parenthetically, we have here a clue to the greater appeal of Marxism as compared to the classical and neo-classical economics and even Keynesian economics in Far Eastern countries today.[1]) The Russian tyranny has contributed to some disillusionment in recent years, and there can be no doubt that the European labor movement has been shaken by it.

Perhaps even more important than Russia is the fact that with the general triumph of the welfare state in the form of highly progressive taxation and comprehensive social legislation, and with the decline in popularity of state ownership as a panacea, most of the historical objectives of the socialist-labor movement (putting aside the revolutionary objectives of Communism) seem now to have been won. With this in mind, together with numerous other factors, among them the considerable adverse effects on the public welfare of the restrictive practices of unionism and the contribution which it makes to the forces of inflation, Peter Wiles, fellow of New College, Oxford, wrote a challenging article in the British magazine *Encounter*[2] entitled "Are Trade Unions Necessary?" "The social conscience," he says, "has claims upon one's purse and one's emotions, not upon one's reason." Since I have myself written on the anachronistic intellectual heritage which impairs our thinking about unionism today, perhaps I may be pardoned for savoring especially Mr. Wiles' objection to what he calls the paying of "intellectual ransom" to trade unionism. It does seem to me that the time has come to take a fresh look at the economics of labor unions and to try to do it in a truly intellectual spirit. As intellectuals let us hew to the line, and let us agree with Mr. Wiles at least in this: no intellectual ransom to outmoded clichés.

Unionism in America has also been a "movement" in some sense historically, or perhaps it should be said that it has been a number of

[1] See E. Stuart Kirby, "The Reception of Western Economics in the Orient," *Quarterly Journal of Economics,* Vol. LXVI, No. 3 (Aug., 1952), p. 409.

[2] *Encounter,* Vol. VII, No. 3 (Sept., 1956).

movements. A recent book by Mark Perlman, *Labor Union Theories in America,*[3] considers historically five facets of unionism: unionism as (1) a moral institution, (2) a revolutionary institution, (3) a psychological reaction, (4) a welfare institution, and (5) a social institution—a "part of the democratic process." It is significant that the book deals almost entirely with the period prior to 1933, at which time union membership was only about three million, and that in his closing brief reflections on "The Great Depression and Thereafter" the author finds the first three "institutions" of little relevance. "The American heritage emphasizes social opportunity and material advancement," he says. On the one hand, "the backbone of the trade-union movement" over the years consists of those unionists who are concerned with job security—the *right* to the job, jurisdiction and seniority. On the other, "the bulk of union membership . . . after fifteen years of unrivaled prosperity . . . may have forgotten the historical mission of elevating workers to the rights of full industrial citizenship. Instead, they are concerned with material plenty in the here and now." (P. 240.) No doubt the contrast between early and more recent unionism can be overdrawn; early unions were not indifferent to material aims, nor are contemporary unions to problems of industrial citizenship. But there can be no doubt that for a number of reasons—among them mere success and growth of power—the spirit of unionism today has undergone some striking changes.

To return to the contrast with Europe, unionism was never a "class" movement in this country to the degree that it was over there, and the revolutionary and socialist phases never achieved the same importance. With a continent to be occupied and developed, one may say without romanticizing that the idea of class, though not absent, has never played the same part here, that mobility both social and geographic has been vastly greater, and that in the development of the West there were always opportunities for the ambitious so that the ideal of a high accessibility of opportunity has remained a part of the American "way of life" long after the frontier was gone and right down to the present day. This abundance of resources and of opportunities has played a major role in the success of "capitalism" in the

[3] *Labor Union Theories in America* (Evanston, 1957).

United States—so much so that the word itself has a very different meaning to the average European worker from what it has to the American worker (and clearly it has a totally different meaning in the under-developed areas of the Far East). Samuel Gompers made the obvious decision in turning his back on radical unionism and holding for the pragmatic principle that in this country unions should accept capitalism and seek at the bargaining table to improve their own wages and working conditions within it. It was the obvious decision because radical unionism clearly had no future here. It laid the basis for what has now come to be described as "business unionism": unionism as efficiently preoccupied with selfish economic gain as any business enterprise is commonly supposed to be. Indeed there seems to be abundant evidence now that a new generation of labor leaders has at last become fully aware of the tremendous economic power which is actually in their hands, and are prepared to exploit it as never before. Only an old-timer, Richard Gray, President of the Building Trades Department of the American Federation of Labor, could have the statesmanship to recognize that labor has done very well in recent years and to propose that wage increases now be foregone for a year as a contribution to tiding over the present recession. Of course, he was promptly howled down. Evidently such a position could hardly be popular either with dues-paying members who expect to get value for money or with ambitious labor leaders who expect to deliver the value and to advance to positions of still greater power by showing that they can.

I believe that many who sympathize by tradition with the labor "cause," including many professional economists, are profoundly disturbed by the fact that it has ceased to be a cause in any meaningful sense. Indeed, as Mr. Wiles has pointed out, even in a revolutionary union there may be a certain idealism which one can admire as such, even though not agreeing with it. But I must confess that, although I do not hold with him for the abolition of unions, I see nothing in particular to admire (either in the labor field or elsewhere) about the full-blown power process of income maximization *per se*. Dave Beck has said, "I am a business man. I sell labor," (and he seems to have deducted some commissions in the process). The extent to which

American trade unions have ceased to represent a social movement and have actually become businesses, complete with holding companies at the top, is only beginning to be realized by the general public. In conducting the affairs of these businesses, the typical union member is as indifferent (and as powerless) as the typical stockholder in a large corporation. He merely contributes an automatic monthly deduction from his pay check as a service fee for the annual package increase. Although Mr. Gompers may well have regarded strong unions as the counterparts of the trusts of his day, it is to be doubted if he ever imagined their operating within the context of power which has actually developed.

What is this context of power? Here I must be brief because a good deal has been said on labor monopoly by others, and I have myself written about it in some detail elsewhere.

What might be called a traditional view has been that labor unions have the power to gain only or mainly at the expense of other laborers. A union with monopoly power—so the argument runs—gains by restricting its numbers in any of several ways, by high initiation fees, apprenticeship limitations, etc., and by setting levels of wages such that all those who seek employment in the area controlled by the union cannot find it. As a result, workers who are excluded must find employment elsewhere, so that labor supply in other areas is greater and wages there consequently somewhat lower. On this ground, a number of critics of unions have made their case in terms of labor's own interest. Unions are bad because they are bad *for labor.* I think it would be hard to convince most laborers of this. And it is hard to convince me.

Consider the same argument as it might be applied to the field of industrial monopoly. Monopoly profits are bad, it would be said, because by restricting output in a monopolized industry, entrepreneurial activity in that industry is reduced; entrepreneurs are thus diverted to other industries and profits elsewhere will be lower. Industrial monopoly is therefore bad because it is bad for business men themselves. What some gain in the monopolized areas is at the expense of others in the more competitive areas. This doesn't sound right, and indeed it isn't right. Although there is probably some element of truth in the line of argument in *both* cases, it is "wrong" mainly because it is not important, and because it turns attention away from another line of reasoning which is the more fundamental one. It is wrong because it is confined to describing what happens in the factor market (labor or entrepreneurship), and does not carry through to include what is much more important: what happens in the product market.[4]

Why is industrial monopoly, by general agreement, against the social interest? And why have we in this country been particularly active in trying to control it? Because it creates a maldistribution of resources, is a common answer. This is a sophisticated argument, which incidentally applies equally to labor monopoly. A monopoly of building materials raises the cost of building and so discourages the construction industry. So does a monopoly of the International Brotherhood of Teamsters hauling building materials in the construction industry. No difference. Either one maldistributes resources as between the construction and other industries.

But I believe the chief source of objection to industrial monopoly is in the matter of incomes—in its exploitation of the public through charging what are generally regarded as unduly high prices and deriving therefrom an excessive income. People do not like to be held up. In more technical terms, the business monopolist by raising his price produces less and yet increases his aggregate income. This means that the social dividend is smaller, and that with his own in-

[4] Incidentally, the argument in the labor field loses much of its importance, and may indeed even be reversed by reason of union policies with respect to the amount of work done. These embrace a whole spectrum of working rules which have the effect of controlling in a variety of ways the amount of work done per laborer. Evidently, if less is done, more laborers are required to do any given job. As a very simple example, consider the demand for a shorter work week—at the same weekly pay, of course. This means a higher rate per hour, and so in the end would have the effect of reducing the number of *hours* which the employer would wish to buy. But if such reduction of hours of work purchased is 10 per cent and if the new work week is 36 hours instead of 40, the employer will require exactly the same number of *laborers* as before. If because of the higher hourly rate he purchased only 5 per cent fewer hours, he would require even more laborers than before. The whole question of such non-wage elements in the labor bargain is a very important one, of course. The incidence on costs of restrictive practices in the field of working rules is probably greater than that of money wages, and the public stake in them is correspondingly great. But public awareness of its interest in this phase of the problem seems to me to be almost exactly zero.

creased money income he is able to buy a larger portion of it. The net effect on others is adverse in both respects: they get a smaller portion of a smaller total.

Let us turn this argument around and try it on the labor field. The New York multi-million-dollar construction industry has been at a standstill for several weeks from a strike of 3500 truck drivers. A portion of these, the sand and gravel drivers, have settled (in the midst of a recession, and in a labor market where supply exceeds demand by over five million according to the latest figures) for (roughly) a 12 per cent increase (over two years) plus fringe benefits, bringing their wage rate to well over three dollars an hour (or about $25 a day), and the others are holding out for the same increase. I can see no reason why they will not get it, for by bringing the entire industry to a virtual standstill they have demonstrated their power to inflict untold damage as the alternative, and there is no reason why they cannot go on almost indefinitely. Their ability to obtain such an increase, and in the face of substantial unemployment, is evidently based on a position of power. And it is far greater in this case than that of the industrial monopolist. But more of this later. The point here is that the cost and hence the price of construction is correspondingly raised so that less construction will be done, and that the income of the truck drivers is increased. On the one hand, the social dividend is smaller, and on the other, the drivers with their increased money incomes are able to buy a larger portion of it.

It is of prime importance to note that this argument, unlike the earlier one, is not confined to the labor market, thus representing the gains of union labor as being at the expense of other *laborers*. On the contrary, it recognizes that the gains of labor monopoly are, *like the gains of any other monopoly*, at the expense of *all* other elements of society, in other words, of the general public. This is so because the higher prices resulting from higher labor costs are paid by consumers generally. And they are paid by those of all income groups, including the lowest. The real incomes of all are diminished for the benefit of a particular group of laborers. The principle involved is extremely simple. There is no mystery about it, and labor monopoly is in this respect no different from any other monopoly.

This proposition is, however, the last thing which organized labor will want to admit, since unions depend heavily on public favor, and must persuade the general public that labor interest and public interest are simply two different names for the same thing. So it is that Walter Reuther even invites the public in, like one of the neighbors, to have a cut in the hypothetical raid which he will engineer on automobile profits. This is economic warfare, of course, and nobody can blame Mr. Reuther for sending up a smoke screen of this sort if he thinks it will help him. But I am afraid that, no matter what judgment one may pass on profits in the automobile industry, higher labor costs will in the end be added to the price of automobiles. We ought to look through the smoke screen if we can.

In sum, the objection from a public point of view to labor monopoly is no whit different from the familiar objection to industrial monopoly. Certainly the public does not enjoy being held up by truck drivers any more than it does by, say, the railroads. But the difference is that it is more aware of railway rates and hence has developed over many years a machinery for controlling them in the public interest, whereas in the wage field it appears hardly to be aware at all of what happens. Indeed, it is not too much to say that there is a widespread positive aversion to finding out and to recognizing the full extent and significance of labor monopoly power, since this would do violence to one of the most cherished of popular beliefs, viz., that the labor cause is unqualifiedly "good."

There are many reasons why the public is virtually immune to an awareness of labor monopoly, some of them connected with points made earlier in this paper, for instance, the heavy tradition that wages are by their very nature highly competitive, that labor is the "underdog," etc. But one very fundamental reason is that the wage bill is paid *immediately* by an employer and only finally and indirectly by the public through the mechanism of the cost structure on which prices are based. Although the main principles involved in the law of cost do not seem very difficult to anyone trained in economics, they are nevertheless sufficiently remote to be difficult for the average citizen. And nothing is easier than for him to sympathize with the laborers who get the higher wages, since this objective seems desirable *per se* and is directly translatable into his own economic world: he would like to have higher wages himself. A banal plea for economic education is evidently in order. But let me restrict myself to a plea for a revived emphasis in economic theory and in the elementary course on economic *structure,* on micro-economics if you will, as against the aggregative and the "macro." No doubt both are important, but it does seem to me that a major consequence of the Keynesian onslaught has been to put a very bad squeeze on the study of what used to be called the theory of value.

An important difference, then, between monopoly power in the hands of labor and in the hands of business is that the former is more easily covered up—buried in the cost structure and forgotten. It does not take much imagination to realize that this is one of the chief sources of its strength: those who might otherwise oppose it are less aware of it.

There are in addition other sources of strength beyond those attributable to mere collective action *per se.* I have dealt elsewhere with some of them under the headings of "accretions of power" and will only summarize them here in passing. The main point is that they are peculiar to the labor market. They include: (1) violence and intimidation, both actual and potential, (2) picketing as a phase of intimidation and also as a means of putting pressure on, or entering into collusion with, other unions, (3) boycotts, both secondary and primary, (4) compulsory unionism, and (5), perhaps the most important of all, the "right," or at least the *de facto power,* in the case of a strike, to deny to an employer access to alternative bargains.

All of these are major factors in the market power of labor unions, and that is the point for the present. Some of them will be discussed later on in connection with the question of remedies.

Before passing on to questions of public policy, it is necessary to say something about inflation as it relates to the wage problem. I know that this subject has been discussed by others in this joint study, yet it would be artificial and misleading to omit it from this chapter. It is inseparably a part of the general problem of labor union power and, indeed, a part of the machinery through which a strong union makes its gains. I have commented earlier on the strength of the tradition in economic thinking that the wage area is one of competition so that the idea of monopoly is associated only with profits. It follows almost by definition from this way of thinking that unions could have no effect on the *general level* of wages and so on the general level of prices. Whatever influence they may have will, according to this view, be on *relative* wages only, and the whole question of the *general* level of wages and prices—in short, of inflation—falls automatically into another compartment, that of monetary and fiscal policy. Wage-push inflation is in this sense a relatively new idea. But the observed fact that unions *can* push up money wages and so prices, over substantial areas of the economy, is rapidly making it respectable. It is, after all, a simple and rather obvious consequence of the recognition of labor union power.

It should be perfectly clear that an upward *push* to prices administered by rising costs does not exclude the fact that prices may also be *pulled* up by increased monetary demand or by increased spending induced by fiscal policy. This is not an either-or proposition. In particular circumstances, it may be mainly one or mainly the other, but in general we have merely to recognize that prices may be either pushed or pulled or both, and that the proposition that they may be pushed is a thoroughly legitimate one from a theoretical point of view.[5] After all, there is nothing novel in the principle that in the long run price must cover cost of production.

An unconscious force working strongly against recognition of the role of labor power in inflation must be that it is not exerted on the whole economy at once but works its way through it piecemeal. In this it is, of course, quite unlike monetary and fiscal policy, the impact of which is (in either case) much more general. But pattern wage setting is increasingly prevalent, and the phenomenon of successive rounds of wage adjustments is a familiar one. Clearly, the social significance of negotiations in the steel industry, for instance, is not merely that of a wage adjustment for steel workers, but of a much more general movement for which their gains will help to set the

[5] For an excellent discussion of the interrelationships between union power and inflation, see James R. Schlesinger, "The Role of the Monetary Environment in Cost-Inflation," *Southern Economic Journal,* Vol. XXIV, No. 1 (July, 1957), and "Market Structure, Union Power and Inflation," *ibid.,* Vol. XXIV, No. 3 (Jan., 1958).

pattern. Even without this phenomenon of pattern increases, the summation of many individual gains by particular unions would add up to a general price increase. But pattern setting quickens the process, makes it more automatic, and enhances greatly the prestige of the particular labor leader who can set the pace.

Higher wages and prices over a substantial segment of the economy within which a round of wage increases takes place will spread their influence more or less and in a variety of ways into the whole price and income structure. But the process is uneven, for the economic system is strung together in a loose way with many backwashes; many incomes will fall far behind and some may never move at all. At this latter extreme are contractual incomes including those of life insurance beneficiaries, pensioners, etc. It is the moment to recall the famous Keynesian quip that "in the long run we are all dead"; some stay behind permanently. It is a familiar phenomenon in inflation that prices and incomes move unevenly so that some gain and others lose. A peculiarity of wage-push inflation is that those who gain most are those who are able to push the hardest. At the other extreme are those who cannot push at all and therefore whose real incomes fall because of price increases elsewhere. It cannot be urged too strongly that this process of uneven price and income movements is of the very essence of the mechanics whereby those unions which are in a strong power position increase their real incomes. It is, in fact, merely a more general application of the earlier reasoning in which it was argued that the gains of labor monopoly are at the expense of the rest of the economic system and in this respect are no different from the gains of business, or any other, monopoly.

In one other very important respect, however, they are different. And the difference is contained in Mr. Gompers' famous reduction of the aims of the trade union movement in "capitalist" America to the single word "more." In other words, the objective is a dynamic one and not to be contained merely within the static concept of income maximization. It is certainly easy enough for any economist familiar with the basic notion of a static state to conceive of such a state in which monopoly power existed very generally in particular markets, where each monopolist had found his position of maximum profit, and where all such positions had been incorporated into the endless and unchanging "circular flow," to use J. A. Schumpeter's expression. But the same could not be said for labor monopoly. Laborers who went on year after year receiving the same wages, however good, would soon be aware that they were getting them without any intervention on the union's part. Either they would cease paying dues and the system would disintegrate, or they would elect a new set of officers who would get on the job. This is simply calling attention to one of the most familiar phenomena of the labor market, attested to both by history and by general analysis, that the service performed by a union is a dynamic one, and when it is not performed, members lose interest. This being the case, a further development is the competition which naturally arises between union leaders under pressure from the rank and file as to which one can deliver the most. All this is natural enough. The point here is that such constant upward pressure is *peculiar* to the wage-push type of inflation, and must be recognized as one of its major elements.

The foregoing description is general and without reference to a special factor in recent years, the virtual institutionalization of the annual wage increase, often incorporated into contracts extending over several years. It would be a serious mistake to associate this institution with increases in the productivity of the economy. If this were the principle, increases would be gauged with some precision to productivity, and when this latter stopped increasing or declined, wages would be adjusted accordingly. What we find is that when productivity does not increase, the ground shifts instead to something else, as to a revival of another (and seriously discredited) principle—ability to pay—a principle, incidentally, which is naturally never mentioned for industries which are in the red, such as metropolitan transport for instance. At the same time so-called escalator clauses are yielding other increases according to still another principle, viz., the rising cost of living. It would surely be little short of fantastic to maintain that there is any principle whatever behind the steady upward pressure except simple opportunism. Mr. Gompers really said it all in the one word "more." It is a matter of using such power as there is to make whatever gains can be had. Anything else is, in Mr.

Reuther's own words, purely a matter of public relations. It is important to realize this, for it would indicate that the remedy is not to be found in terms of a principle, but very simply in terms of reducing the power.

Since so-called "labor productivity" is so much talked about, however, I should like to comment on it parenthetically. Actually, it is the productivity, not of labor, but of the whole economy, with the adjective labor attached to it. Its statistical measure is national income (corrected for price level) divided by man-hours of labor. If the same figure were divided instead by management hours, it would become management productivity. Divided by an appropriate measurement of investment it would become capital productivity, by acres of land, land productivity. Divided by miles of highway it would become highway productivity, and so forth. For any particular increase in national income it would be extremely interesting and important *really* to know just who it was whose increased efficiency was responsible for it. But the common phrase which gives the credit to labor is simply a sly bit of Marxism, as if *only* labor were productive. It is evidently quite possible for the efficiency of any agent of production, say labor, actually to decline while the productivity of the economy as a whole (and hence so-called "labor productivity") increases, and so on.

Turning finally to the question of what might be done, let me first comment briefly on a number of familiar ideas before adding a very simple one of my own.

In dealing with a monopoly problem in one field, it is only natural to think of methods which have been tried with respect to monopoly in others. Two leading examples are the attempt to "preserve competition," as by the anti-trust laws in industry, and the acceptance of monopoly with direct government regulation, as with public utilities.

Since the latter is not seriously proposed in the wage field, it may be disposed of very easily. It may be acceptable and even necessary in time of war. As a peace-time proposal, Fritz Machlup has written, "I shudder at the mere suggestion," [6] and I add my shudder to his.

[6] Fritz Machlup, *Monopolistic Wage Determination as a Part of the General Problem of Monopoly* (Washington, 1947), p. 29.

The political element is heavily in the picture as things stand. The problem is to reduce it, not to open the flood gates. It seems not too much to say that government wage-setting on any comprehensive scale could be the end of a free enterprise system.

Labor unions are, as we know, specifically exempted from the anti-trust laws, and so the proposal is natural enough merely to remove the exemption. This would clearly be desirable in a number of situations in which unions do with impunity in the product market what business men may not do, and in others where unions become virtually agents in mutually beneficial deals with business men whereby the law is circumvented. But it is not clear to me how the courts would apply the law in the crucial areas of collective bargaining, strikes, boycotts, and picketing, for instance. The anti-trust laws as they stand are not directed to these matters, and sooner or later a set of principles appropriate to them must be evolved. It would seem to me that it is specific legislation designed for the labor area that is needed, and that only the greatest confusion could result from merely asking the courts to apply the anti-trust laws as they stand to labor unions.

The proposal to abolish industry-wide bargaining is closely related to the conception of applying anti-trust laws (and ideas) to the labor field. I think it would be no more than a misleading gesture if it were confined to *mere* bargaining, and if unions themselves were not also reduced to the scale of the individual enterprise with collusion between them successfully prevented. This latter especially would be a large order.

It is often to the advantage of a large union to concentrate its power and bargain with a single firm in an industry, thereby gaining a leverage which can be turned against the others. This kind of "whipsawing" has been used with notable success by the U.A.W. in the automobile industry. It might be regarded as a corollary of pattern setting, one of the ways in which a pattern is set and extended. Indeed the question must be faced squarely whether this general phenomenon of pattern setting, which bears some analogy to price leadership, tacit collusion, and other related forces in the industrial field, is not the real bogey, instead of industry-wide bargaining in the literal sense. It seems at least an open question whether the sweeping abolition of industry-wide bargaining would have the results that some seem to think it would. In particular, it might have little if any effect in industries where the units are already large on the employers' side, like the automobile or steel industries, or where the monopoly power of even a small union is overwhelming, as with the teamsters, and it might have the greatest effect in more atomized industries where union power is less anyway. In sum, it seems to me quite possible that it would not change the picture very much. But the matter clearly deserves further study.

Another answer to the question of what might be done is "nothing at all." It has been held that union strength sufficient to force a steadily rising wage and price level—a creeping inflation of 2 to 3 per cent a year—is simply one of the facts of life and unavoidable in the sense that it could be avoided only at the heavy cost of substantial unemployment and loss of output. I know that Gottfried Haberler has discussed this thesis in his chapter, and perhaps I should merely comment that what he said about it seems sensible to me, and pass on. But let me add a point or two.

I do not believe that *anything* in the field of social policy is "inevitable," and it seems to me wholly pernicious to spread the idea that it is. If something is inevitable there is no use opposing it. Indeed, we should recall that it is a well-known tactic of dictators to convince not only their own subjects but the rest of the world that destiny is on their side, and that it is useless to stand in their way. I once heard a well-known Marxist, when asked at the close of a lecture on socialism what was the most useful contribution that a socialist today could make to the cause, use this word in replying. The most useful thing, he said, and seemingly with complete ingenuousness, was to persuade as many people as possible of the inevitability of socialism; and we all know that this is good Marxist theory—and tactics. The surest way to guarantee creeping inflation is for the idea to take hold that there is no alternative. Then there will be no resistance. One should add the next stage: that as soon as this idea is generally accepted, increases will be correspondingly easier to get and the pace will be accelerated.

The line of thought which I should like to suggest as a remedy is not so much to exert counterpressures or to rely on countervailing powers as to attack the problem at its source and seek means to diminish labor power itself. Such an idea does not seem to require great imagination, although it does appear to be almost completely novel in the labor field. I have summarized above some of the matters discussed in my booklet, *The Economic Analysis of Labor Union Power,*[7] under the heading of "accretions of power," in the sense that they are not a part of mere collective bargaining *per se.* I believe that, on the whole, these accretions have fallen into the lap of labor with tacit public approval, or at least indifference, as a part of the prevailing belief that the labor cause is in some global sense "good," and therefore that the measure of the powers and immunities which labor unions should enjoy is simply "enough to win." It will be necessary to gain wider acceptance for the thesis that labor unions, economically speaking, are partly good and partly bad, and that perhaps they should therefore be allowed to win only half of the time. This will involve removing or diminishing some of the accretions, and perhaps in the case of particularly powerful unions, taking some further steps beyond this.

I must interject at this point that I do believe that comprehensive study of this whole range of problems by economists from a *public* point of view is desperately needed. On many fundamental issues of policy in this field, we lack the right kind of knowledge to proceed because the problem has been studied and analyzed almost entirely from a labor, and not from a public, point of view.

Some will say that the political power of labor is an effective barrier to any regulation of labor unions in the general social interest, and of course this political obstacle is not to be denied. Yet the precedent of the Taft-Hartley Act is encouraging. The revelations of the McClellan Committee have again put unions on the defensive and have perhaps created another opportunity for constructive action beyond the worthy though limited objectives of protecting union members themselves from abuse of power within their organizations and from corruption. It seems to me that the immediately urgent problem (invoking the principle of least resistance) is to find measures which will

[7] Chamberlin, *The Economic Analysis of Labor Union Power* (Washington, 1958).

reduce union power and which will also gain general support from their inherent reasonableness, fairness, or appeal to other values *not* directly related to unionism.

Here are some proposals which seem to conform to this criterion. They should be regarded as suggestive, rather than as constituting a program in any adequate sense:

(1) Outside the field of employer-employee relations, unions should be subjected to the anti-trust laws in exactly the same way as are other business entities. This will certainly require a careful definition and restriction of the meaning of the phrase "employer-employee relationships," and of the related concept of a "labor dispute" so as to preclude some of the global interpretations of this latter which seem now to prevail.

(2) Means should be found for achieving union responsibility as legal entities on a par with employers and other organized groups with respect to contracts, to acts done under union aegis by its member, etc. A familiar proposal is compulsory incorporation, although I know there is disagreement as to whether this is really the best means to achieve the objective. Legal and other issues are involved here on which I do not myself feel competent to pass judgement.

(3) If and where the union shop is permitted, much more needs to be done to protect union members from the abuse of power by union authority.

(4) Picketing should be subjected to substantial restrictions and to effective penalties, with reference especially to the obstruction of access to property and to passage on highways. It should be recognized for what it has in fact become in most cases: a highly perfected means of intimidation of workers, of denying economic access, and of forcing the collusion of laborers not a party to a dispute.

(5) Loopholes in the Taft-Hartley prohibition of the secondary boycott should be effectively closed. Since it was the intention of the earlier law to prevent this abuse, it is hard to understand why the loopholes still remain open. All power of a union to put pressure either on an employer, another union, or on unorganized workers, through the "hot cargo" abuse, or any other form of denial of normal economic access should be decisively eliminated. Penalties should be

severe enough to secure compliance and to open up the channels of trade and opportunity to all on equal terms.

(6) There is certainly an anomaly in allowing a large union to concentrate resources drawn from its entire membership on the objective of ruining a single employer. The analogy with "local price cutting," whereby a large firm takes losses in one small area in order to eliminate a local competitor—a practice forbidden to industry by the antitrust laws—seems complete to me, and I think means should be found to protect individual businesses from this abuse of big-union power.

In addition to these six suggestions, it appears to me as a matter of principle that the size of unions and the size of bargaining units in different areas of the economy—in short, the structure of labor organization—should be dictated by the public interest rather than by the desires of the laborers concerned. The application of this principle might involve diluting the strength of some unions which are powerful because they are small and strategically situated, by merging them with larger units. In other cases, it might involve the breaking up of large units into smaller ones. The criterion should be not mere size but size in relation to industrial structure. The public interest should also prevail in the matter of collusive action between unions.

This is perhaps the most revolutionary proposal of all. The prevailing conception seems to be one of "freedom"—freedom, that is, for any group of laborers, large or small, industry or trade, local, regional or national, to engage in joint action in their common interest merely if they find it to their advantage to do so. Applied to the field of industry, this would mean that any group of business men or corporations would be similarly free to engage in joint action, including merger, merely according to the dictates of their own advantage. Of course, the general principle of the supremacy of the public interest in the business area is well established. What reason can there be for exempting labor from the same principle?

2

Wages and Labor Union Action in the Light of Economic Analysis

Frank H. Knight

Over his keys, the musing organist,
  Beginning doubtfully and far away,
First lets his fingers wander as they list
  And builds a bridge from dreamland for his lay.

THE FIRST QUATRAIN of this poem, which impressed me deeply in my youth, comes to mind in connection with my task here. Some mental bridges are to be built, and quite long ones. And while I fondly hold to a distinction between critical reflection and musing, and between dreamland and sound generalizations as a starting-point, I realize that the different terminology of "theorizing" and "assumptions," as popularly used, suggest a kinship. Further, if the occasion runs true to type, voices will be raised to place my performance in the realm of fancy, not of fact.

I am a theorist in economics and more generally in the study of human and social problems. For this role I make no apology, and shall offer no sales-talk. To many, "theory" is a sort of "cuss-word," as is its virtual synonym, "abstraction," both of which go with all rational thinking. I think I know why this attitude is taken. People commonly prefer to make their own theories to support conclusions already reached on grounds other than reasoning from premises critically scrutinized. Moreover, after living so long in the world and in modern academia, I must expect to be accused of doing that myself. But I know no way of refuting either prejudice or the accusation of prejudice except to discuss issues as candidly and clearly as one can. So that is what I propose to do, hence necessarily to theorize. The task is to build or sketch out the bridge of logic and critical reflection between some axioms—propositions taken as not in dispute—to such conclusions as they validly support respecting the matter at issue. At the outset I mention prejudice to stress the conviction that it is the most fundamental fact in connection with problems of social policy in a free and progressive society. The crucial matter is attitudes, the process by which beliefs are established in minds, and the way in which people argue for their beliefs in attempting to persuade others to agreement. Agreement is the objective, but is commonly taken to mean that others shall agree with "me." Hence the procedure followed, and presumably expected to be effective, is not discussion as a cooperative intellectual quest of truth but use of psychological techniques of persuasion. The major desideratum, then, is intellectual morals, but that problem cannot be treated in the scope of a single chapter.

It should be noted that there is another type of bridge needing to be built for any adequate treatment of the problems arising in a free and progressive society. That is a historical bridge. Its construction cannot be undertaken here in any detail. But it is important to recognize that the type of society in question in which we live and find our problems is a very recent arrival on the historical scene. Only a few generations old, it evolved with revolutionary suddenness out of the social order of medieval western Europe, which was very different and was committed to ideals antithetical to freedom and progress, i.e., to conformity to sacred traditional norms and obedience to a sacred authority as their interpreter. The supreme ideal was expressed in the monastic vows to poverty, chastity and obedience. The obviously parasitic nature of such a life, its manifest impossibility for society at large by which it must be supported, led to a dual system of norms—counsels of perfection and precepts for worldly behavior. The main tenets of the latter have been noted: conformity to an eternal and immutable law interpreted by a divinely ordained absolute authority. Most pertinent here is the static character of the culture and its ideals, for this means that the ordinary man would know the right in conduct, hence his choices were not intellectual, but moral—between conformity and obedience and sin. With the advent of ideals of freedom and progress, the norms are practically inverted—the main problem is intellectual, i.e., to know what is right in a dynamic sense—the "best" direction of change.

It should also be noted that the cultural transformation went through an intermediate stage. For a few generations public thought and expression in morals, politics and economics were directed to enhancement of the power of absolute monarchical states under monarchies ruling by divine right, these having replaced the Church as the main seat of power. These societies were still unfree, but a secular authority is less opposed to rational change than an ecclesiastical one, and this fact turned out to be crucial. Diplomatic and military competition forced the states to tolerate and even encourage commercial and scientific movements as sources of new wealth and the sinews of war—science as the basis of a rational and progressive technology. Both of these activities seem to go naturally with individualism, at least under the conditions then prevailing. They furnished the main dynamic of further political change leading to the democratization of the monarchies in and following the revolutionary period of the late eighteenth century, the "Age of Reason" or "Enlightenment." But the fundamental freedom established in the passage from medieval to modern culture is freedom of thought and expression. The west-European mind had to be liberated from the dictation of belief by prescriptive authority, ecclesiastical and political. The crucial break was made by science, specifically the new astronomy of Copernicus and Galileo. This destroyed the view of all truth as divinely revealed and eternally immutable, subject to interpretation by a divine authority, the uneasy partnership of church and the political order.

The final liberation established a new norm of conduct and new conceptions of the individual and society. The former may be described as utilitarian or pragmatic or as "economic rationality." It means the free, intelligent or effective use by individuals of means in achieving freely chosen ends. In politics, democratic society is ideally a free association of such individuals, each the final judge of his own values and of the use of means for realizing them. But this freedom is necessarily subject to his respecting the similar freedom of others, all cooperating for increased efficiency in the use of means. Since individualistic efficiency can be indefinitely increased by specialization, free society is characterized by the organization of economic activity through exchange (purchase and sale) of goods and services in markets. In fact, that is the one completely free form of cooperation possible to human beings with differing tastes that is practicable on any considerable scale. The market organization was fairly developed before 1776 when Adam Smith effectively launched a propaganda for more completely freeing it from the shackles of state control—that of the Church being virtually obsolete—and incidentally founded political economy as a theoretical science. A main aim of the political democratization that went on apace was to reduce governmental power in favor of freedom, economic, religious, intellectual and cultural.

The market system must be understood as a method of organizing intelligent cooperation for mutual advantage, but it is motivated by individual interests and values—selfish or generous, and material only in the sense that specifiable means are used, more or less effectively, in promoting them. Mutual advantage, with advantage defined by each person for himself, is the substance of Adam Smith's famous "invisible hand," which he contrasted with "benevolence" as the individual's reliance for getting his dinner—assuming a free society. It must be stressed that the heart of the "Liberal Revolution" was a new ethic, the nominally Protestant right of private judgment in belief and conduct, subject to the principle of mutuality. In private conduct the new ideal was the intelligent, hence inherently free, use of means. It is individualistic, but mutuality requires free agreement with all other parties in any associative action.[1] Implied and equally to be stressed

[1] Discussion of markets, analytical or practical, must describe them in general terms, i.e., as *theoretically* simplified or idealized (not ethically judged). Thus arise the concepts of "perfect competition"—a market with a large number of independent buyers and sellers—and its antithesis, "monopoly." The word means "one seller," but may be generalized to include "monopsony"—one buyer, and kindred monopoloid situations. "Competition" is ambiguous and misleading. As motives, both competition and cooperation are incompatible with end-and-means rationality. The meaning relevant for economics is not a psychological attitude but the figurative, purely impersonal, competition of alternatives open to individual choice.

is the ideal of improvement or progress. It involves introduction of new ends and new means as well as new ways of using means. The ethical postulate is (in Adam Smith's phrase) the right of every man to strive to improve his condition (always subject to the mutuality principle). It was assumed and argued by the proponents of the new view of man and society—the utilitarians and classical economists—that in the main the requirement of agreement would assure continuous harmony of interests between individuals and between the individual and society, hence social progress as well as individual.

Thus, in terms of economic relations the new conception of society was dualistic. It consists of the economic order of competitive buying and selling in markets and a (vastly changed) political order, providing the necessary framework of law in which the former could operate. We need not trace the democratization to the basis of one vote for each adult member (citizen) of a national state. Minimizing the role of government in favor of individual freedom (*laisser-faire*) would *in the limit* reduce its function to policing the market, to guaranteeing freedom by preventing force and fraud. (We must pass over international relations.) Even in theory the early economist-propagandists by no means went so far, but under their urging policy went to excess and soon produced a reaction, the early Factory Acts (in Britain, the main home of the revolution). With changing conditions, democratic states have gone on to "interfere" more and more in market relations, regulating, controlling, supplementing and displacing the economic order until this task has become the main, or most controversial, function of government as the instrument of social policy. The primary changes in conditions have been the rapid advance of technology, accumulation of capital, and appearance of new wants.

Even by 1776 the advance of technology had reached a point where efficiency required production by fairly large units, specialized both as to products and internally as to functions performed by different individuals, with different tools. Such enterprises also clearly required direction by responsible leaders, constituting in fact the most important specialization of personal roles. The result is the entrepreneur, who hires labor and property services in one set of markets—at prices fixed by competition with other entrepreneurs—makes products and sells these in another set of markets at prices similarly determined. Thus (in a much simplified view) the bulk of the members of a modern economy get money incomes by selling productive services—one or both of these forms, for wages or rent-or-interest—and converts these into real income, partly buying products for consumption, partly creating property in one form or another, through saving and investment. The entrepreneur, however, shares in a very different way. His profit is not the price of a service and not properly a reward for performing a function, though he plays the key role in the economic order. For the purposes of this chapter, his activity and income especially need analysis, but only a sketch of high-points can be given. In short, the role is to make the responsible decisions necessary to production, and his income is what is left from the receipts of the enterprise (the residual) after he pays for the labor and capital services as costs of production. The point to be stressed is that the residual may be positive or negative, a gain or a loss. For that reason, words like "share" and "income" must be put in quotation-marks, as should "profit" itself, as long as it popularly stands for a positive quantity. Profit, as gain *or loss,* is closely related to "monopoly," an even more opprobrious term, though a monopolist also may not make a gain, but incur a loss. Before carrying the analysis a bit farther, it is well to revert briefly to the relation between the political and the economic order as two parts of the mechanism of social-economic control, the economic order in the inclusive sense, for every judgment respecting policy involves a comparison between the two.

The system as a whole is to be judged as a means for achieving certain social values. Of these, the first in rank is *order;* that is of the essence of any society, hence of any human life, since man is a social being. But order inevitably conflicts with *freedom,* the novel and distinctive value of liberal society. A rigid order—more or less characteristic of pre-liberal society, as it is even more of a beehive—excludes all freedom for the individual, while literal absolute freedom would be anarchy, a chaos without either order or effective freedom. The general aim of policy must be to harmonize order and freedom through the best compromise. But still other values and value conflicts must be considered. Economic activity must be *efficient* as a condition of life itself and of all values, and especially for *progress,* notably growth in efficiency through time. Individual *security* is a fifth value which conflicts with freedom, since freedom for one involves insecurity for others. Security would in a sense prevail in a rigid order, assuming that it possessed efficiency. Sixth and finally, a free economic order must satisfy the human demand for *justice,* in some sense and some degree, otherwise it will not persist but will be overthrown and replaced by a compulsory order or by chaos. The most serious conflicts are between freedom on the one hand and order-with-security, and justice on the other, while progress is everywhere a complicating factor. The task of reconciliation through compromise falls to government, which is especially the custodian of order. In a politically free society, government operates through the making and enforcement of laws by agents held responsible to the people as a whole.

In comparing the political and the economic order, the main difference is that the latter is in theory (i.e., ideally) free, while political action always involves more or less compulsion. In a perfectly competitive market, everyone is free in the sense that no one can exercise arbitrary power over anyone else, since each buyer or seller faces equally good alternatives. But government, even when most democratic, means at least coercion of minorities by a majority, and this ideal cannot be closely approximated in practice. The laws must apply to all alike, and men will not in fact agree on what laws are desirable, otherwise jural law (requiring enforcement) would not be needed. (We here ignore crime, defiance of law not held to be wrong.) The market organization has the supreme merit of enabling men to cooperate without agreeing in their specific tastes and value judgments. This also they will not do freely, but they do agree in desiring efficiency in the use of means to achieve their various ends, and this the market system does provide, along with freedom, through the coordination of specialized activities.

Real markets do not conform strictly to the theoretical ideal, but they conform much more closely than denouncers of the system allege. One main economic task for government is to produce closer conformity by removing the main causes of divergence. However, it has other tasks, and harder ones, than dealing with monopoly and otherwise making competition effective. It must regulate, supplement or displace market relations where these would lead to intolerable results or where, in the judgment of the people expressed through the political order, political action will lead to improvement.[2]

In terms of basic values, the root of our problem is an inherent conflict between efficiency and freedom, i.e., a *minimum of power relations* between persons. Especially in question is freedom to organize. To secure the boundless increase in production made possible by modern technology requires establishments of considerable size. But such a unit requires management with power, and the more so as the size is greater and as progress is stressed. No sizable human group can be ideally, anarchistically, democratic and be active. In fact, power relations arise in connection with an advanced and advancing technology, quite apart from the scope of associative action, even where only two persons are involved. Power comes to exist because the specialization of tasks is associated with differentiated knowledge and skill. In consequence, modern society is a veritable tissue of *agency* relations. Individuals with specialized competence everywhere make decisions for or on behalf of other persons who more or less freely appoint them as agents in a more or less definite role. But an agent has power over his principal; he gives orders which the latter obeys. This is particularly true of all group action, since a group must act through some leader. It is true above all of democratic government, which consists in the making and enforcement of laws by deputized representatives, who inevitably have power over the governed in varying degree. Literal and pure self-government means anarchy—chaos. A principal, particularly a group, faces the problem of holding the agent responsible, as far as may be, in his exercise of power.

[2] The idea of a society with literally and purely individualistic relations is a monstrous absurdity. No population is made up of individuals with the maturity and qualifications necessary for responsibility. Children and other dependents must be provided for, the young educated, and many "public services" furnished for the group by group agencies. However, development of that set of problems is neither possible here nor directly relevant to our topic. The present discussion must be limited to some aspects of market competition, in relation to monopoly or monopoloid situations.

The situation may be illustrated in principle by a simple if extreme case involving only two parties—hence no organization in the usual meaning—the case of patient and his doctor. Here the doctor has power, actually power of life and death, when and so long as the relation exists. The only freedom possible to the patient is free choice of his doctor, and freedom to change doctors at will—precisely the freedom of a competitive market (for medical services). But the most complete freedom will not enable patients to get the best medical service available, still less the best possible. That objective depends on power (knowledge and skill) that they do not possess—else they would not need doctors. Here we meet with rather the most serious fallacy in the argument of radical critics of the market organization; that is defining freedom to include power, even the ability to make completely intelligent choices. That knowledge is a means, but choice is universally limited by scarcity of other means, of a more tangible sort—such as the money to pay the doctor preferred. Access to means of any kind presents a power problem distinct from that of freedom; only confusion can result from defining freedom to include power, as being in a position to get what one wants—as negative critics of the market-economy commonly do. (They do so because "freedom" has become a word to conjure with in argument—inverting the social ideal of conformity and obedience accepted in our culture only a few generations ago.) It should be noted, too, that a doctor or other expert has a degree of monopoly power—a monopoly of his own services, subject to imperfect competition from other specialists offering more or less similar services—with a corresponding power to fix his price. And the nature of agency is management of affairs of others in some area.

At the same time we find an equally serious fallacy on the part of advocates of market competition as the sole and sufficient organizational ideal on the ground that it means maximum freedom. This it does—assuming an ideally free market, but the fact does not support the conclusion drawn. There are essential values other than freedom, and other rights, notably some right to access to means or power, which is required to live decently. Freedom is ineffective, empty, without power to act and to act in some desired way; it is relative to both means and ends, as given conditions. All three are data, different dimensions, in an individual's range of choice. Correct analysis must define freedom in the old-fashioned negative way as the absence of arbitrary coercive interference by others in doing what one wants to do and would otherwise be able to do. The right to means must of course be limited, as must freedom and all individual rights; the "right" scope of each right must be discussed on its merits, in view of the harmonies and conflicts among values underlying all problems of group action. In the theoretically ideal perfectly competitive market, interference by one with another's use of means in his possession does not occur; in that situation, means are means of production and represent power over things rather than over other persons. But this view becomes unrealistic when the means possessed by different persons are quantitatively very different. In human terms the possessor of vast means clearly has power over the person with narrowly limited means —partly because there cannot be an approximately perfect market for the means of one at or near the subsistence level. Moreover, we all know that power corrupts—corrupts character, and, in fact, excessive weakness is equally corrupting. Social policy cannot ignore the ethical import of these facts. Free exchange does not require equality or near-equality, but it does require limits to the degree of inequality.

The belief of the early economists that not much more than policing of the markets would be necessary by the governments rested on some major oversights. We have mentioned their fatal neglect of the fact that freedom of exchange has meaning only in so far as one has something to sell for which others will give something that one wants. Another serious matter is that economic power is used to get more power, giving rise to a tendency to progressive increase in inequality and, especially, that inheritance of unequal means and opportunity gives children of the next generation a correspondingly unequal start in the economic race. This is clearly unfair by individualistic standards, and gives rise to the major policy problem of justice.[3] But the

[3] Failure to see limitations inherent in economic freedom lays the early economists, and some later ones, open to the criticism of too much reliance on an over-simple theory and even to suspicion of conscious or unconscious sympathy with the position of the "vested interests," the possessors of superior economic power at the time. They are naturally disposed to belief in freedom to use it.

present discussion is limited to the simpler issue of the use of economic power in market relations, notably by an entrepreneur, or by someone else in opposition to him. The latter is allegedly needed to offset his *monopoly* power, the source of profit, especially in large industrial units where the entrepreneur is now usually a corporation. In point here is the claim of labor organizations—unions or their leaders and sympathizers—to countervailing power, a point still to be discussed. What is certain is that no price can be raised arbitrarily without changing the supply.[4]

Our analysis may proceed by bringing the illustrative case of patient-and-doctor nearer to reality. We change the situation to one in which a number of doctors are employed for a fixed remuneration (wages or salary) by an institution such as a hospital or clinic conducted as a private enterprise. An entrepreneur now buys the services of the doctors in one market and sells them to patients in another, both more or less perfectly competitive. Such an organization arises because an entrepreneur can function in establishing intercommunication between individual patients and doctors better, in their judgment, then they can do in any other way. Apart from separate exploration and negotiation, the result might be sought through other forms of organization, usually distinguished as cooperative. There are two familiar types. The patients might organize a consumers' cooperative, or the doctors one with the producers' label. In internal organization, specific services provided, and methods, innumerable alternatives are open to either form, but illustrative here is the hiring of doctors on a salary and hiring them out to prospective patients.

[4] The classical economists talked nonsense about monopoly price, holding that it is the highest the seller can charge. In fact, of course, he tries to balance loss through reduced sales against gain from the higher price per unit so as to secure the maximum monopoly revenue or profit.

As regards social policy, it is a question how far Smith was wrong in thinking that monopolies would not present a serious problem if governments would not support their position in one way or another. And the doubt is greater if we imagine the government doing what it could to maintain the conditions of effective competition. However, the urge to monopolize is strong, and in some fields action against business monopoly will doubtless continue to be needed—though the magnitude and importance of this evil are grossly exaggerated in the public mind (and especially of course by reformist thinking).

The point for emphasis is that this model is a type for all specialized production—in particular, that the same alternatives are open to the parties concerned, the consumers and producers of any good or service. The cooperative forms—so miscalled as distinguishing them from the entrepreneurial, reflecting a prejudice—have been both advocated (on idealistic grounds) and repeatedly tried. Even with the benefit of much unpaid labor, they have generally failed to survive for long. A limited success in retail merchandising is an unimportant exception.

The illustration would be still nearer to what is typical in industry if some entrepreneur were to undertake the education of potential doctors, establishing a claim to their services afterward—paralleling the fixed investment in plant. The institutions of free society bar making such a claim effective (it would be "involuntary servitude") and education is generally left to the family of the individual or to his own devices. Much individually and socially precious opportunity is thereby sacrificed to freedom, narrowly interpreted, but such details are not to be elaborated here. The essential fact is that modern civilization depends on somebody performing the functions that in our society are the role of the profit-seeking entrepreneur, who is in principle the *agent* of both consumers and ultimate producers. That employees are thought of by themselves and others as working for this party, merely reflects ignorance and prejudice. That is no more true in any other case than it is true that the patient is working for the doctor in obeying his orders. Before going in more detail into the problems presented, another common and fundamental misunderstanding—also rooted in a prejudice—may be pointed out. An entrepreneur hiring doctors for "wages" and selling their services to patients would nominally and in law "own" the institution or organization rendering the services but not, in a free society, the doctors—though it would be true to form if some of them contended that this were the case. In manufacturing (for example) he (or it, a corporation) may own much or little of the equipment used—or none, or less than none. His ownership may be, for a time or on the whole, a liability and not an asset.[5]

[5] Usually only for a time, and that because of contractual or other factors limiting the possibility of dissolving the enterprise and withdrawing without loss the productive

As the facts respecting ownership make clear, the entrepreneur sometimes makes a positive profit, a gain, and sometimes incurs a loss. He sets up and conducts the enterprise in the hope and with an expectation of gain, through selling his output of services or material products for more than he pays for the productive services employed —labor and/or property services. The fulfillment or disappointment of his hope and expectation may extend over a wide range, from very large gains to loss of everything put into it or more, leaving him in debt or bankrupt, involving loss to other parties. In our simple case, where only doctors' services are bought and sold, the hope of selling these for more than is paid for them suggests exploitation to many people—exploitation of the doctors or the patients or both. But the illustration should make it clear why this view is false. Manifestly, the entrepreneur renders a service to both parties in making a more effective market, or making it available at less effort-cost, than either or both together can do, or think they could, for themselves; otherwise they would adopt some of the alternatives we have pointed out.

Secondly, an entrepreneur makes a gain only if he does better, not merely than any alternative method, but better than competing entrepreneurs. Entrepreneurs take chances or bear uncertainty as to the quality of the responsible decisions they make, which determine success or failure. It is true that one may hire a manager paid a salary for the more routine decisions. But such a person is the agent of the real entrepreneur, who hires him, sets his powers and duties and (by agreement) fixes his remuneration; these are the responsible decisions on which the entrepreneur takes the risk, and the hired manager is essentially a laborer—like the doctors in our illustration. Besides coordinating the ordinary, more or less routine, specialized functions, the major managerial decisions include anticipating such contingencies as may arise in the course of operations; and, in industrial production, the most important task of all is to find or devise and

capacity committed to it, when it ceases or fails to yield the returns to be had from such resources in other employments. This point will be stressed later.

We should note that the entrepreneur function is only more or less specialized in a particular individual or group. Nearly everyone participating in an enterprise or having dealings with it shares to some extent in both management and the peculiar contingent character of entrepreneurial profit.

introduce improvements, successful innovations in the technology of production or more appealing products. Economic growth, progress, is necessary for any improvement in living standards or the maintenance of tolerable standards for an increasing population. The hope and expectation of profit is the lure (as it has been well described) which induces men to undertake the entrepreneur's role, perform its functions and take the risks of success or failure.

It is a trivial observation—for anyone understanding the A.B.C.'s of economic analysis—that in so far as there is perfect competition in the markets in which entrepreneurs buy and sell—and between all entrepreneurs in both—all costs tend to equality with selling-prices, and no one will either make a gain or incur a loss. Such competition, however, can only be approximated, men and the conditions of human life being at all what they are. That would require perfect foresight to the indefinite future on the part of all.[6] The entrepreneur's functions have to be performed by somebody; the question is how the directors of production are to be selected, motivated, and held effectively responsible to the ultimate principals, the producers and consumers, as their agents. We have seen why private profit-seeking entrepreneurship has become the overwhelmingly predominant method of securing their performance in industrial civilization in comparison with other alternatives freely available to the parties concerned.[7]

[6] Ideal competition can be somewhat closely approximated on the part of buyers of products and sellers of productive services; between entrepreneurs themselves, a comparable approximation is theoretically impossible as well as practically. That would require every entrepreneur to foresee the decisions and acts of all others (as well as other contingencies). But for that, universal collusion would be necessary, which would destroy the conditions of individualistic (competitive) organization.

[7] A further alternative is conceivable, has been strenuously advocated, and should be mentioned. That is socialism: that "society as a whole" should take over all the entrepreneurial functions, together with ownership of all productive wealth. Since a group of considerable size can act only through individual agents, this means control of economic activity in detail by the personnel of government, i.e., by agents selected (in a democracy) by competitive campaigning and voting in place of "market competition," by politicians instead of businessmen. ("Society" is a euphemism chosen for propaganda effect.) Detailed analysis is impossible here, but one or two observations may be offered for what they are worth.

First, the larger the group the more arbitrary coercive power its government personnel as agents will inevitably have—the more government will be by men rather than laws—and the degree is multiplied as progress is stressed as an objective. Secondly,

After noting that perfect competition would eliminate all profits—gain or loss—it is appropriate to glance at imperfect, beginning with the facts (as far as known) about profit in our economy of today. First, to the utter confusion of thinking, the anti-business prejudice causes the public mind largely to overlook, ignore or flout the well-known fact that profit is often loss, or to ask how the balance works out. A mere honest use of words would dictate that the organization be called not the "profit system," but one of profit-*seeking*, or profit-*and-loss*. As to the over-all balance, accurate knowledge of gains and losses is, in the nature of the case, not to be had. The evidence available makes it certain that there is no large predominance of gains, and indicates that losses are at least equal to them, if not greater, in the aggregate (or on the average) and in the long run. This would follow theoretically from the familiar facts as to the psychology of risk-taking, or gambling; and this motivation applies to profit-seeking activity. It is notorious that human nature often elects to gamble when the odds are known to be strongly in favor of loss. Laws are considered needful to prevent people so wasting their means and impoverishing their families. The fairest lottery or game of chance has costs, and the players' losses must exceed their gains. In business life this result is supported by the empirical evidence available. Our best statistics of income distribution find no net-profit share, and in many fields—particularly where risk is greatest, such as prospecting for rare minerals—it is notorious that losses far exceed gains.

It thus appears that "society," the economy as a whole, gets the services of entrepreneurs as a class at little cost, or less than none. Yet the service is literally indispensable, for efficiency and progress, and any other method of securing it would be both less effective and quite costly. The entrepreneurs (like gamblers) are motivated and recom-

reflection on the powers a socialistic government would have to have in a modern nation will surely indicate that it could not tolerate the free criticism and organized partisan opposition required for even formal democracy; it would quite certainly be a dictatorship of a single "party" monopolizing power and suppressing freedom, not only in economic matters, but wherever it might find such action expedient in its own interest. And this even if its personnel were people abhorring irresponsible power—while the likelihood that such persons would be the ones to achieve power should give pause to anyone believing in freedom and having a voice in deciding between "socialism" and the organization through free markets and free enterprise.

pensed by the excitement of the game. It is true that a typical entrepreneur makes a gain some of the time, and many do so on the whole —matched by losses at other times or by other profit-seekers. The advisability of confiscating gains when and where they are found must be discussed from two standpoints—these of the public and of a special-interest group, such as labor. As to either, it means playing the game with business on terms of "heads I win, tails you lose." Strictly speaking, it is a matter of how far this practice can wisely be carried, for much profit is now taken by taxation and by the union action in question here.

Everything said so far is introductory to the question set by our title. Such length has seemed necessary to define the problem, which can now be disposed of rather briefly. In general, a society must choose between voluntary cooperation, organized in whatever way the parties can freely agree upon, and either no-organization or compulsion, by an over-all majority vote or by a dictator. At best, much political compulsion is unavoidable, and a democracy must draw a line somewhere, between business and politics. However, the issue of our title relates directly, not to public policy, but to interference in the working of the competitive-enterprise economy through dictation to entrepreneurs by a particular interest-group, the wage-earners, organized in unions of some scope. The scope may be a plant or single enterprise, an industry somehow defined, or the economy as a whole. It is clearly the ambition of typical labor-leaders to make it as broad as possible, to maximize their power. Public policy is finally involved to determine how much power unions or their leaders are to be granted or allowed to exercise.

To keep the discussion within bounds, it must be considerably narrowed. As to power relations between union leaders and the rank-and-file (or non-member wage-earners), i.e., the internal politics of the labor movement, only a few general observations can be offered. The government of a union—especially a large one—cannot be "democratic" in approximately the sense of a modern nation, politically free. Sumner H. Slichter has noted three features which are generally lacking: an organized opposition, an independent judiciary, and a free press. Union policy calls for compulsory membership as a condition of earning a livelihood within the jurisdiction covered. (We must ignore jurisdictional disputes, as well as the internal problem of fixing wage differentials, i.e., pooling of benefits.) The unions claim that compulsory membership is necessary to make organization effective, and largely "get away with it"—more formally in this country, but equally in practice in Britain. This may make their power greater than that of the state itself, or in some cases practically absolute. As to scope, the limit would be the whole "working class," of which an effective organization would obviously control the state. We shall consider only "collective bargaining" over *wages*—obviously including fringe benefits— and, to be concrete, shall take as a type case, the United Automobile Workers under the leadership of Walter Reuther. It is national in scope, an industrial union, covering a field much wider than the production of motor vehicles. We must also ignore the supervision over wage bargaining by governmental agencies.

Incidentally, "bargaining" is a misleading, essentially dishonest, use of a word. A producer under effective competition does not bargain over prices in either of the two sets of markets in which he operates. His activity consists in making offers at some price, which are accepted or refused by the other party, on the basis of comparing other (competing) offers. (Normally, an offer is made at the going prices or a very little less or more—the process by which a market price gets changed.) Nor does a monopolist bargain; he sets the price which in his estimation will maximize his long-run net gain—to be accepted or refused, or accepted for a variable quantity of the good in question. The honest meaning of bargaining is use of persuasion, i.e., "salesmanship" (or buymanship).

What "collective bargaining" obviously means in our case is simply monopolistic action on the part of a labor union. And the union, like any other seller, can secure a price above the free-competitive level only by arbitrarily restricting the quantity offered for sale, obstructing access to work in the union's jurisdiction. It matters not at all whether a monopolist formally sets price or quantity if there is effective competition on the other side. (If there is not such competition on at least one side, the condition is bilateral monopoly, the price is economically indeterminate and must be settled by force in some form.)

A union's first defence is that the employer bargains as a unit (monopolistically) and if employees act as individuals they are practically helpless; any one of them is unimportant to him, while he is indispensable to the worker. The latter is "free"—to starve, if he will not work on the employer's terms. There is a little truth in this reasoning—not much, and only with respect to an enterprise in being, a going concern, with its actual employees. The case needs to be examined in other aspects as well as short versus long-run conditions. The importance to the employer of an individual employee is obviously a matter of degree, depending on his replaceability. But good management must assure that no one is "very" important—because of contingencies of health and life, and especially because the worker is always free to "quit"; if he is highly specialized—normally trained by the employer at considerable cost—*his* monopoly creates a serious problem, that of turnover. The opponent-critics of "business" of course think nothing of all that, and the public attitude is much the same. On the other side, and more important, an employer cannot afford high-handed action toward an employee; other workers will know about it, and productive efficiency requires worker morale. His labor relations must be fairly satisfactory to the bulk of his employees —up to or a little beyond reasonable expectations—and also he must constantly recruit replacements.

In a longer-run view, the arbitrary (monopolistic) power of both sides decreases rapidly in favor of the impersonal process of competition unless, that is, there is an appeal to overt coercion. This is now done, practically speaking, only by unions through a strike based on monopoly power on a scale to stop operations, and various actions in support of a strike. That is considered a natural right and held to justify any steps deemed necessary to make and keep it effective, beginning with compulsory union membership. (We shall return to this in a moment.) Unionists and their partisans among the public refuse to look very far ahead, since to do so would destroy their case—the demand for "more, now"—as the introductory argument of this chapter has shown. In a moderately long run (still with respect to a going enterprise), another argument, somewhat more serious, is advanced. It is that the employer (or group) from whom higher wages are demanded (above those voluntarily offered) has a monopoly in the market for the product. This is "proved" by his making a profit or "excessive" profit, which is no part of necessary cost, unearned, and constituting "exploitation" of "labor"—or possibly consumers, or both. Ignored, of course, is the fact that always, even at the moment, other employers of similar labor are making no profit, or even incurring loss; that is "irrelevant." Again, there is some literal truth in the contention. Any enterprise making a (positive) profit has a degree of monopoly at the moment due to frictional considerations. If resources were completely and instantly mobile and prices perfectly flexible, shifts would occur immediately eliminating any gain, hence preventing any from appearing. (This mobility would also prevent loss—and an enterprise may be a monopoly in any degree and suffer loss to any extent; but that also is ignored or viewed as irrelevant.)

The mere fact that competition is imperfect means that there will be gains and losses greater or less and over longer or shorter intervals. Any proposal to appropriate gain raises the question, first, of whether there is a gain that admits of confiscation, and then of who has the right, or for whom it is expedient, to assess and take it. Here one must have in mind the nature of profit and the profit-seeking motive and their complex role in the economy. The most important function of the entrepreneur is in connection with innovations; together with thrift, this motive is responsible for economic growth, a condition of preserving a high civilization or advancing it. To be an effective lure, the gain hoped for and expected must be large enough and endure long enough to overbalance the chance of loss, also as estimated by the profit-seeker. As things stand in our economy, gains do not appear to exceed losses without any net compensation for risk-taking. This factor seems to function not as a subjective cost but rather as an incentive to entrepreneurs. If this motive is to be destroyed, or seriously weakened, "society" must consider the possible alternatives or face the consequences in stagnation and decadence.

Undoubtedly, there are "bad" monopolies—contrived for reasons of gain not connected with improved methods or products—or unduly prolonged beyond the need for assuring performance of their function. Usually these are rooted in "unfair competition," implying some coercive restriction of access to the market. The need for dealing with them by the public agency and in the public interest has long been recognized, and various policies energetically pursued; such are anti-trust laws, regulatory commissions, and public ownership. The question of who should identify such monopolies and choose and execute appropriate action—whether it should be the legal organs responsible to the public as a whole or the particular special-interest group of wage-earners, organized by "leaders" in any enterprise or sector of industry (or even the economy as a whole, i.e., syndicalism)—we submit, is not a question to be seriously considered. Surely, it is self-answering in favor of the former alternative, from the standpoint of the public interest. And the same answer should undoubtedly be given from the standpoint of wage-earners as an inclusive class. (As Mr. Slichter in particular has observed, and he is more friendly to union claims to power than is the present writer.) Whether it is expedient in the self-interest of its actual members for a limited group, such as the United Automobile Workers, to undertake this task is a question too complex for detailed consideration here. It involves public policy and the public attitude, and relations between union leaders and the rank-and-file, and other matters of internal policies of unions.

What needs emphasis most of all is that in the final long-run view we get entirely away from the going-concern-in-being in which alone anybody has power over prices or wages or conditions of work—either the entrepreneur or unions or other participants in enterprise (property owners) or consumers. We are then in the realm of really perfect competition affecting all parties concerned—as far as human limitations and the conditions of life make possible this theoretical ideal. Here we confront the conditions of growth (and maintenance) of productive capacity, and must stress, too, that decisions affecting the future in these respects are being made at every moment. In fact, all decisions of policy must look to the long run in this sense. It is in this connection that the power of unions to interfere with entrepreneurial policy presents the greatest menace. It goes without saying that any danger of strikes is an additional risk, which must reduce the incentive to engage in enterprise and be offset by a greater prospect of gain. It also enters into any plan for expansion or introduction of a substantial improvement. Nor is it negligible that wrangling with union representatives—called "collective bargaining"—is a serious handicap in managerial activities, an additional cost to be borne, and risk to be allowed for.

Calling for mention is still another method of dealing with "excess profits," namely, taxation. This has been advocated and been tried by our national government. It was immediately found unworkable, as elementary economic analysis would have shown in advance; no "excess" can be measured or defined. The only real case is "bad" monopoly, and that is better treated as such and dealt with by the other procedures mentioned before. The now famous demands of Walter Reuther on the Big Three makers of autos (and many other products) represent a "generous" offer on his part to do what the government could not—to determine the excess in this case and bestow the proceeds of confiscation in accord with his judgment (and interests). That such a proposal is taken seriously by the public suggests to a student of economics the need for education in good sense rather than in the principles of the "dismal science." The course of events in a mere few months following publication of the demands might contribute something to the enlightenment of some, if not that of labor leaders and partisans. One lesson that economic reformers will doubtless keep on refusing to learn is that imperfect competition between buyers of labor does not open the way to raising wages forcibly without causing unemployment, but rather makes matters worse for that project. A wide range of gain and loss among enterprises means that more of them are on the margin of bankruptcy or beyond it but holding on at a loss in the hope of better times. Accordingly, there is the more certainty that an increase in costs will force closing down or do so on a more extensive scale.

The possibility of mulcting enterprise, by the government or by a labor union able to call a strike of workers necessary to operations, depends on the length of the interval considered and on a wide range of factors, impossible to list or classify. The scope of incomes in jeopardy from a sudden and unexpected stoppage will extend far beyond pure profit and its recipients. As we have noted, the entrepreneurial function itself can be but very incompletely specialized. The profit receiver normally furnishes both labor and property services that "could be" hired from others and could be sold to others and paid for by wages and rent-or-interest, as the case may be.[8] On the other hand, anyone who makes any "commitment" of labor or property to an enterprise shares more or less in the entrepreneur function, especially in the risk of any untoward occurrence, such as a strike, cutting off its income or reducing it so as to impinge on his normal expectation of a share in its earnings.

The limit to the mulcting of enterprise by threat of a strike is fixed, of course, by the loss the employer can afford to take—or inflict on others for whom he acts as an agent, rather than to fight it out with the striking organization—or ultimately through bankruptcy and liquidation. It will depend on the complex commitments of the profit-receiver, which cannot be stated in general terms, also on the degree to which he holds himself responsible to other interests. A list of these might begin with the owners of property committed on various terms and effectively for various intervals, from lessors to holders of various categories of securities and business creditors. Included also are employees not directly parties to the strike and the social interest in order and the maintaining of free institutions. The most important interest of all may be that of the consumers of the product. It is standard union policy to inflict as much inconvenience and loss as possible on the largest group of these, expecting them to exert pressure on the management to yield to the strikers' demands. And popular prejudices are such that this tactic is often effective—in the face of the

[8] A full analysis of profit would have to go into the relations between rent and interest, i.e., between leasing property and paying rent and owning it and paying or imputing interest. More might also be said about the relations between property and personal services as sources of income, from the standpoint of the justice or expediency of taxation. Popular prejudice exaggerates the difference, from the standpoint of justice, even to the absurdity of contrasting property rights with "human rights"; also into that of the law (the Clayton Act) solemnly declaring that labor is not a commodity.

obvious fact that in no very long run consumers must pay the bill in a mixture of higher prices and reduced supply. (The "bill" including the costs of strikes, as already pointed out.)[9]

As to what happens when the fight psychology enters into a labor dispute—as it usually does in varying degree—again, little can be said in general terms or beyond what is familiar to newspaper readers. A fight is, of course, normally costly to all parties involved. Unions or their leaders and to a large extent the public hold, quite logically, that the right to strike implies the right to do anything judged necessary to make the strike effective. (The right itself is sacrosanct, though corresponding action by an employer is wicked.) The result can rarely be achieved without coercive action to prevent the management from securing replacements. (As is the case with monopolies in general.) The first recourse is normally appeal to public opinion, whipped up by propaganda, working on the popular prejudice in favor of "workers" against "business" and "property"—but the end justifies the means. This goes on to political action and (as news readers also know) to personal intimidation and often to overt violence against both property and persons. In politics, informed people know that the laws (in the U.S. and Britain) purposively give unions the maximum advantage against employers, and encourage the former to inflict damage, even suffering, on consumers and others not parties to a dispute; thus they increase the arbitrary power of unions and their leaders. When general laws are not enough, special legislation may be enacted to deal with special situations, as in the case of railway labor in the U.S. Incidentally, the current plight of these necessary agencies and the inadequacy of their services are in no small part due to legally sanctioned "featherbedding" and other wasteful practices imposed by unions; and similar conditions are notorious in the building trades and elsewhere.

To bring this chapter to a conclusion, three points may be stressed. First, all that has been said in no way implies condemnation of organizations of wage earners, as such, and for activities consonant with

[9] The writer recalls a strike of operatives of the street cars in the city where he was living, when the companies were in receivership and not making expenses. The agent of the court reportedly asked the strikers' representative where he was expected to get the money to meet the wage demand, and received the reply, "That is your problem."

the public interest. Such action would not conflict with the interests of management—with the same qualification, that the latter acts honorably and intelligently as the agent of the ultimate producers, both wage-earners and property owners, and of the consumers. In the large, they are all obviously the same people; all are members of the vast cooperative which we call the competitive economic order. Preferably, the relations between labor and management should be consciously cooperative as their substantive interests are complementary. When particular interests do come into conflict, as they will on many occasions, the relation should be at least peaceful, leaving the adjudication of differences to impartial arbitrators or finally to the one agency which at all effectively represents all interests in the economy, the democratic state.

The rightful positive role and scope of labor organizations is a topic too vast to be taken up in detail here. They quite certainly should not exercise monopoly power, and the state should as far as possible prevent their having it—especially the right to strike (in concert, collusively)—as it should do with respect to enterprise. Monopolistic action by labor unions inevitably interferes with the working of the enterprise system, particularly with the performance by entrepreneurs of their necessary functions—the anticipation of changes and adaptation to change, and especially the selection and introduction of innovations on which growth depends. Monopolistic action by labor is possible only in an established and "going" situation, and can be effective only against a profitable employer monopoly; in general this is an exceptional and short-run phenomenon, offset by operation at a loss at other times or by other firms. In any case, a bilateral or countervailing monopoly is a pernicious arrangement, as it can only lead to deadlock and throw the decision into the field of force. In cases where market competition cannot be made reasonably effective, or where its results can be improved upon by political action, that should of course be adopted.

In general, the only wise course for society and for all the main special interests is to make the best possible division of labor between the two systems, the economic and the political order, recognizing that the relation between them as forms of social control is properly cooperative. On the positive side, labor organizations have two indubitable rights, among others. One is bargaining in the honest meaning already stated, the practice of persuasive salesmanship—though the objective of such activity in general is to establish a degree and kind of monopoly. The other is the right to conduct political propaganda, under reasonable and lawful standards—like any interest group or any individual in a free society. Its merits, the democracy must judge. The need for grievance machinery and promotion of various common interests not calling for monopoly power calls for no comment.

The second point to be stressed is implied in stating the first. The term "wages" should be honestly used; that is, it should refer to the price of labor service, determined in the open market where independent able and willing buyers and sellers are brought into communication to make offers and freely accept or reject offers made. But this suggests the third point, which was stated earlier. There is no implication that wages, the economic value of a human service, determined by demand and supply under the most idealized competitive conditions and expressing the free choices of consumers and producers, measure the income a worker ought to get. That is a matter for the democratic government to decide, along with the method and all details of desirable redistribution out of incomes judged too high, in view of the needs where they are inadequate. All this, of course, after allowing for voluntary private charity—including paying workers more than they earn, provided the excess comes out of the incomes of those responsible for making the payment.

A final word: The supreme social need, as this chapter should make clear, is—again repeating—more widespread understanding of and respect for the truisms of the economics and politics of free society. Specifically, that means the comparative merits and limitations of competitive-profit-seeking and competitive vote-seeking as the foundation of economic organization. Decisions of social policy are finally made by political action, but as they affect economic activity, intelligent decision requires a comparison between the two, in terms of the consequences of action or inaction, and of what is judged by the political order to be desirable.

3

Unions, Inflation, and Profits

F. A. Hayek

TENDENCIES are observable in the field of labor economics which most seriously threaten our future prosperity. The developments which are bringing this about are not of recent date. They extend at least over the last twenty-five years. But for most of that time, and particularly during the long period of great prosperity through which we have recently passed, it may have seemed as if the United States could take in its stride even those new hurdles which only a few alarmists regarded as serious. But there are strong reasons for thinking that things will soon be coming to a head. It may be that already those new demands of labor which I want later to examine in some detail will prove to be the critical point. Or Walter Reuther may decide that this is not a favorable moment for a decisive test of strength and the fatal struggle will be deferred a little further. Whichever it will be, I have little doubt that we shall soon have to face fundamental issues which we have managed to avoid for so long and which have not become easier to solve because the practices and institutions which raise them have been allowed to continue for such a long time.

Before turning to the more specific problems which the new union demands raise, I must explain how I see the more general problem of policy which the powers of modern labor unions create, and describe the character of the particular phase of business fluctuations in which it seems those problems will now have to be decided.

The first of these tasks divides itself into two distinct yet closely connected ones: the character which labor organizations have gradually assumed, and the new powers they have obtained, not as a result of anything *they* can do, but as a result of the new conceptions of the tasks of credit and fiscal policy. With regard to the first, though it contains the crux of the union problem, I can be very brief. The essential facts are here so well known that I need merely mention the chief points. Unions have not achieved their present magnitude and power by merely achieving the right of association. They have become what they are largely in consequence of the grant, by legislation and jurisdiction, of unique privileges which no other associations or individuals enjoy. They are the one institution where government has signally failed in its first task, that of preventing coercion of men by other men—and by coercion I do not mean primarily the coercion of employers but the coercion of workers by their fellow workers. It is only because of the coercive powers unions have been allowed to exercise over those willing to work at terms not approved by the union, that the latter has become able to exercise harmful coercion of the employer. All this has become possible because in the field of labor relations it has come to be accepted belief that the ends justify the means, and that, because of the public approval of the aims of union effort, they ought to be exempted from the ordinary rules of law. The whole modern development of unionism has been made possible mainly by the fact that public policy was guided by the belief that it was in the public interest that labor should be as comprehensively and completely organized as possible, and that in the pursuit of this aim the unions should be as little restricted as possible. This is certainly not a public interest. But all this has been so admirably treated by Sylvester Petro of New York University in his recent book *The Labor Policy of the Free Society* [1] that I need merely refer to that work.

I must take a little longer in discussing the particular circumstances which have made the power of unions over wages so especially dangerous in the present world. It is often said that successful general union pressure for higher wages necessarily produces inflation. This is not correct as a general proposition. It is, however, only too true under the particular conditions under which we now live. Since it

[1] *The Labor Policy of the Free Society* (New York, 1957).

has become the generally accepted doctrine that it is the duty of the monetary authorities to provide enough credit to secure full employment, whatever the wage level, and this duty has in fact been imposed upon the monetary authorities by statute, the power of the unions to push up money wages cannot but lead to continuous, progressive inflation. It is the blessing that J. M. Keynes has showered on us which we enjoy in this respect.

We are not concerned here with the niceties of his theory. What we are concerned with is the factual assumption on which his whole argument rests: that it is easier to cheat workers out of a gain in real wages by a reduction in the value of money than to reduce money wages, and with his contention that this method ought to be employed every time real wages have become too high to allow of "full employment." Where Lord Keynes went wrong was in the naive belief that workers would let themselves be deceived by this for any length of time, and that the lowering of the purchasing power of wages would not at once produce new demands for higher wages—demands which would be even more irresistible when it was recognized that they would not be allowed to have any effect on employment.

What we have achieved is a division of responsibilities under which one group can enforce a wage level without regard to the effects on employment, and another agency is responsible for providing whatever amount of money is needed to secure full employment at that wage level. So long as this is the accepted principle, it is true that the monetary authorities have no choice but to pursue a policy resulting in continuous inflation, however little they may like it. But that in the existing state of opinion they cannot do anything else, does not alter the fact that, as always, it is monetary policy and nothing else which is the cause of inflation.

We have behind us the first long period of such cost-push inflation, as it has come to be called. It has been one of the longest periods of high prosperity on record. But, though the upward trend of wages has not yet stopped, the forces which have been making for prosperity have been flagging for some time. We have probably reached the point when we must reap the inevitable harvest of a period of inflation. Nobody can be certain about this. It may well be that another massive dose of inflation may once more get us rapidly out of the recession. But that, in my opinion, would merely postpone the evil day—and make the ultimate result much worse. Inflation-born prosperity has never been and never will be lasting prosperity. It depends on factors which are nourished, not simply by inflation, but by an increase in the rate of inflation. And though we may have permanent inflation, we clearly cannot for very long have inflation at a progressive rate.

Such inflation-fed prosperity neither comes to an end because final demand becomes insufficient to take the whole product off the market, nor can it be perpetuated by simply keeping final demand at a sufficiently high level. The decline always begins, and did begin this time, in the field of investment, and it is only as a consequence of the decline of incomes in the investment goods industries that final demand is later affected. It is true that this secondary shrinkage in final demand may become cumulative and tend to become the controlling factor; it may then turn what would otherwise be merely a period of recession and readjustment into a major depression. There is, therefore, every reason to counteract these tendencies and to prevent them from setting up a deflationary spiral. But this does not mean that by merely maintaining final demand at a sufficiently high level we can secure continued full employment and avoid the readjustment and incidental unemployment made necessary by the transition from inflationary to stable monetary conditions. The reason for this is that investment is not, as is often naively believed, coupled in any simple manner with final demand; a given volume of final demand does not always evoke a proportional, or perhaps even more than proportional, change in investment in the same direction. There are other factors embodied in the whole price-cost structure which determine what rate of investment will be evoked by a given level of demand. It is a change in these factors which brings about the primary decline in investment and incomes which then produces a decline of final demand.

I cannot here examine this highly complex and very controversial mechanism in detail.

I will confine myself to two considerations which seem to me to prove that the predominant "lack of buying power" theory of depression is just wrong. One is the empirical fact that not only have declines of investment often started when final demand and prices were rising rapidly, but also that attempts to revive investment by stimulating final demand have almost invariably failed. The great depression of the 'thirties was indeed the first occasion when, under the influence of such "purchasing power theories," deliberate efforts were made from the very beginning to maintain wages and purchasing power; and we managed to turn it into the longest and most severe depression on record. The second point is that the whole argument on which the purchasing power view rests suffers from an inherent contradiction. It proceeds as if, even under conditions of full or nearly full employment, an increase in the demand for final products would lead to a switching of resources from producing final goods to producing investment goods. Indeed, it suggests that if at any one time the demand for consumers' goods should become very urgent, the immediate effect would be that fewer consumers' goods and more investment goods would be produced. I suppose that in the extreme case, because people want more consumers' goods very urgently, no consumers' goods and only investment goods would be produced. Clearly there must be a mechanism which will bring it about that the opposite happens. But unless we understand that mechanism, we cannot be sure that it may not also operate under conditions of less than full employment. We evidently cannot accept the current popular view on these matters, which not only offers no answer to that crucial problem, but which, if consistently pursued, leads into absurdities.

I now come to my main subject. The reason why I have spent so much time in diagnosing the economic situation in which the new demands of labor are presented is, partly, that they are presented both as non-inflationary and as a safeguard against (or a remedy for) depression, but mainly because in the present situation the greatest pressure will be brought on the employers to avoid a labor dispute, which at this juncture may have very serious consequences. But the decisions which the corporations facing the new demands will have to make are decisions of principle which may have tremendous long-term effects, indeed, may do much to shape the future of our society. They should be made entirely in consideration of their long-run significance and not be affected by the desire to get out of our momentary difficulties. But with the power the unions have acquired, the capacity of the corporations to resist any harmful demands depends on what support they get from public opinion. It is therefore of the greatest importance that we clearly understand what these demands really imply, what their satisfaction and the general acceptance of the principle underlying them would mean for the future character of our economy.

As my readers know, Mr. Reuther has presented the demands of the United Automobile Workers for 1958 as a "two-package" program, consisting of a set of "minimum basic demands which will be common for all employers" and of supplementary demands "in addition to the minimum for those corporations or companies in a more favored economic position"—or, in other words, one set of demands applying to the automobile industry generally, and further demands directed to the Big Three. The first package constitutes in general only "more of the same as before"—although we have been told that it will be the biggest wage increase demanded in the history of the automobile industry—and I shall consider it only briefly as an illustration of what I have already said about the inflationary character of these demands and especially about their significance in the present phase of business. It is the second set which raises the interesting new problems and, I believe, constitutes a real threat to the future of our economy.

Of the first part of the demands, I want to examine only the claims that wage increases proportional to the increase in average output per head of the employed are non-inflationary, and that "increasing mass purchasing power" through wage increases is an effective means of combatting depression. They are easy to dispose of. Changes in output per head are, of course, not the same as changes in the productivity of labor. To see this clearly we need merely consider an extreme but by no means impracticable case, such as the replacement of present power stations by highly automatized atomic energy stations. Once one of these modern stations is erected, a handful of men would appear to be the sole producers of a colossal amount of electric energy and their output per head may have increased hundreds of times. But that does not mean that the productivity of labor in that industry has significantly increased in any sense relevant to our problem, or that in that industry the marginal product of a given number of workers has increased at all. The increase in average productivity of labor in the industry is the result of the investment made and in no way reflects the value which a man's work contributes to its product. To raise wages in proportion to the increase in average productivity in that industry would raise them to many times their marginal product in other industries of the economy. Unless we assume that the particular men employed in that industry acquire a vested right in a share of the product of that investment and are entitled to earn much more than exactly similar labor elsewhere, it will mean a general rise in money wages far in excess of what can be paid without a general rise in money incomes, that is, without inflation.

This does not mean, of course, that labor may not succeed in pushing up money wages to that level, but it means that this would be highly inflationary and could not mean a significant increase in their real wages for the workers of this kind as a whole. Since the illustration just given throws much light on one of the crucial aspects of the power of modern labor monopoly, I will dwell on it just a little longer. Where very large and very durable investments have once been made, it is today the owner of these investments who is almost completely at the mercy of an effective monopoly of the supply of labor. Once such plants have been created, and so long as they can be kept going without substantial renewal or re-investment, labor is in a position to appropriate almost any share of the returns due to the investment of the capital. The demand for a definite share in the increase in the average productivity of labor due to the investment of capital amounts, in fact, to nothing less than an attempt to expropriate that capital. There is no reason why a really powerful union monopoly should not succeed in this to a large extent so far as investments irrevocably committed to a particular purpose are concerned.

This, however, is only a relatively short-run effect and the advantages that labor as a whole can derive from such policies look very different when we consider what effects such policies must have on the attractiveness of new investment once they come to be anticipated. Personally, I am convinced that this power of union monopolies is, together with contemporary methods of taxation, the chief deterrent to private investment in productive equipment which we have allowed to grow up. We must not be surprised that private investment dries up as soon as uncertainty about the future increases after we have created a situation in which most of the gain of a large, risky and successful investment goes to the unions and the government, while a loss has to be born by the investor. Man is so made that in times of great prosperity he still tends to forget about these deterrents. But we must not be surprised that as soon as prospects darken a little, these reasonable fears revive in full strength and we face another apparent "exhaustion of investment opportunities" which is entirely the result of our own follies.

This brings me to the second aspect of the general demands of the U.A.W.: their significance at a time of threatening depression. It is contended that an increase of wages at this juncture will result in an over-all increase in purchasing power and thereby reverse the tendency towards a shrinkage of incomes. I do not wish to deny that at a time when there is danger that we may be entering a deflationary spiral, it is desirable that aggregate spending power should be prevented from falling further. What I question is that raising wages is a sensible or effective method to achieve this. What we need in the first instance is not that some people earn more but that more people earn an income, and particularly that employment revive in the capital goods industries. There is every likelihood that in the present phase of business an increase of wages will lead immediately to a decrease of employment in the industries concerned—even if it is not achieved through a labor dispute and work stoppage which, at present, would react even more rapidly on employment. And it seems certain to have even more harmful indirect effects on employment in the investment industries. I believe that under conditions of more or less full employment an increase of real wages of the final producers may act as an incentive to investment—crudely speaking because it induces the producer to substitute machinery for labor. But this is certainly *not* true in a situation where a large part of the capacity of the existing equipment is unused. In such a situation, investment does depend solely on how much of the final product can be sold at a profit, and that prospect can only be worsened by raising money costs first.

I must not enlarge any further, however, on the first part of Mr. Reuther's "packages" since, after all, they do not raise any problems with which we have not all been long familiar. Even if some of the consideration I have mentioned cannot be stated often enough, or emphasized strongly enough, there is nothing new in them.

The interesting part of the proposals is the second "package," the special, discriminatory terms for the more successful enterprises in the automobile industry. It is not quite easy to say what their aim is or what Mr. Reuther expects to achieve by them. But it is well worth while to ask what the consequences would be if they were successful.

It will doubtless be remembered that before the U.A.W. put forward this demand they had asked that the Big Three reduce the price of their cars by $100 and promised that if this were done, the U.A.W. would take this into account in formulating their new demands. The fact that this suggestion has not been acted upon is now advanced as a justification for the new demands. I do not believe that that demand for price reduction ought to be taken very seriously, and it is probably more correctly seen as a public relations job—intended to prepare public opinion for the demands subsequently put forward. The union had, in fact, used exactly the same tactics twelve years earlier. But it will help to understand the present issue if we examine for a moment the significance of that demand.

For the purposes of the argument, let us assume that General Motors and perhaps also the two other big automobile manufacturers could, in fact, profitably sell their cars at the reduced price, and that perhaps over a limited period this would even turn out to their advantage. There seems very little question but that this would rapidly mean the end of the remaining independent producers and leave the Big Three alone in the field. If that is so, the first question on which we must form an opinion is why they do not go ahead and reduce their prices. One obvious answer is, of course, that such action would probably bring them rapidly into conflict with the anti-trust authorities. We have reached the ridiculous position where an attempt to act competitively will lay a particularly efficient organization open to the charge of aiming at monopoly. I do not know what advantages Mr. Reuther imagines his workers would reap from this result, if he really wanted it. I merely mention this to point out that it would almost certainly bring about results which are contrary to one of the accepted objects of public policy.

In fact, it seems very doubtful whether the Big Three regard it as really in their interest that the independent producers should be eliminated. If any one of them did think it desirable, he could quickly force the others into a course of action which would have that result. But it seems to me much more likely that a concern like General Motors, which takes such pains to preserve active competition between its divisions, would for the same reasons regard it in its long-run interest to preserve the independent experimentation of the smaller producers. After all, the men inside the big corporations probably understand better than many outside observers that the exceptional efficiency of a particular organization is not the necessary result of size, but rather that size is the result of the exceptional efficiency of a particular organization. They doubtless know also that such exceptional efficiency does not only not follow automatically from size, or from any device or design which can be established once and for all, but only from a constant and ever-renewed effort to do better than can be done by any other known method. I feel very strongly that in this sphere the simplified schemes which the economic theorist legitimately uses as a first approach, and which treat costs as a function of size and approach the problem in terms of economics of scale, have become an obstacle to a realistic understanding of the important factors. Many of the individual and unique features of a particular corporation which make for its success are of the same character as the similar features of an individual person; they exist largely as an intangible tradition of an approach to problems, based on a tradition which is handed on but ever changing, and which, though it may secure a long superiority, may be challenged at any time by a new and even more effective corporate personality. I must say that if I were responsible for the fate of one of these corporations I would not only feel that I was acting in the best interest of the corporation if I sacrificed the temporary gain from the control of an even larger share of the market in order to preserve the stimulus which has kept the organization on tip-toe so long. I should also feel that in my efforts to prolong this leadership as long as possible, and use for this purpose part of the differential profits which this greater efficiency allowed my corporation to earn, I was acting in the interest of the community at large. An advantage of an individual or a corporation which cannot be duplicated remains an advantage to society even though nobody else has it; it ought to be made full use of so long as nobody else is prevented from bettering the result by different and even greater advantages. To think of such positions in terms which are appropriate to monopolies based on obstacles to entry into an industry leads to an altogether distorted approach to the problems of policy.

It will be useful to remember this when we now turn to the specific demand of the automobile workers directed only to the three dominant corporations. I am not a little puzzled to understand what Mr. Reuther really expects to achieve by them, and from what parts of them he expects to derive any real benefit for the employees, and what part has been put in rather for its optical effect, that is, to gain the support of public opinion. The result of the acceptance of these demands would depend on certain decisions on the part of the management of the corporations, the character of which is by no means obvious. I shall, therefore, have to consider the consequences of these demands being accepted on the basis of alternative assumptions about how the corporations would respond to the new conditions.

The "supplementary economic demands" directed to the Big Three are that one half of all profits in excess of ten per cent on what is called "net capital" should be divided equally between employees and the consumers so that one quarter of these "excess profits" during any one year should be given as a rebate to the buyers of cars, while another quarter should be handed over to the unions to do with it as they please. It is this last feature which distinguishes the proposal from all other profit-sharing plans and particularly from the profit-sharing plan which was offered by some automobile manufacturers to the workers and was turned down by them. It is not a plan to give the individual worker a determinable share in the ownership of the enterprise and therefore in its profits, but rather a plan to give the union, or the representatives of the workers employed in the corporation at a given time, control over, in the first instance, one quarter of the profits in excess of ten per cent on net capital.

There are various grounds why the idea that the workers in a corporation should be given a favored opportunity to invest their savings in the corporation seems attractive, and there are also good reasons why the great hopes which some people have set on such plans have scarcely ever been justified. Though the worker may find greater satisfaction in working for a corporation where he has a share in the profits, however small, and take a greater interest in the prosperity of the corporation, it is also natural that, if he has any savings to invest, he would normally prefer not to stake them on the same enterprise on the prosperity of which all the rest of his income depends.

It is, however, an entirely different matter if it is demanded that the body of workers employed by a firm at any one time, without having contributed to its capital, be given a share in the profits. The effect will in part depend on how this share is to be distributed among the workers or otherwise used for their benefit. On this the proposal as published leaves us largely in the dark. It merely tells us that the workers of any company "would determine democratically how they chose to allocate the money available from their companies through this supplementary package" and adds a list of purposes for which they may be used which ends with "any other purpose which they deem advisable." I sometimes wonder whether this is not the most ominous sentence in the whole document, since it leaves open the possibility that the individual worker may get little if anything for his free disposal and that the money will be used mainly for the collective purposes of the union, i.e., further to increase its power.

So far as the effects on the position of the companies affected are concerned, we must distinguish between the short- and the long-run effects. In the relatively short run, the companies would have the choice between absorbing the loss of net profits and continuing essentially the same price policies as before, or at once trying to recoup themselves by an adjustment of prices. The former would mean that they would both be in a stronger position in the labor market compared with their weaker competitors and also offer the consumers what amounts to a lower price—though how significant the expectation of an uncertain and at best small rebate at the end of the year would be in affecting the choice of the purchaser seems doubtful. At any rate, so long as they followed this policy, the tendency would necessarily be to strengthen their superiority over the less successful companies and to increase the likelihood of the elimination of the latter. If, on the other hand, the companies concerned decided that they could not afford the reduction of profits but that it was expedient to raise prices sufficiently so as to restore them (so far as practicable), the car buyers would not only have no advantage at all—they would have to pay more than before, because they would have to provide the additional profits which would have to be obtained to satisfy the demands of labor.

In the long run, however, the managements of the corporations would have no such choice. Mr. Reuther is here obscuring the main issue by calling all profits in excess of ten per cent on "net capital" before taxation (i.e., 4.8 per cent after taxation) "excess profits." I will not examine here the difficulties which the vague concept of "net capital" raises in this connection but, for the purposes of the argument, shall assume that it can be given a sufficiently definite meaning. Whatever this basis of calculation, it is difficult to see in what sense the profits actually earned by the successful industries can be called "excessive." It is true they are high in comparison with those companies in the industry that are struggling for survival, but hardly in any other sense. The commonly accepted measures of profitability scarcely suggest that the profits earned by the three companies are more than is necessary in such a highly risky field to make the investment of new capital attractive: at the end of last year the value of the shares of both Ford and Chrysler was below the book value of the assets of these companies, and only the price of General Motors shares exceeded the book value of the assets by more than the average for all the companies included in the Dow-Jones index number of the prices of industrial stocks.[2] But even if it could be seriously

[2] See the Statement by Theodore O. Yntema, Vice President-Finance, Ford Motor Company, before the Subcommittee on Antitrust and Monopoly of the Committee on the Judiciary, United States Senate, Washington D.C., February 4–5, 1958.

maintained that the profits of these companies were in some meaningful sense "excessive," surely this would only constitute a case that, in the general interest, more capital should be invested in the companies concerned and not a case for making investment in them less profitable. Or, assuming there were any grounds on which it could be contended that the big firms in the automobile industry were making "monopoly profits," this would seem to me the strongest possible case against giving the workers a vested interest in the preservation of such monopoly profits.

This brings me at last to the general principle involved in those demands, the question of what would be the significance for the character of our whole economic system if the principle underlying them were generally applied. This is a question which must be examined without any regard to the particular figures mentioned in Mr. Reuther's "packages." If it is in any sense right that the employees of a particular firm should get one quarter of the profits in excess of ten per cent, it would seem equally right that next time they should demand one half, or that they should claim some even larger percentage of all profits. It is, of course, a familiar and only all-too-often successful practice to establish a new principle by putting forward at first what may seem quantitatively a not very important demand, and only when the principle has been established to push its application further and further. It may be that Mr. Reuther was not very wise in asking in the first instance as much as one quarter of what he calls excess profits. The danger that he would gain his point would probably be much greater if in the first instance he had asked a modest ten per cent and only after the principle had been established had pushed for a higher participation. Perhaps because he has on the first occasion asked for as much as he did, the public will be more ready to grasp what the establishment of the principle would mean.

The recognition of the right of the worker of a firm *qua* worker, to participate in a share of the profits, irrespective of any contribution he has made to its capital, establishes him as a part owner of this firm. In this sense the demand is, of course, purely socialistic and, what is more, not based on any socialist theory of the more sophisticated and rational kind, but on the crudest type of socialism, commonly known as syndicalism. It is the form in which socialist demands usually first appear but which, because of their absurd consequences, have been abandoned by all of the theorists of socialism. It is at least possible to put up a rational argument in favor of nationalizing all industrial capital (though I believe it can be demonstrated—and is confirmed by all experience—that the consequences of such a policy would be disastrous). But it is not even possible to construct a rational argument in support of the contention that the workers employed at any one time in a firm or industry should collectively own the equipment of that industry. Any attempt to think through the consequences of such an arrangement soon shows that it is utterly incompatible with any rational use of the resources of society, and would soon lead to complete disorganization of the economic system. The final outcome would, no doubt, merely be that some new closed group of established workers would entrench themselves as the new proprietors and endeavor to get out of the seized property as much for their benefit as they could. The expropriation of one groups of capitalists would have been achieved, but only to give some other group an equally exclusive (and probably equally temporary) right to the particular assets.

This is not the proper place, nor should it be necessary once more to demonstrate the unworkability of a syndicalist system. What needs to be brought out is that the fulfilment of Mr. Reuther's demand would be a step towards syndicalism and that, once the first step were taken, it is difficult to see how further demands in the same direction could be resisted. If the U.A.W. has now the power to appropriate part of the capital of some of the biggest enterprises in the country, there is no reason why the same power should not next time be used to appropriate more and in the end all of it, and why the same should not happen in other industries. Nothing, indeed, brings home more vividly the dangers of the situation we have allowed to grow up over the last twenty-five years than the fact that it is necessary to examine such demands seriously and to explain at length why they must on no account be accepted if we are to preserve the fundamental character of our economy. I hope it is due to the fact that most people believe that these demands will not be pressed seriously and that, at least this time, they have been put forward as a bargaining maneuvre, that they have not caused more concern. But I fear that it may be more due to the fact that the public have not yet realized that much more is at stake than the prosperity of three big corporations. What will be tested when these demands are seriously put forward is the crucial issue of how far the organized groups of industrial workers are allowed to use the coercive power they have acquired to force on the rest of this country a change in the basic institutions on which our social and economic system rests. This is no longer a situation where we can afford the detached view which assumes that in a conflict of interests there is always something to be said for both sides and a compromise to be desired. It is a situation when even the fear of the grave consequences which at this juncture a prolonged labor dispute and perhaps a long stoppage of production might have must not be allowed to influence our position. It is, it seems to me, a moment at which all who desire the preservation of the market system based on free enterprise must unambiguously desire and support an outright rejection of these demands without flinching at the short-run consequences this may produce.

Many people probably still feel that the great automobile manufacturers are able to take care of themselves and that we need not concern ourselves about their problems. This is scarcely any longer true. The fact is that we have permitted a situation to develop in which the unions have grown so powerful, and at the same time the employees deprived of any effective defense, that there must be grave doubt about the outcome if Mr. Reuther, according to his favorite practice, singles out one of the Big Three for attack. We have reached a point when the question of how we can still enable one such corporation effectively to resist demands which, if satisfied, would place us straight on the road to syndicalism, must be a major public concern. Mr. Reuther may, indeed, be in a position to bring most severe pressure, not only on that corporation but on the public at large, because it may depend on him whether the present decline is turned into a major depression. It should be clearly recognized that the responsibility is entirely his and that no threat will frighten the public into a compromise which in the long run could be even more fatal. It seems to me that in this situation the economist must not shirk this duty of speaking plainly. This is not a pleasant task for one who as a scientist must aim to be impartial and whose inclination is either not to take sides in a particular dispute of interests or, if he has to, to favour the side on which are the relatively poorer. I have admit that I have my doubts whether the predominant concern of so many economists with what they regard as justice in the particular case rather than with the consequences of a measure for the structure of society as a whole has on the whole been beneficial. But I am quite sure that the present issue has nothing at all to do with questions of justice between the particular parties involved but that it raises a question of principle which should be decided in the light of the consequences which its general adoption would have for our society. If this means that the economist, whose chief duty it is to think through and explain the long-run consequences, has to take what may be the unpopular side, particularly the side which is likely to be unpopular among the general class of intellectuals to which he belongs, I feel it becomes even more his duty to do so unreservedly and unequivocally. Perhaps I may conclude with the words of one of the wisest and most detached of economists, which have been quoted before at the head of a well-known essay called "Reflections on Syndicalism" which is now proving to have been dreadfully prophetic. The passage by Alfred Marshall which Henry Simons quoted at the head of that essay runs as follows: "Students of social science must fear popular approval; evil is with them when all men speak well of them. If there is any set of opinions by the advocacy of which a newspaper can increase its sales, the student, who wishes to leave the world in general and his country in particular better than it would be if he had not been born, is bound to dwell on the limitations and defects and errors, if any, in that set of opinions: and never to advocate unconditionally even in an *ad hoc* discussion. It is almost impossible for a student to be a true patriot and to have the reputation of being one in his own time."[3] It is probably equally impossible in our time for a student to be a true friend of labor and to have the reputation of being one.

[3] Henry C. Simons, "Some Reflections on Syndicalism," *Journal of Political Economy*, Vol. LII, No. 1 (March, 1944), p. 1.

4

Wage Policy and Inflation*

Gottfried Haberler

THE PROBLEM OF INFLATION and its relation to wage policy is very crucial and timely. In fact, barring the outbreak of a shooting war or a great intensification of the cold war, chronic creeping inflation and the role of wage policy in the inflationary mechanism will probably be the most important domestic economic problem with which the United States will be faced in the next few years.

The United States is now in its third postwar depression (not counting the drop in industrial production from early 1944 to the end of 1945). I am not going to speculate at length how long it will last nor how deep it will go. Let me simply state my conviction that it will not last very long nor go very deep for the simple reason that if it did show signs of getting out of hand we can be reasonably sure that measures would be taken, some combination of monetary and fiscal policies, to bring it to an end.

The cyclical pattern after World War I differed significantly from the cyclical pattern after World War II. The first postwar depression, 1948–49, was much milder than the first depression after World War I in 1920–21,[1] and the second major postwar depression has been conspicuous by its absence.

* Written in February, 1958.

[1] Alternatively, one might say that this time we have skipped the first postwar depression, equating the recession of 1948–49 to that of 1923–24, and the recession of 1953–54 to that of 1926–27. The present depression would thus correspond to the Great Depression of 1929–33. But we can be sure that it will not become nearly as bad.

On the whole we can say, I believe, that things have been better managed, or at any rate have worked out better, this time than the last time. The rise in output and employment has been faster and more sustained than after World War I and if a catastrophe like the Great Depression can be avoided, which I am sure will be the case, the record of the period of 1945–65 will be tremendously better than that of the period from 1918 to 38.

But now let us look at the price development. Here too we find a profound difference between the trend during the two periods of 16 years from the beginning of the two world wars. The price rise during World War II was a little less precipitous than during World War I, but the difference is not as great as a superficial glance at the index would suggest because inflation was partly hidden by price control and rationing, at least until 1946.[2] There was, however, a sharp drop in prices after World War I in 1920–21 and then after a fairly stable period of almost 8 years another sharp decline occurred from the middle of 1929 to the end of 1932. After World War II nothing of this sort happened. The consumer price index shows only a very slight decline in 1948–49 and a pause from 1952–56. Wholesale prices fell a trifle from the middle of 1948 to the middle of 1949 and then again a little after the end of the Korean War. During the mild recession of 1953–54 the wholesale price index did not change at all, a drop in prices of farm products being offset by the continuing rise of other items.

It is true that, as Arthur Burns has pointed out in his remarkable lectures *Prosperity Without Inflation,*[3] the increase in wholesale prices of 8 per cent during the last boom (between December, 1954, and August, 1957) or the 6 per cent rise in consumer prices during the same boom are not extraordinary by historical standards. According to Burns, the average rise of wholesale prices during the ascending phase of 18 peacetime cycles between 1850 and 1950 (not counting war years and immediate postwar years) was 17 per cent.

[2] If one takes 1948 as the peak year of the war inflation (which is not unreasonable on the theory that the price rise from 1946–48 was a delayed war effect) there is no difference between the two war inflations. But considering the fact that the economic effort in the second world war was much greater than in the first, we can say that a better job was done in restraining inflation on the second than in the first world war.

[3] Arthur E. Burns, *Prosperity Without Inflation* (New York, 1958), p. 13.

But despite this fact, we can say, I believe, that a profound change in the cyclical and long-run pattern of prices has taken place since about the Great Depression of the 1930's. It finds its expression in the fact that in the past cyclical price rises, even when greatly aggravated by wars, were followed by price declines. This seems no longer to be true. The difference is dramatically revealed when we compare the price curve, whether at wholesale or at retail, for the period from 1914 to 1931 with that for the period of 1940 to 1958. In the first case, we find the picture of a wave, in the second case, the picture of a rising flight of stairs.

What it means is, of course, that we live in a period—it would perhaps be a little presumptious to say in "the age"—of creeping or chronic inflation. I am now going to discuss the role of wage policy in the process of creeping inflation, and I think it will help to guard against the danger of overstating the case if I try to put the problem in proper perspective by briefly recounting some salient facts of recent economic history.

In the United States, as well as abroad (especially in Europe), it has become more and more popular in recent years, first among economists, but now also among journalists and politicians, to distinguish between wage-push and demand-pull inflations. It is said that in the past, before the emergence of powerful labor unions, when prices rose it was because they were "pulled up" by rising demand either in the ascending phase of the business cycle or during periods of war inflation or gold inflation. To-day, on the other hand, prices are often "pushed up" by rising costs due to wage increases forced upon the economy under the threat of strike by powerful labor unions, often with the active help of governments. Usually the conclusion is drawn, explicitly or implicitly, that while the proper treatment of a demand inflation is a tightening of the money supply, monetary policy is not the appropriate answer for a cost-push inflation, because it would be either ineffective or be effective only with very costly side effects in the form of an intolerable amount of unemployment.[4]

[4] It is interesting to recall that J. M. Keynes in his *A Treatise on Money* (1930) distinguished between "profit inflation" on the one hand and "income or wage inflation" on the other. A mere profit inflation is, however, a transitory phenomenon because wages

The theory that there is such a thing as a wage-push inflation as distinguished from a demand-pull inflation, and that we now suffer from the former rather than from the latter, has not remained unchallenged. It is natural that it should be rejected by the unions themselves and their economists. But it is also more or less discounted by economists who are beyond the suspicion of pleading for special interests and who have anything but a soft heart for labor monopolies. I am thinking here of some members of the Chicago School, notably of Milton Friedman.[5] In England, men like Sir Dennis Robertson[6] and Lionel Robbins[7] have expressed the opinion that the current in-

---

and other income will ordinarily be quickly pulled up when profits are inflated; that is, a profit inflation will draw an income inflation in its wake. This is what Keynes calls an "induced income inflation," to be distinguished from a "spontaneous income or wage inflation" that exists when wages are pushed up by trade unions or government action.

These useful distinctions were unfortunately not carried over into *The General Theory* (1936) where the treatment of the wage-inflation problem is much more rigid and unsatisfactory than in the earlier book.

On Keynes' discussion of inflation in the *Treatise,* see the interesting article by James R. Schlesinger, "The Role of the Monetary Environment in Cost Inflation," *Southern Economic Journal,* Vol. XXIV, No. 1 (July, 1957).

[5] Milton Friedman, "Some Comments on the Significance of Labor Unions for Economic Policy," in D. M. Wright (ed.), *The Impact of the Union* (New York, 1951). See also the interesting article by Walter A. Morton, "Trade Unionism, Full Employment and Inflation," *American Economic Review,* Vol. XL, No. 1 (March, 1950).

[6] One may surmise that Sir Dennis' views are faithfully represented by the "Cohen Committee," in its *First Report of the Council on Prices, Productivity and Income.* This report (Feb. 17, 1958), one of the great economic state papers of our time, deals extensively with the issues here under discussion and leans, as far as the past is concerned, towards a demand-pull explanation of inflation. It makes it quite clear, however, that now, when one may hope that the inflationary demand pull on prices has been stopped by disinflationary policies and by the waning of the boom, there is danger that price stability and full employment may be upset by a continuing wage push. It is very likely that matters will come to a head very soon in the United Kingdom as well as in the United States. If wages continue to be pushed up in the face of stable or falling effective demand we surely are confronted with a wage push *pure et simple.* Is it not plausible to assume that this would have happened earlier if effective demand had been controlled then? If this hypothetical question is answered in the affirmative it seems to me to follow that we had wage-push inflation all along.

[7] See his masterly summing up of recent events: "Thoughts on the Crisis," *Lloyd's Bank Review,* New Series, No. 48 (April, 1958). Robbins argues very persuasively that for the greater part of the postwar period it is "the explanation in terms of the pull of demand which has the greater plausibility." (P. 5.) He admits that "towards the end of the period and at the present time the picture tends to change." (P. 6.) But he is inclined to regard the wage push after the demand has ceased to pull as a hangover from the previous period. It takes the unions time to get adjusted to the different climate.

I sincerely hope events will prove that Mr. Robbins is right, but I greatly doubt it.

flation in Britain is, or until recently was, primarily a demand inflation and ought to be cured by monetary policy.

Now, the disagreement between the two schools, the demand-pull and cost-pull theories of inflation, should not be exaggerated. The proponents of the wage-push theory do not deny that demand-pull plays an indispensable role and that in many cases it is the dominant factor. I have mentioned the fact that during the first World War, when unions were much weaker than in our times, prices rose at least as much as during the second World War. Milton Friedman has shown that during the Civil War prices rose probably about as much as during the two World Wars. This does not prove conclusively that in our time the wage push did not contribute much to inflation, because it would seem to me likely that the resistance of monetary policy against inflation was stronger in the later cases than in the earlier ones so that prices would have risen less, if it had not been for the strong wage push. But nobody would deny that even in the last-mentioned case there has been also a strong demand pull. In fact, both groups would agree that a wage push could not result in a price rise if effective demand did not sufficiently expand. A sufficiently tight money supply could always prevent prices from rising, even if wages are pushed up.

The problem of wage push versus demand pull is, nevertheless, not entirely of the hen or egg variety. The crucial operational question is this: Suppose demand to be sufficiently controlled to prevent a rise in the price level—would this stiffen the employers' resistance to union wage demands to such an extent that wages would be held to that level which is compatible with the given price level *and* the maintenance of full employment? Or would the unions succeed in pushing wages beyond that level, in which case the inescapable result would be unemployment?

The optimists of the demand-pull theory believe that the mere threat of unemployment or a little unemployment would be sufficient to restrain unions. The pessimists, e.g., Sumner H. Slichter and Edward H. Chamberlin, believe that with the present mood of the unions, the methods of collective bargaining and the encouragement that the unions receive from various government policies, it would require a large amount of unemployment, at any rate an amount which would not be tolerated by our society, to maintain price stability.

I need not add that Slichter and Chamberlin draw different conclusions. Slichter resigns himself to a slowly rising price level. He thinks creeping inflation of 2 or 3 per cent per year is unavoidable and is the lesser evil than unemployment and loss of output. Chamberlin does not reconcile himself to this prospect and demands that the evil be eradicated at the source by clipping the monopoly power of unions to push up wages in excess of the gradual rise in *average* labor productivity which results from technical improvements and the accumulation of capital.

All this raises many important issues of which I can take up only a few. The question whether continuous creeping inflation is feasible I shall discuss only very briefly. Let me simply state my opinion that, contrary to what Slichter thinks, a price creep, if pursued long enough as a declared policy, would become a trot and then a gallop and if monetary policy then tried to keep it down to a creep, unemployment would result despite the rising price level. This reasoning, with which the Federal Reserve Board has been defending its policy of tight money, has been often attacked and ridiculed and called hysterical on the grounds that galloping or even trotting inflation is "unthinkable" in the United States. I agree that in the United States galloping inflation is very unlikely (at least in peace time). But this criticism of the Federal Reserve policy is nevertheless irrelevant and irresponsible. If runaway inflation is "unthinkable" it is only so because the Federal Reserve will not allow the money supply to expand sufficiently. What the critics overlook is the possibility, which to my mind is the most probable, almost inevitable, outcome, that if creeping inflation goes on a few years in succession, the mere attempt to keep it down to a creep will produce depression,[8] either unemployment

[8] This is exactly what happened in 1956–57. The tight money policy did not prevent the rise in prices altogether, it only kept it down to a creep. This was sufficient, according to the critics of the tight money policy, to bring on the depression.

I myself would not say categorically that the tight money policy was the only cause of the depression. The boom would have come to an end anyway sooner or later. Probably the Federal Reserve, however, could have kept it going a little longer if rising prices caused by the wage push had not forced its hand.

combined with slowly rising prices or more unemployment with stable or falling prices, in other words, stagnation or cumulative depression. A third possibility, in the long run just as—or even more—pernicious than the others, is an increasingly controlled economy.

But I cannot pursue this problem any further. I return to the question of whether the dilemma actually exists which the pessimists assert and the optimists deny—namely, that without a change in the present methods of collective bargaining, full employment and stable prices cannot be had both at the same time.

Let me now describe the position of the optimists as represented by Milton Friedman.[9]

In the opinion of the Chicago School, the power of labor unions to raise wages or change the wage structure has been greatly exaggerated. Nobody can, of course, deny that in many important industries unions exert a tight control over the supply of labor and conditions of work. In that sense, unions are surely labor monopolies. But Friedman shows, applying Marshall's theory of joint demand, that in order that unions be able to push up wages, it is not sufficient that they control the supply of labor; demand for labor must be sufficiently inelastic. Now, the elasticity of demand for labor for an industry or a firm depends (a) on the elasticity of demand for the product and (b) on the proportion of wage cost in total cost. If, to take up the second condition first, the share of wages in the total cost of the product is small, as in the case of some highly skilled workers in key positions, demand for that kind of labor will be highly inelastic, and a tightly organized union of that kind of labor will be able to raise the wages of their members very high. This explains why the craft unions and, according to Friedman, *only* the craft unions, have been so successful.

The industrial unions, on the other hand, which organize all labor in a particular industry, are not in such a favorable position. They can

[9] Friedman's theory has been subjected to a searching criticism by Lloyd Ulman, "Marshall and Friedman on Union Strength," *Review of Economics and Statistics*, Vol. XXXVII, No. 4 (Nov., 1955), p. 389. Ulman's paper, which also cites a wealth of empirical material, is one of the most illuminating discussions of the union wage problem I have seen. See also Friedman's rejoinder, *ibid.*, p. 401.

raise wages only if demand for the product of the industry or firm is inelastic. For only in that case can the employers pass on the wage rise to the consumers. But since the Chicago School believes that the American economy is highly competitive, it follows that the elasticity of demand for the products of any particular firm in most industries is large. Thus, their optimism with respect to the prevalence of competition in the American industry leads them to be optimistic also with respect to the lack of monopoly power of labor unions.

It is not surprising that Chamberlin, who stresses the ubiquity of monopoly in the form of monopolistic competition, does not share this optimism.

I, too, cannot share this optimism, although I agree with my friends in Chicago that the fear of monopolies, other than labor monopolies, in the American economy has been greatly overdone. I believe, however, that the difference between Chicago and Chamberlin on this point is much smaller than they both are willing to admit. Since I agree with both to a large extent, they cannot be so far apart from one another (if I am right). But I realize that I am in danger of being crushed between two millstones.

The main reason why I think that the two disputants are closer to one another than they think is this: It seems to me that the Chicago critics of monopolistic competition overlook that what Chamberlin calls "monopolistic competition" is competition (and not monopoly) as far as welfare and policy implications are concerned. That is to say, in my opinion, and this is, I believe, also the position of Chamberlin himself, monopolistic competition in his sense does not, or at least does not necessarily or to a great extent, imply a misallocation of resources, as ordinary monopoly does, and does, therefore, not call for extensive regulatory action on the part of the government.

However, this is really a side issue. Even if there existed in every industry the purest of pure competition so that demand for the product of each firm were perfectly elastic, demand for the industry as a whole need not be elastic; hence, demand for labor as a whole, when labor is represented by an industrial union, is *not* perfectly elastic, and may be very inelastic, although there can be no doubt that wages are a large part of total cost. Thus the inflationary dilemma posed by the existence of labor monopolies does exist even if the economy is otherwise very competitive. Friedman is quite right in saying that the monopoly power of unions is much greater in the short run than in the long run, the short-run demand curve for labor being necessarily much less elastic than the long-run demand curve. But this is quite sufficient for the wage-price mechanism to produce inflation. If unions in a few key industries are able to push up wages without immediately causing much unemployment, we can rely on others to follow suit after a while. The American economy is sufficiently competitive to generalize wage increases (notwithstanding temporary or even some permanent distortions in favor of a few tightly organized groups) and to maintain a fairly uniform level of wages.

The mechanism by which wage increases in certain key industries are gradually generalized over the whole industry may be intricate and will not always and everywhere be the same. But that there is such a tendency there can hardly be a doubt. The key industries are likely to be progressive industries where productivity (output per man-hour) rises fast.[10] It clearly is easier for unions to get wage rises if they can point to increases in productivity, especially if prices are sticky (at least temporarily), and hence increases in productivity in the absence of corresponding wage increases would lead to rising profits.

Wages in many other industries will follow almost automatically. Firms of industries where labor is not unionized often adjust their wages automatically to union wages elsewhere because they are afraid any lag would pave the way for unionization. If there are independent unions, adjustment must be delayed because contracts have to expire. But unless there is much unemployment and depres-

[10] It should be observed that in a single industry wages cannot go up in proportion to the increase in "labor productivity" there (i.e., output per input of labor) without pushing up the cost of production and the price of the product *unless* the capital output ratio remained constant (and there was no change in the "degree of monopoly power" or more generally in the market structure of the industry).

The same is true for the economy as a whole. But there is this difference: While for the economy as a whole the capital output ratio may be assumed to be fairly constant in the short run or to change only slowly, for individual industries significant changes, mostly upward, of the capital output ratio are possible even in the short run. Moreover, the share of wages (including salaries) in national income is remarkably stable in the short run, which is not always the case in particular industries.

sion in an industry, no union will long stay behind the wage increases secured by unions in the progressive industries.

Thus, if wages are first pushed up in progressive industries, prices of the products of those industries may not rise at all, because the wage rise is absorbed by rising productivity. But when this wage increase then spreads to less progressive industries which have no margin to spare, prices are immediately pushed up.

Aggregate effective demand must, of course, keep up or quickly catch up with the rising level of wage cost. If it did not, unemployment would result and at some level of unemployment the wage push would presumably cease. At what level is a difficult question, where the answers of the optimist and pessimist diverge.

The mechanism by which demand keeps up or catches up with rising costs—or occasionally runs ahead of it—is easiest to understand if and when, as at present in most countries, deliberate and solemnly declared policies of full employment are being pursued. In the absence of such policies, the mechanism is more complicated because it then is blurred by the vagaries of the business cycle. However, these vagaries are not entirely absent today, because the cycle is not yet dead, although it has recently as so often in the past been pronounced dead by very prominent experts. The cycle necessarily confuses and complicates the situation because it causes demand (and profits) frequently to run ahead of costs (during business cycle upswings) or to fall below them during the downswing, rather than simply following the relentless upward push of wages.[11]

But I shall refrain from going into the intricacies of the cycle. The

[11] For that reason I am not convinced by some of Mr. Robbins' arguments for the proposition that inflation in Great Britain was for the most time of the demand-pull type. "If the prime movement had been on the side of costs, the prospect of profits would have been continually threatened, the index of wage-rates would have tended to rise faster than the index of weekly earnings, the volume of vacancies would have tended to fall below the level of applications. And these things did not happen." (*Op. cit.*, p. 5.)

In a world which is subject to cyclical swings this is, I believe, not necessarily true. In a business cycle upswing rising wages simply lead to higher prices, leaving profit margins and the number of vacancies unchanged. Thus the fact that profits are satisfactory does not necessarily exclude the wage push.

It goes without saying that the rising price level makes the boom more precarious. It may lead to speculative buying and invites restrictive monetary measures. Either development is apt to shorten the life of the boom.

existence of full-employment policies greatly simplifies the problem from the analytical standpoint.

It might be pointed out in passing that the problems of the wage-push inflation pose themselves with special clarity and crudeness in underdeveloped countries and, interestingly enough, not only in countries with leftist regimes. In Franco Spain, for example, last year the government raised minimum wages by 50 per cent, which has led, after abortive attempts to keep prices—or rather the price index—down by price control measures, to a sharp rise in prices and a balance of payments crisis. In Latin America it happens frequently that governments raise minimum wages by 50 or 100 per cent at a time. The late Brazilian dictator, Getulio Vargas, before he committed suicide in 1954, left a time bomb for his successor by hiking wages by 50 per cent. Since this wage push could not be undone, Vargas' successor had no choice but to let prices rise to catch up with the higher wage level.

I shall now discuss what could be done to prevent or stop cost-push inflation and what the proper policy might be once it has led to depression and unemployment.

The first line of defense must surely be monetary policy. On that our optimists and pessimists should be able to agree. Even the pessimist who foresees trouble and does not believe that monetary policy can be the full answer will agree that tight money is necessary to prevent creeping inflation from degenerating into runaway inflation. Moreover, there is always the chance that the optimists may be right after all, at least at times, and a little unemployment turn out to be sufficient to stop the cost push. The most prominent pessimist, Sumner H. Slichter, has been emphatic in saying that tight money is necessary to prevent the creep from becoming a trot. But he has also been saying that tight money policy must not be overdone. By that he means that money must be just tight enough to allow prices to rise on the average parallel with the irresistible upward thrust of money wages—that is, 2–3 per cent a year, not more and not less. More than 3 would lead to galloping inflation, less than 2 would spell unemployment.

At this point I am afraid I must part company with him because I believe it is impossible to keep a price rise for any length of time at a rate of 2–3 per cent. But I lack the time to argue this point in greater detail. Let me simply say that Mr. Slichter's prescription for monetary policy cannot be carried out. It amounts to telling the Federal Reserve Board not only that they have to walk continuously a tight rope—at times that is probably unavoidable—but, in addition, to walk it bent over to one side!

Let us now assume that the pessimist is right, that is to say, that monetary policy will run into this dilemma: either to let prices rise or to allow an intolerable amount of unemployment to develop. What can be done to avoid or avert this dilemma?

Fiscal policy, that is to say, creation of a budget surplus to counteract inflation, is no solution for the particular dilemma caused by wage push. Fiscal policy may have certain advantages over monetary policy from other standpoints.[12] But if wage increases exceed the growth of average productivity of labor and the government, by means of a budget surplus brought about by higher taxes, keeps demand at a level which prevents prices from rising parallel with cost, unemployment will develop, even if the higher taxes are such as to fall entirely on wage income.

It is sometimes suggested that price control could solve the problem or at least conribute to the solution. Here we have to distinguish between areas where competition, including monopolistic competition in the Chamberlinian sense, prevails and the case of monopolies such as exist in the public utility field.

In the first case, which covers by far the larger part of the economy, any attempt to control prices would make things worse. Price control would disorganize markets, necessitate formal and informal rationing and the creation of a costly bureaucracy and red tape; this would waste productive resources and divert them from their optimal uses. Hence the margin available for higher real wages would be reduced and thus inflationary pressures intensified.

[12] It can be argued, for example, that anti-inflationary monetary policy has its impact primarily on private investment while fiscal policy can be made to bear on public expenditure and private consumption.

The case of monopoly (other than labor monopoly) is different. Most economists agree that the existence of monopolies, such as in the public utility field, justifies and requires public action. The extent to which monopoly positions actually exist (outside the public utility field where rates are controlled anyway) is a matter of dispute. I myself am inclined to agree with G. W. Nutter and others who believe that the fear of monopolies has been greatly overdone. As mentioned before, this is partly based on the belief that Chamberlinian monopolistic competition, which certainly does exist in many areas, has to be classified (from the policy and welfare standpoint, not from the analytical point of view) as competition. But this is again a side issue which I do not want to pursue, because it is not essential for my argument.

From the point of view of the inflation problem, business monopolies seem to me entirely different and less dangerous than the labor monopoly of trade unions. While the latter are continuously pressing for higher wages for their members and thus, if they have sufficient bargaining power, are a continuing threat for price stability, the same cannot be said of business monopolies.[13] Suppose monopoly is introduced in a field where until now competition prevailed. This will lead to a rise in price and a reduction in output. [14] The introduction of a monopoly can thus be said to have an inflationary effect. But once it exists, it does not, as labor unions do, exert a continuing inflationary pressure. Similarly, the dissolution of a monopoly and the *introduction* of competition can be said to have an anti-inflationary effect.

It follows that an attempt to cure wage-push inflation by a drive against "monopolies" (other than labor monopolies) is like trying to prevent the explosion of a boiler in which the steam pressure is building up in consequence of excessive fuel intake, not by reducing the

[13] In passing, let me emphasize, although I have no time to elaborate, that I do not wish to pass a moral judgment. I would not blame the unions for exploiting their bargaining power. It is society that is to be blamed for giving them excessive monopoly power.

[14] I leave open the question whether and to what extent J. A. Schumpeter and J. K. Galbraith are right when they contend that a certain degree of monopoly (Schumpeter says a temporary monopoly position in new industries) is conducive to, or a condition for, rapid technological progress. To the extent that they are right, the monopoly problem, including its inflationary implications, is further reduced in importance.

fuel and steam pressure, but by trying to increase the capacity of the boiler so that it may stand the rising pressure a little longer. Inflationary pressure is a short-run phenomenon like steam pressure in a boiler, while attempts to eliminate monopoly and to make the economy more competitive, like changing the shape or capacity of a boiler, is a structural reform which, although it may be very desirable, most certainly takes a lot of time.

What holds of an attempt to make the economy more competitive holds also of other types of policy that might be expected to increase output per man-hour and to that extent counteract inflationary pressure. For example, a significant reduction in government outlays involving the release of productive resources that were so far absorbed for unproductive purposes by the government, coupled with a corresponding cut in taxes, would increase the margin available for non-inflationary wage boosts. Suppose it were possible to reduce substantially defense expenditures or farm support payments. This would give some temporary relief, but could not provide a complete answer to the problem of continuing inflationary pressure exerted by the upward thrust on wages.

There exists, however, one type of reaction which is often emphasized as a powerful *continuing* offset to inflation and according to the defenders of labor unions can be relied upon either to make wage-push inflation self-limiting, or at least to offer real advantages in the form of greater over-all productivity outweighing, at least partly, the obvious disadvantages of inflation. What I am thinking of is the theory that the wage push, so long as prices are not allowed (presumably by financial controls) to outrun the rise in cost, will spur managers and production engineers to greater efforts to increase output per unit of labor input by means of introducing better methods of production, labor-saving devices, improvements in products and so forth. This same argument is also used for justification of labor unions as such, when their wage and cost raising activities stay inside the limit imposed by stable prices.

I regard this type of reasoning as largely fallacious. It attributes to labor unions and their wage policies or to creeping inflation what ought to be attributed to the competitive mechanism. Suppose we had an entirely different type of wage policy; suppose we succeeded in what many economists thought (and some still think) would be a much better system—namely, letting prices slowly fall under the impact of gradually rising production and output. In other words, suppose progress took the shape of real incomes (including real wages) rising in the form of falling prices with constant average money wages (incomes) rather than as now in the form of rising prices and still faster rising money wages. By and large this system would produce the same incentive as the present one. The incentive comes from the ever-threatening squeeze on profits, irrespective of whether this squeeze results from falling prices or rising costs.

I realize that this is a crude treatment of a very subtle and difficult problem, as the problem of incentives must inevitably be. I would submit, however, that the refutation of a theory need not be subtler and more refined than the theory which it purports to refute!

I now come to the last problem on which I should like to make some comments. Suppose the attempt to stop creeping inflation due to wage pressure by means of financial controls, whether successful or not, has led to unemployment and depression. What would be the proper wage policy to alleviate the depression?

The present depression obviously is a promising candidate for being explained that way. Also the depression of 1937–39 can, I believe, plausibly be said to have been triggered by the mechanism in question. But I would admit that it is often difficult to diagnose a concrete situation and especially difficult to distinguish between the "trigger" and the "basic" cause. The present depression may have come anyway, though perhaps a little later if the Federal Reserve had not been forced by the boom intensified by the wage push to step violently on the credit brake.

Moreover, I am emphatically not of the opinion that most depressions in the past have been caused or triggered in the way described. We have not yet outlived or conquered the business cycle, although we know a good deal more than we did twenty years ago how to deal with a depression—and especially how *not* to treat it—once it has started. In my opinion, an eclectic or pluralistic explanation of how depressions are started is indicated, although once started and well under way they have many essential features in common.

Fortunately, however, it is not essential for our problem to decide this question. I think the place of wage policy in anti-depression strategy is very much the same whatever the cause of the depression—except in one respect which I shall mention presently.

I believe that today there is fairly general agreement among economists on how to deal with a depression. To put it briefly and therefore bluntly and apodictically, it is that by some combination of monetary and fiscal policy measures aggregate expenditure on goods and services ought to be strengthened. This still leaves enough room for disagreement concerning the diagnosis of a concrete situation and on the timing, dosing, and composition of the package of measures to be recommended. Some wish to rely primarily on monetary policy, others on fiscal policy; some would like to reduce taxes, others raise expenditures; some would put their faith mainly in "built-in stabilizers" because they work automatically and minimize the role of fallible judgment. I cannot, and fortunately need not for my purposes at this point, go into these details. I think it is a fact that a large group of economists could agree on that—a group stretching almost across the whole rainbow of opinion, from Milton Friedman on the one end of the spectrum, via J. M. Clark, A. C. Pigou and D. Robertson in the middle to, let me say, Alvin Hansen at the other end. Moreover, and this is the point I wish to make, all of the economists mentioned should agree, and all of those mentioned up to and including Robertson have more or less clearly said so on various occasions, that a general forced rise in wage rates is definitely not among the acceptable anti-depression policies. In other words, the "purchasing power" theory, which says that a depression is a good time to raise wages on the ground that this will strengthen purchasing power, effective demand or, as I have called it, aggregate expenditure on goods and services, a theory which is very popular among labor leaders and some labor economists, is or should be entirely unacceptable even for orthodox Keynesians.

On the face of it, it goes against the grain of the free market economy to raise the price of a commodity which is in excess supply as labor is in a depression. It should be clear that raising wage rates (by government decree or union pressure) is not on the same level as an increase in effective demand by means of monetary or fiscal policy measures. Purchasing power, i.e., income and expenditure of the working class, may or may not increase when in a depression wages are pushed up, depending upon the elasticity of demand for labor. The crude purchasing power theory of wages overlooks a basic fact which among others Keynes kept emphasizing, namely, the double role of wages as cost, on the one hand, and as income, on the other. The most effective method of rekindling expansion in a depression is to reduce cost and increase expenditure.[15] That could be done by reducing wages and at the same time increasing expenditures by financial policies. As a bare minimum requirement, the wage *level* should be left unchanged.[16]

It would be easy to cite examples where recovery policies were mismanaged by sharply raising costs and others where this mistake was avoided. The ineffectual American New Deal policy, especially in its early phase when the stimulus on economic activity resulting from expenditure increases was largely offset by forced cost increases, or the French "New Deal," also called the "Blum Experiment," after

[15] It is easy to think of cases where within limits and in the short run wage increases in certain areas may stimulate aggregate demand. Assume a given firm very liquid and demand for labor inelastic, output having fallen to the irreducible minimum short of the firm shutting down altogether. Then a wage push may induce the firm to spend some of its idle funds.

It is clear, however, that this wage push will not induce the firm to expand. Moreover, a policy of pushing up wages would impede price cuts and induce price rises and thus reduce the real purchasing power of all consumers.

Obviously, an expansion brought about by easier money, tax cuts, and public expenditure is an entirely different thing.

It should perhaps be added that the proposition that a general wage push in the climate of a depression is likely to be deflationary or at best neutral does not contradict the proposition that in the climate of a business cycle upswing it is likely to add to the fires of inflation, although it makes the boom more precarious.

[16] This statement will be qualified below. While I would not recommend a policy of deliberately reducing the over-all wage *level* (if that could be done), surely *relative* wages (as between different types of labor, secularly declining and expending industries, and so on) should remain flexible. And while in periods of general expansion (business cycles upswings) the flexibility of relative wages can be largely achieved by selective wage *increases,* in depression periods it should be brought about by selective wage *reductions,* thus reducing the wage level. Any reductions in the wage level incident to the policy of maintaining flexibility of *relative* wages should be welcome.

the Socialist leader Léon Blum, prior to the outbreak of the second World War, which disastrously weakened the economic strength of France at a decisive point of her history, are glaring examples of mismanagement. The Nazi recovery directed by H. G. Hjalmar Schacht avoided this mistake and was a great success. Needless to say, it was misused for dangerous, detestable, and ultimately disastrous purposes, but from a technical economic standpoint it was well conceived and well executed. I might mention in passing that Schacht was very conservative in financial matters and did many things *contre coeur*. He could even prove it, which saved his neck at the war criminal trial in Nuremberg. This illustrates the historical truth that radical or, better, unconventional policies, when they are required, are always better carried out by conservative statesmen. For the obverse it is much harder to find convincing examples.

In a depression brought on as a reaction to wage-push inflation or, in fact, in any depression, however triggered or caused, during a period of chronic inflation, it would be especially unwise to allow wages to be pushed up. The reason is that such a policy would strengthen the inflationary poison which permeates the economic atmosphere in such a period.

Chronic creeping inflation carries the double danger, first, that it is likely to precipitate a depression and, second, that it impedes the alleviation of a depression which has been caused by other factors. The present depression is an example. Suppose we take the view that it had to come anyway, that it is not merely the unavoidable consequence of creeping inflation. The mere fact that it is embedded in a period of chronic inflation makes it obviously much harder for the monetary and fiscal authorities to counteract it vigorously by financial measures. If prices had not risen so much and for so long as they actually did, it would not matter so much if energetic anti-depression measures led to price rises or prevented a price fall. This makes it doubly important to avoid any unnatural and unnecessary rise in costs such as a policy of pushing up wages in a depression would involve.

Finally, let me draw a few conclusions for wage policy. I shall divide what I have to say into two parts. First, I shall try to set out the ideal objectives that ought to guide wage policies and, second, I shall say a few words on how to approach the ideal. Not being a specialist on labor problems, my remarks on the second problem will be very tentative and general.

We can be sure that the American economy will continue to expand in the sense that output per man or man-hour will have an upward secular trend. If deep depressions can be prevented, the secular growth rate will be larger. I think we can be confident that at least in peacetime the problem of inflation as well as that of the business cycle (at least that of major fluctuations including deep depressions) can be solved with a tolerable degree of efficiency by means of monetary fiscal policy, *provided* we can somehow reduce the upward pressure on wage rates.

The aim should be to let the over-all wage level rise not more than the gradual rise in over-all productivity. Some rise in the money wage level would be even compatible with a slight downward secular trend in prices.

The basic difficulty is that the wage level, even the wage level in a large segment of the economy, say, in industry or manufacturing industry as a whole, is an abstraction and cannot well be made the subject of government control, at least not in the United States.[17] From the policy standpoint it is not an operational concept. The rule concerning the over-all wage level must therefore be translated into rules concerning wages in particular industries.[18] Only a few hints can be given here on how such a transposition may be effected.

[17] Some foreign countries such as Holland, Sweden, Great Britain, have come much closer to being able not to control effectively but at least to speak meaningfully of controlling the over-all wage level.

[18] It need hardly be stressed that from an analytical point of view (waiving the difficulty of operating by policy upon the wage level) the rule to the effect that price stability requires that the wage level changes with changes in the average productivity of labor (output per man or man-hour) cannot be regarded as a precise, theoretical law. It is a rather crude rule of thumb, but good enough for the crude problem with which we are confronted. If average productivity rises by, say, 2 per cent a year, wages cannot go up on the average by, say, 5 per cent or more for any length of time without pushing up prices or creating unemployment. This does not, however, exclude that wages may rise, say, by 2½ per cent or 3 per cent for a while, the difference coming from a squeeze on profits. Or under a different set of circumstances (for example, starting from a situation of abnormally low profits) a rise of wages by not more than the rise in average productivity may be too much in the sense that it would drive up prices

Of crucial importance are, it would seem, the progressive manufacturing industries. The danger is that in these industries wages are driven up in excess of the gradual rise in *over-all* productivity, even if prices in the progressive industries themselves are not pushed up. If this happens, a rise in the general price *level* is sooner or later unavoidable, even if the wage increase in the progressive industries remains well within the limits set by the increase in productivity in these industries themselves, because of the fact discussed earlier that wage rises in the progressive industries will sooner or later spread to the less progressive parts of the economy.

One obvious corollary of this should be emphasized. If the progressive industries that have been able to reduce their cost of production (or to produce better products at the same cost) do not reduce their sales prices,[19] the general price *level* is bound to go up. The reason is that industries that have been able to reduce cost of production (without reducing their prices correspondingly) will hardly be able to avoid sharing the resulting profits with labor. That is to say, wages will go up, and this wage rise will then spread to the less progressive industries which cannot absorb the rise in cost without immediately marking up the prices of their products.

---

or lead to unemployment. As was pointed out earlier, what makes the rule workable is the historical fact or accident that the capital-output ratio and the labor share in national income is fairly constant over moderate periods.

This makes it possible to speak of average rather than marginal productivity of labor. Alternatively, we could also say that the workability of the rule depends on the assumption that the percentage gap between marginal and average productivity remains fairly constant.

The theory could, of course, be refined *ad libitum:* If output per man rises because more and more capital is used per worker, the share of labor may or may not go up according to whether the marginal rate of substitution between labor and capital is greater or smaller than unity, according as to whether inventions are capital- or labor-saving, according to the changes in the degree of monopoly in the pattern of oligopolistic and monopolistic competition and so on and so forth.

I do not believe, however, that much would be gained from such refinements for the solution of the kind of problem we are confronted with: A rise in average productivity in the neighborhood of 2 per cent per year and a rise of money wage rates up to 10 per cent in major sectors of industry.

[19] If the price of improved products is kept stable (i.e., the same as the price of the previously produced inferior products), we have, of course, a hidden price fall. It would be interesting to investigate whether the consumer price index makes sufficient allowance for that. Obviously, the appearance now of new types of products raises similar questions.

A related complication is that in a rapidly changing, progressive economy, relative wages should be kept flexible to facilitate and stimulate the redistribution of labor between declining and expanding industries.[20] In a growing economy, flexibility of relative wages can be achieved by differential wage increases. (This implies, of course, a temporary deviation from the rule of rapid generalization of wage increases.)

But for the maintenance of long-run stability of prices and short-run stability of output and employment, it would be highly desirable not to rule out downward adjustments in wage rates. For example, in rapidly declining industries, a reduction in wages would slow down the decline and enable a slower and less costly adjustment. The railroads are a good example. If through a wage reduction railroad rates could be reduced, the spiralling losses of traffic to other types of transportation could at least be slowed down and more gradual and orderly adjustment achieved.

In a depression, with unemployment and overcapacity existing almost everywhere, flexibility of relative wages should be achieved entirely or predominantly by selective wage reductions in industries exceptionally hard hit by the depression, especially if there are reasons to believe that the decline of those industries is partly structural and not purely cyclical. This implies, of course, a reduction in the wage *level*. It would be a grave mistake to insist in the midst of a general depression on wage increases elsewhere so as to keep the wage level unchanged.

It should be observed that even with the present downward rigidity of wage rates, there still exists some downward flexibility of hourly earnings, wage cost and efficiency wages as a consequence of the abandonment of expensive overtime, reduction in costly labor turnover, elimination of inefficient workers and improvements in labor discipline. But these adjustments are imperfect and insufficient substitutes for a downward flexibility of money wage rates. I should perhaps add that in an age in which vigorous anti-depression policies by

[20] It goes without saying that the adjustment of the labor force is easier in case the labor force is growing rapidly because it may then be sufficient to regulate the influx of new recruits to the labor force making actual transfers unnecessary.

means of public works and tax cuts, built-in or *ad hoc* contrived, are routine there is no danger at all that a mild selective downward flexibility of wages could start or intensify a cumulative process of deflation.

If it is impossible to prevent prices from rising during cyclical upswings, long-run price stability requires that prices fall during cyclical downswings. And with wages completely rigid downward, this is impossible to achieve.[21]

It is easier to say what the ideal behavior of wages is in theory than to suggest how the ideal should be approached in practice. When it comes to the question of how to make the labor market more competitive, to reduce the upward pressure of wages and lessen their downward rigidity, I am not in a position to give a detailed program for action or to hold out hope for an easy solution. One cannot refrain from expressing the hope that in the future more guidance and advice than in the past will come from qualified experts, that is to say, from labor economists.

Appeals to union leaders to be more modest and exhortations of employers to resist wage demands and to reduce prices, even when they come from the highest quarters, unless accompanied by real action, are certainly quite useless and may be positively harmful, because such utterances, by creating the impression that something has been done, tend to weaken the resolve for real action which is weak anyway.

Legislative reforms would include prohibition of mass picketing and closed shop agreements, protection of those who are willing to work, prevention of violence and coercion, and application of the Sherman Act to labor unions. Probably more important than new legislation would be stricter enforcement of existing laws. If corrective action, either legislative or executive, is taken in time, more drastic measures will probably be unnecessary. If nothing is done until creeping inflation has become intolerable, the reaction may

[21] The reduction in efficiency wages brought about by the factors mentioned in the preceding paragraph will enable some price cuts even if money wage rates remain unchanged. But these price reductions will be short lived and insufficient to compensate for price increases during the preceding boom.

become violent with the danger of subsequent reversal. In this connection, President Truman's attempt in 1946 to draft striking railway workers into the army, which was strongly opposed by Senator Robert Taft, comes to mind.

An indispensable prerequisite for wise remedial action is that public opinion should be alerted to the danger of creeping inflation and to the necessity for keeping wage rises within the bounds of the gradual rise in over-all productivity. I find it difficult to believe that it should be impossible to persuade labor that if wages rise faster than over-all productivity, either prices must rise or unemployment result and that, in either case, the economy as a whole including labor itself will suffer.

5

Collective Bargaining and the Maintenance of Market Competition*

James W. McKie

LABOR MONOPOLY has only recently become a matter of widespread public concern. In past years public opinion has been more tolerant of labor monopoly than of business monopoly. Public policy has reflected little concern for the effect of various kinds of collective action in the labor market on consumer welfare.[1] The epitome of this viewpoint is the famous statement in the Clayton Act that "the labor of a human being is not a commodity or article of commerce."

But this difference in policy toward labor and business monopoly cannot rest on the notion that labor unions necessarily have less monopoly power than business firms. Monopoly is a matter of degree. Some unions have little power because they cannot control entry, substitution, or the access of employers to non-unionized labor. There are degrees of monopoly in business also; there are almost no pure monopolies.

* I am indebted to George W. Stocking and Paul Sanders of Vanderbilt University and to Rita Ricardo Campbell for helpful criticism and suggestions. Responsibility for the views expressed in this chapter is, of course, entirely my own.

[1] Professional economists have often called attention to these interconnections, for example, John T. Dunlop, *Wage Determination Under Trade Unions* (New York, 1944), Chapters V and VI. See also James R. Schlesinger, "Market Structure, Union Power and Inflation," *Southern Economic Journal,* Vol. XXIV, No. 3 (Jan., 1958). Others have dwelt on the political implications of unionism, e.g., Henry C. Simons, "Some Reflections on Syndicalism," *Journal of Political Economy,* Vol. LII, No. 1 (March, 1944). But the methods of partial analysis not infrequently lead economists to treat labor markets in isolation.

Labor unions do not, of course, *behave* like business monopolies. They do not maximize "profits." They pursue many objectives that may partially conflict with one another, like higher wage rates, higher incomes for employed workers, more employment within the trade, and more leisure. It is not easy for economists to determine analytically how the union's attempt to achieve optimum "welfare" for its members distorts the optimum allocation of resources. Different assumptions about the dimensions of the workers' welfare lead to different conclusions about the degree of monopoly. Nor is it any more apparent to the public how the laboring man's efforts to improve his lot impinge upon the general welfare. Public opinion has commonly conceived of the monopoly problem in labor markets as an opposition between worker welfare and profits, not primarily as an opposition between labor welfare and consumer welfare. In recent years it has become more aware that the consumer interest is involved in labor-management relations because of the apparent connection between wage increases and general price inflation. But for a long time a large segment of the public favored the organization of unions to give working men collective power to resist the market power of business firms. This doctrine of countervailing power has probably been the most important influence shaping anti-monopoly policy toward labor unions.

Attitudes toward countervailing power often reflect some confusion concerning what it is that the power in question is supposed to countervail. Those who advocate countervailing power for labor groups believe that it is a tolerable substitute for competition and possibly the only practical remedy for business power in labor markets. Informal applications of the doctrine often assume that *any* business firm possesses a high degree of market power in purchasing labor; they also often disregard the distinction between monopsony power in purchasing labor and monopoly power in selling products.

If a business firm has monopsony power to depress wages below labor's marginal value product, the union *may* redress the distributive balance by raising wages without itself creating monopolistic distortion in consumer markets. If the firm sells its products under competitive conditions but has monopsony power in purchasing labor, unionization of that firm's employees will have no monopolistic effects in the product market. Cases like this must be rare even when we allow for inevitable impurities in competition in the product market. To meet the requirements of the case, the firm would have to sell in a very wide market while buying labor in a local market, perhaps a company town. It would have to be insulated against wage competition from other employers, perhaps by distance—but not by distance from the market, since this would merely create differential costs and distance-rents, not monopsony profits. And it would have to be protected against entry from other employers seeking low-wage labor, as well as from exit of its employees seeking higher-paying jobs. If all firms were unionized, the product market would remain unaffected only if each firm's employees organized into a separate union which acted independently of all others, while each firm acted independently of all other firms in determining its wage policy and its price policy. Essentially, what we are visualizing here is a small seller who is a relatively big employer in a very small labor market dealing with a union including only the local employees of that one firm. The relevance of this case to the actual labor movement is remote.

In all other cases the power of union and employer in the labor market is intermingled with monopolistic elements or effects in subsequent markets toward the consumer. This intermingling perhaps is responsible for the confusion of monopoly power and monopsony power. It may account for the frequent citations of concentration ratios in particular industries in support of assertions that labor organizations merely countervail the power of business firms. The view that unions counteract the monopsony power of employers is no doubt partly true, but when the employer has monopoly power in product markets the monopoly power of the union is not merely countervailing but concurrent or even additive. Once the union has wiped out the employer's surplus from monopsony, higher wages in the short run can come from only three sources: The union may benefit at the expense of other factors of production sold in competitive markets. It may share in a monopolistic employer's profits. Or it may raise the wage-costs of employers (whether monopolistic or competitive), causing product prices to rise. And in the long run the union may capture for itself the gains from increasing productivity, which might otherwise have been passed on to consumers in the form of lower prices. In realistic cases the countervailing power of the union is likely to overreach the monopsony power of the employer.

The ultimate effects will vary depending on the objectives of the union and the degree of monopsony power and monopoly power that the employing firms possess.[2] If the union tries to promote more employment without reducing the efficiency of the labor unit, the ultimate monopolistic restriction will be less than if it tries to maximize the wage bill for the workers already employed.[3] But when a union attempts to capture a share of a monopolistic employer's profits for itself, it may create a double monopolistic distortion in consumer markets. When factor monopoly is loaded on top of product monopoly, the factor price goes up and the employer maximizes profits with reference to those higher costs. The outcome depends on whether the demand curve for the product is more or less elastic than the demand curve for labor. While we cannot generalize on the long-run elasticity of substitution among factors, the creation of union power in such a situation would probably in the short run raise prices to consumers and restrict output more than the monopolistic firm had done when there was no union.[4]

The union is clearly not exercising "countervailing" power when it sets wage levels in industries consisting of competitive or monopolistically-competitive firms that have no market power in the purchase of labor. In such market structures the union wage is transmitted in large part to the consumer market (and in part to other factors of production) through its effect on costs. Entry and exit of firms regulates the price effect on the product market. If the industry is initially in equilibrium, the upward push of wages must result in the

[2] See the conclusions of Dunlop and Benjamin Higgins in Dunlop, *op. cit.*, Chapter V.

[3] W. Fellner, *Competition Among the Few* (New York, 1949), pp. 255–62.

[4] It would also reduce the total joint monopoly gain to firm and union. See Fellner, *op. cit.*, Chapter X, and J. J. Spengler, "Vertical Integration and Antitrust Policy," *Journal of Political Economy*, Vol. LVIII, No. 4 (Aug., 1950).

elimination of firms before the cost curves of the remaining firms again reach tangency with the demand curve at a higher price. In the long run the union does not gain at the expense of profits in a competitive industry.[5]

We do not know how extensive monopsony power in the labor market would be if the unions were not there to counteract it. Possibly it would be considerable, as many labor economists assert. But strong unions can also create or share in monopoly in the product market. This is not necessarily a purely short-run effect. Shifts in demand for the product, expansion of industry investment in response to higher demand, and increases in productivity will all create opportunities for the union to gain if its strategic position enables it to control the business response to these changes. The result will be a different set of prices in the consumer market than would exist if the labor market were competitive.[6]

A policy of limiting and reducing the monopolistic effects of labor union activity on product markets can make little use of theoretical models except to develop general norms. It must look to the more tangible elements of market structure and the practices that monopolists use to secure and maintain market control. Union strategy varies greatly from one industry or employment to another, depending among other things on the skill of the workers in the employment and on the structure of the industry that employs them. Basically, the union tries to maintain and improve its wage standards and other benefits by controlling the supply of labor and preventing competition from firms having lower standards. In pursuit of these objectives it tries to prevent wage competition among workers and to organize employees of non-union establishments. It may also attempt to control entry to the labor force, to prevent access of employers to non-unionized labor, to limit price competition among firms or exclude competing firms from the market, or even to control product prices

[5] E. H. Chamberlin has suggested inverting the usual analysis of the theory of the firm by treating minimum profits as a cost and examining the "maximization" of wage income. E. H. Chamberlin, *The Economic Analysis of Labor Union Power* (Washington, 1958), p. 35.

[6] Schlesinger, *op. cit.*

directly. Some of these practices are now recognized as legitimate and legal if carried on in certain ways; others are not.

The simplest case of direct price control is the market in which the unionized labor sells services to the consumer at rates fixed by the union. There may be no "firms" involved at all; an example would be the hire of house-painters by home-owners. In a few cases the employers themselves, such as master barbers, are also members of the union. The union fixes the price of the service and all details of the relative compensation of the master and his journeymen "employees." The union controls the consumer market by controlling employers and self-employed persons. There have been occasional instances of unionization of self-employed entrepreneurs operating businesses without any identifiable labor interest—service stations, for example.[7] While unionization of employers is not at present an important means of cartelizing the consumer market, it could become so if unchecked.

A strong union may also attempt to cartelize independent employers who are numerous and weak. When the union has had the power to withhold labor from price-cutting employers and from prospective entrants to the industry, it has in some cases set the price of the product or enforced a "code of fair competition" on employers.[8] In some areas unions have been able to control (or at least influence) state and local licensing and inspection of certain kinds of business, which enables them to control entry and competition in these lines.

If the union is powerful enough, it may reach through a layer of numerous small employing firms to control the supply of the commodity directly by controlling the amount of work actually done. The United Mine Workers, for example, controls the supply of soft coal more effectively than a loose cartel of coal producers could do.

[7] "The Des Moines local picketed eight service stations . . . in July 1939 for posting prices $0.002 below the rest of the retailers. . . . At the time of the strike about 385 of the 425 dealers were reported to be members of the teamsters' union." (Dunlop, *op. cit.*, p. 109.)

[8] The construction trades and the photoengravers' union are prominent examples. Dunlop, *op. cit.*, pp. 104–9. The teamsters' union of course has been most active in cartellizing local trade. See Corwin D. Edwards, *Maintaining Competition* (New York, 1949) for a quotation from the by-laws of the Bakery and Confectionery Workers' Union providing for withdrawal of labor from firms engaged in "unfair or unwarranted competition."

To suppress wage competition in the labor market, the union tries as a rule to eliminate price competition from non-unionized employers. One way to do so is to organize the unorganized firms. If it is unable to organize them directly, the union often proceeds to the commodity market. There it may apply pressure or persuasion on users of the commodity to exclude non-unionized employers from their markets, either to force them to unionize or to eliminate them altogether. This is the secondary boycott. But the secondary boycott is not only used as an organizing weapon by unions in the same trade as the workers they are attempting to organize. "Stranger" unions having no economic interest in common with the unorganized workers have also used it. The teamsters, for example, have used their control of truck transportation to cartelize retail trade that depends on trucking. The union can spread through unrelated labor markets and bring product prices and entry under its sway. In extreme cases this kind of pressure lends itself to racketeering, where the stranger union signs what amounts to a protection agreement or "sweetheart contract" with the employer and guarantees the docility of his employees. Other unions, notably the construction trades, have used the secondary boycott in conspiracy with employers as a means of sealing a local market against outside competition, whether the outside competitors were unionized or not.[9]

Employers in substantially competitive industries, when they must deal with the union anyway, are frequently willing to turn over to the union the job of policing competition, and indeed must usually depend on the union to protect them from non-unionized firms. If union and employers succeed in cartelizing the industry, they may both share in the monopoly gains. If the union were powerful enough, of course, it would not have to depend on cooperation with employers. If it could control the labor supply perfectly, monopolistic practices might never become visible in the product market at all. The union could regulate entry and determine the "competitive" price through its control of labor costs. Conspiracy with employers and

[9] *U.S. v. Brims,* 272 U.S. 549 (1926); *U.S. v. United Brotherhood of Carpenters and Joiners,* 313 U.S. 539 (1941); *U.S. v. Employing Plasterers' Association of Chicago,* 347 U.S. 186 (1954).

direct interference with entry are symptoms of imperfect union monopoly.

In other types of product market, the union has little or no influence upon business policy, and does not attempt to control the price of the product nor entry to the market. Not surprisingly, these are usually markets in which the business firms already have an appreciable degree of short-run monopoly power. It is not necessary for the steelworkers to prevent "disorderly" competition in the steel market; the steel firms can stabilize their own markets. The relation between the two market levels varies depending on the importance of the labor group in question. Electricians performing highly skilled work in a steel mill, for instance, account for a small proportion of the total wage bill, and can increase their wage rates considerably without appreciably affecting the price of the product, if they take care to keep their craft organization separate from the union of the steelworkers at large. If there are only a few small craft unions within a large firm, neither the union nor the firm need concern itself with the relation of price policy to the wages of these special groups. A union such as the electricians may adopt one strategy in dealing with large employers such as steel manufacturers and quite another in dealing with small employers such as electrical contractors. Union policy responds to the structure of the product market and to the composition of the employing company's labor force.

The great industrial unions, on the other hand, have not the protection of insignificance. The wage rates they obtain are linked in some way to product prices. The large employing firms will try to protect their own profit margins by transmitting the unions' wage gains forward to the price of the product, and possibly try to enlarge them by making larger-than-compensatory price increases on these occasions. Just how oligopolistic market structures in the post-war economy have linked product prices and the wage level together is controversial. Some economists hold the view that wage increases in oligopolistic industries have pushed prices up, while others think that monetary inflation has pulled both prices and wages up. Many have expressed the conviction that industrial unions have not secured materially larger wage increases in the post-war period than their members would have secured in a competitive labor market, and that industrial unions may in truth have held them down.[10] I have no wish to enter the controversy about cost-induced versus money-induced price inflation.[11] The monetary theorists' viewpoint is not inconsistent with different relative movements in wages and prices, depending on the manner in which different labor market structures transmit inflationary forces. The view that organized labor cannot secure higher than competitive wages depends of course upon an assumption that competition is really effective in both the product market and the labor market in the long run—in other words, that both the demand curve for any one firm's product and the demand curve for any kind of labor are highly elastic in the long run. Those who hold this view acknowledge that *if* there are barriers to entry or restrictions on competition in product markets, or if the union can control the supply of labor, it can secure non-competitive wages. They generally agree that craft unions can often establish these conditions, but deny that they are important in the relations between large industrial unions and oligopolistic firms. In my own view they tend to underrate the barriers to entry in oligopolistic industries and to discount too much the importance of the short run.[12] However, craft unions may indeed be typically stronger than industrial unions, owing to several factors such as their greater power to control entry to the labor force. They may also typically encounter much less monopsony power in the hands of their employers. Any formulation of policy should take account of the differences in the sources of their strength and in the market effects of their behavior.

Public policy designed to deal with the monopolistic consequences of union activity faces a fundamental difficulty. Unions have a de-

[10] Milton Friedman, "Some Comments on the Significance of Labor Unions for Economic Policy," in D. M. Wright (ed.), *The Impact of the Union* (New York, 1951), especially pp. 215–26.

[11] For a comprehensive review of the various approaches to the incidence of collective bargaining, see M. Bronfenbrenner, "The Incidence of Collective Bargaining Once More," *The Southern Economic Journal,* Vol. XXIV, No. 4 (April, 1958).

[12] See also the arguments presented by L. G. Reynolds and C. Taft, *The Evolution of Wage Structure* (New Haven, 1955), and Bronfenbrenner's comments, *op. cit.,* pp. 405–6.

fensive as well as an acquisitive role. Many large firms and some local small ones do have some monopsony power in the purchase of labor; short-run frictions do impede the mobility of labor. Union power may typically over-compensate this monopsony power. But if individual workers had to sell their labor services competitively they would lose their protection against it in many labor markets. And more is involved than wage rates. Without the union, the individual worker would be powerless to influence those elements that strongly affect his conception of the *fairness* of his employment relationship. Although in an unorganized market mere competition among firms for labor and growth of productivity might produce not only rising wages but rising fringe benefits for the worker, they would be less likely to create adequate grievance procedures, protection against arbitrary firing, seniority rules, and the like. These problems seem to weigh more heavily on the industrial worker than on unorganized white-collar workers, who have shown no great desire to have unions to solve them. The fundamental attitudes of the blue-collar worker towards his employment, of course, are not even explicable on economic grounds.

But meritorious objectives like fair grievance procedures go hand in hand with less meritorious ones. There appears to be no special reason why public policy should give unions *carte blanche* to create and exploit monopolistic positions while attempting to enforce competitive standards elsewhere. However, a dogmatic condemnation of monopoly of any sort wherever it occurs would condemn unions as unions, for they can achieve nothing without monopolizing the labor supply or at least restraining competition in the labor market. A workable labor policy cannot declare all unions to be criminal conspiracies, nor can it exempt unions from all restraints. Yet these two extremes are the only perfectly consistent policies. Anything in between will be partly inconsistent or even contradictory as it will encourage monopoly and competition at the same time.

The drift of public policy during the period 1933–1947 was toward the second extreme: no limit on unions' monopoly power. Since then the various agencies of government have begun to impose checks on union practices and the spread of union power without aiming at a return to completely un-organized labor markets. In the following examination of policy we shall not question the right of employees of a plant or firm to organize in unions and to bargain collectively with the employer on wages, hours, working conditions, and related matters, even though collective bargaining is a monopolistic process and not a competitive one within the scope of the agreement. Anti-monopoly policy should seek to restrain *extensions* of this monopoly in both the product market and the labor market.

In formulating public policy we must start from where we are, and the present is full of the accidents and inconsistencies of history. Public policy must seize on particular circumstances or convenient points of departure. It must aim at attainable objectives. In other words, its application will be opportunistic. One cannot base such a policy on universals in such a way that every reasonable man would construe the results as an ideal state of affairs. It will not lead to a perfect balance of monopolistic and competitive elements, nor to a perfect symmetry of monopoly power among labor groups and employers. All that one can hope is that it will produce a more workably competitive market economy.

Every element of labor market structure and union practice is relevant to our problem, but we shall concentrate on the elements of structure and behavior which have had important monopolistic effects. Effective control of the spread of monopoly does not require a complete revolution in labor policy. Two statutes already on the books—the Sherman Act and the Taft-Hartley Act—are powerful anti-monopoly weapons. Some important changes and additions would strengthen anti-monopoly policy, but would not take the determination of wages out of the process of private collective bargaining.

If the association of employees in collective bargaining is to be immune from Section 1 of the Sherman Act, the immunity should be strictly confined. It is not, or should not be, a license to cartelize the product market. The law already restrains cartelization of the product market in several ways. Under the rule of the *Allen-Bradley* decision,[13] unions lose their immunity to the Sherman Act when they

[13] *Allen-Bradley Co. v. Local Union No. 3, IBEW,* 325 U.S. 797 (1945).

conspire with employer groups, even though a "labor dispute" is involved. The union may not aid such groups to suppress interstate competition. And a local combination may not stop the free flow of materials or competing products into the state.[14] The law distinguishes between agreements relating to wages, hours, and supplementary conditions of employment and agreements relating to the product market. However, it should define "labor group" more strictly and impose stricter limitations on permissible agreements. Businessmen-employers should not be permitted to clothe themselves in the guise of union members, nor to fix prices in the guise of collective bargaining.[15] It is not clear, to the layman at any rate, whether the law prohibits the union from making price-fixing and market-control agreements severally with individual employers or from forcing them to comply with such arrangements set up on the union's initiative. The sweeping rule of the Hutcheson case,[16] that labor acting alone is exempt from the anti-trust laws, seems to indicate that unions can do these things. But other cases have appeared to limit the immunity to cases arising out of "labor disputes," a term which has had an elastic and shifting definition. The Taft-Hartley Act has deprived labor of certain weapons that it could formerly use with impunity. But the whole matter needs clarification. The law should explicitly provide that no contract or bargain between employer and union may contain any clause or agreement relating to the price of

[14] *U.S.* v. *Chattanooga Chapter, National Electrical Contractors Association,* 116 F. Supp. 509 (1953); *U.S.* v. *Employing Plastering Association of Chicago,* 347 U.S. 186 (1954).

[15] The District Court held in *U.S.* v. *Fish Smokers Trade Council* (C.C.H. 31 Labor Cases, 70,291, 1956) that the jury should determine whether a group of jobbers in the smoked fish industry was a labor or a non-labor group. Obviously some statement of legislative policy would help to narrow the scope for such decisions.

[16] "So long as a union acts in its self-interest and does not combine with non-labor groups, the licit and illicit . . . are not to be distinguished by any judgment regarding the wisdom or unwisdom, the rightness or wrongness, the selfishness or unselfishness of the end of which the particular union activities are the means." *U.S.* v. *Hutcheson,* 312 U.S. 219 at p. 232 (1941). What the Court did was to grant a general immunity to labor (acting alone) from the anti-trust laws by analogy to the immunity from *injunctions* granted by the Norris-La Guardia Act to unions pursuing a labor dispute. See C. O. Gregory, *Labor and the Law* (New York, 1949), pp. 269–79. ". . . Justice Frankfurter virtually took organized labor entirely out from under the Sherman Act. This, in effect, repealed that act as far as labor was concerned, on the strength of the Norris-La Guardia Act."

the product or its quality, the volume of the firm's output,[17] the mode of sale, or the channels of distribution. Unions and employers who make such agreements should be subject to the penalties of the Sherman Act. These additions would strengthen the existing rules against joint conspiracy of employers and union to cartelize markets and bar outside competitors.

A related issue is the administrative jurisdiction of the National Labor Relations Board. Its power to define labor disputes and regulate labor practices should not of itself exempt any practice from the prohibitions of the anti-trust laws.[18] The law should provide that an unfair labor practice may also be a violation of the Sherman Act just as price discrimination by a business firm may simultaneously be a violation of the Clayton Act (restrainable by cease-and-desist orders of the FTC) and a violation of the Sherman Act. And it should also declare that certain practices which are *not* unfair labor practices and hence exempt from injunction under the Norris-La Guardia Act may nevertheless violate the Sherman Act if the union weaves them into a pattern of control or cartelization in the product market.

Of course the Sherman Act would not apply to many labor-cartelized product markets that are strictly local. State anti-trust laws have proved to be very weak indeed in application if not in concept. Doubtless local markets would continue to escape, just as local price-fixing arrangements involving no labor association have escaped. This local exemption from the Sherman Act would help to solve by default the difficult problem of the self-employed fringe. If carpenters work for contractors, they may bargain collectively and fix a union rate of

[17] Except, perhaps, an agreement to smooth out seasonal fluctuations in output. Cf. Neil W. Chamberlain, *The Union Challenge to Management Control* (New York, 1948), Chapters 5–6.

[18] "During the past few years it has apparently become accepted usage to regard as a labor dispute any situation in which a union uses its monopoly power . . . simply to promote economic controls in order to promote the financial positions of itself and its constituent unions. Such activity is termed a labor practice in order to bring it within the jurisdiction of the National Labor Relations Board. . . . It is not a legitimate purpose of labor law to free unions to do whatever their leaders conceive to be the general advantage of organized labor in the way of restraining trade and commerce and destroying competition." Roscoe Pound, *Legal Immunities of Labor Unions* (Washington, 1957), pp. 45–7. See also the *Report of The Attorney General's National Committee to Study the Antitrust Laws* (Washington, 1955), p. 305.

wages; may carpenters employed directly by a private householder fix the price of the service they sell? Does the householder become the employer, even though not involved in any collective bargain, or does the carpenter become a "business man"? The law could probably draw the line between self-employed persons fixing the price of "services" and fixing the price of products, and set up some arbitrary categories that would prevent non-labor groups from using the exemption as a screen for price-fixing. Most of the borderline cases would simply escape the federal law because of their intra-state nature.

Secondary boycotts are efforts to extend or to insulate a local or partial monopoly. The Taft-Hartley Act defines them as unfair labor practices. They are not all alike. The law might well exempt secondary consumption boycotts in which an aggrieved union by peaceful publicity attempts to persuade the public not to consume the employer's product and does not attempt to coerce third parties or picket distributors' premises. The employer is free to persuade customers to the contrary. The troublesome secondary boycotts and secondary strikes are those in which the union attempts to prevent other firms from using or selling the product. When a local group uses them to exclude the goods of all outside competitors merely to strengthen local monopoly and maintain product prices, it is clearly attempting to cartelize. But suppose a union merely uses the secondary boycott to organize non-union shops? Public policy at present permits the union to organize non-union employers directly. Only the means are different.[19] Why did the Taft-Hartley Act make this sharp distinction of means?

One reason is undoubtedly that the secondary boycott violates equity by injuring innocent third parties. Another is that unions have

[19] This ambiguity of means and ends is reflected in past court pronouncements on secondary boycotts and other means of organizing non-union plants. *Loewe* v. *Lawlor*, 208 U.S. 274 (1908); *United Mine Workers* v. *Coronado Coal Co.*, 259 U.S. 344 (1922); *Coronado Coal Co.* v. *United Mine Workers*, 268 U.S. 295 (1925), where the issue turned on the subjective *intent* of the union in striking against non-union producers; *Apex Hosiery Co.* v. *Leader*, 310 U.S. 469 (1940). Cf. also Gregory, *op. cit.*, Chapters VIII and X.

used them all too often to cartelize rather than merely to organize the trade. The teamsters' union and the construction trades are the ones that have displayed outstanding virtuosity in using the secondary boycott, and it is in these areas that cartelization has been most frequent and most objectionable. A third reason is that public policy already provides machinery for employees to organize by election if they wish to have a union. The secondary boycott as an organizing weapon puts pressure on the *employer* to sign a union contract whether his employees want it or not. Stranger unions use boycotts to force organization upon disparate trades. Unions in different lines of work or different industries use them to reinforce each other. Secondary boycotts enable power to breed power. Their prohibition does not deprive the workers of any of their basic rights of organization and bargaining.

In curbing secondary boycotts, secondary strikes, and "hot-cargo" clauses,[20] public policy must also put restraints on some forms of picketing. Picketing of third parties is itself a form of secondary boycott. Although its purpose may be merely to inform the consuming public or the employees of the existence of a labor dispute, the labor dispute is sometimes not within the picketed establishment. To prevent this form of secondary boycott the law should confine picketing to establishments where a lawful strike is taking place or where a dispute exists between the employer and the union legally certified to represent the employees. Organizational picketing should be permitted only for a brief period before a scheduled election, and should in effect be confined to propaganda at the employees' entrance to the premises.

Picketing in furtherance of a secondary boycott has been declared

[20] The Interstate Commerce Commission has ruled that common carriers may not refuse "hot cargo" shipments blacklisted by the union because they have been handled in transit by a non-union truck line or have originated in a plant against which some allied labor group has a grievance. But the ICC ruling does not determine the legality of hot cargo clauses in contracts signed by any class of shipper. The NLRB has taken an ambiguous position on hot cargo clauses. Several cases are now (March, 1958) before the Supreme Court. (*NLRB* v. *General Drivers Local 886, International Association of Machinists* v. *NLRB*, and *Carpenters* v. *NLRB*.) The Court may rule that hot cargo clauses of all sorts for all kinds of carriers are illegal; if it does not, Congress should do so legislatively.

unlawful,[21] but organizational picketing by stranger unions has been upheld.[22] The only other suggestion offered here is that the NLRB should be empowered to proceed against secondary boycotts, secondary strikes, and secondary picketing on its own initiative, without waiting for a complaint from an injured party who may be too cowed to make one. Defining these as unfair labor practices should not estop the government from proceeding under the Sherman Act against unions which use them in a pattern of monopolistic control of the product market.

Public policy should not only prevent cartelization of the product market and union restrictions on entry of firms but also union restrictions on entry of persons into the labor force. Since unions can limit the supply of labor only by closed-shop agreements combined with restrictions on entry into the union, it appears that the present restrictions on closed shop agreements and excessive initiation fees are essential elements in anti-monopoly policy. Of course, even when the union does not have a closed shop, the wage rates it negotiates with the employer may be higher than competition would have set them, and this may of itself restrict the number of jobs; but the long-run pressure of persons seeking employment will tend to restrain the monopoly power of the union if it cannot close the trade against them. Since union-shop agreements, unlike the closed shop, do not give the union power to control the labor supply, they are not nearly as offensive to anti-monopoly policy as long as the union cannot force the employer to discharge anyone simply by expelling him from the union. (Anti-monopoly policy has no bearing on the moral issue of the "right to work.")

The Taft-Hartley Act curb on the closed shop, as everyone knows, was a dead letter for ten years, but the Board seems at last to be bestirring itself to enforce it. Recently the general counsel of the NLRB informed the Building Trades Department of the AFL-CIO that closed shop agreements and other illegal hiring arrangements would have to be eliminated in the near future; both union and employer

[21] *Electrical Workers, Local 501* v. *NLRB,* 341 U.S. 694 (1951).

[22] *A. F. of L.* v. *Swing,* 312 U.S. 321 (1941).

would be subject to the reimbursement remedy of the Brown-Olds Case if they did not comply.[23] This is drastic indeed. It remains to be seen whether the craft unions will be hard hit by the new policy. Some skeptics believe that craft-union control of labor is already so firm that the hiring practices will continue as before by tacit agreement. Yet some unskilled trades have had closed-shop agreements; in some areas many skilled-craft workers are not members of unions. The effects will be spotty. The new policy should in any event loosen up some tightly controlled local monopolies in the long run. It will also put an end to the practice of some union locals of excluding qualified members of other locals from jobs within its jurisdiction or extorting fees for "work permits" from outsiders—a type of guild restriction which public policy simply cannot countenance.[24]

The employment relation for craft unions and some unions of unskilled workers employed by small enterprises is different from the employment relation for the large industrial union. In the past the craft unions have guaranteed the skill of the workers they "supplied" to employers, and employers have found this beneficial. Furthermore, the union membership of a worker has often been entirely independent of his relation to any employer. Employment may be casual or short-term. A building contractor, for instance, may employ several plumbers for two or three weeks and then need no more for a month. Obviously the NLRB cannot hold new elections in his "establishment" every month or so for two or three employees in a craft. Instead the employer uses *already* unionized labor. In trades like this a union shop may not be altogether distinct from a closed shop. If these unions continue in the future to "furnish" labor to employers, they must not sign exclusive contracts, but they may still retain substantial control over the labor supply. Public policy should guard against

[23] *Wall Street Journal,* February 26, 1958. In the Brown-Olds case, which involved a closed shop contract, the Board ordered the unions to refund all dues and assessments collected from its members during the period of the illegal contract. *Local 231, Plumbers and Pipefitters,* 115 NLRB 594 (1956).

[24] If union carpenters will not work on the job with non-union painters, the law can probably afford the employer no recourse. There appears to be no way to prevent "conspiracy" among different craft unions to use the market power of the strongest to sustain unionization of the weakest, without infringing the right of the union worker to leave his employment.

tacit monopolization in these situations by ensuring by all possible means that union membership remains open to every applicant, without excessive initiation fees or unduly restrictive apprenticeship rules.[25] The hiring hall should be a special kind of labor market, not an exclusive preserve.[26] The NLRB has recently taken a strong position (in the Hodcarriers and Associated General Contractors case) against closed-shop hiring halls, requiring them to offer their services henceforth to all applicants on a non-discriminatory basis whether the applicants are union members or not. This may further weaken the power of certain craft unions to control the labor supply.

The policies already outlined would prevent conspiracy between unions and employers to control the product market. They would prevent unions from controlling product prices directly and from restricting either entry to the product market or entry to the labor force. They would inhibit restraints on the opportunity for non-union employers to link up with non-union workers. But they would not restrain the spread of union organization directly so long as the union organizes new establishments in the permissible ways. Under the Wagner Act, public policy actively encouraged the extension of unionization. Present policy is more neutral. It permits labor and management to find their own equilibrium of forces. It denies to each the use of certain practices and requires them to bargain in good faith. It does not encourage the spread of unionization, but permits a union to find what affiliates it can in an orderly process of persuasion and election.

But suppose the union succeeds in organizing all establishments

[25] A strong craft union might attempt to restrict entry by tacitly restricting the number of apprentices it trains. One may doubt whether there are many skills so occult that newly-entering workers could not pick them up somehow and improve them by practice, especially if employers and trade schools set up training programs.

[26] The same problem of casual employment exists in some unskilled trades like stevedoring. A recommendation to keep the union open looks very pallid compared to the fierce evils that have afflicted the longshoremen's trade. A union which tries to organize and control unskilled laborers who are not continuously employed in definite establishments may resort to violence and intimidation to enforce its demands and maintain 100 per cent membership. The remedies for violence and extortion are beyond the scope of our discussion.

and in fixing uniform wages and other conditions of employment throughout an industry. Where then is the check on monopolistic exactions? Declarations of policy have not really indicated what the limits to union monopoly power should be. It is clear that a union's power to get higher wages and other benefits from any one employer will be strengthened if it can organize all the firms in the industry. If public policy encourages the union to take wages out of competition, there is no apparent stopping place short of industry-wide control of wages. In the past both Congress and the courts have often assumed that this was the legitimate end of labor policy. Because collective action in wage determination was guaranteed, unions pursuing their own self-interest were given more or less free rein to eliminate *all* competitive influences on their wages, if they could.

The idea that labor must suppress *all* competitive influences on wages in order to gain its rightful ends confuses one end with another. The rationale behind public guarantees of the right of collective bargaining is that individual workers have no bargaining power, that they suffer from immobility and ignorance of alternative opportunities, that they need to act collectively to offset the monopsony power of employers and secure fair treatment. No doubt their actual need for unions to protect themselves against exploitation varies from one labor market to another. But in no case does it follow that the unions must eliminate all competitive influences *outside* their employment relationship with the individual firm to protect their members against exploitation. Their right to bargain collectively with their employer is not tantamount to an unlimited right to suppress price competition among firms, even though this competition indirectly effects their wages.

Competition may indirectly and implicitly limit the power of a union even when an industry is virtually completely organized. If the union can require all existing employers to observe union wage scales, workers seeking jobs at the union wage may be excluded by lack of employment opportunities. This potential supply of labor may affect the policy of the union, causing it to accept lower wage rates and more employment than it might otherwise have favored. If it does maintain wages above the "competitive" level, not all the potential supply will be employed. Workers may be displaced to non-union trades. But the power of the union might be undermined if new firms can enter and existing firms can break away from the union scale to take advantage of this potential supply of workers.

Craft unions dealing with many small employers are likely to try to reinforce marketwide control with ancillary restrictions on entry. Unions faced with many small employers must constantly grapple with the problem of the unorganized firm or the firm that breaks discipline. By various techniques they try to organize all firms, make them conform to a common wage pattern, and bring mavericks to heel. The competitive problem for the industrial unions in large-scale industry is somewhat different. We have said more about craft and other small-unit unions than about large-unit industrial unions because the former practice exclusion and conspiracy more frequently than the latter. It is easier to frame public policy toward cartelization and exclusion in terms of the traditional categories of anti-trust law. Moreover, many small-unit unions try to impose monopoly on industries that otherwise promise the public the benefits of competition: their effects are more visible. In general, large industrial unions have less control over entry to the labor force. In their greater concern for employment, they have occasionally even urged a low price policy upon their employers in order to expand markets and create more jobs. But the structure of the employing industry insulates them better than small-unit crafts from product-market competition. Oligopolistic firms are in a better position to secure monopolistic revenues from the product market and to share them with organized labor. Once all the firms in an oligopolistic industry are organized, there is less danger of competition from wage "chiselers" than there is in unionized competitive industries. Non-unionized firms are less likely to enter and undercut both prices and wages. It is futile to expect entry of non-unionized employers in many trades even when the union maintains high wage rates and the firms hold prices well above the competitive level. Competition in both labor and product market depends on the existing firms.

Anti-trust policy can attempt to limit joint monopoly in these large-scale industrial structures by attempting to create effective competition among firms. It can also prevent secondary control practices by unions such as restraints on entry into the labor force. A double-edged anti-monopoly policy can undoubtedly do much to promote effective competition among existing firms and to prevent vertical combinations of labor and management against the consumer. But many would question whether indirect competitive checks have much effect on a powerful union which can set wage patterns for the whole industry at once. The same question arises in less concentrated industries that are completely organized by a single union. In both cases wages and prices may settle into an inflexible and non-competitive pattern. Competition may be severely handicapped when a union represents the employees of all firms and engages in multiple-unit or industry-wide bargaining.

The term "industry-wide" bargaining covers many different bargaining arrangements.[27] It may mean that all the employers bargain with the union at once through chosen representatives. The bargaining may be nationwide in scope or cover markets somewhat less extensive. It may mean that the union bargains with a group of several key employers and then imposes the agreement on other employers without negotiation. It may mean only that the union enforces the same terms on all employers individually without negotiation with a group. Usually, however, it refers to some sort of "multiple unit" bargaining carried on between the union and a group of employers which results in substantially identical wage rates for all the employers in the market—meaning the product market, regardless of whether the labor market has the same scope.

Market-wide bargaining is not universal. Not all labor groups favor it. Employers often use it defensively to resist "whipsawing" by a union which threatens each employer in turn with a strike and loss of his markets to competitors. But unions do, practically without exception, favor multiple-unit *representation,* whether they bargain with employers individually or collectively. Their aim is industry-wide

[27] See the *Proceedings of the Conference on Industry-Wide Collective Bargaining* of the Labor Relations Council of the Wharton School of Finance and Commerce (Philadelphia, 1949), pp. 22–24.

organization of the trade by one union and an industry-wide wage pattern that will prevent price competition from firms with lower wage costs. To further this interest some unions do promote market-wide or multiple-employer bargaining. Whether unionized employers bargain with unions willingly or unwillingly, they frequently welcome standardization of wage rates and elimination of the kind of price competition that stems from lower wages.

Proposals to prohibit industry-wide or multiple-unit bargaining would forestall the double incidence of collusion from the management side and cartelization from the union side, which strengthens monopoly not only in the labor market but in the product market. These proposals would forbid the employers to bargain in a group or to coordinate their employment policies explicitly. But they go beyond elimination of formal multiple-employer bargaining. They would also forbid the same union to bargain with different employers. While these proposals would not make national unions unlawful, only the unit consisting of a single firm's employees could represent them in economic bargaining, and the national union would be forbidden to coordinate or control the policies of their locals.[28] A labor union as a bargaining unit would be confined to the bounds of a firm. Most of these proposals would allow a single union to represent the employees of different plants of the same employer, even though widely separated geographically. Most would exempt local markets from the prohibition of multiple-unit bargaining, within some strictly-defined limits.[29] Clearly, craftsmen working intermittently for contractors and other small groups employed by small firms cannot set up "local" bargaining units within the firm; while these craftsmen may not need

[28] See the provisions of the Hartley Bill (HR 6074, 80th Congress, 1948), the Gwynn-Fisher Bills (HR 7697, 7698, and 8449, 82d Congress, 1952, and HR 437, 83d Congress, 1953) and the Lucas Bill (HR 2545, 83d Congress, 1953).

[29] Cf. the Gwynn-Fisher Bill: "[The prohibitions against combinations of employers in collective bargaining and against labor unions representing the employees of more than one employer] . . . shall not apply with respect to any employers of labor organizations whose concerted activities or arrangements are confined to the wages, rates of pay, hours of employment, or other terms or conditions of employment, of employees employed in a single bargaining area, provided such employees do not number more than five thousand and the National Labor Relations Board has found a unit of such employees to be appropriate . . . , and the employers of such employees have designated an association or other agency as their collective-bargaining representative. . . ."

unions to resist exploitation, the proposals would not go so far as to break up craft locals into tiny fragments.

A "limitist" policy [30] in this form would, of course, greatly reduce the power of some national unions whose individual units are weak. It would also put a brake on their efforts to organize non-union establishments, since they could not control such local units even after organizing them. The units would not benefit much from affiliation with a national union. In some cases the national unions would be reduced to insignificance and their organizing drives would stop dead.

Unions have often claimed that employees of different firms must join together because otherwise large employers would tacitly collude to keep wages down. There is really no reliable evidence to support or refute this claim. Advocates of a limitist policy properly deny that the *product* market is the relevant unit for measuring monopsony in the *labor* market. If multiple bargaining in local labor markets were exempted from the proposed ban, unions would be free to resist collusive monopsony without reaching out to control competition on national markets.

Some form of limitation on industry-wide bargaining would help to maintain a fluid and competitive economy. From the point of view of the economist, industry-wide bargaining not only is likely to encourage collusion and cartelization but also is likely to interfere with the long-run optimum use of regional resources. Regional differences in wage levels are not entirely due to the presence or absence of unions; they also reflect differences in resource endowment. Public policy should encourage mobility of resources. A low regional wage level is better corrected by emigration of labor, immigration of capital, and long-run growth in productivity than by an artificially imposed uniformity of wage scales.[31]

However, it is not clear what form of limitist policy is appropriate for dealing with the problem. A prohibition of multiple-unit union

[30] The term has been used by H. Gregg Lewis and others. See "The Labor-Monopoly Problem: A Positive Program," *Journal of Political Economy*, Vol. LIX, No. 4 (Aug., 1951).

[31] Unions claim that industry-wide bargaining can take account of local differences in labor markets. But one may doubt whether it takes enough account of them to prevent regional distortions.

representation in collective bargaining would be a major break with past national policy, unlike the other policies reviewed earlier. In some respects it would be a "union-busting" policy. It may be possible to restrict bargaining to sub-industry units without prohibiting multiple-unit representation, but the policy would have to be adapted to specific industry structures. It is difficult to see how a general rule such as Section 2 of the Sherman Act could be used to limit union size. A test of excessive or unreasonable monopolization in the *labor* market under the Sherman Act could not rest on the convenient distinction between union practices in the labor market and union practices in the product market, a distinction which supports other kinds of restrictions on union monopoly. Nor could it depend on a distinction between legal and illegal *practices;* organizing and collective bargaining under present statutes are perfectly legal. And it would hardly be equitable to forbid employers to band together in collective bargaining if their several groups of employees can do so. Further research into labor-market structures might indicate better ways of limiting the power of individual unions. The proposals offered up to date are not likely to become official policy.

The objective of anti-monopoly policy[32] toward labor unions should be to maintain workable competition in product markets and to restrain the development of undue concentration of power in the labor market. It is a complement of anti-monopoly policy toward business firms. The elements of such a policy are:

(1) To prevent restraints on entry into product markets;
(2) To prevent control of product prices and output by labor unions, whether acting alone or in collusion with employers;
(3) To prevent restriction on entry into the labor force;
(4) To limit the scope of union power by encouraging a large degree of structural flexibility in labor markets.

This policy could avail itself of the following means:

(1) Enforcement of the provisions of the Taft-Hartley Act on closed shops, secondary boycotts and secondary strikes. The ban should ex-

[32] See the *Report of the Attorney General's National Committee to Study the Anti-Trust Laws, op. cit.*, pp. 293–306.

plicitly include secondary picketing. The NLRB should be empowered to act on its own initiative against these restrictive practices.

(2) Elimination of union control of local licensing and inspection.

(3) Reversal of the Hutcheson decision, by legislative amendment of the Clayton and Norris-La Guardia Acts if necessary, to subject union control of product markets to the sanctions of the Sherman Anti-Trust Act. The policy should spell out prohibitions on union control of output (other than by lawful strikes), product prices, channels of distribution, market areas, or customers. It should make union restrictions of entry to the product market illegal. Use of the secondary boycott to control product markets should be an offence against the Sherman Act as well as an unfair labor practice.

The need for a curb on multiple-unit bargaining is becoming urgent, but we cannot specify a "limitist" policy without further research into the circumstances of individual markets. But even without a direct curb on the scope of union organization in the labor market, the public authority can prevent restrictions on entry to the labor force and restrain cartelization of the product market by unions or combinations of unions and employers. Some effective means of restraining monopoly power are at hand or easily provided. By using them, public policy can arrest further movements of the industrial structure toward monopoly.

6

Regulating Unions

David McCord Wright

PRACTICALLY EVERYBODY now agrees that unions should be regulated in some way or other and for some purposes or other. Thus in the summary of *The Impact of the Union,* Part Two, we find the following, "We all further agree that labor power, like corporate power, must be subject to restraints for the general welfare."[1] But where trouble starts is in wondering *how* and for what *purpose* the union should be regulated. In this connection there is an important bit of wording in the *Impact* summary just quoted which the reader may have missed. It does not say "labor" should be subject to restraints but labor *power.* Why is this? The answer lies in the basic philosophy with which the problem is approached. And in working out the implied philosophy we will get valuable guides both as to the reasons for regulation and the types of regulation to be applied.

First of all, let us try to set the problem in general perspective. For a number of years and in numerous books and articles I have argued that there is, over the long run, a close association between the values of economic growth, political freedom, democratic opportunity and the free market. If men are made relatively free, economically and politically, some of them will become creative. And if they become creative they will tend simultaneously to create growth and disturbance. Indeed disturbance inheres in the very nature of the process since, inevitably, and no matter what economic and political system reigns at the moment, the process of expanding total output per

[1] D. M. Wright (ed), *The Impact of the Union* (New York, 1951), p. 379.

head implies *disproportionate* expansion in some lines and contraction in others. Furthermore, if growth is to retain its impetus, there must constantly be added new ideas and new methods. But these new ideas and new methods are evolved and—still more important in many cases—applied by special types of men—men requiring a good deal of independence. I have argued that in the last analysis this independence demands—again over the long pull—that there be a reasonable possibility of voluntary transfer between independent and competing policy centers.[2]

But it is precisely in the matter of independence and freedom of transfer that the principal argument for the free market lies. Where the market is centrally controlled and policies are set from the center, mere geographic transfer is useless. The same basic authority and the same basic preconceptions will be operative everywhere. Freedom of experiment will be proportionately hampered. Such, in a nutshell, are some of the major elements of the problem of economic growth and one of the principal arguments for the free market. Let us now, however, go on to apply these ideas to labor policy. I will assume that we want rising living standards per head, democratic opportunity, political freedom. There are other values. But the values given are the ones most generally stressed today.

Accepting the point of view just outlined, in what way are labor unions today likely to need restraining for the public good? We obviously need to know the problem before we can decide what to do about it. Roughly, in addition to questions of simple honesty, which have been much in the public eye, we find the following economic areas in which union action and public welfare (as defined above) may sometimes conflict: wage demands, disputes over standards of economic "security," variously defined, managerial organization, the incentive problem, compartmentalization of the labor market. We may begin with wages.

Again in *The Impact of the Union,* K. E. Boulding summarized the discussion of wages as follows:

[2] D. M. Wright, *A Key to Modern Economics* (New York, 1954), Ch. II; ———, "Adventure of Routine," *Harvard Business Review,* Vol. 33, No. 5 (Sept.–Oct. 1955); ———, "The Open Secret of Economic Growth," *Fortune,* Vol. LV, No. 2 (Feb., 1957).

We all, or nearly all, consent
If wages rise by ten per cent
It puts a choice before the nation
Of unemployment or inflation.[3]

In other words, a rate of increase of money wages substantially in excess of the rate of increase of productivity will induce an economic crisis—as outlined in Boulding's jingle. Unions, on the other hand, tend to preach a doctrine which assumes: (a) a rise in wage *rates* must mean a rise in labor income, (b) a rise in labor income must mean a rise in total expenditure, (c) a rise in total expenditures must mean a rise in employment and in investment demand. Hence the way to get out of a depression is by raising money wages. But only the middle step of the argument, if that, is at all reliable. And it is clear that if unions ignore these limitations great conflicts with public welfare may ensue.

But the potential conflict of labor action and the general welfare is far broader than just wages. Growth we have seen comes through change and causes change. This, it should be remembered, is just as true under socialism or Communism as under capitalism. Now it follows that if every man is to be guaranteed, not merely an unchanged pay cheque, but an *unchanged routine of life;* that is, if no one is to be under any necessity of changing the type of work he is doing, it will become virtually impossible to have growth. I remember discussing this problem with a European labor leader. He said he was in favor of industrialism but against the introduction of *any* machine which would offset the "psychic equilibrium" of any worker. The reply to such an idea, of course, must be that the person advancing it is really opposed to industrialization of *any* kind. For inevitably, in the process of growth, there must be somebody whose love of skills, power, friends, or places is disturbed in the process of technological change. I believe it was William James who said that if there existed one cockroach with an unsatisfied desire, the perfection of the universal harmony would be spoiled. Few of us carry our standards out to cockroaches! But the regime of smooth continuity advocated, say, by Thorstein Veblen must be a stagnant one. And to the extent that

[3] *Op. cit.*, p. 79.

the labor movement moves in that direction, to that extent it conflicts with growth and opportunity. Our analysis, therefore, leads to the conclusion that if we want growth we must discourage "featherbedding" whether in the form of simple gouging or in the shape of the more high-minded advocacy of serene routine for its own sake.

A good many labor people will, however, grant this much—at least in theory anyhow. "But," they will say, "admitting that change is needed, let us *plan* change in advance so that we can be sure everything will dovetail nicely." To this there are at least two objections. In the first place, as growth occurs on any substantial scale, we inevitably move into regions of the unexplored. Our best information becomes less and less reliable, and with the best of available knowledge unexpected technological quirks may nevertheless arise which can be highly unstabilizing. In addition, if any important effort is being made to meet the desires of the consumer, it will be found that these will shift and shift unexpectedly as growth takes place. Furthermore, as explained, for example, in the writer's *Economics of Disturbance*, conflicts between growth and stability are possible transcending the power of *any* planning wholly to reconcile.[4] I have in mind "accelerations," "back logs," and "front logs." The result of all this is that the planning board which desires to be sure that expansions will always dovetail together will inevitably be forced progressively to extend the area of its controls in order to exclude the unexpected. Furthermore, and for the same reasons, pressures will be very great to slow down growth to a "*manageable*" rate—which may be less than could be obtained under a freer, if less tidy system, or what is needed if population is growing rapidly.

Cumulating all these technical objections leads on, however, to a yet more fundamental political point. That point is one frequently expressed by the author as the "law of decay of self-perpetuating non-competitive groups." In deciding *what* shall be produced and *when*, we inevitably also decide who shall hold power and when. *Spontaneous* opportunity, the life blood of science, democracy, and sustained growth, disappears. Thus, the central coordination which looks so sensible in the short run becomes, over the long run, the best

[4] Wright, *Economics of Disturbance* (New York, 1947), Ch. VI.

means of slowing down growth and cutting off opportunity.[5] The history of France and of French Canada in the century following Colbert's great "rationalization" scheme is a case in point.[6] Thus, again, if unions insist upon a system of advance planning designed to ensure that there will never be any loose ends in the process of growth-change, they will to that extent be putting across a method of social stabilization which over the long pull will lead to social stagnation—political as well as economic.

There are two other more or less high-minded types of union policy which curtail growth and opportunity. One of these is the use of the seniority standard for promotion. As unions take over the power of management they also inherit the problems of management and one of the most important of these is the envy problem. Where promotion goes to the more able men—as it should for efficiency's sake and for the sake of democratic opportunity—the resentment of those who have not been promoted can become very great. If a manager says a man has been promoted because he is "better," the un-promoted are apt to take that as a reflection upon them. "Solidarity" of morale is best ensured by using "objective" standards of promotion which do not reflect upon the capacity of others. Seniority is the obvious answer, with all that it implies in the way of frustration and the stultification of fresh points of view. As Mrs. Honor Croome puts it, "Excellence is suspect; he who excels might constitute himself a pace maker . . . all must travel in convoy at the pace of the slowest; whoever follows a privately charted course is almost by definition a pirate." [7]

It will be seen that in the case of seniority we have the union venturing into what was once the domain of management—namely, promotion policy. The same feature is found in the second high-minded "non-economic" value which tends to cut down growth. That is the desire for "participation" in management by the rank and file. Thus Bishop Fielding Bayne of the Episcopal diocese of Seattle, Washing-

[5] See note 2.

[6] See, for example, T. B. Costain, *The White and the Gold* (Garden City, N. Y., 1954), Chs. XXIV–XXVII.

[7] Honor Croome, "Liberty, Equality and Full Employment," *Lloyd's Bank Review*, New Series, No. 13 (July, 1949), p. 21.

ton, has said, "The slave obeys because he is ordered to obey, or because he is paid to obey. The son obeys because he wishes to." But why should a slave be *paid?* One inference might be that Bishop Bayne was following the philosophic principle sometimes stated (roughly): "He is a slave who follows rules not of his own making." [8]

Repercussions of such a doctrine upon the structure of management and upon labor relations could be profound. To many—if not most—people in the United States and Canada the fact of *payment* or wages is the index, not of slavery, but of freedom. For the fact that a man is paid means that he is legally able to leave and that his service is voluntarily given. Of course, if there is unemployment, leaving may be difficult. But the business cycle is a separate problem which we will touch on later. The idea quoted would lead to demands for sharing of management, the "one man, one vote, one dollar" idea of democracy. It could also be developed into the Marxian notion of "alienation"—that a man who works for the market rather than himself is enslaved or "alienated." [9] However one takes it, the explosive possibilities of the idea are obvious, and its popularity in some labor circles not very reassuring for the future of the competitive economy. It must be asked, furthermore, whether if we split society up into "self governing workshops" ruled by the majority and between which transfer is difficult, the man who has new ideas but is compelled to follow the vote of the majority on work policy is any less a "slave" than the man who chooses to be paid to work according to someone else's instructions but is free to leave if he "can't take it."

Returning to management, the trouble with the self-governing idea is, again, the fact that in a growing society we are constantly venturing into the unknown where risk bearing and quick decision are essential. For the same reasons that ships are not governed by committees of the whole crew voting and discussing before each shift of the helm, industrial organizations are not run effectively by votes of

[8] I have been unable to find the idea stated in the precise wording given. Plato comes close to it in the *Republic* and the *Symposium*. In any case, what is a valid philosophic distinction between the obedience of a free man who understands the need for authority and that of the man who merely obeys in spite of himself, should not be taken as a criterion for social organization.

[9] Alasdair C. Macintyre, *Marxism, an Interpretation* (London, 1953), Chs. V–VI.

the workers. Committee government, dual control, greatly reduces the adaptability and energy of an organization. On these fronts let me quote Lord Lindsay of Birker, a noted political theorist, former Master of Balliol College, Oxford, created a peer by the Labour Government and hence an extremely friendly critic. He writes: "One of the most persistent ideals of early trade unions was that of the 'self governing work-shop,' in which the distinction between the management and the managed had entirely disappeared. Unfortunately experiments made of setting up such work-shops have always, or nearly always, been inefficient. It is interesting to note that the Russians started with the same idea—that the worker, the ordinary simple worker at the bottom should run the business and they have had, in the interests of efficiency, progressively to give up any such notion." [10]

Closely allied with problems of promotion and management is the general problem of economic incentive, both for economic activity and economic saving. No matter what system one has, if an economy is to grow, people must somehow be persuaded or forced not to consume. Again there is a cyclical problem here, but again we leave that aside for the moment. In the free market the principal inducement toward accumulation is found in inequality of income and of wealth, plus profit, plus interest. The recent reaction of savers in the United Kingdom to increased interest rates shows that orthodox doctrine upon these points is by no means wholly out of date.[11] But the union movement tends to develop an intense jealousy of income differentials (except possibly for union leaders), profits and interest. To be sure, as indicated, there are from time to time periods in which "saving" seems redundant. This is due to the fact that we simply cannot expect the rise and decline of various industries always to cancel one

[10] F. S. C. Northrop (ed.), *Ideological Differences and World Order,* (New Haven, 1949), p. 261.

[11] "In 1952, however, there came a remarkable increase in the rate of personal saving. It jumped to 6½ per cent of personal disposable income—a slightly higher figure than in 1938. It stayed around this level in 1953 and 1954, and then again rose fast to 8 per cent in 1955 and 10 per cent . . . in 1956. Estimates for the whole of 1957 are not available yet, but quarterly figures suggest that there was a further increase, to around eleven per cent in the first nine months. . . . High interest rates are likely to have encouraged many people to save more." From *Economic Record,* issued by the U. K. Information Service, Vol. 12, Number 3 (April, 1958).

another smoothly. The same phenomenon can occur in a socialist state.[12] But if serious deflation be avoided, the motive to accumulate will soon once more be needed. And in the meantime the intense attacks upon "inequality" often begun by equalization-minded union leaders during depression may, by discouraging the inducement to invest, actually prolong the crisis rather than halt it. In this connection, Messrs. Boulding and Samuelson make the point that while wage demands usually have some relation to market condition, pension plans do not. Therefore, they are potentially far more pernicious, since they could be carried to the point of seriously impairing a needed (on average) flow of corporate saving.[13]

One final set of union policies has already been implied and must again be briefly mentioned before we can summarize. This set of policies concerns the splitting of the market into independent and closed groups. We have said earlier that the right to transfer on a relatively independent basis was one of the most important guarantees of personal freedom and opportunity. But by means of the closed shop, pension and other benefits, large parts of which are lost on transfer, and other restrictions upon and discouragements to the right of transfer, the labor market is increasingly being cut up into more or less watertight sub-markets between which it is becoming increasingly difficult and expensive to move. In return for an often vague and tenuous right to "influence" the leadership of the union which "represents" him, the worker is severely crippled in the far more effective and immediate right of switching his job.

We are now in a position to stop and summarize the various ways in which union policy may conflict with the general welfare. The public is usually most conscious of such things as violence and goon squads, or (at the moment) racketeering and dishonesty. But the problem is never really grasped until one recognizes that violence, dishonesty and racketeering, while bad enough in themselves, are not really the basic problem. Even if there were no racketeering, no violence, no goon squads, no sit-down strikes—even if every pension

[12] National Bureau of Economic Research, *Conference on Business Cycles* (New York, 1951) p. 396.

[13] *The Impact of the Union, op. cit.,* p. 79.

fund were honestly and intelligently administered—even if every union leader were a personally honest and high-minded man—there still could be a need for restraints upon union action. Why? The answer is that practically none of the lines of action we have been describing involve moral dishonesty. Honest men can force the economy into inflation or into unemployment—by mistakenly asking too high a level of money wages. Honest men can high-mindedly prefer security in work routine to technical change and thus hold back the standard of living of the poor. Honest men can advocate tight, centralized planning and misguidedly destroy independent opportunity and scientific innovation. Honest men can think seniority the only moral basis of promotion. Honest men can ham-string management and efficiency for the sake of "participation." Honest men can, in the name of equality, destroy incentive, opportunity and saving. Honest men can cut down capital formation by excessive pension demands. Honest men can prefer union "solidarity" to a fair chance, and set up closed shop and other obstacles to transfer. The fundamental dilemma is thus not racketeering and dishonesty, but the basic philosophy of much of the modern labor movement itself—a philosophy which tends always and everywhere, albeit often unconsciously, to work against growth, incentives, change, opportunity, continuing political democracy and development. Well now, what shall we do about it?

There are, it is submitted, three possible general lines of approach toward the set of problems we have outlined. They are as follows: First of all, we might make the unions and union policies directly subject to government control. Secondly, we might hope to educate union rank and file and union leaders in the economic facts of life so that unions would act "intelligently" or "responsibly" or with "self restraint." Thirdly, we might try to keep the unions from becoming powerful enough to be a serious danger. There is no possible line of approach which does not come under one or more of these three heads.

Those who are familiar with economic history and have trained themselves to look beyond labels will be struck by the resemblance between the summary of possible methods just given and the "big business" problem in Canada and the United States seventy years ago. There, too, there was a lot of talk, not all of it justified, about dishonesty and coercion. But there, too, full understanding was only attainable when one recognized that the problem went beyond mere "greed" or "bad" intention. There, too, the general available strategies of approach were the same: "social control," "self restraint," limitation of power.

Of course, it is obvious that if we attempt to limit power we are in a sense imposing social control. By the same line of reasoning, some political theorists will employ the quip that because we use traffic lights we live in a "planned society." This sort of verbal gymnastics is true enough on its own plane but overlooks all those questions of degree by which men really live. Following out the basic philosophy already outlined and the fundamental assumption of the liberal state, I submit that the principal line of approach toward union regulation should be in the direction of limiting power rather than government control. It was for this reason that the summary of the *Impact* symposium with which we began was worded as it was.

To have the government fix wages, whether directly or through a board, enormously increases the power of the state, is by no means always a way of getting wise action economically, and is often the way for every sort of political skullduggery. As in the case of so many controls, one control leads to another as more and more power is demanded to make the original scheme "workable." If, for example, one fixes a wage "level" or a permissible percent or formula for wage increases (and only those who have studied—worked with the problem—will know how difficult this is, especially if any sort of "objectivity" is being aimed for), immediately the question will arise of when is an increase an increase. What about re-classification of jobs? What about promotions? If a wage increase is granted will that make a price increase permissible? justified? inevitable? desirable? And if we get into prices what about shifts in the quality of goods, compulsory extras, black markets?

"Self restraint" and "responsibility" are equally unsatisfactory. There are several points here. First of all, in a growing world—which means a changing world—what is reasonable today need not be reasonable tomorrow. Unless there are some independent sources of policy around to see the change in circumstances and act on it, adaptation may not take place. Yet to appeal to the unions for self-restraint is open to nearly all the objections that can be made to similar treatment for business. It unduly penalizes the conscientious and puts a premium on evasiveness. Furthermore, like wage control, it almost inevitably leads to demands for more and usually centralized power. For the cooperating union will ask for methods to restrain the "chiseler." Still more important, union leadership will almost inevitably be compelled to ask for more control *over the rank and file*. If they can't control the rank and file it is unfair to ask them to act "responsibly." How familiar in "collective bargaining" is the formula: "Well if you turn me down you will have somebody worse back here tomorrow making even worse claims." Nor can moral suasion or appeals deal with the man who is high-mindedly convinced that growth is a bad thing.

For all these reasons we are forced back, therefore, upon one of the basic tenets of the liberal state: namely, that it is better on balance and safer to limit power than to appeal merely to the moral sense and information of those who wield it. This may appear a cynical doctrine to people of romantic leanings. Yet the writer submits that the historical record amply justifies it.

Coming down, therefore, to a more practical level, it is submitted that what we want is a union movement strong enough to prevent real exploitation but not so strong as to be an exploiter itself—of its own members, or of other unions, the public, or management. Such a standard is, of course, easier to state than to implement. Therefore, one further philosophical footnote must be given as to the nature of desirable power diffusion. There is a confusion often encountered here between mere checks and balances of "countervailing power" which simply keep everyone immobilized in a general stalemate and the fluid *diffusion* of power which permits opportunity and adjustment. It is the latter type of diffusion which is desirable. We don't want entrenched labor or entrenched industry locked in an eternal deathgrip. Rather, we want a system of free centers of experiment and power none of which is strong enough to block off the general current.

With this final qualification we come to specific measures. We have spent so much time outlining the problem and the standards by which one approaches it because, so far as mere legal gadgets are concerned, there are plenty of measures available, and what is really lacking is not legal machinery but public opinion and public understanding. Laws, even when enacted, are usually futile if not backed up by public opinion, something each generation seems to have to discover all over again for itself. Thus to go into legal minutiae without giving reasons is not very helpful. And to the present state of American opinion, it is the understanding which *is* still, to a considerable extent, lacking. The general structure of legislation which our analysis calls for may, however, be briefly indicated.

From our analysis we definitely want measures outlawing featherbedding, secondary boycotts, violence and goon squads, and compulsory union membership. The reasons for all these measures have, in effect, already been stated and there is no reason to repeat them. A more knotty problem is posed by the question of industry-wide bargaining. If a union is industry-wide in membership it obviously is an industry-wide bargainer *de facto*—and if the firms in the industry cannot get together then the union obviously has a great advantage through "artichoke" tactics and that sort of thing. On the other hand, industry-wide bargaining by both sides is clearly an open door first to stalemate and then to government regulation or to cartelization. Whether a firm-wide union would be strong enough is, on the other hand, debatable. Yet the logic of such a conclusion is difficult to escape. The problem, then, of what constitutes the appropriate size of a union is one which deserves much more careful consideration.

But beyond and behind all question of machinery are two more fundamental problems: education of public opinion and fiscal policy. Concerning the first of these, education, there is no hope for intelligent union policy until the public has been brought to the degree of sophistication concerning union power that it now has concerning business power. Once the public and its leaders fully realize that unions can, in Sumner Slichter's phrase be "over-dogs" as well as underdogs then we can sit down to a discussion of details. In this connection unions today probably derive a great part of their appeal in the United States from the notion that they are a "respectable" way to be radical. Our generation is largely disillusioned concerning socialism and Communism—particularly the latter. But the criticism so far has been almost wholly negative. It is still not too respectable, intellectually anyhow, to believe in competitive capitalism. The stereotype of the business man as necessarily predatory confronting the labor leader, necessarily altruistic, is still strong, particularly in clerical circles. There is a vacuum here that urgently needs filling.

However, beyond the question of education is the question of performance and the business cycle. Here the community may find itself, in the slang phrase, really over the barrel. If we do not underwrite excessive wage demands we will probably get unemployment and if we do underwrite them we will certainly get inflation. The attempt to break union power, as such, by unemployment strikes me as futile, dangerous and very nearly immoral. But on the other hand, if the union movement itself forces us into the choice of underwriting endless inflation or permitting more unemployment, then the public interest, it seems to me, lies in the soundness of the dollar. There is a problem of balancing alternatives here which involves elements of judgment and probably, in the real world, of compromise. Such judgments can be reached intelligently and probably harmoniously if both sides realize that no standard can be fully satisfied. But they will never be reached if we think of the matter as one of knights in shining armor fighting devils. Once the public sees the contestants as free from haloes there is more hope. It is much easier to deal with a wolf than with a wolf in sheep's (or angel's) clothing.

7

Some Non-Wage Aspects of Collective Bargaining*

Albert Rees

MY ANALYSIS will concern two non-wage aspects of collective bargaining: grievance settlement and seniority. Although grievance procedures and seniority can be found in many diverse industries, they have perhaps reached their fullest development in mass-production manufacturing. I shall confine my discussion to the manufacturing industries except where I explicitly indicate otherwise. However, many of my generalizations would not apply to the garment trades, while most would apply to mining and to transportation.

In the past two decades there has been a fundamental change in the relation of the manufacturing worker to his job. Where he once held his job at the pleasure of his supervisor, he now has rights in it which are jealously guarded. That these rights are tremendously important to workers has been documented in several recent studies of worker attitudes.[1] Ask an older worker what his union has done for him, and he is very likely to tell you that in the old days he constantly had to do favors for the foreman to keep his job—his choice of language will be much more colorful than mine—while now he is not beholden to anyone. Worker folklore about the pre-union period

* I am indebted for helpful suggestions to the members of the Research Group in Labor Economics and Industrial Relations, University of Chicago, and in particular to H. Gregg Lewis, Joel Seidman, and George P. Shultz.

[1] See, for example, Joel Seidman, Jack London, Bernard Karsh, and Daisy L. Tagliacozzo, *The Worker Views His Union* (Chicago, 1958).

undoubtedly exaggerates the extent of favoritism by foremen and the use of managerial authority in ways that seem arbitrary to workers. Nevertheless, I believe that this folklore has a substantial basis in fact. The necessity for buying the foreman's drinks or for painting his porch represented a kind of tangible exploitation of the workers. However, the psychological freedom from fear of reprisal in the union situation is probably much more important than any tangible gain.

The protection afforded workers by the non-wage aspects of collective bargaining is not without costs, and this protection raises both analytical and practical problems. I shall touch on several of these costs and problems as I proceed.

First, let us ask what the relation is between the union power to protect job rights through seniority and grievance procedure and union power to raise wages. In my view, strong grievance machinery and strong seniority rights may accompany general economic power but can also exist in its absence. Indeed, in many of the mass-production manufacturing industries where grievance machinery has perhaps reached its greatest importance, we have as yet almost nothing in the way of research findings that suggest substantial union power over relative wages. In the terminology of H. Gregg Lewis in Chapter 9, strong grievance machinery and seniority rights are compatible with competitive unionism.

The view I have just expressed has been challenged from two sides. Sumner H. Slichter, the foremost student of the non-wage aspects of collective bargaining, has argued that unions that have the power to win dramatic changes in the non-wage terms of employment must surely also have substantial power over wages, even though we have not been able to measure it.[2] This position, I think, does not recognize sufficiently the implications of the union's role as an innovator in the non-wage aspects of collective bargaining. Employers have always paid wages the amount of which has been governed within rather narrow limits by the operation of competitive labor markets during peri-

[2] Sumner H. Slichter, "Do Wage Fixing Arrangements in the American Economy Have an Inflationary Bias?" *American Economic Review*, Vol. XLIV, No. 2 (May, 1954), p. 330.

ods of full employment. It therefore requires real union strength to get employers to pay wages substantially higher than they otherwise would pay. But employers in the pre-union period did not, for example, grant seniority rights. When they agreed to do so, they may have found that the costs of the reform were small, or that they fell on the foreman or on workers not in their employ rather than on the firm. The employers could thus come to accept these practices rather willingly, however hostile they may have seemed before the fact. This hostility may have arisen from employer fears that seniority was somehow part of a union attempt to get higher real wages. From the union point of view, however, a strong emphasis on seniority in the early days of collective bargaining might mean less use of the union's limited bargaining power in raising wages.

It may even be possible that some of the non-wage aspects of collective bargaining are so desirable to workers that they create net advantages for the first firms to adopt them by attracting the best workers to these firms. But if this is so, why did not employers institute these practices on their own initiative? In the pre-union period, when a manufacturer was short of labor he raised his wages. Perhaps he could have attracted the labor he needed at less cost by, for example, instituting a seniority system and thus making his factory a better place to work. But this idea would never have occurred to him. Competitive labor markets will insure the spread of a successful major innovation in personnel practice once it occurs, but they cannot guarantee that it will occur. If the practice in question lies outside of the thinking of any of the competitors, it can only be introduced by an outside institution that takes a very different view of the problem.

In stressing that grievance procedures and seniority systems are union innovations, I do not mean to say that they cannot exist without a union. Practices of this sort were part of many employee representation plans instituted by employers.

A few such plans began before World War I, many more emerged during and after that war, and the National Industrial Recovery Act of 1934 inspired a large number.[3] More recently, when company sup-

[3] For a summary of the early plans, see E. R. Burton, *Employee Representation* (Baltimore, 1926).

port or domination of employee organizations has been illegal, there have still been a fair number of non-union companies with grievance procedures and seniority systems.[4] Although there is little information on when or under what circumstances these practices were adopted, it seems fairly clear that most of them were responses to the threat of unionization, whether immediate or remote.

Moreover, non-union grievance procedures and seniority systems seem on the whole to offer workers less protection than their counterparts under collective bargaining. Non-union seniority clauses typically qualify seniority rights more severely than clauses in collective agreements, and no union is present to oversee their administration. Present non-union grievance procedures seldom terminate in arbitration. In crucial discipline cases they thus require some executive of the firm to judge a dispute between a worker and his supervisor, and he may be biased toward upholding the supervisor's view. Perhaps for this reason, workers seem to make little use of most of the non-union grievance procedures.

I do not conclude from this that good non-wage conditions of employment in large firms can only be got through collective bargaining. There are several large manufacturing firms whose workers have repeatedly voted against unionization in free elections. These seem to be cases in which a determined company maintains an unusually able personnel department and treats workers generously. I do conclude that collective bargaining has a strong comparative advantage in producing desirable non-wage conditions. Local union leaders are free of the conflict of interest that besets the worker-oriented personnel man, and they have closer contact with the workers' views. The large company that seeks to produce acceptable unilateral substitutes for collective bargaining for manual workers incurs costs not unlike the costs to a nation of producing behind tariff walls a commodity in which it has a comparative disadvantage.

Let us now turn to the opposite view of the relation between the non-wage aspects of bargaining and union economic power. It has

[4] See J. J. Bambrick and J. J. Speed, *Grievance Procedures in Nonunionized Companies* and *Seniority Systems in Nonunionized Companies* ("National Industrial Conference Board Studies in Personnel Policy," Nos. 109 and 110 [New York, 1950]).

been argued that since some unions have no demonstrable monopoly power over wages, they must be powerless in general, and therefore cannot improve non-wage conditions for workers as a group. All they can do is to benefit some workers at the expense of others by solving conflicts among the interests of different members in particular ways. This view is especially appealing with respect to seniority, since it would appear that whatever the senior man gains the junior man must lose. In a sense, students of seniority have invited this view by stressing that seniority issues can create bitter internal strife in unions. But this view neglects the role of seniority in preventing favoritism and arbitrary action by supervision, and in reducing uncertainty for everyone. It is true that many grievances involve essentially claims of one worker against another. But this does not mean that workers as a group have nothing to gain from the presence of a machinery for settling such claims. One might as well argue that the larger democratic society gains nothing from a system of civil courts, since any damages awarded the plaintiffs must be paid by the defendants.

Not long ago I had occasion to discuss seniority with an outstanding economist who has had little contact with labor matters. He was appalled to learn that the overwhelming majority of layoffs and promotions of manual workers are now made on the basis of seniority. Are not ability and incentive stifled by such a system? It is natural for an economist to take this view of the much discussed conflict between seniority and ability. The answer, however, is less simple than it appears.

First, we must remember that seniority did not replace selection according to measured ability. It replaced practices that at best were much more subjective and at worst were open to grave abuse. If seniority represents a sacrifice of ability, it is in relation to an ideal that is largely unrealized. Second, the conflict between seniority and ability is reduced by the natural positive correlation between ability and experience, which may be higher in manual jobs than elsewhere. Third, where a worker has leadership ability as contrasted with mechanical ability, there are two natural outlets for his talents that lie outside the seniority system. One of these is election to union office, the other is promotion to a supervisory position. In both there are often ample opportunities. Finally, promotion according to seniority is almost always subject to some qualification in terms of merit, and is subject to satisfactory performance during a trial period on the higher-rated job. This may still permit the promotion of a man who is barely adequate, and it may impose unnecessary training costs on management, but these problems do not appear to be severe. James J. Healy of Harvard University has investigated 46 arbitration awards in which the arbitrator had set aside management's decision to promote a junior employee over a senior employee on the grounds of superior ability. In most of these cases the senior employee soon proved able on the new job, and in almost half the supervisor later doubted whether the junior employee would have done better.[5] However, such findings, even if based on more evidence, would not necessarily imply that ability should not be a stated criterion for promotion. To discard it might have adverse incentive effects.

A fifth factor is frequently mentioned as reducing the costs of seniority in terms of the sacrifice of ability. It is said that a seniority system makes management select employees more carefully and with a view to future promotion. Thus Mr. Slichter writes:

> In several important respects union control of layoffs tends to promote efficiency. In the first place, it tends to promote improvements in employment practice. As long as an employer can drop a man at any time for any reason, he may tolerate inefficient hiring practices, but when it is difficult for him to drop men, he is likely to exercise greater care in selecting them.[6]

Without questioning the facts asserted, it can be pointed out that this channel of adjustment may in large part merely alter the nature of the costs imposed by seniority rather than avoiding them altogether. Greater selectivity implies that a higher starting wage must be offered to get qualified applicants. A special form of these costs is

[5] J. J. Healy, "The Factor of Ability in Labor Relations," *Arbitration Today,* Proceedings of the Eighth Annual Meeting of the National Academy of Arbitrators (Washington, 1955), p. 51.

[6] Sumner H. Slichter, *Union Policies and Industrial Management* (Washington, 1941), p. 160.

incurred when exceptionally able men are hired as laborers because they will one day be eligible for promotion to skilled jobs. This involves an uneconomic reduction in the specialization of labor.

If management seems to be bearing the costs of seniority systems rather cheerfully, I think it is not only because it lacks alternatives. Seniority produces an important benefit for management by cutting down voluntary quitting. Such turnover, especially among skilled workers, is costly to management. But to say that seniority involves little net cost to the firm is not to say that it is costless for society. The reduction of mobility involves social costs to which I shall return later.

In addition to its use in determining the order of layoff and promotion, seniority is also used for such purposes as assigning overtime work or shifts. Here it is often a rationing device in the face of bad internal pricing, and better results for both workers and employers could generally be obtained by altering the relevant prices. Consider, for example, a contract provision requiring double-time for work on holidays. When in the face of such a provision an employer finds it necessary to schedule holiday work, it is generally much sought after and will go to the senior employees. This is clear evidence that the premium is too high—that at this premium rate the workers on the whole would prefer more holiday work and less leisure. There exists some lower premium at which the number of people who prefer the holiday work to the extra leisure would be about equal to the number the employer would want to use, and rationing by seniority would be unnecessary.

Similarly, it can be shown that most premiums for second and third shifts are too low, since senior employees will almost always choose to work day shift.[7] In this case it may be harder to see what the employer would gain by raising the premium. He would be able to attract better workers at the same wage since he would not have to require new workers to work nights unless they chose to. In general, if seniority is in principle used to assign workers to shifts, the internal pricing will be optimal if the distribution of workers by seniority is in

[7] The commercial airlines offer an interesting exception to this generalization. Night differentials for pilots are so high that senior pilots almost always choose to fly at night.

fact uncorrelated with the distribution by shifts. This will show that the wage inducements present just offset the average difference in tastes for the different kinds of work, so that senior workers will exercise rights to choose shifts according to the way their individual tastes differ from the average. This will leave room for the junior employees to do the same.

The grievance procedure is in many ways simpler to discuss than seniority. This procedure provides an avenue of redress for the worker whose rights or privileges under the collective agreement have been interfered with. The provisions of the agreement governing the employer's rights to discipline or discharge workers are especially important in this connection. In situations where the approach to grievances is not legalistic, the procedure can also be used as a channel for solving problems not covered in the agreement. Such channels of communication are very important in large organizations. In the chain of command within management there are strong incentives not to take problems to a superior because they may tend to make the subordinate "look bad." The grievance procedure offers the worker a way around such roadblocks, and often the higher levels of management may be more willing to act favorably on his complaint than those lower down. Indeed, it is not unknown for foremen to encourage workers to file grievances as an effective way for the foreman to get a problem in his department considered by someone higher up than his own superior. The solution of problems raised through the grievance procedure can lead to the removal of inequities in wage rates, to improvement of lighting, ventilation, or safety devices, to reductions in the speed of an assembly line, or to many other such changes in the conditions of work.

One possible indication of the importance of grievance machinery is that within a given industry a higher proportion of small firms than of large firms is generally unorganized. This is due in part to the higher costs per member to the union of organizing small firms. However, it is also true that informal procedures for settling grievances are much more effective in small firms where the worker can have relatively easy access to higher levels of management.

The costs of grievance settlement seem to be of a different kind than the cost of seniority. For the most part they are simply operating costs—the time spent by both parties in handling grievances and the costs of arbitration. There may also be costs in the reduction of managerial flexibility and discretion and in increasing management's reluctance to take disciplinary action. However, the main shortcoming of the protection afforded by grievance machinery is not that it is too expensive, but that it is to some extent incomplete. There are still times when the rights of individual workers are not secure.

Without any attempt to be exhaustive, I should like to list a few of the kinds of cases that experienced arbitrators have mentioned in discussing this class of problems.[8] First is the case of the non-union man within the bargaining unit. Although the union is supposed to handle his grievances, in practice it may refuse to do so or may not do so with its usual care and vigor. Second is the case of the union member who is in some sense a minority member—perhaps a political opponent of the union leadership, perhaps a member of a racial or ethnic minority. He, too, may sometimes have difficulty in getting his grievances heard. Third is the case of the logrolling of grievances—one grievance is settled in favor of management so that another can be settled in favor of the union. If the first grievant's case was just, his rights have been infringed. Fourth is the case of the union member whose grievance is dismissed by the union for lack of merit. Though unions are undoubtedly right in the great majority of such cases, they will be wrong in some, perhaps increasingly as union-management relations grow more amicable. Some union members may feel that the union has not protected their interests whenever a grievance involves conflicts of interests among workers, as almost all seniority grievances do.

In any case in which a member's grievance is dismissed by the union for reasons he feels are unsound, he in effect has a grievance against his union. Some unions have an effective internal machinery for handling such complaints, but many do not. Even where such procedures exist, they may be very slow, and by the time the worker's case has

[8] I have learned much about these problems from speeches by Charles O. Gregory of the University of Virginia Law School and Willard Wirtz of Northwestern University Law School. However, they bear no responsibility for these remarks.

been won within the union, his rights to have it considered by management have expired.

An extreme problem, fortunately rare, is raised by the "sweetheart agreement" in which an employer recognizes one union to keep another union out, and the recognized union then fails to protect workers' interests. Such cases usually involve financial corruption in the union that is recognized.

In a rather different category are cases in which the grievance process seems to produce justice that is too heavy-handed. Suppose that company rules or a collective agreement provide for automatic dismissal for some offense, such as drunkenness on the job, fighting with a foreman, or theft of company property. A long-service employee violates such a rule for the first time with no mitigating circumstances and no room for doubt about the facts. If the employer chooses to exercise his rights under the agreement, there is little or nothing that the union can do about the particular case, though it can later try to revise the relevant parts of the agreement. Yet the penalty may be much heavier in relation to the seriousness of the offense than penalties for comparable offenses outside the plant. Perhaps such cases create problems because disciplinary rules and the disciplinary provisions of collective agreements have not yet fully reflected the increasing cost of discharge to the worker.

I have been deliberately sketchy in referring to these problems because others are much better able than I am to discuss them in detail. They are mentioned here only as an introduction to the discussion of two very different ways of strengthening the rights of individual workers.

Most proposed solutions to the problems I have been discussing run in terms of improving the internal government of the union, the processes of grievance settlement, or the law governing collective bargaining. I am somewhat skeptical about the possibilities of making substantial gains along these lines. Legislation protecting the rights of non-members or minority members would be extremely difficult to administer. We all hope that attempts to increase democracy within unions will be successful in some cases where autocratic rule is now extreme. However, in many unions now moderately democratic, the natural tendencies are in the other direction—the tendencies of a maturing organization losing its original sense of idealistic mission. The recent establishment by the United Automobile Workers of a Board of Review made up of prominent outsiders is a promising development. However, such a board will probably be able to consider only the most important cases of member grievances against the union. Something might be gained by increasing the safeguards to the individual grievant in arbitration, perhaps making his rights in discipline cases more like the constitutional rights of a defendant in a criminal trial. Such a tendency, however, would eventually make arbitration slower, more formal, and more expensive. Carried to extremes, it could have adverse effects on management's authority and on efficiency.

Competition between unions, if carried on by persuasion rather than by economic pressure, can help solve some problems of individual rights within the union. From this point of view, it is desirable to make it as simple as possible for the majority of workers in a bargaining unit to change to another union or to no union, if they so desire, though some care must be taken not to disrupt bargaining relations by very frequent elections. Also from this point of view, unity of the labor movement, long a goal of many unionists, must be considered a rather mixed blessing.

It is desirable to explore all such institutional devices, and especially for the unions to explore them for themselves. But I feel that simultaneously we must explore another avenue. The real difficulty is that in the crucial cases involving discharge by the employer or expulsion from union membership,[9] much too much is now at stake. Discharge for cause can cost a worker many thousands of dollars in seniority rights and pension rights. In addition, in many states it can cost him his rights to unemployment insurance benefits. Because

[9] Under the Taft-Hartley Act, expulsion from union membership except for failure to tender regular union dues and initiation fees cannot be used to require an employer to discharge a worker under the terms of a union shop contract. However, the provision may at times be circumvented if the employer cooperates by discharging an expelled worker "for cause." Such collusion may be tempting in the case of Communists or other radicals whose views are abhorrent to both the employer and the union.

of this, arbitrators may be justifiably reluctant to uphold management in discharging workers unless the case against the worker is iron-clad. Management, in turn, becomes reluctant to take strong action against workers who make trouble or court accidents, for fear that an arbitrator will not uphold the action.

Is there any need for the stakes to be this high? One would think not. There should be another line of defense available to the worker that would prevent him from ever being too dependent on a particular employer, a particular union, or a particular arbitrator. That line of defense is the labor market. If a worker is discharged or aggrieved in some less serious way, he should of course have rights of appeal. But if he feels, for whatever reason, that these rights are inadequate or that the remedies are too slow, he should be able to get similar work elsewhere at no substantial sacrifice.

Job protection through the market and through seniority rights and grievance procedures are now often thought of as alternatives. The market is the shield of the skilled craftsmen, of the worker in the building trades where jobs are short-lived, or in the garment trades where work is seasonal and employer turnover is high. All others have institutional protection instead of market protection. But why should they not have both? Is there a necessary conflict between the two?

A basic reason why workers fought so bitterly for unions in the 1930's was that the labor market offered them no security. Loss of a job meant joining the eight million or more others already unemployed, with every prospect that the unemployment would last a long time, and that there would be no income except relief or charity. Small wonder that job security was more important than wages or hours to the new industrial unions. Even during the prosperous 1920's, though unemployment in most years was not high, there was no insurance system to help tide over the unemployed worker until he found work.

In the postwar period we have had generally high levels of employment interrupted by recessions like those of 1953–54 and 1957–58, which have so far been brief and, by the standards of earlier periods, not severe. We have a system of unemployment insurance that is far from perfect, but far better than none. Workers surely have a higher level of asset holdings than ever before and they can draw these down or borrow against them at times of adversity. The widespread ownership of automobiles and the improvement of roads permit workers to travel further to work without changing their residence. It would seem that the costs of losing a job permanently would be lower than ever before. But for many workers this is not true.

In the 'thirties the market offered no protection because the economy was sick. In the 'fifties the economy has been vigorous, yet the market often offers the worker only inferior alternatives because the institutional system of job protection erected by unions has limited its operation.

We used to worry about the tyranny of employers over workers, and today there is growing concern about the tyranny of certain unions over their members. Of course, the fact that in addition to an autocratic employer there is now sometimes an autocratic union does not mean that the worker is no better off than before. So long as the two autocracies do not collude, the worker may be protected by their competition for his loyalty. Few unions are as openly, colorfully autocratic as the United Mine Workers, yet this union seems to do an effective job of processing grievances. Moreover, job security is largely provided by local unions, and local unions are on the whole much more democratic than national unions.

It is clear, however, that neither an employer nor a union, nor any collusive combination of the two, could have any substantial power over a worker who could always at little cost get an equally good job with another employer or in the jurisdiction of another union. How can the costs of mobility be reduced to provide more of this natural defense to the individual?

One line of attack is clear. In recent years, workers have built up very substantial private pension rights that in most cases are lost if the worker leaves a particular employer. The vesting of pension rights in the individual has been widely advocated as a solution to this problem. It must, of course, be admitted that it is more expensive to provide vested pensions than unvested ones of the same amount, since the funds paid in behalf of employees who leave the firm cannot be used to pay the benefits of those who do not. In my judgment, the social advantages of vesting justify this cost. Some unions have already won vesting of pensions to a limited extent.

A second avenue by which mobility can be improved is to strengthen the United States Employment Service and its affiliated state agencies. For reasons too complex to explore here, and through no fault of its staff, the employment service still falls far short of its potential.

But I should like to return now to the main thread of my discussion —to seniority rights. Seniority today seems to be the single most important barrier to mobility, and the one about which it is by far the most difficult to make constructive suggestions.

The problem we now face was clearly foreseen by the early students of seniority in mass-production industries. Thus in 1941 Mr. Slichter wrote:

> One of the most obvious and most important effects [of seniority] is to discourage the voluntary movement of men from shop to shop. When a man resigns from his position, he loses, of course, the seniority which he has accumulated. When he accepts a position in another shop, he is a junior man and in danger, therefore, of being laid off at the first lull in business.[10]

Frederick H. Harbison of Princeton University foresaw in particular the effects of seniority on older workers. The long-service worker, he reasoned, was most likely to be immobilized by seniority. The average age of employees under seniority systems would tend to rise when seniority governed layoffs and reduced the quit rate of older workers. Harbison predicted that, to offset this tendency, employers would increasingly give preference in hiring to younger men to preserve a normal age distribution. He concluded:

> If technological change and market shifts tend to make seniority districts unstable, the displaced long-service workers who were previously "married" to such districts may find it very difficult to secure new jobs because the employers will want to avoid hiring middle aged and older workers. In such cases the "compartmentalization" that follows from widespread application of seniority results in automatic discrimination against long-

[10] *Union Policies and Industrial Management, op. cit.*, p. 151.

service workers who have the misfortune to be displaced from their regular jobs.[11]

The situation that Mr. Harbison feared now seems to be a reality. While seniority may reduce the incidence of unemployment among older workers, it makes it harder for older displaced workers to find new jobs. That displaced workers over forty-five experience difficulty in finding work is suggested by statistics on the duration of unemployment by age. In 1956, 29 per cent of unemployed men age 45 to 64 years had been unemployed 15 weeks or longer at the time of the labor force surveys. For unemployed men age 25 to 44, the comparable percentage was 21. In 1955, 38 per cent of unemployed men age 45 to 64 had been unemployed 15 weeks or longer, while only 26 per cent of unemployed men age 25 to 44 had been unemployed this long.[12] We cannot tell how different these proportions would have been when pensions and seniority were rare, for comparable statistics were not published before 1954. It should be noted that the differences adverse to the older group exist in the face of the prevalent practice of laying off the junior employees first and rehiring them last, which tends to reduce the duration of unemployment of the senior workers.

Despite the considerable discussion of the effect of seniority and pensions on mobility, I know of no thorough research study on this point. Such a study is certainly needed, but it would be difficult to design. One cannot be certain of the findings, for employers may be reluctant to hire older workers for reasons entirely unrelated to seniority or pensions.

In the early studies of seniority, it was felt that insistence on strict seniority was a natural but perhaps temporary reaction to the arbitrary behavior of supervision in the past. As objective measures of ability were developed, they would gradually play a larger role, especially in promotion. As unions became more secure, they would become more flexible in their attitude. Such considerations led Mr.

[11] F. H. Harbison, "Seniority in Mass-Production Industries," *Journal of Political Economy*, Vol. XLVIII, No. 6 (Dec., 1940), p. 858.

[12] U.S. Bureau of the Census, *Current Population Reports*, Series P-50, No. 72 (March, 1957), p. 11.

Harbison to conclude that "it is quite possible, therefore, that seniority systems in the mass-production industries may be modified substantially as unions are accorded more complete acceptance, particularly if they share with management some responsibility for the determination and measurement of skill and ability." [13]

Unfortunately, this prediction has not been borne out by events to the same extent as Mr. Harbison's less cheerful prediction about mobility. If anything, seniority systems seem to be giving less and less weight to ability rather than more. This was Mr. Healy's conclusion from a study of changes in the language of seniority clauses in 85 uninterrupted bargaining relationships between 1940 and 1953.[14]

Perhaps the continued emphasis on seniority reflects in part the disappointment of earlier hopes about the ease of measuring ability scientifically. The tests and measures that seemed to have such promise to psychologists and personnel administrators may have less predictive power than was once believed; in any case, the skepticism of unions toward them has not been overcome.

The present situation seems to be that an experienced worker who is permanently displaced can get new work readily at his old level of skill only if his skill is very high, easily transferable, and in short supply—for example, if he is a tool and die maker. Otherwise he must start his new employment, not only at the bottom of the seniority list, but at or near the bottom of the skill ladder and the wage structure, and work his way slowly up the channels of promotion from within. Often he would have to start in a common labor pool. It is this problem that makes discharge by the employer or expulsion from union membership followed by discharge such a severe penalty in industries where seniority rights are important. Of course, a worker who has invested in specialized skills that are no longer needed is bound to suffer a capital loss, and deserves no more protection than any one else who makes an investment that turns out badly. But the present situation goes beyond this; it imposes capital losses on workers whose skills are valuable to other employers, but who cannot get the chance to use them.

[13] F. H. Harbison, *op. cit.*, p. 862.
[14] J. J. Healy, *op. cit.*, p. 47.

In my judgment, both management and unions have a larger stake in doing something to modify this situation than is generally recognized, not only in the interests of displaced individuals, but in their own interests. From management's point of view, the value of the policy of promotion from within as an advantage in recruiting new entrants to the labor force has probably been overemphasized relative to the value of frequently bringing new blood into the work force at all levels. The man from outside has a great advantage in seeing ways of doing things better than the "way they have always been done," and this ability is by no means confined to engineers and executives. Moreover, there may be instances when management considers all the men in line for promotion to a particular vacancy to be in one way or another poorly suited or inadequately qualified. In this case the gain in efficiency from the right to hire from outside is expected to exceed the gain from the right to skip over a senior employee in favor of a junior one, though it is the latter about which management has usually been concerned.

From the union point of view, the growing sacrifice involved in the loss of job rights invites governmental supervision and regulation of internal union processes whenever the loss of such rights can in some way be laid at the door of the union. To be sure, this is by no means the most important cause of the renewed interest in regulating the affairs of unions. But because unions oppose extensive and detailed government regulation of their internal political processes, they may have an incentive to strengthen the impersonal protection afforded union members by the market so long as the market protection does not altogether eliminate the need for union protection.

It would be fine if I could conclude with some workable and specific suggestions for dealing with some of the issues I have raised about seniority. Unfortunately, I cannot, and must leave this to those more familiar with the intricacies of the collective agreement. What I have tried to do is to sketch a framework within which such detailed thinking could proceed.

We might consider the possibility that some of the costs of seniority in promotion, like those of seniority in the choice of shifts or overtime assignments, could be reduced by better internal pricing. If senior men often turn down their rights to a trial on a higher paid job, this is evidence of an inadequate skill differential. The opposite case, however, is much more likely. The higher paid job or assignment is often much more attractive in other ways as well. If senior men always exercise their rights to a trial on such a job and almost always can perform it to the full satisfaction of management, the skill differential may be too large. In extreme cases, where the job at the top of the progression is attractive enough, voluntary mobility will be reduced throughout the progression even more sharply than it is already reduced by seniority rights in layoffs. The result will be a long wait to get to the top, and the most responsible jobs may be filled by men so old that they have passed their peak efficiency. Cases of this kind are frequent in the railroad train and engine service.

In such a situation there may now be no difficulty in attracting men into the job progression, yet better results might be achieved by paying more at the bottom and less at the top. Such a wage structure throughout an industry would reduce somewhat the costs to individuals of having to change employers. At present, individuals of equal ability and experience may get very different wages in different companies solely because the companies have been growing at different rates. Narrower differentials might also encourage senior men not to bid on higher-paying jobs if they disliked increased responsibility or had any doubt about their capacity to perform the job. In effect, this would increase the weight given to ability in promotion.

Unions of skilled craft workers are responsible for most pay differentials that seem clearly too large. The tendency of industrial unions has generally been to compress differentials. Yet occasional excessive differentials exist in manufacturing industries that bargain with industrial unions. These may result from the faulty operation of job evaluation plans or incentive plans or from technological change that has outmoded differentials which were once well-founded. While seniority systems are not responsible for such faulty internal pricing, they tend to make it more viable by increasing the certainty for the worker who is now underpaid that he will one day be overpaid.

Outside the area of collective bargaining, there are two places where first steps to improve mobility might be easy to take. First, those companies that believe strongly in promotion from within as a rule of policy for nonunion workers and even for executives might do well to take a fresh look at their policy. Here companies have freedom to act whenever they decide to do so. The deliberate policy of promotion from within seems to be quite widespread among railroads, utilities, banks, and insurance companies. Second, we might re-examine the emphasis we give to job security in education and in vocational guidance. Perhaps the lesson of the Great Depression was learned a little too well.

Of one thing I am certain: The answer to these problems for unionized workers lies in the constructive modification of the system of job security the unions have built and not in its destruction. The freedom that job security has given the manual worker cannot be lightly put aside.

8

The Freedom of the Individual under Collectivized Labor Arrangements

Philip D. Bradley

> Experience in the last half century has driven us to the realization that, after all, we live in a factual world where organized groups, whether for production, commerce or propaganda, are too powerful to permit the feeble forces of the individual to survive . . . Regretfully but inevitably we must adjust our lives and our government to modern needs and find, in a Constitution written for a simpler era, guidance for the problems of our present age.
>
> *Justice Stanley F. Reed*[1]

> There is no inevitability in history except as men make it.
>
> *Justice Felix Frankfurter*[2]

IN FEBRUARY, 1951, sixteen non-operating railway labor unions notified the Santa Fe Railway Company that they wanted a union shop agreement. Not until seven years later did the unions and the company adopt a modified form of the union shop. To anyone interested in the position of the individual under today's collectivized labor arrangements, the Santa Fe case is both significant and instructive.[3]

Passage by the United States Congress in January, 1951, of an amendment to the Railway Labor Act provided the grounds for the

[1] Quoted in the Washington *Evening Star*, January 31, 1957, p. 1.

[2] Felix Frankfurter, *Mr. Justice Holmes and The Supreme Court* (Cambridge, Mass., 1938) p. 9.

[3] The word "case" is not used in the legal sense here but as the term is employed in business and other schools for the purpose of designating a particular set of facts and conditions.

unions' demand for a union shop. Under the provisions of the amendment, railway labor unions and the carriers were permitted to make union shop contracts. Within a month of its passage, approximately 390 carriers, among them the Santa Fe, had been notified that the non-operating unions demanded a basic change in the relationship of the individual worker to the unions. At that time the individual employee was free to decide for himself what value, if any, he placed upon the services offered by the unions. The unions proposed that the railway companies join with them in taking this freedom to choose from the individual.

To forward their purpose the unions held a series of conferences with the individual carriers. Upon discovering that the negotiations were not productive, the unions asked for the assistance of the National Mediation Board, as provided for under the Railway Labor Act. At this point the first major break developed in the ranks of the carriers. Three major roads, two in the east and one in the west, accepted the union proposals for the introduction of compulsory unionism and, therefore, did not participate in the mediation proceedings.

But mediation likewise failed and, in accordance with the procedures of the Railway Labor Act, President Truman on November 15, 1951, appointed a three-man Emergency Board to hear the arguments of the unions and the carriers and to make recommendations for settlement of the dispute. Following hearings the Emergency Board on February 14, 1952, submitted a report to the President recommending that the parties adopt union shop agreements.

By the end of 1952 the unions, armed with the Emergency Board's recommendation, had very largely broken carrier opposition to the spread of compulsory unionism. In August an agreement had been reached with the eastern carriers as a group. Although agreements had not been negotiated with the western and southeastern roads as groups, agreements had been made with a number of individual carriers in both areas. Finally, by April, 1953, all carriers west of the Mississippi had submitted to the unions' demands for involuntary participation in unionism except for the Santa Fe.

This, in brief, was the background when the union leadership and the Santa Fe management met in Chicago on May 5, 1953, at the unions' request, to discuss once again the union shop issue. The conference was not to be a long one, for on the same day fourteen non-union employees of the Santa Fe asked a District Court in Texas to restrain the Santa Fe and the non-operating unions from entering into a union shop contract and asked further that the unions be prevented from striking or using other economic force in an attempt to compel the Santa Fe to sign such an agreement. The court granted the employees' request and consequently the Santa Fe withdrew from the conference with the unions. Subsequently the company also asked the same court to restrain the unions from striking or otherwise using force to compel it to accept the unions' terms. The effect of this action by the Santa Fe was to align the company with the non-union employees in resisting the unions' demands for compulsory unionism.

Once transferred to the courts, the dispute was to remain there for over four years. According to the calculations of the trial judge, the presentation of the case to judge and jury alone took five weeks. Based upon jury findings which overwhelmingly favored the position taken by the non-union employees and the Santa Fe and upon his interpretation of the law, the judge issued an injunction against the unions, as requested by the non-union employees and the company. From this decision the unions appealed, thereby starting the case on its way to the Supreme Court of the United States.[4]

That the management of the Santa Fe made an all-out effort to prevent unwilling employees from being impressed into the union movement is suggested by a mere description of the time factor in the case. But beyond this it is apparent from the record that the company committed every necessary resource to the struggle. Obviously the case was an expensive one in the usual financial sense. Much greater must have been the cost resulting from the extensive degree

[4] The Court of Civil Appeals of Texas, Amarillo, reversed the Trial Court and dissolved the injunction. *Sandsberry* v. *International Association of Machinists* 277 S.W. 2d 776 (1954). The decision was affirmed by the Supreme Court of Texas, three Justices dissenting in 295 S.W. 2d 412 (1956). The majority considered itself bound by the previous decision of the Supreme Court of the United States in *Railway Employes' Dept.* v. *Hanson* 351 U.S. 225 (1956).

The Supreme Court of the United States refused to review the case, denying a writ of certiorari. *Sandsberry* v. *International Association of Machinists* 353 U.S. 918 (1957).

to which management committed its time and effort to the formulation and execution of company policy in this prolonged engagement with the union. Surely, any employee who wished to retain his freedom must have been satisfied that management cooperated to the full in their mutual attempt to resist the extension of union control.

Smaller companies have also sometimes tried to protect their employees' freedom. A bill of complaint filed by Automatic Merchandising Corporation against officers of the Teamsters' Union, the Chemical Workers Union and the Central Labor Union of Boston demonstrates that the Santa Fe kind of behavior is not limited to large corporations or to the union shop issue. Automatic, founded in 1950 by two recent college graduates, sells food, beverages and similar products through coin-operated machines. Many of its vending machines are placed in industrial plants where they replace cafeterias and other older methods of feeding plant employees. They operate in a highly competitive market. In addition to the several traditional methods of in-plant feeding, plant managers could choose the services offered by anyone of the many direct competitors of Automatic in the Massachusetts market area. Despite rugged competition, Automatic, due to excellent management, has had a remarkable growth and today is the dominant firm in the Massachusetts market for this kind of service.

The bill of complaint filed by Automatic states that in July, 1957, two officers of the Teamsters came to the company's office and demanded that Automatic recognize Local 841 of the Teamsters as the exclusive bargaining agent of all machine service and repair employees. Automatic did not know how many, if any, of its employees wanted to be represented by this union and consequently refused to sign a contract giving Local 841 bargaining rights for its employees. The officers of the company took the position that the wishes of the employees regarding representation must govern and that these should be ascertained through an election conducted by an impartial agency. The bill states further that the union officers rejected the idea of an election, refused to permit an election to be held for the purpose of determining whether the employees wanted to be represented by it, threatened to picket the company's plant and, if the company continued to resist, threatened to take various actions against the vending machines Automatic operated in industrial plants and elsewhere.

Apparently the threats voiced by the union representatives were not empty ones for the bill of complaint goes on to allege acts of violence, intimidation and coercion engaged in by the Teamsters, aided and abetted in some cases by the officers of other unions, in their attempt to compel Automatic to deliver its employees to them without benefit of an election. By way of relief, Automatic asked the Superior Court of Massachusetts to restrain the unions from engaging in the acts described and for an award to cover all damages suffered.

The Santa Fe case illustrates one type of managerial reaction to the demand that employees be compelled to participate in unionism. A very different kind of management behavior is revealed by the Forstmann Woolen Company case. The essential facts in the Forstmann situation are contained in the following announcement which the company management posted on all union bulletin boards:

UNION SHOP
(April 18, 1947)

For nearly three years, the Textile Workers Union of America, C.I.O., has been official bargaining representative for mill workers of our company. During that time, the union and its leadership have demonstrated their dependability and readiness to recognize the common interests of the company and its workers.

Because the conduct of the union has been such as to deserve the confidence of the workers, the membership in the union has experienced steady growth, to the point where now more than 95% of workers in the bargaining unit have joined the union. In this way our workers have themselves demonstrated by overwhelming numbers their faith in the union. Therefore, it seems only fair that the management also should indicate its confidence in the union and its leadership.

The management, therefore, is voluntarily demonstrating its faith in the future of cooperative relations by granting to the union the privileges of a Union Shop, to be effective on the first of June.

In the meantime, those few remaining workers in the bargaining unit who have not yet joined the union, will have the opportunity to voluntarily do so.

> The management hopes that those who have not joined will recognize that the constructive efforts of the union in behalf of all workers in the bargaining unit will deserve their support as members.
>
> As of June 1, when this becomes a Union Shop, all workers in the bargaining unit who have been with the company for thirty days or more, will be expected to be members of the union as a condition of employment.

Thirteen years after General Motors recognized the United Automobile Workers as a bargaining representative for its employees, it entered into a modified union shop agreement with the union. Under the terms of the agreement arrived at in the bargaining sessions of 1950, old company employees were not required to join the union. Nor were new employees committed to its perpetual care. They were required to become union members upon acquiring seniority, but they were also permitted to escape from the union towards the end of the first year of seniority. In the bargaining session of 1955 these escape provisions were traded away. Thereafter an employee's service with the company, no matter how long, did not provide him with protection against the claims of the union.

Markedly different types of corporate behavior are illustrated by the cases cited. Needless to say, scores of other cases would serve to make the same distinction. In an earlier phase of our history, in the 1930's, for example, any explanation of the behavioral differences noted which ran in terms of the willingness or unwillingness of companies to accept unionism would have been widely believed. Thus, at that time the behavior of Santa Fe and Automatic would have been written off as the reactions of managements unwilling to recognize that unions are here to stay while the behavior of the other companies, of which Forstmann and General Motors are examples, would have been attributed to the fact that their more progressive managements were prepared to live with the unions. The Santa Fe and Automatic cases cannot be disposed of, however, on such grounds. One cannot read the testimony and other statements of the company officials in the Santa Fe case without coming to the conclusion that management was as much in favor of voluntary unionism as it was opposed to compulsory unionism, a not altogether unexpected attitude given the long history of the unions in the industry. In the case of Automatic the management's insistence upon holding an election taken with the union's opposition to it would suggest, on the present test, that it was Automatic and not the union which accepted unionism as a permanent part of the American scene.

Had those who advised management in the Forstmann and General Motors cases been given the facts in the Automatic situation, what counsel would they have given Automatic? At this point it may be said that the Automatic situation contains an element not present in the other cases. Obviously the demands made upon Automatic were illegal, whereas that condition is not present in the other situations. Before McClellan [5] the naive might have counselled Automatic to resist on the ground that what the Teamsters demanded was illegal, but after McClellan only the cynical would contend that a company in Automatic's position should resist for this reason. Automatic is vulnerable in the market. Its automatic cafeterias are located in plants employing hundreds of times as many workers as Automatic employs. A picket line thrown around one of these plants might well induce the manager to ask himself why he should share the burden resulting from Automatic's unwillingness to deliver its employees to the Teamsters. Nor would the manager encounter any difficulty in finding vending companies which were entirely willing to step into Automatic's shoes. McClellan shows that firms with vastly greater resources and better protected market positions than Automatic's had little difficulty in devising formulas which permit adjustment to illegal union demands.

Although the Forstmann Woolen situation developed a decade before the Teamsters served their demands on Automatic, it is the earlier situation and not the Automatic one which displays novel managerial behavior in the area of union-management-employee relationships. A fair inference from the announcement posted on the bulletin board is that Forstmann management was pleased by the union's behavior during the period in which it enjoyed the right to represent Forstmann employees. Apparently someone in managerial

[5] *Investigation of Improper Activities in the Labor or Management Field,* Hearings Before the Select Committee on Improper Activities in the Labor or Management Field, United States Senate, Senator John L. McClellan, Chairman (Washington, 1958).

circles was struck with the thought that the firm's feeling toward the union should be expressed by something other than words. The thought here was that the company's "acceptance" of the union needed confirmation through the performance of a specific and tangible act. The problem then reduced to one of ascertaining exactly what management could give to the union in order to express its faith and confidence.

Superficial analysis might suggest that in this management had a rich range of choice. Why not, for example, raise the wage rate above what it would be if this feeling of apparently mutual warmth did not exist? Or, possibly, shorten hours? Advantages are to be realized from the adoption of either alternative. Measurability is one. Thus the union leaders would not have to speculate as to the depth of management's feelings, they would know in dollars and cents or in hours and minutes exactly how much their cooperative and responsible approach was appreciated by management. Unfortunately, either approach also has its inherent dangers. An increase in wage rates or a decrease in hours adequate to reflect fully the company's confidence and faith in the union might well undermine the firm's competitive position. The consequent decrease in sales, output and employment could easily be misinterpreted, particularly by those who lost their jobs and, more importantly, that loss might have unfortunate repercussions for the union leadership. On the other hand, an increase in rates or decrease in hours so small that it did not handicap the company marketwise might be taken by the union leaders as an intimation that the company regarded its union relationships rather lightly.

Fortunately, the wage-hour approach to a solution of the company's problem of how to express its feelings is only one of many possibilities. Thus an invitation to participate to a significant degree in the making of managerial decisions would probably persuade even rather belligerent union leaders that they had finally been accepted. Or, consider the varied ways in which profits can be used as an expression of confidence. One possibility would be the payment of a year-end bonus, a payment appropriately adjusted both to the level of profits and to the intensity of management's feelings. Leaving its distribution or use to the discretion of the union leadership would reinforce the impression to be conveyed. Better still, taking a cue from others, the company might offer to share with the union all profits over the amount required to give the company anywhere from, say, a five to a fifty or greater per cent return on capital. The rate established would serve as an excellent index of management's union attitudes. By setting the rate in the neighborhood of five per cent, management would be suggesting an almost unlimited faith in unionism, whereas a rate set around the fifty per cent level might convey to the union the notion that it had been rather uncooperative. These brief comments on how tangible expression could be given to company feelings are intended to suggest the wide range of alternatives available to the firm.

Compared to the alternative actually adopted by Forstmann, all of these schemes, and the many more which might be included in the list, such as guaranteed annual incomes, suffer in several respects. By comparison with the Forstmann formula they are uninspired. To demonstrate this, consider the elements with which Forstmann worked.

Among its employees there was a group, estimated by the management to be about five per cent of all employees, which refused to join the union. How long the average employees in the group had worked for Forstmann is not stated in the bulletin board announcement. But from that document it can be learned that the Textile Workers had been in action at Forstmann for almost three years. Most likely the non-union group had seen the union in action; possibly some of these workers had been at Forstmann for many years. They knew what the union offered. Nevertheless, exercising their freedom to buy or not to buy what the union offered, they refused to buy.

Apparently management felt that this was a poor decision. In the minority's place, management would recognize that the "constructive efforts of the union in behalf of all workers in the bargaining unit" deserve the support of *all* employees. This is a commonplace situation. Who has not felt, often very deeply, that some other person has made an unsound or an incorrect decision? But, while the feeling is universal, the power to do anything about it—to substitute one's correct decision for another's incorrect decision—is definitely limited in free countries. In fact among private parties it is a power largely associated with differences in age, like the case of the parent straightening out the mistakes of the child.

Curiously enough, the individual in the labor area is treated very much like a child, and very often, particularly by union leaders, as a juvenile delinquent. The Forstmann conclusion that a minority of its employees was incapable of making a "correct" appraisal of the value of the union's services would be shared, especially in recent years, by virtually all union leaders, by many corporate managements and by officials in all divisions and strata of government service. Elsewhere I have shown that an individual's refusal to support the union representing him may rest upon entirely rational grounds.[6] Were it not for situations like Forstmann, one might think it entirely superfluous even to attempt to show that a citizen can be, at one and the same time, both rational and unwilling to join a private organization.

However, these latter considerations are aside from the main point. The fact is that our laws take a most important traditional freedom from the individual employee and place it in the custody of management. Under these provisions the individual employee exercises his previous freedom to join or not to join a private organization subject to the will of management. At any time management may exercise its power for its own advantage. This is what Forstmann did. By delivering the minority to the union, Forstmann succeeded in giving expression to its faith and confidence in a dependable, constructive and confidence-inspiring union leadership.

Nor should another element in the transaction be overlooked, for it is this which displays the genius of those who conceived the trade. To Forstmann management the freedom of choice enjoyed by the employee was not important. One may suspect that on any scale of management values this freedom would rank very low, possibly at the bottom of the scale. On the other hand, the power to control all employees in a bargaining unit would rank very high, probably at the top, on any union scale of values. In effect, the bulletin board announcement meant that the company was giving up what it valued least while the union was getting what it wanted most. On the basis of

[6] Bradley, *Involuntary Participation In Unionism* (Washington, 1956).

what it cost the company the arrangements made were obviously superior to any of the unimaginative wage-hour, management-sharing or profit schemes considered in a previous paragraph.

Forstmann's delivery of its minority employees was made in response to management's satisfaction with the general conduct of the bargaining process. The General Motors case adds another element to the delivery process. In this case control over the individual employee's freedom to choose was put on the table in a *given* bargaining session. In exchange for this control, management wanted the union to yield or give up some specific thing. It was to be a trade. Management would deliver the free minority to the union if the union gave management something it wanted. Both parties would benefit and that is about all that can be expected from an economic transaction. Management happened to possess the power to terminate the minority's freedom. The power was of no great value to management, but it was wanted very much by the union leaders. A swap could be arranged as soon as the unions put something on the bargaining table management wanted.

Two sets of questions arise from an examination of the cases cited. One concerns the great diversity in managerial reactions to a common problem.Why did Santa Fe fight for almost seven years to preserve what Forstmann disposed of by way of a bulletin board announcement? Why did Automatic stake its very existence on a refusal to deliver its employees to a union which comes very close to being "all-powerful." And, why did another company trade off the minority in a single bargaining session? A second group of questions concerns the employer's power to deliver an employee minority to the union. How, for example, did this power come to be lodged with the employers? And, why is one private party allowed by law to profit from the sale of another's freedom?

An analytical account of these matters may conveniently begin with the factual observation that no group has ever believed that the Congress of the United States could be persuaded to introduce compulsory unionism by law. The observation holds for the economically dreary days of the first Franklin Roosevelt administration and for all subsequent years up to the present, including 1951, when the Railway Labor Act was amended to permit the union shop in that industry. To require a citizen to join and support a private organization if he is to earn a living, is an act apparently not easily reconciled with the consciences of those who must appeal to the voters of a free society every two or six years.

The Congressional attitude forms a solid barrier to those who want to introduce compulsory unionism via the fast route of federal fiat. In the early 1930's there were many groups who wished to achieve precisely this objective. Even in those days, a period when any scheme, no matter how weird, could get a serious hearing, the advocates of compulsion realized that they could not hope to destroy the Congressional barrier in their path in any acceptable number of years. Since they could not take the high road, they did not hesitate to take the low one.

To reverse national traditions and to destroy freedoms whose origins are to be found in pre-Constitutional times must have appeared as a mammoth challenge even to people who had the advantage of being able to maneuver in the chaotic conditions of the early 'thirties. Powerful tools would be needed. Moreover, they could not be used openly lest the impression be conveyed that it was the Congressional barrier itself which was to be removed.

To get Congress to lower the barrier against compulsory unionism it was considered necessary to dress the proposals for its enactment to look like something that was a part of the American tradition. Thus the statements of the principal Congressional spokesman for the cause were designed not to inform but to soothe his listeners when he said "the national labor-relations bill, which is the Wagner bill, does not present a single *novel* principle for the consideration of Congress." [7] Who, if the "novel" is taken in the sense that "there is nothing new under the sun," could object? Moreover, "since this bill is so permeated with principles of freedom," the good senator was astounded, "to encounter the wide-spread propaganda that it imposes new forms

[7] Senator Robert F. Wagner, Hearings Before the Committee on Labor, House of Representatives, Seventy Fourth Congress, First Session on H. R. 6288, p. 9. Italics added.

of restraints."[8] He was particularly distressed by those who did not understand that "majority rule does not even imply that any employee can be forced to join a union except through *the traditional method* of a closed shop agreement with the employer."[9] Personally he held "no brief for or against the closed shop."[10] But, after all, "it is legal in New York, in Massachusetts and in many other states—no sufficient reason has been advanced why Congress should change *the status quo*."[11]

Taken narrowly and literally the senator's propositions concerning "traditional," the "status quo" and "closed shop" might pass the examination of a wary and expert economic historian. Concededly the closed shop agreement was a *method* of compelling individuals to participate in unions. To say this is to say nothing about how *frequently* the method was employed. Likewise, to point to certain states which permit such agreements is not to indicate the number of workers affected by them. In exactly the same way, one might say that disrobement is the method traditionally used by the Dukhobors of Western Canada to express discontent with the political authority. Canadians could be forgiven, however, if they failed to grasp how the nude cavortings of this sect establishes a basis for the conclusion that Dukhoborism is a typical religion in Canada or that its practices, if extended to other areas of Canada, would not be regarded as, at least, a bit novel. Or, one might say with equal force that inasmuch as people die in electric chairs in various of our states, this is a typical American way of dying, and the extension of the practice would introduce neither novelty nor new restraints.

These unsubtle distinctions between "traditional" and "typical" and "representative" were not alluded to by those who wanted to make an uncommon condition of employment commonplace. Nor were they caught by many of those who voted to support Wagner. The indisputable fact is that at the time Wagner's bill was being debated, unions as a whole could claim as members only a very small

[8] *Ibid.*, p. 15.
[9] *Ibid.*, pp. 16-17. Italics added.
[10] *Ibid.*, pp. 15-16.
[11] *Ibid.*, pp. 15-16. Italics added.

part of the total working population, while the number of involuntary participants in unions at that time is best described as numerically insignificant.[12] Perhaps it is a tribute to those who created the myths of the Wagnerian theme that they are repeated in many of today's text books.

To create a theme is one thing. To get people to practice it is another and much more difficult thing. Only in a few industries, primarily in printing and construction, was the "traditional" requirement widespread that a worker must join and support a union in order to earn a living. Those who do not believe in the inevitability of any given historical course may even now debate the wisdom of choosing the closed shop as the vehicle by which to make compulsory unionism universal. For several years it appeared unable to carry the load imposed upon it. Nor could those who had confidence in it claim that its eventual successes confirmed their judgment, for the promise of success when it came was largely due to unanticipated events.

There were, in the early 'thirties, a number of factors which made almost inevitable the choice of the closed shop as the method of spreading compulsory unionism. This technique creates or sets up a struggle between two parties. It does this by vesting in the employer the ultimate power to establish closed shop conditions. Hence, to get closed shop conditions the organized employees must first compel the employer to exercise his power over the unwilling minority.[13] The

[12] In 1935 about 7 out of every 100 members of the civilian labor force were union members while fewer than 3 out of every 100 members of the civilian labor force participated in union activity on an involuntary basis.

[13] To use the words "minority" and "majority" in this chapter without pointing out that they have entirely different meanings in the union world from the meanings they carry in everyday life in the United States would be entirely misleading. The difference is that which exists between a majority or minority as determined by an election held in Communist Russia or Fascist Germany and a majority or minority as determined in one of our national elections. In each case a vote is taken. But, a few unions excepted, the procedures followed in a union before a vote is taken are those of totalitarian states and have little in common with the practices of American political life. National union leaders support their claim that the unions are "democratic" by pointing to the patent fact that a vote is taken. They say nothing about events preceding the vote. But the fact is that any group within the union which systematically opposes the union leadership on any major issue will be charged with dual unionism and will be treated, to the degree our laws permit, in the same manner as counter-revolutionaries are treated in

extension of compulsory unionism would thus be marked by a series of victories in which the employers were defeated by organized labor. To many advocates of compulsion during this period these were seen as but local engagements in the great over-all conflict between Labor and Capital.

To whatever degree the advocates of compulsion derived their facts from the world of make-believe, they nevertheless built enduringly. For almost thirty years every new closed or union shop contract has been hailed or interpreted as a victory for the employees and a defeat for the employer. Such is the standard newspaper treatment and thus is it seen by persons in all walks of life.

In the years immediately following passage of the Wagner bill involuntary unionism in any form spread slowly. The reasons for this are debatable. Possibly the vehicle of class struggle was less efficient than it had been imagined, or possibly unionism must be powerful, its leadership entrenched, before it can compel purchase of what it has to offer. These and other explanations cannot be assessed here. Suffice it to say that doubts must have developed among the advocates of compulsion as to the wisdom of those who in the turbulent early days of the New Deal chose the indirect rather than the direct route to involuntary unionism.

War in Europe and defense preparations at home profoundly affected labor market conditions. Employment rose sharply and so did the number of strikes. To eliminate this obstacle to the flow of war material, President Roosevelt in March, 1941, established the National Defense Mediation Board. Although nothing more than a voluntary mediatory instrument without real powers of its own, the mediation board might well have coped with all the emergencies created by strikes for higher pay. But apparently everyone underestimated the determination of some union leaders to use the national emergency for the promotion of their objective in the area of compulsory unionism. Thus the war between nations was used to achieve what the war between classes had failed to produce. Confronted by a union ultimatum to extend the closed shop in the coal industry or else, the me-

Russia. With few exceptions the "majorities" and "minorities" of so-called democratic unions have the same significance as do those of totalitarian countries.

diation board refused, whereupon the CIO members of the board deliberately destroyed it by walking out.[14]

Three weeks after Pearl Harbor, when it was clear beyond any question that the life of the nation was in peril, union leaders again demonstrated their determination to use the nation's fight for freedom as an opportunity to reduce freedom at home. This time the scene was Washington where President Roosevelt had called a conference of union and industrial representatives for the purpose of developing a program to settle the wave of strikes which followed the wrecking of the National Mediation Board. The conference was stalled for almost a week by the refusal of the union leaders to give up the notion that the national crisis could be used to get new closed shop agreements. No mystery attaches to what they were after. They knew that the public was fed up with strikes called for the purpose of forcing management to sign such agreements. They wanted to make sure that any government board formed as the result of the conference would have the power to consider and to settle disputes arising from their attempts to spread compulsory unionism. In brief, they wanted to substitute government for union coercion.

Following the conference, the President by executive order, established the National War Labor Board, a tripartite group composed of union, industry, and public members, and vested in it the power to dispose of disputes that "might interrupt work that contributes to the effective prosecution of the war." Subsequently the industry partici-

[14] That the Congressional and Executive attitudes toward compulsory unionism had not changed since 1935 is attested to by President Roosevelt's declaration, made in response to John L. Lewis's strike threat, that: "I tell you frankly that the government of the United States will not order, nor will Congress pass legislation ordering, a so-called closed shop. . . . The Government will never compel this 5 percent to join the union by a Government decree. That would be too much like the Hitler methods toward labor." (*Labor Relations Reporter,* November 17, 1941.) On this husband and wife spoke as one, for in her column in the Washington *Daily News* of March 13, 1941, Mrs. Roosevelt put the matter as follows: "I do not believe that every man and woman should be forced to join a union." However, readers not familiar with the literature on compulsory unionism should be warned that the Roosevelt views are suspect on at least two grounds. Thus the Reverend Reinhold Niebuhr of the Union Theological Seminary concludes a spirited defense of compulsory unionism with the observation that: "The implausibility of the so-called 'right to work' laws is so obvious that one must come to the conclusion that their proponents are either stupid or dishonest in their pretensions." (*American Federationist,* February 1957, p. 14.)

pants in the conference denied that they had ever agreed to give any board this power.

In demanding that the new board be given this broad authority, the unions sought to transfer the power to compel individuals to participate in unionism from the employer to a government agency. Moreover, they intended that the board use the power given it. Exploiting the nation's peril to the full, the union leaders pushed their campaign for a change in union status. Caught between this production-crippling campaign and the public and Congressional opposition to union tactics, the War Labor Board came up with the maintenance-of-membership formula. The Board's use of this device is often defended on the grounds that it represented a necessary compromise between the views of unions and employers and that the degree of compulsion involved in such agreements is minor. However phrased, the fact remains that due to the board the compulsory principle was extended to a very large number of contracts where it had never been found before. Both pre-war and post-war experience suggests that the unions' campaign for compulsory unionism was advanced by the Board during these years well beyond the point it would have reached had this been a period of peace and had it been impossible for the unions to arrange a transfer of the power to compel participation in unionism from the employer to a government agency.

Between V-J Day and the outbreak of the war in Korea on June 25, 1950, the unions attempted to develop the involuntary element in agreements where it had been introduced through the artificial insemination activities of the War Labor Board. As in the pre-war period, progress was slow. Employers proved to be far better guardians of individual freedom of choice than government boards.

Although the union leadership had shown itself to be adept and expert in using the nation's peril as an instrument for changing union status in World War II, even more skill at extending compulsory unionism under the national emergency umbrella was exhibited in the Korean War. By the time it was evident that Korean activities were not to be an overnight affair, the union high command had announced the formation of the United Labor Policy Committee. Once organized, this (voluntary) union of unions wasted little time. A thousand union leaders were brought to Washington in March, 1951, to protest the economic policies of the Administration. Among the Presidential measures designed to placate the United Labor group was a reorganization of the Wage Stabilization Board, which added dispute powers to the Board's already existing wage stabilization powers.[15] Once again, as in World War II, the unions successfully maneuvered to transfer from the employer to a government agency the power to compel participation in unionism.

While the unions covered by the Taft-Hartley Act were deploying their forces in this manner for an all-out attack upon the freedom of the individual, the non-operating railway unions were acquiring weapons for a similar assault upon the workers covered by the Railway Labor Act. Prior to its amendment, on January 10, 1951, that Act prohibited compulsory unionism. Upon amendment, it provides substantially the same method for compelling participation in unionism as does the Wagner Act.

Having through their own efforts added to the advantages which a state of war gave them, the union leaders went on to demonstrate the vast improvement which had taken place in their operational skills since World War II. Regrettably, the ensuing operations cannot be given the detailed consideration which their importance and technical excellence merit. Fortunately, two cases, those in steel and railways, capture the spirit and illustrate the techniques of the over-all campaign.

On November 1, 1951, the steel workers' union served its new contract demands on the basic steel companies. Given the fact that the existing contract was to terminate in less than two months, namely, on December 31, the extent and novelty of the demands are highly significant. In its report submitted in March, 1952, the Wage Stabilization Board classified the union's demands under seventeen headings and then added an eighteenth to cover "all other" demands. All told, acceptance of the union program would have required over one hundred changes in the existing agreements, but more significant than

[15] The Board's stabilization authority derived from The Defense Production Act, but its jurisdiction over disputes, including disputes over non-economic issues, rested on nothing more than a Truman decree, namely, Executive Order 10233.

their number was the controversial nature of the principles involved in several of the union's requests. Certainly that was the case in the demand for a union shop and for a guaranteed annual wage plan.

Why, when time was so short, did the union confront the industry with so many and such controversial demands? The answer would appear to be that the union wanted to provoke a dispute. This conclusion is supported by a variety of additional facts. Among these was the union's unwillingness even to consider alternatives to its own program and its failure to announce its money demands until December 15. Inevitably the industry rejected the demands, as the union knew it would.

On December 22 the dispute thus created was referred by the President to the Wage Stabilization Board. On March 20, 1952, after hearings, the Board reported to the President. Among its recommendations was one to the effect that the new steel contracts should contain union shop provisions. Predictions that this would be the outcome and that it would be produced when the public members joined the union members to out-vote the industry members were made in Washington simultaneously with the referral of the dispute to the Board.

Why a wage stabilization agency was ever given the power to consider "non-economic" issues—such as compulsory unionism—can only be explained by the obvious fact that in this case the unions wanted the Board to have that power. Other questions remain. Granted that they had the power, why did the public members use it to break a long-standing dead-lock between the unions and the companies, and why did they use it to support the union's demands for a radical change in union status? For answers to these questions we turn to the report submitted by the Board. In an explanatory statement the chairman, who was also a public member, states that the public members recommended a union shop "after they found themselves unable to secure a majority in favor of their own proposal to return the matter to the parties for collective bargaining . . ."[16] Collectors of such statements believe that this one by itself justifies the inclusion of the re-

[16] Statement of Chairman Nathan P. Feinsinger, *Report and Recommendations of the Wage Stabilization Board in the Matter of United Steel Workers of America CIO and Various Steel and Iron Ore Companies* (Washington, 1952), p. 9.

port on any list of the three or four most interesting documents produced by the union movement. One can only speculate as to why the chairman felt it worth while to put a perfectly simple proposition so obscurely. He could have said: "We find that union and industry disagree on the subject of the union shop." This discovery would have astonished few possessed of the capacities to read or hear. He could then add: "The public members recommend acceptance of the union demand." His justification for the action taken is concise and to the point. The public members, he states, "decided that *fairness* and *equity* in the circumstances of this case required that the union shop be recommended." [17]

All things considered, it might have been advisable to let the union shop recommendation rest on the simple assertion that in making it the public members were guided by nothing more than their feelings about what is "fair and equitable." However, the chairman goes on to say that "in *all* its recommendations, the board has sought to arrive at a conclusion conforming to its *best estimate* of what the parties would have arrived at in free collective bargaining subject to the principles of wage stabilization." [18] Here is another of those remarkable statements which give the report such a singular reputation. Accepted at face value it is a confession of incredible incompetency. How could the public members, given the long history of the dispute and, for that matter, given the facts to be found in their own opinion, as well as the chairman's statement, have guessed, estimated or otherwise arrived at the conclusion that the parties, if left to their own devices, would voluntarily agree to impose compulsory unionism on the steel workers?

An opinion is not expressed here as to what it was that motivated the public members to take the position they did.[19] Opinion at the

[17] *Ibid.*, p. 9. Italics added.

[18] *Ibid.*, p. 9. Italics added.

[19] One of the public members offers a possible clue. Writing in collaboration with a member of the Harvard Business faculty, J. T. Dunlop states it is their experience that "The union security issue [compulsory unionism] is never resolved in a particular contract as long as the parties debate general issues of principles. Only when this level of discussion is abandoned and the parties seek practical solutions to the questions raised by union security is agreement possible. Which group of employees should be included and which excluded?" John T. Dunlop and James J. Healy, *Collective Bargaining* (Chi-

time was less restrained. A distinguished member of the United States Senate charged that the public members were biased. In a public speech the president of a steel company stated that "It is a reasonable inference that this was a political deal and that the public members of the Board participated in it." [20] Sumner Slichter disagreed with Senator George's charge and, in turn, raised the question "How could such good men produce such a bad decision?" [21] His answer is that the Board was assigned incompatible functions and used inappropriate methods. Of course this answer does not meet or dispose of the charges of bias and politics. It was the President, not the Congress, who, in response to union ultimatums, gave the Board authority to consider non-wage disputes and it was the President who picked the public members of the Board. Thus the process through which the Board acquired its dispute functions reenforces rather than refutes the charge of a political deal.

Almost invariably American corporations accept and act on the recommendations of the boards created by Presidential order. To do otherwise would be to show disrespect for the office and to invite public and Congressional condemnation. In the steel case the weight of Congressional and public opinion supported neither the President nor his board. Later in the year, after hundreds of thousands of workers had been delivered to the unions, the Congress stripped the Board of all non-stabilization powers. In the meantime the companies refused to come to terms with the union on the basis of the Board's recommendations. Stunned by the companies' defiance and reacting blindly to the ever-mounting evidence that the Presidential office was held in less respect than it had been in decades, President Truman on April 9 seized the steel industry. On June 2 the Supreme Court, a majority of whose members were Truman appointees, held

---

cago, 1953), p. 186. (Bracketed words supplied in quotation.) The obvious inconvenience of having principles has been noticed by others. This might be appropriately named the Dunlop-Healy effect after its latest discoverers.

[20] Clarence B. Randall, *Seizure . . . the New Push-Button Warfare on Business*, an address before the National Press Club (Washington, April 25, 1952), p. 14.

[21] Sumner H. Slichter, *Wage Stabilization and Emergency Disputes*, reprinted from *The Commercial and Financial Chronicle*, April 24, 1952, p. 5. This is an excellent analysis of the stabilization and dispute functions of emergency boards.

that the President in seizing the steel plants had exceeded his constitutional powers. The reaction of the union leaders was immediate. They called a strike which was to last almost two months. Thus they closed the steel industry in a period of national emergency and with no more support for their action than the opinion of four professional arbitrators who had been chosen and clothed with authority by a President who was politically beholden to the unions.

On August 15 the union and the company entered into an agreement which provided for an extension of compulsory unionism. What label should be used to identify the provision agreed to is a matter of dispute. Text books frequently refer to it as a "modified union shop," but the Bureau of Labor Statistics "classifies it as a maintenance of membership provision because new employees have the option of choosing whether or not to join the union."[22]

Although the steel and railway unions shared a common objective, namely, the capture of the free employees in their industries, their tactics differed in several basic respects. In the steel case the union decided to include the compulsory unionism demand in a package of many wage and non-wage demands; the idea was to force first the companies and then the Stabilization Board to act on the package as a whole. The package approach was designed to give the public members of the Board an opportunity to look like reasonable and impartial judges. By accepting certain demands while rejecting others the Board would convey the impression of balance. In brief, the desired impression would be created when the public members gave the union only "half" of what it wanted. In his statement the chairman couples the union shop and guaranteed wage demands in a section entitled "Union Shop and Guaranteed Annual Wage Issues." He then recommends the union shop and sends the guaranteed wage back to the parties for bargaining. How could even the dull-witted and insensitive possibly miss this demonstration of impartiality?

In their campaign the railway unions rejected the package or "shotgun" approach in favor of the "rifle" approach. Thus Emergency Board No. 98, created by President Truman on November 15, 1951,

[22] Rose Theodore, "Union-Security Provisions in Agreements, 1954," *Monthly Labor Review*, U. S. Department of Labor, Washington, Vol. 78, No. 6 (June, 1955), p. 655.

was authorized to investigate and report on only two issues, namely, the union shop and check-off of union dues. Given the inequality in the importance of these issues, the Emergency Board could not hope to create an impression of impartiality by rejecting one issue while recommending the other. In this sense the Emergency Board enjoyed fewer degrees of maneuver than the Wage Stabilization Board.

From this it should not be inferred that the railway unions divorced their campaign for compulsory unionism from their drives for other objectives. Due to union activity, the period 1950–52 was one of near chaos on the railroads. Disputes arising from demands for higher wages and changes in working conditions ended up before emergency boards. In turn, union rejection of emergency board recommendations was followed up by threats of strikes, strikes, "wildcat" strikes, White House-called conferences between unions and management, and government seizure of the roads. In fact Emergency Board No. 98 held hearings and submitted its report recommending adoption of compulsory unionism while the roads were being operated by the Secretary of the Army. Under cover of a barrage of headline-producing events, the unions pushed through the amendment of the Railway Labor Act permitting compulsory unionism, served their union shop demands on the roads and then took the issue to Emergency Board No. 98 when the roads upon demand refused to deliver their employees to the unions. Thus although Emergency Board No. 98 enjoyed little freedom in which to maneuver it did operate under a heavy covering fire.

By almost any test the rifle proved superior to the shotgun in these engagements. Although the Emergency Board's recommendation of compulsory unionism preceded the Stabilization Board's similar recommendation by more than a month, it produced a much smaller public and Congressional protest. Moreover, as indicated in the opening paragraphs of this chapter, the railroads very largely accepted the Board's recommendations without prolonged opposition. Possibly this passive attitude is to be expected from an industry which is being inexorably strangled by government regulations. In any case the "Santa Fe type of reaction or behavior" was the exception. Finally, there can be no question but that the Emergency Board fathered a union shop form of compulsory unionism whereas the debate continues as to what it was that the Stabilization Board produced.

Between 1935 and 1957 union ranks were swollen by millions of unwilling draftees. Exactly how many workers were conscripted in this period and how many volunteered are questions which cannot be answered on the basis of published studies. Nor, looking at the present rather than the past, can we estimate with any great accuracy the number of workers who would leave the union cause if they were free to do so. "Almost none" we are sometimes told by the union high command but then we are also told that there can be no security for unions as long as there is freedom for individuals to choose.

Of those drafted how many could charge their loss of freedom to the conscription procedures established by the Congress and how many were the victims of Presidential actions? Exact numbers are difficult to ascertain but something can be said about the relative importance of these two routes to involuntary participation in unionism. Of the two branches of government the executive proved to be a more effective instrument than the legislative. Over fifty per cent and possibly as many as seventy five per cent of all those compelled to participate in unionism during this period could attribute their loss of freedom to actions taken as the result of Presidential orders.

To recognize that the administrative branch of government rounded up more conscripts for the union cause during this period than would have been delivered if the unions had relied entirely on the procedures established by the Congress is not to prove the superiority of this approach to compulsory unionism. It has potential weaknesses. One is that the three steps in the process are so easily understood. (1) In a period of national peril union leaders refuse to cooperate in the defense program until jurisdiction over non-wage disputes is given to a Presidentially appointed board. (2) Unions then demand what they could not get in time of peace. (3) The resultant dispute goes to the board and the public members recommend compulsory unionism in one form or another with the traditional weight of the Presidential office behind their recommendation.

Once understood, will modern unionism's drive to consolidate its power position continue to receive approval? A final answer may be years in coming. However, the tactics and objectives of unionism in this area can be compared with other historical drives to acquire or consolidate power. Rockefeller, for example, sought money. To get it he forced transportation companies to grant rebates and, thereby, drove many of his competitors out of business. Through the trust form of organization he consolidated the market positions thus won. Rockefeller has long been a principal exhibit in our "liberal" censors' museum of industrial horrors. Tested by the same implicit standards do the leaders of the compulsory unionism movement merit exhibition in the same museum? An answer to this requires the making of a number of comparative judgments. Is great economic and political power a higher goal than great wealth? Does the planned destruction of the individual freedom of millions of workers find a defense in the principles of a society which condemns the planned destruction of market competitors? Are the freedoms lost in the first process inferior in some sense to those destroyed by the second process? Are the methods used by union leaders in the pursuit of their objective ethically superior to those of Rockefeller? What principles protect political deals involving the executive office of the nation in a time of national peril from the censure visited upon rebate deals involving the executive office of a railroad in a time of peace?

The strength of the Wagner approach to compulsory unionism derives from an application of the proposition that "the hand is quicker than the eye." While the attention of everyone is held by what is represented as another engagement in the long struggle between "labor" and "capital" the union strips the individual of a basic right. Nowhere in history can a magician be found whose act rivals that staged by the Congress. For almost twenty years almost every member of the audience has identified the corporation as the loser in the repeated capital versus labor dramas.

Were the union leaders well advised when they abandoned the protection afforded by this misleading performance and turned instead to the extension of unionism by executive fiat? By transferring the power to compel participation from the employer to a government board they destroyed the Wagnerian myth that there was something inevitable or necessary about the grant of this power to the employer in the first place. Moreover, the ease with which the power was first given to and then taken from the employer points up the irresponsibility of government in the labor area. Apparently this is a power the Congress is willing to let almost anyone exercise. What the Congress has been willing to "permit," so long as the Congress itself is not directly involved, is astounding. Thus the Congress permitted a dozen or so professional arbitrators to compel millions of individuals to participate in unionism. But the degree of irresponsibility in this instance was no greater, possibly it was less, than that involved when the Congress first "permitted" employers to trade off their employees' freedom for whatever the union leaders were willing to offer. Irresponsibility will end when the Congress reserves this power for itself.

Much of the nature of Wagnerian unionism is revealed by the compulsory unionism campaign. In fact, were it not for the contribution it can make to an understanding of the procedures and objectives of modern unionism, the analysis of compulsory unionism today would lose much of its contemporary significance. In the literature compulsory unionism is treated as a distinct subject, one different in basic respects from other union objectives. Of course such differences exist, indeed they would be difficult to overlook. But largely overlooked are the common elements shared by this and other union programs.

Today, under our system of compulsion by Congressional courtesy, common thugs substitute their judgment for that of individual workers in deciding whether a union's services are of value to the worker. The service may consist solely of the union's demonstrated ability to collect five, ten or more dollars from every member each week. Or it may be a promise to refrain from committing a specific act, like knocking out the member's teeth or throwing acid in his face.

Almost everyone becomes mildly indignant, for a time at least, over "this kind of unionism." But what kind of unionism is it and on what grounds is it condemned? Is there an undefined subtlety to be caught in the words of the respectable union leader who says "This kind of unionism gives all labor a black eye."? Probably it is the kind of force applied, certainly it is not the use of force, which irks our solid union leaders, although one cannot be certain of this given the number of times baseball bats and shotgun slugs have worked up support for respectable unions. In this respect the decent union leader is like the decent slave owner who while pocketing the profits from his plantation spoke out with equal moral force against those who whip their slaves. Moreover, "this kind of unionism" is obviously not condemned on the ground that it takes from the individual the right to decide whether or not the union offers anything worth paying for. Rather, the objection is to the thug who now makes that decision, not to the loss of freedom. If it were Reuther, say, rather than the thug pictured by McClellan, who decided that what was good for the union was good for every worker, then most of those who become indignant at "this kind of unionism" would go back to sleep.

Through unions, thugs now control vast quantities of purchasing power. Their expenditures suggest that the officers of thug-controlled unions are often impressed by the varied and extraordinary hazards the members face. Their attendant concern is inferred from the correspondingly unusual insurance protection provided the rank and file. Thus the widow of a beneficiary may find that she cannot collect on her husband's life insurance because, for all practical purposes, he was not garrotted by a Hungarian executioner. Or, the taxi driver who breaks his leg while working may find that insurance-wise he would be better protected had the accident occurred while he was going over Niagara Falls in a canoe. But insurance protection is probably most needed by those who protest that their needs could be better satisfied through other uses of their money. Unappreciative beneficiaries of union action are either thrown out or told that the insurance does not cost them anything, for, after all, the insurance is bought with the extra five or ten cents per hour the union wrung from the employer.

To find grounds for condemning the expenditures of thug-controlled unions requires no greater ethical perceptivity than that developed by our ancestors three or four hundred years ago. In this case the thug-controlled union offers the worker a choice between losing his job or buying its insurance, and this is precisely the principle involved when the armed robber says to his victim "your money or your life." By depriving those they confront of acceptable alternatives, the alley thug and the union thug destroy freedom.

Other and quantitatively more significant applications of the same principle are rarely, if ever, condemned. By way of example, consider a number of the non-wage benefits which have emerged in recent years. These, we are told, represent defeats for reluctant and reactionary employers at the hands of progressive, democratic unions. In this view private pension plans were established when unions forced employers to recognize the needs of those "too old to work, too young to die." Likewise, private unemployment compensation became a reality only after employers were compelled to "share the risks and costs of unemployment" hitherto borne entirely by their employees. Through a variety of different insurance programs employers have unwillingly accepted responsibility for other specific employee needs. These are major exhibits in any demonstration of how unions benefit those whom they represent. In each of these cases the union took "something" from the employer and gave it to the employees.

To measure the "something" taken from the employer a knowledge is required of the "arithmetic of collectivism." Newspapers occasionally carry stories describing the development of mathematical systems in which parallel lines behave in non-Euclidean ways and in which two plus two is not equal to four. Fully as novel and useful results are produced by the arithmetic of collectivism. Consider the case of a union operating in an industry where new contracts are written every three years. Suppose the union gets a 25 cents an hour increase for its members. Is this a "big deal" and does it prove that big dealers run the union? To answer such questions facts are required on past and anticipated price movements. Possibly 25 cents does no more than offset the increase in living costs over the past three years. Or it may just balance anticipated increases in living costs over the next three years. Suppose that in fact the increase exactly offsets past living cost increases so that real employee income remains unchanged. In this case can the membership and public be persuaded that the union has scored again, particularly when there is a growing suspicion that union activity is itself a principal cause of inflation? In other words, can a union which is barely maintaining its position on the treadmill of wage-push inflation create the impression that it is really moving ahead? To know how to do this is to reveal a command over the arithmetic of collectivism.

The 25 cents could simply be added to the real wage rate. This unimaginative operation would do nothing more than add to the employee's "free" income. To create the effect it desires, however, the union must see to it that the employee does not gain control over the entire 25 cents the union has wrested from the company. In other words, control over a part of the 25 cents must be withheld from the employee. Private pension plans and private unemployment compensation programs are conspicuously successful examples of "controlled" income devices. In the arithmetic of collectivism

$$15\text{¢ (rate increase)} + 10\text{¢ (pensions)} > 25\text{¢},$$

where the inequality sign should be read "is worth more than." To whom is this combination of free and controlled income items worth more than 25 cents? Obviously it is worth more to the union for it can now feature the claim that it not only got an increase in the rate but *pensions,* as well. Writers on labor affairs for newspapers and magazines will see to it that no one overlooks the union's latest triumph. Certainly it is worth more to the company, for management may not only save a few cents by agreeing to the pension (or other) principle but, in addition, any alert management will seize the opportunity to write provisions into such schemes which will benefit the company in a number of other ways.

Except in highly unusual circumstances, 15 free cents plus 10 controlled cents would be worth *less* to the employee than 25 free cents. This proposition reduces to the statement that 10 controlled cents are worth less to the employee than 10 free cents. The validity of the proposition can be tested whenever a union is prepared to let those they represent choose freely between the alternatives. If "rights" to controlled income could be bought and sold in a market, they would soon sell at a discount, the amount of the discount varying with a number of factors studied in any elementary course in economics. With 10 free cents the employee can buy anything that can be bought with the 10 controlled cents. And, alternatively, he can buy other goods and services which cannot be bought with the 10 cents set aside for pensions or similar services by the terms of the collective agreement. The satisfaction he would derive from the combination of goods and services he could buy with 10 free cents might be greater, and generally it would be greater, than the satisfaction he would derive from the goods or services whose purchase the union arranges with the 10 controlled cents. This proposition derives from the application of the basic economic premise of a free society to a particular situation. The premise is that the allocation an individual makes of a given income will yield him more satisfaction than he would experience if his income were allocated for him by anyone else.[23]

That the principle involved in the operations of the union thug is essentially the same as that involved in those of the alley thug is apparent to most observers of contemporary unionism. Each operates by confronting his victim with an unacceptable choice. One says "hand over your wallet or you will be beaten up." The other says "pay your dues or you will be beaten up." Or the more sophisticated racketeer may say "buy our union insurance or work some place else." Growing recognition that the only real difference between the two kinds of thugs is that one operates in an alley whereas the other operates in a union will produce legislation, eventually, adequate to cope with the activities of the union racketeer.

While most observers of contemporary unionism catch the common principle in the operations of alley and union thugs, few of them see that the same principle is inherent in many of the "benefits" provided by respectable unions. In terms of principle does it really make any difference whether the command "buy our insurance or find another job!" comes from a thug or a respectable union? What differentiates the two cases? Attempts to do so on the ground that the union thug sells the worker something that is worthless or something that is worth less than the amount the worker is forced to pay for it necessarily fail unless it can be shown that respectable unions do not do these things. But does the respectable union in the illustration given above use the 10 controlled cents to provide exactly those things which the individ-

[23] Allocation refers to the division of income between consumption and savings and, in turn, to the division of the portion to be spent among alternative goods and services and of the portion to be saved among alternative forms of saving.

ual workers would buy for themselves if they were free to spend the 10 cents as they please? Of course it cannot do so if it represents more than one worker. Even identical twins have different wants or preferences. To meet the preferences of one is to fail to meet the wants of the other. The twenty-year-old worker in excellent health might say that the union in taking 10 cents out of his hourly pay for a retirement plan is spending the money exactly as he would if he had control of it while his cancerous twin with six months to live would feel that anything set side for retirement was a complete misuse of income. Differences in individual wants or preferences arise not only from differences in health but from differences in age, sex, occupation, skills and myriad other factors too complex to be allowed for in the plans of even the most systematic collectivist. These considerations suggest why one worker might be willing to pay 10 cents for the retirement plan written into the contract by the union whereas another worker, if not compelled to do so, would not pay one cent for it. Still other workers might willingly pay one or more cents but less than 10 cents. Whenever a union sets aside an amount greater than the amount the individual would willingly pay for the purpose it is behaving in essentially the same manner as the thug union. Both unions force the individual to take something that is worthless or worth less to him than the amount he has to pay for it.

From the standpoint of a free society how significant are these substitutions of union for individual judgments? Judged by the resistance offered to them, the almost universal opinion would appear to be that they are not very important matters. The Congressional attitude is clear. While the Congress itself will not take these freedoms from the individual it will raise no objection when others do. Thus it permits unions and corporations to pluck the individual to the limits of their self interest. Nor can the individual rely upon the executive branch of government for protection. The Truman administration, in particular, displayed a remarkable capacity for doing that which the Congress refused to do. Management resistance to the union campaign against the individual is now reduced to a few scattered fronts. The intervention in two wars of union-oriented public officials made many a corporate official take a second look at the high price they were paying for refusing to deliver their employees' rights to the union leaders. Why not toss those rights on the bargaining table, as the Wagner Act encourages them to do, in exchange for things a corporation, as opposed to a citizen, really wants? That this is what happened is obvious to almost everyone but the students of the subject.[24]

Any account of what has happened to the liberties of the individual under labor collectivism would be incomplete if reference were not made to the position taken on these matters by that institution to which all Americans instinctively look when individual freedom is endangered. To provide a case history of the Supreme Court's interpretation of what can be done to the individual under Wagnerian unionism would take us well beyond the spatial limits set for this chapter. Fortunately, the position of the Court can be fixed without resort to the case method.[25]

Writing in 1938, Professor Frankfurter noted with approval that "Naturally, therefore, Mr. Justice Holmes attributed very different legal significance to those liberties of the individual which history has attested as the indispensable conditions of a free society from that which he attached to liberties which derived merely from shifting economic arrangements. These enduring liberties of the subject, in the noble English phrase, were, so far as the national government is

[24] See Lloyd G. Reynolds, *Labor Economics and Labor Relations* (New York, 1954), pp. 228-232, for the standard discussion of this subject.

An excellent index of the general loss of interest in protecting employee freedoms is the emergence of the millionaire candidate for the office of governor, senator or president. Throughout his life this social phenomenon has found, with few exceptions, that anything he wanted, he could buy. But now he wants public office and money is not legal tender for the purchase of this. To get the support he needs, he must pay off in the currency potential supporters accept. A principal reason for the success of the type is his discovery that union leaders will accept his promise to participate in the further destruction of the liberties of the individual worker as a down-payment for their support. Trading in the liberties of employees apparently provides him with the same kind of satisfaction his father or grandfather derived from commodity manipulations; but, whereas his ancestors were cursed and reviled by the press for making a profit out of commodities, he is hailed by it for making political profit out of individual freedom. The avidity with which he joins the union high command in devouring the liberties of the "working masses" almost forces one to choose between protecting our inherited freedoms or his inherited wealth.

[25] For reasons of space, only one of the elements determining the Court's position is commented on here.

concerned, specifically enshrined in the Bill of Rights."[26] In this view, one which Justice Frankfurter has made decisive in the Wagnerian period, liberties divide into two sets, kinds or classes. Liberties of the first class are distinguishable from liberties of the second in terms of the different impacts their extinguishment would have upon a free society. Whereas a free society could not survive the loss of one set of liberties, no such consequence would follow from the loss of other freedoms. Hence, in terms of the survival of a free society, there are necessary and unnecessary freedoms. Classic examples of such necessary liberties are the Constitutionally enumerated freedoms of speech and religion. From this view it follows that Congressional activity will not be limited by the Court unless it can be shown that it impinges upon a necessary freedom.

Imbued with this theory, judges could remain calm in the face of the freedoms lost under Wagner. Suppose employer and union do get together to take a nickel out of the employee's hourly pay. In putting it aside to buy accident insurance for the employee they are only substituting their judgment for his as to how he should protect himself, if at all, against a specific risk. Merely to compare what is lost by the employee in this case with what would be lost if even the least important of the liberties specifically noted in the Bill of Rights were impaired is to prove how unessential this freedom is to the maintenance of a free society. Nothing more need be said when union and employer take another nickel out of the employee's hourly pay for health insurance. Complaints against this sort of thing should be filed in the plaintiff's economic brief where it can be looked at by the more intellectually curious of the justices' clerks. But it would be better still if the plaintiffs took their complaints to the Congress, for the freedoms whose loss is complained of are simply by-products of economic arrangements which the Congress has the power to change at any time.

The principle being so clear it would be a waste of time and money for an employee to ask the Court to intervene when union and employer make other dispositions of his income. He may not want to allocate a dime out of his hourly wage to build up a retirement fund.

[26] Felix Frankfurter, *Mr. Justice Holmes and the Supreme Court* (Cambridge, Mass., 1938), *op. cit.*, p. 61.

Or he may not feel it worthwhile to set aside another dime to finance unemployment compensation. But as against union-employer preferences, his preferences regarding the allocation of his income count for nothing insofar as the Court is concerned.

Nor are there any limits to which this process can go, provided only that the basic distinction between classes of freedoms is observed. When they set aside funds to provide for the worker's illness, accidents, unemployment and old age, union and employer have very largely decided how much and for what purposes the worker should save. Thereby they also decide how much he should be allowed to consume. Judges in the grip of the Holmes-Frankfurter doctrine [27] would be as astonished to hear a worker claim that his freedom to allocate his income between savings and consumption had a Constitutional foundation as would have been Ptolemy had a contemporary advanced the claim that the sun did not revolve around the earth.

Union and employer can also determine how the employee spends the amount of income they permit him to use for consumption purposes. Thus they can decide that the services provided by a union are good for the employee, as in the Forstmann case. Having made that decision, they use the check-off of dues to guarantee that the employee never falls behind in his payments for union services. Among the services provided are political ones. Union dues support candidates for public office. Frequently unions use funds extracted from Republican employees to elect Democratic candidates and funds of Democratic employees to elect Republican candidates.[28] Here, where

[27] This is a convenient phrase but it may not be an altogether accurate one and it will not be to the degree that Professor Frankfurter's interpretation of Holmes' position differs from Holmes' position.

[28] This illustrates but does not state the objectionable principle involved. What is objected to is the union's power to usurp a role traditionally and necessarily reserved for the individual.

The constitutional validity of the use of dues moneys taken from workers under the force of a compulsory union membership contract is presently involved in three law suits: *Looper* v. *Georgia Southern & Florida Ry. Co.*, 99 S. E. 2d 101 (1957), *Allen* v. *Southern Railway Co.*, Super. Ct., Mecklenburg County, No. Car., May 15, 1958, and *Phillips* v. *Louisville & Nashville R. Co.*, Civ. No. 3697, U.S. D.C. W.D. Ky., filed Oct. 13, 1958. In the *Looper* case, the Supreme Court of Georgia held that Congress could not, consistently with the First and Fifth Amendments to the Federal Constitution, compel railroad employees, as a condition of employment, to pay to a union political and economic preferences overlap, the intent logician might infer that the Court, however indifferent it might be to economic preferences, would already have acted to prevent suppression of the employee's political preferences, since in this case the distinction between necessary and unnecessary freedoms is clearly ignored.

By contrast this points up the Court's inability to find that modern unionism suppresses any preferences whose expression is essential to a free society. Provided they do not overstep certain obvious bounds, union and employer in a Holmes-Frankfurter world are permitted to exercise fantastic powers. Thus by mutual agreement they can transfer all of an employee's income from the "free" to the "controlled" category. They can add to the employee's savings at the very time he might prefer to save less and spend more. Or they can decree the opposite. More can be spent on the employee's housing even though he prefers more clothing. And when he wants to get drunk he may find the funds necessary for the purpose have been put aside to educate him on the benefits of Wagnerian unionism. While these few examples suggest certain possibilities they do not begin to exhaust the countless ways in which union and employer can act to deny the individual employee freedom to express his preferences. The full development of a Holmes-Frankfurter society does not depend upon the passage of additional enabling legislation. Existing legislation contains principles, ones scrutinized and accepted by the Frankfurter Court, adequate to provide for the fullest development of a social system in which union and employer express all the economic preferences formerly expressed by the individual.

To call this society a "free" society is the privilege of anyone who wants to give new meanings to old words. To hold further that the system is one of many which the Congress might appropriately build

---

initiation fees, dues and assessments which would be used in part for the support of political candidates or causes to which the employees are opposed. Upon remand to a trial court, the evidence unmistakably showed such use of dues extracted under union shop agreements. The unions agreed by stipulation that they used substantial portions of dues compulsorily exacted from employees for the support of political candidates and causes to which they are opposed. The Court so found and enjoined enforcement of the union shop contracts involved on the ground that such exaction was unconstitutional. The case is being appealed again to the Supreme Court of Georgia and like the others cited is expected ultimately to reach the Supreme Court of the United States.

on the foundations provided by the Constitution is equivalent to maintaining that there would be nothing inappropriate in the construction of an outhouse on the foundations of the Parthenon. For what Holmes does via Frankfurter is to specify conditions *necessary* but not *sufficient* for the maintenance of a free society, although the insufficiency involved is not traceable to the Constitution. Sufficient conditions are provided by it. Among these is the declaration that "The enumeration in the Constitution of certain rights shall not be construed to deny or disparage others retained by the people." [29]

[29] To anyone who takes more than a casual glance at the Constitution, the treatment accorded the Ninth Amendment by the interpreters of the Constitution is puzzling. One is tempted to conclude either that the Amendment does not mean anything or that it does not mean anything to narrowly trained specialists in Constitutional law, a very different breed from those who drafted the document itself. Although the annotated edition of the Constitution prepared for the Congress by the Library of Congress and published in 1938 runs to more than 1200 pages it disposes of the Ninth Amendment in less than one full page and even then the space is used to comment on an erroneous citation of the Ninth made in 1833. The appearance of the new annotated edition in 1953 suggests that the Amendment has acquired little new Constitutional significance in the intervening period, a period more likely than any other in our history to suggest obvious uses for this particular amendment.

Part II

9

Competitive and Monopoly Unionism

H. Gregg Lewis

MANY OF THE DIFFERENCES among economists in the positions they hold regarding public policy toward trade unions, as well as in their assessments of the importance of unionism as a labor market factor, stem from disagreement on the answer to the question: What is the impact of unionism on relative real wages? If we knew the answer to this question, we would surely know much about the extent to which unionism is monopolistic, the conditions that strengthen or weaken monopoly unionism, and the consequences of unionism for the distribution of wage and salary income and for the allocation of labor and other resources among uses.

We now have fairly good estimates of the relative real wage effects of about a dozen individual unions and studies now in process will add perhaps another dozen to this sample of estimates. For many unions, however, the wage and related data needed for *direct* estimation of their wage impact are not available. This is particularly true of many of the old AFL craft unions. For a substantial proportion of these unions, however, historical and descriptive studies are available that provide information on a wide variety of "non-wage" variables. Can some of this information be used to indicate *indirectly* the relative wage effects of these unions? This is the question to which this paper is addressed.

Are union dues a good indicator of the relative wage effects of unionism? Does the fact that a union is an industrial union rather than a craft union tell us anything about its wage impact? What about the closed shop, seniority rules, "make-work," "share-work," "featherbedding" rules and the like? Is the extent to which a union has organized the employees in an industry a useful index of its power to increase real wages in the industry? And so on. In principle there is only one way to find out which of the many non-wage variables of unionism are useful indicators and that is to test them on the sample of unions for which we have direct estimates of relative wage effects. Nevertheless, here as elsewhere in problems of positive economics, we must look to economic theory for guidance in selecting among the many possible variables those most likely to be useful.

The first half of this chapter applies competitive theory to unionism; the second half, monopoly theory. In this sense the first half of the chapter may be said to contain a theory of the "competitive union"; the second half, a theory of the "monopoly union." The competitive union and the monopoly union, however, are ideal types used for purposes of analysis rather than mutually exclusive descriptive categories for the classification of real unions. Throughout the chapter I use these analytical constructs to classify the *data* of unionism, not *unions.*

Let me illustrate. Competitive unionism, as we shall see, produces no real wage effects; monopoly unionism, on the other hand, does produce such effects though in particular cases they may be imperceptible. Now suppose that one of the implications of competitive unionism is that union dues will be equal to zero, while the corresponding implication of monopoly unionism is that union dues will tend to be greater, the greater a union's impact on real wages. Theory thus would point to union dues as likely to be a useful indicator of relative real wage effects of unionism.

In view of the common assertion that the purpose of unionism is "to take competition out of the supply side of the labor market," it may seem strange to think of unionism as conceivably having some aspects that may be quite compatible with competitive theory. Students of industrial relations tell us, however, that unionism often provides a set of rules and procedures for employee-employer relations (a "system of industrial jurisprudence"), opportunities for social relations among employees, a way of life for the worker at his place of work, that are substitutes for those offered in non-union employments. We have never viewed "labor relations" in non-union plants as something which by its very nature was incompatible with competitive theory. In the same way we need not view "collective bargaining" as having no aspects consistent with competitive theory.

In order to isolate the effects of competitive unionism, assume that unions have no monopoly power. In other words, treat unionism simply as a technique by which a distinct set of non-pecuniary aspects of employment, a substitute for the set in non-union firms, is produced in a competitive labor market. To begin with I shall use a simple model that makes the assumptions that:

1. Unionism produces non-pecuniary conditions of employment—call them "collective bargaining"—the same in kind and amount from one union employment to another and the absence of unionism produces conditions—call them "individual bargaining"—homogenous in the same sense from one non-union employment to another. For both employers and employees there are only two "industries": union which produces collective bargaining and non-union which produces individual bargaining.
2. Collective bargaining costs the same to produce in real terms as individual bargaining and neither enters the production functions for other outputs produced by union and non-union firms.
3. Employees sell labor services that are perfect substitutes for each other; each employee supplies a fixed quantity of labor services, the same for all employees; and each employer demands a fixed quantity of labor services, the same for all employers.

The problem is to find the relative *money* wage which will compensate employees and employers for any net non-pecuniary advantages or disadvantages of collective bargaining relative to individual bargaining and the distribution of employment between union and non-union firms. This problem is essentially the same as one treated by Gary S. Becker in his *The Economics of Discrimination*[1] and I refer you to Becker's work for a full statement of the framework for analyzing non-pecuniary aspects of labor markets.

Consider first the relative supply of labor to the union industry.

[1] Chicago, 1957.

Let *k* measure an individual employee's relative tastes for collective bargaining in the following manner:

If W is the market ratio of money wages in union firms to money wages in non-union firms, the individual employee will act as though the market *real* wage ratio were kW, where k is a positive number that is larger, the greater the employee's preference for collective bargaining relative to individual bargaining.

The employee will supply his labor services to the industry with the larger real wage; thus he will supply his labor to the union industry only if kW is not less than unity—that is, only if W is not less than 1/k. Thus 1/k is his minimum relative money supply price of labor to the union industry.

Employees to some extent will have different tastes for collective bargaining. Thus for some, probably few, the minimum supply price will be substantially less than unity, say 0.9 or less. These individuals will be willing to sacrifice money wages ten per cent or more higher in non-union firms than in union in order to enjoy collective bargaining. There will be others, also few, whose minimum supply prices may be quite high, 1.1 or more, who would have to be paid wages in union firms ten per cent or more higher than in non-union firms to compensate them for their relative distaste for collective bargaining.

The market relative supply curve of labor to union firms is now easily constructed. Calculate the fraction s(W) of all employees whose 1/k is less than or equal to any specified relative money wage, W. This fraction is the relative supply of labor to union firms at the wage W. If tastes differ, s(W) will be greater, the greater is W. The curve $\overline{SS}$ in the diagram below shows for each W, the corresponding fraction s(W) of labor services supplied to union firms. It is thus the relative supply curve of labor to the union industry.

The relative demand curve for labor in the union industry can be developed in much the same way. Let k_e measure an employer's tastes for collective bargaining relative to individual bargaining as follows:

He acts as though the real wage cost "per hour" of union labor relative to non-union labor is k_eW where k_e is a positive number that is *smaller* (not *larger,* as for employees) the greater his preference for collective bargaining relative to individual bargaining.

He will choose to demand union labor—that is, to be a union employer, only if the real wage cost of union labor does not exceed that of non-union labor; that is, he will demand union labor only if k_eW does not exceed unity. Thus $1/k_e$ is his maximum relative money demand price for union labor. The maximum demand prices for some employers, surely a small fraction, may be quite high, 1.1 or more. These employers are willing to buy union labor services even though it may cost them ten per cent (or more) more than non-union labor because they very much prefer collective bargaining relative to individual bargaining. There will be other employers whose maximum demand prices for union labor will be quite low, 0.9 or less. These will choose to be union employers only if they are compensated for their relative distaste for collective bargaining by a money wage for union labor that is ten per cent or more below that of non-union labor.

The fraction of employers, d(W), whose maximum demand prices, $1/k_e$, exceed a specified relative money wage, W, is the relative de-

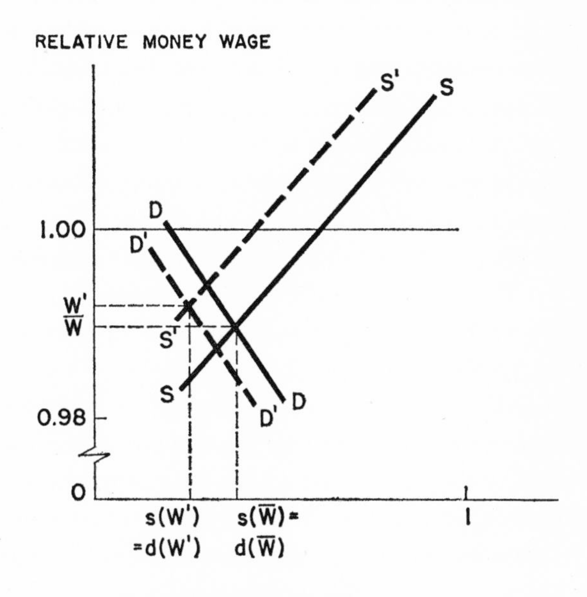

FIG. 1

mand for union labor at the relative wage W. If employers' tastes differ, the relative quantity of labor demanded, d(W), falls as the relative money wage, W, rises. The relative demand curve for labor in the union industry is the curve $\overline{DD}$ in Fig. 1.

Market equilibrium is at the point of intersection of the relative demand curve and the relative supply curve. The equilibrium value of W is $\overline{W}$, with the fraction $s(\overline{W}) = d(\overline{W})$ of employees and employers in the union industry.

The difference $(1-\overline{W})$ is the "equalizing differential" in money wages. If this differential is positive, it measures the percentage excess of non-union over union money wages; if it is negative, its numerical value measures the percentage excess of union money wages over non-union. Whatever its value, it is the differential in money wages that compensates employees and employers at the margin for any net non-pecuniary advantages or disadvantages of collective bargaining relative to individual bargaining.

Is a $\overline{W}$ as large as, say, 1.05—an equalizing excess of union over non-union money wages as large as five per cent—likely? I think not. It should be clear from Fig. 1 that a $\overline{W}$ this high implies either that (a) at least half of the employees dislike collective bargaining so much relative to individual bargaining that they are willing to sacrifice at least five per cent of the income they could earn in union firms (at least $150 per year at union yearly wages of $3,000) in order to avoid being employed in the collective bargaining industry, or that (b) at least half of the employers like collective bargaining so much relative to individual bargaining that they are willing to incur wage costs as union employers that are at least five per cent higher than they would incur as non-union employers. Neither of these implications seems plausible to me as a general characterization of the tastes of employees or employers in the United States.

Similarly a $\overline{W}$ as low as 0.95—an equalizing excess of non-union over union money wages as high as five per cent—implies either that (a) at least half of the employees like collective bargaining so much relative to individual bargaining that they are willing to sacrifice at least five per cent of the money income they could earn in non-union employments in order to enjoy collective bargaining or (b) that at least half of the employers dislike competitive—not monopoly—unionism so much that they are willing to incur wage costs at least five per cent higher as non-union firms than as union in order to avoid collective bargaining. These also seem to me to be implausible general characterizations of the tastes of employers and employees. On the other hand, it seems quite possible to me that $\overline{W}$ might be one or two per cent below unity, and this seems more reasonable to me than any figure above unity.

The persistent use of the "union label" suggests that consumers in a given product market are not completely indifferent between supply produced under union conditions and supply produced under non-union conditions. Assume that all consumers are alike in being willing to pay a price per unit for output produced under union condition that is, say, five per cent higher than the price per unit of non-union output. For simplicity, suppose that labor is used in the same fixed ratio to output in both union and non-union firms and that labor costs amount to 50 per cent of total costs. The effect of the consumer tastes then is to raise the demand curve, $\overline{DD}$, in Fig. 1 by ten per cent along the vertical axis, increasing both $\overline{W}$ and $s(\overline{W}) = d(\overline{W})$. Conversely if consumers generally were to prefer non-union to union output, this would cause the demand curve to be lower than it otherwise would be.

It is surely true, however, that the unionism tastes of individuals as consumers will tend to be in the same direction as their tastes as employees or employers, but very much smaller in magnitude. The great bulk of consumers, I would argue, are essentially indifferent between union and non-union output. Thus I believe that the unionism tastes of consumers have negligible labor market effects.

In the preceding analysis the equalizing differential was made to depend only upon the distribution of relative tastes for collective bargaining among employees, employers, and consumers. Let us now drop the assumption that collective bargaining costs the same in resource terms to produce as individual bargaining.

In two respects collective bargaining will tend to cost somewhat more to produce than individual bargaining. First, union employees, unlike non-union workers, must bear the costs of the union that represents them. We may view the competitive union as an organization providing collective bargaining services to its members, covering its costs through its membership dues. Second, union employers may be subject to somewhat larger resource costs directly in manning larger "labor relations" staffs and indirectly through the effects of such rules as seniority rules on the utilization of labor in production.

The effect of the costs borne by employees is to raise the supply schedule (before dues) to the position $\overline{S'S'}$ in Fig. 1. The effect of the resource costs borne by employers is to lower the demand curve to the position $\overline{D'D'}$. Both factors work to lower the equilibrium fraction of employment in union firms from $s(\overline{W}) = d(\overline{W})$ to $s(W') = d(W')$. They have opposite effects, however, on the equilibrium relative money wage (before dues).

Notice that neither union dues nor the check-off *per se* are incompatible with competitive unionism. It is not possible, however, simultaneously to have high union dues, say 5 per cent of wages before dues, significant costs of collective bargaining borne by employers, and a substantial fraction, say 25 per cent, of employment in union firms unless 25 per cent of the employees and 25 per cent of the employers together are willing to bear costs of collective bargaining amounting to more than 5 per cent of wages before dues. Furthermore, even if this implication were plausible, dues this high would not emerge unless the costs of producing collective bargaining to the union were this great. It is my impression that the costs borne by unions to produce collective bargaining are very much less than five per cent of the payroll of union employees.

The upshot of the preceding line of reasoning is the expectation that *competitive* unionism in general will lead to negligible equalizing differentials in money wages between union and non-union firms. The differentials in wages between union and non-union firms observed in some empirical studies of the wage impact of unionism, in general, I believe, do not consist in any important part of the equalizing differentials of competitive unionism.

Thus far there has been no place in the analysis for any distinction between employers who are competitive in their product markets and employers who are not. In order to deal with this problem it is necessary to define employer tastes for collective bargaining even more precisely:

Let W_u and W_n be the money wages per unit of labor service in union and non-union firms respectively. An employer with a k_e less than unity is assumed to act as though his real wage cost as a union employer is W_u, his real wage cost as a non-union employer, W_n/k_e. In Becker's language he "discriminates" against individual bargaining. An employer with a k_e greater than unity acts as though his real wage cost as a non-union employer is W_n, as a union employer, k_eW_u. He "discriminates" against collective bargaining.[2]

If $W' = W_u/W_n$ is less than unity, W_u must be less than W_n. But then it follows from the above definition and from Fig. 1 that non-union firms will have higher *real* wage costs than union firms except "marginal" union firms with k_eW_u equal to W_n. Now remove the assumption that all firms have the same fixed employment per firm, but instead have negatively inclined demand curves relating quantity of labor demanded to real wages. Furthermore, assume that there are no systematic differences in these labor demand curves between union and non-union firms or between firms that are competitive and firms that are monopolistic in product markets. Union firms, having lower real wage costs, will tend to expand employment, non-union firms to contract employment. This will cause both W' and $s(W')$ to rise. Thus the fraction of employees employed in union firms will be greater than the fraction in firms with k_e less than $1/W'$.

Notice that this proposition holds for firms that are monopolists in product markets as well as those that are competitors. We have been assuming, however, that employers could choose only between the individual and the collective bargaining industry. In fact they have a third choice, namely that of not being employers at all, save of themselves. Hence let us drop the assumption that employers may choose

[2] The particular meaning given here to the taste coefficient, k_e, is only one of many that might have been given; it was chosen mainly because it leads to somewhat simpler analysis than other definitions of the k_e.

only between individual and collective bargaining. Which employers will have the greatest incentive to move into the third industry—to become "self-employers?" They will tend to be those with the greatest tastes against collective bargaining. Which of the self-employers will have the greatest incentive to become employers? Those with the strongest tastes against individual bargaining. The effects of these transfers will be to raise both W' and $s(W')$. (Notice that the factors discussed in this and the preceding paragraph make it even more likely that W' will deviate little from unity.)

There may be differences between competitive and monopoly firms, however, in these transfers to and from the third industry. Consider, for example, a non-union firm receiving monopoly returns that cannot be capitalized and transferred *in toto* into the third industry. These monopoly returns act as a disincentive to transfer. The same argument holds for a monopolist self-employer who except for the monopoly returns would become a union employer. Thus, in equilibrium, market forces tend to make the ratio of union employment to non-union greater in competitive firms than in monopoly firms. In the equilibrium position monopoly firms will have on the average greater tastes against collective bargaining than competitive firms.

The preceding analysis has dealt with competitive unionism on the average. Even crude inspections of the data show, however, that the extent of unionism, $s(W')$, varies greatly among regions, sizes of communities, occupations, from one time to another, and so on. It is not nearly so apparent, however, that there is correspondingly large variability in W'.

Notice that I have drawn the demand and supply curves in Fig. 1 so that they are quite elastic with respect to W over much of their length. These high elasticities reflect my "hunch" that among both employers and employees tastes for collective bargaining have little dispersion about the average. If this hunch is right, then slight differences in employer or employee tastes, say among regions, will cause large differences in extent of unionism and negligible differences in W'. In what follows I make this assumption a key part of the analytical framework.

We have no way of knowing whether observed differences in extent of unionism are consistent with a competitive view of unionism unless we have indicators of tastes constructed quite independently of the data they are to explain. The discovery of such indicators is an undertaking for which economic theory provides little guidance. Nevertheless, I do not view the undertaking as hopelessly difficult and in the analysis that follows I suggest some indicators of tastes for collective bargaining and the differences in extent of unionism that follow from the differences in tastes in the presence of competitive unionism.

It has often been pointed out that persons in rural and Southern communities tend to have relatively individualistic political views. It seems reasonable to me, therefore, to expect that employees and employers in such communities will have above average relative preferences for individual bargaining which, in the present analysis, leads to the result that $s(W')$ will fall substantially as ruralness and Southernness increase. This result surely fits the data well.

The same general line of argument leads to predictions of differences in the extent of collective bargaining among occupations. The persons who as employees will tend to have the strongest preferences for individual bargaining, I believe, will tend to be those we describe as "ambitious," "enterprising," "nonconformist," "individualistic," and "independent." Persons with these characteristics, however, will tend to be found disproportionately in the upper occupational ranks rather than the lower. Thus it seems likely that extent of organization, on this line of reasoning, would be found to be negatively correlated with occupational rank. This conclusion in one respect fits the data well and in another it does not. White collar workers—professional and clerical—tend to be substantially less unionized than manual workers. On the other hand, the oldest unions we have are those of skilled craftsmen and by and large it is still true that unionization of skilled manual workers is more extensive than that of unskilled. The latter data, as I shall show later, fit better one of the implications of monopoly unionism.

Students of human and industrial relations have often asserted that under non-union conditions, but not to the same extent under unionism, small establishments offer better "labor relations" to employees than do large establishments. The implication of this assertion is that s(W′) will tend to be positively correlated with establishment size.

Among the most commonly emphasized aspects of competitive unionism are the rules and procedures that in one way or another make seniority of service valuable. Such rules and procedures will have least value for those who neither have seniority nor expect to accumulate it. These will tend to be women, particularly young and beautiful women, casual workers and other part-time, part-year workers. The occupations in which such workers predominate we would expect to be relatively little unionized and in fact they are poorly unionized.

Finally, consider the changes in extent of unionism over time. The two periods in which the extent of union membership grew most rapidly in the United States were during World War I and in the decade of the New Deal. The important factor common to these two periods is a change in public policy favorable to unionism. (The World War I change was temporary, was reversed in the early 1920's, and union membership fell off substantially.) In part the changes in policy reflected changes in community tastes favorable to unionism that by themselves would have led to increased extent of unionism. But the changes in policy were more than that. Consider, for example, the Wagner Act. This act made it unlawful for non-union employers to refuse to bargain with the unions chosen by their employees as their collective bargaining representatives. In this respect the law raised the real costs to employers of individual bargaining relative to collective bargaining. Thus the great growth of unionism following the passage of the Wagner Act is not on its face evidence of a growth of monopoly unionism.

On what "scale" will competitive collective bargaining be produced? Consider first the problem of optimal organization of collective bargaining *within the firm*. I have already given some reasons why different categories of employees will tend to have systematic differences in their tastes for collective bargaining. For example, we would expect office employees to have less strong tastes for collective bargaining than plant employees. If these differences in tastes were the only factor involved, we would expect to have collective or individual bargaining units within the plant defined along the lines separating one taste group from another—an individual bargaining unit, say, for office employees and collective bargaining units for plant employees.

Collective bargaining, however, is a system of rules and procedures governing employer-employee relations not only within homogenous "occupations" but also among "occupations" that are closely related to each other through worker transfers, promotions, demotions, hiring, layoffs, work scheduling, and so on.

The consideration just noted surely is not of major importance when the occupations are "office" and "plant." In this case tastes will govern the definition of the "bargaining" units. The same will be true of plants of a single firm that are widely separated geographically and other examples can be cited. On the other hand, efficient operation of the procedures of collective bargaining will tend to require that the bulk of unskilled, semiskilled, and even some skilled "production worker" occupations within the plant comprise one collective bargaining unit rather than several.

Thus, although I would not expect all employees of an establishment generally to belong to one collective bargaining unit, I would expect competitive unionism to resemble "industrial" unionism more strongly than "craft" unionism. This expectation, however, does not fit the history of unionism well; industrial unionism, by and large, is a "Johnny-come-lately."

The considerations that lead to the expectation that the "plant" and "office" and the geographically separated establishments of a single firm will have separate bargaining units—separate unions if the units are *collective* bargaining units—also lead to the expectation that generally the scale of competitive collective bargaining will not be greater than the scale of employment of a single firm.

The mere affiliation of a competitive union with an association of unions, of course, is not in itself evidence of monopoly. In principle, such affiliation may be the means by which a union can purchase counsel on such matters as grievance procedures, time study methods, job evaluation techniques, and other substantive matters of personnel practice. Yet when the firms that are members of a trade association collectively attempt to fix product prices, set output quotas, allot territories, and the like, we suspect the association of attempting to monopolize. Trying, of course, is not succeeding; nevertheless, we are unable to account for the behavior with competitive theory. In the same way when associations of unions—"national" unions—collectively fix the terms of collective bargaining agreements, we suspect an attempt to monopolize.

I have already noted that union dues (if low), the check-off of union dues, and seniority rules are compatible with competitive unionism. It is possible to cite many other collective bargaining practices that also are compatible with the competitive view of unionism: the written, jointly signed, collective bargaining contract running for a term of months and the inclusion in the contract of procedures for handling grievances, job evaluations, time studies, vacation scheduling, worker safety measures, and a host of other details within the scope of the personnel department.

A good many union practices, however, are commonly viewed as evidence of monopoly unionism. I shall examine only two of these here. First, the "union" shop. If the collective agreement does not provide for a check-off of dues of all members of the collective bargaining unit, the "union" shop may be viewed simply as a device to assist the union to recover the costs borne by it in producing collective bargaining conditions of employment. The requirement of membership in the union as a condition of employment may perform another function that is not of necessity monopolistic. An employer with no monopoly power in the labor market may show preferences in his employment practices, nevertheless, for those who "belong to his church." So also a competitive union and an employer may jointly agree to employ only those willing to join the union. Thus I do not view the union shop as evidence by itself of monopoly unionism.

Finally consider the union practices to which the labels "make-work" or "featherbedding" are commonly attached. The effect of many of these practices is to require that certain tasks be performed only by members of a specified union of skilled craftsmen. In some cases these practices may perform the same function as health or safety rules. But in many others there is clearly no health or safety question involved, and I am able to explain them only with monopoly theory.

Private monopolizing may be thought of as a trade, employing both labor and other resources, in which the practitioners—the residual income recipients—earn income by driving the demand price for a commodity or productive service above its supply price. Thus a successful labor monopolist will cause the demand price of labor—the wage rate—to rise along the demand curve for the labor "covered" by the monopoly to a level above that of a competitive unionism. This is the direct relative wage impact of the labor monopoly. Since the demand curve for labor covered by a successful monopolist will be negatively inclined, the rise in the wage rate will cause employment in the covered field to fall below its competitive level. This is the direct relative employment effect of the monopoly.

The rise in the wage rate for covered labor also will cause the demand schedules for substitutes of the covered labor to rise and those for complements to fall. Therefore, "employment" of substitutes will tend to rise, of complements to fall. These are the indirect employment effects. If the supply schedules of the substitutes and complements are infinitely elastic, there will be no changes in their prices, but if the supply schedules are positively inclined, prices of substitutes will rise, prices of complements will fall. These are the indirect relative price effects.

Will there be any tendency for the direct relative wage effects of the same monopolist at different times or among different monopolists at the same time to be correlated with the direct and indirect relative employment effects? In one important sense the answer is surely "yes," for *un*successful monopolists will cause neither wage nor employment effects. But what about the correlation for successful monopolists?

Refer to Fig. 2. The curve $\overline{DD}$ is the demand curve, $\overline{MR}$ the corresponding marginal revenue curve, and $\overline{pS}$ the supply curve of labor

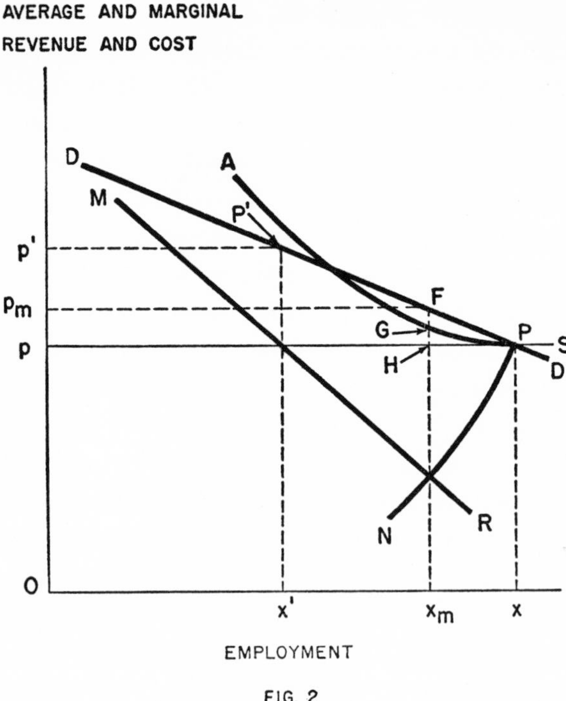

FIG. 2

in the covered area. In the absence of monopoly the wage rate would be Op and employment would be Ox. If monopolizing were a costless activity to the monopolist, he would drive the wage rate to Op′ and employment to Ox′. For some problems it does no harm to assume that monopolizing is costless. But for others, including some discussed in this chapter, it is essential to assume that monopolizing is an expensive business in which the costs of driving the wage rate above Op may in some cases increase rapidly as the wage rate increases.

The curve $\overline{AP}$ in Fig. 2 is the sum of the supply price, Op, and the costs of monopolizing per unit of employment; the curve $\overline{NP}$ is the corresponding marginal cost curve. The monopolist will maximize his net receipts by driving the wage rate to Op_m, employment thus to Ox_m, the employment level at which his marginal costs equal his marginal receipts.[3] The monopolist's net revenue is $\overline{GF} \times Ox_m$.

[3] In Fig. 2 marginal costs $\overline{NP}$ are positive at all levels of employment. This is not necessary, however; both marginal costs and marginal revenue may be negative at some

This section is largely an analysis of certain systematic differences in cost and demand conditions for a given monopolist over time and among different monopolists at a given time. It is clear from Fig. 1 that insofar as the differences are in cost rather than demand conditions, the resulting direct wage and employment effects, taken numerically, will be positively correlated. On the other hand, differences in demand conditions among successful monopolists lead to wage and employment effects whose correlation, plus or minus, is sensitive to assumptions made about the *curvature* as well as the *position* of both the cost and demand curves. Thus I am unable to predict that in general there will be a high correlation between the relative wage and employment effects. The same statement holds for the correlation between the direct wage impact and the indirect effects on the employment of substitutes and complements. The latter effects depend not only on the size of the direct wage effects but also on the cross elasticities of demand and the elasticities of supply of the substitutes and complements.

Where does the union fit into this scheme? For purposes of analysis I make two alternative extreme assumptions about the residual income recipients of monopoly unionism. Consider first the "boss-dominated" union, one that behaves as though the residual income recipients of the monopoly gains were the union "bosses." Employees in the field covered by the monopoly, though they may be "members" of the union, are simply hired hands who are paid competitive wages by the bosses for the monopolizing services such as striking and picketing they perform. Ideally, in such a union there would be a check-off of union "dues" for all covered employees amounting (per unit of employment) to $\overline{GF}$ plus the fraction of $\overline{HG}$ that is not "wages" paid to covered employees for services performed for the

---

levels of employment and even may be equal where both are negative. Thus the monopoly equilibrium point, F, may be one at which the demand curve is inelastic.

Notice also that if monopolizing costs rise rapidly enough as wages are increased above Op, the average cost curve $\overline{AP}$ may lie entirely above the demand curve. Thus monopolizing may fail to occur even in situations in which the demand curve is not highly elastic in the neighborhood of the point P.

union. Given such a check-off, the closed shop and similar arrangements would be superfluous. A complete check-off may be more costly, however, than to require that all covered employees be members of the union and to collect the dues directly from the members. Thus the closed shop and like devices are simply substitutes for the check-off in the boss-dominated union. In either case, the device for rationing employment in the covered area is the dues charge.

Notice that in the boss-dominated union, though the demand price of labor is above the supply price if the union is successful, no part of the difference goes to covered employees by virtue of their being covered employees. Thus in the presence of the boss-dominated union there will be no queueing up of persons eager to become covered employees in order to receive wages higher than in alternative employments.

Now consider the "employee-dominated" union. In such a union, employment in the covered area is the necessary and sufficient condition for receiving the monopoly gains (dues) that in the boss-dominated union go to the bosses. (In the employee-dominated union, the union officers may be viewed simply as employees of the union receiving a competitive wage for the monopolizing services they perform.) The employee-dominated union, unlike the boss-dominated union, will face a queueing up of persons eager for covered employment in order to partake of the monopoly gains and *must* have procedures for deciding which of these persons will be admitted to employment. Furthermore, the employee-monopolizers must have arrangements insuring that the employees who benefit from the monopolizing pay "dues" covering the costs (per unit of employment), $\overline{HG}$, of monopolizing. In addition, if within the covered area some employment opportunities offer greater monopoly gains than others, there must be rules for deciding who is to get the plums.

The list of rules and procedures for solving these problems in the variety in which they appear in the real world is a very long one, including much of what are often viewed as "bad" or "monopolistic" practices: the closed or union shop, union hiring halls, state or local licensing, "proficiency" examinations, seniority rules, many of the so-called "make-work," "share-work," and "featherbedding" practices, and nepotistic and discriminatory rules specifying the race, sex, religion, kinship, etc., of those eligible for union membership.

The boss-dominated union uses price rationing methods, the employee-dominated union non-price rationing methods, to decide who is to be employed in the monopolized field. In general, price rationing is much the simpler of the two systems and offers greater opportunities for capitalizing the monopoly gains. It is reasonable to expect, therefore, that the members of the employee-dominated union at any given time would try to find ways of substituting price rationing for non-price rationing. Thus I would expect the members who play key roles in the rationing process to establish rules, *de facto* if not *de jure,* giving preferences in admission to the union to friends and relatives, and permitting the members to receive gifts in kind if not in money from applicants for membership in the union. Indeed, why should the transformation of an employee-dominated union into a boss-dominated union stop before it is complete?

The rationale for unionism in the eyes of the public is that it protects either the interests of labor or the health and safety of the public. The wage gains brought about by a successful boss-dominated union, however, do not go to covered employees. Furthermore, the public tends generally to be somewhat intolerant toward too handsome rewards for the protectors of its health and safety. The more closely a union comes to resemble the successful boss-dominated union, the more likely it is to be viewed as a "racketeering" union and to be harassed by Congressional investigations, district attorneys, and disgruntled union members. Thus I would expect that, typically, monopoly unions would use *both* price rationing and non-price rationing methods.

The total of the dues, fees, taxes, and assessments per unit of employment levied by a union on covered employees cannot overestimate[4] but may underestimate the wage impact (HF in Fig. 2) of a monopoly union. If unions generally were the boss-dominated, price rationing variety, I would expect union dues, broadly measured, to be a first-rate guide to the differences in relative wage impact of

[4] This assumes a conclusion reached earlier: that competitive unions generally will charge negligible dues.

different unions and of a given union over time. The greater the reliance a union places on non-price rationing methods, however, the greater the extent to which that union's dues underestimate its wage effect.

Fortunately, the amount of this bias can be at least crudely estimated from empirical data. The more a given union relies on non-price rationing, the larger the ratio of unaccepted to accepted applicants for membership in the union. Data on union dues together with data on this ratio, therefore, may provide quite good indexes of relative wage impact.

On the other hand, the non-price rationing rules and procedures will tend to be used both by unions that are trying to be monopolists but not succeeding very well and by quite successful monopoly unions. Hence they will have little usefulness as indicators of the relative wage effects of unionism.

The preceding analysis has taken the degree of success of a monopoly union as a given and has inquired into the effects of monopoly unionism. The remainder of the analysis is concerned with factors that make one monopoly union more successful than another and a given monopoly union more successful at one time than another. I examine first the factors underlying the demand curve for covered labor (DD in Fig. 2).

The more elastic is the demand curve for covered labor at the point P and immediately to the left of P, the lower will be the demand schedule relative to the cost schedule ($\overline{AP}$) *for given costs of monopolizing,* the lower will be the relative wage effect, and the more likely that the monopolizing will yield no return.

The elasticity of demand for union labor will be higher, the greater the elasticity of demand for the output of unionized firms. Let ρ denote the ratio of output of unionized forms to the output of highly substitutable products produced in nonunionized firms, e the elasticity of supply of the latter firms, η the elasticity of demand for the output of union and nonunion firms taken together, and η_u the elasticity of demand for the output of the unionized firms. Then:

$$\eta_u = \eta(1 + 1/\rho) + e/\rho.$$

ρ is, of course, approximated fairly closely by the ratio of union employment to non-union employment in firms producing essentially the same product. If, for example, the union has only half organized the industry producing a specified product, ρ is equal to unity, and the elasticity of demand for the output of the union firms will be more than twice—much more if e, the elasticity of supply in non-union firms, is large—the elasticity of demand for the industry output. Thus unions for which ρ is low will tend to have small relative wage effects. There is good sense, therefore, in the common usage of the extent to which a union has organized its industry as an index of its success as a monopoly union.

This is an appropriate place to discuss the common argument that industries characterized by product monopoly are more likely to be fruitful for monopoly unionism than industries that are competitive in product supply.

There are two factors tending to produce such a positive correlation between product and labor monopoly. First, product monopolists like labor monopolists will tend to be more successful in industries in which the elasticity of product demand is low. To the extent that industries characterized by product monopoly have lower elasticity of product demand than other industries, they will tend also to be more attractive to labor monopoly. The essential factor, however, is elasticity of product demand, not product monopoly; there is "correlation" here between labor and product monopoly, but not "causation." However, product monopolists, like labor monopolists, produce at some expense to themselves lowered elasticity of product demand. Thus there will be some complementarity *on the side of monopolizing cost* between product monopolizing activities and labor monopolizing activities. It is only in this sense that product monopolizing is a "cause" of labor monopolizing.

Three factors work the other way. First, I pointed out earlier in connection with competitive unionism that product monopoly employers on the average may "discriminate" slightly more against collective bargaining than competitive employers. They will, therefore, be more costly to organize. Second, product monopoly lowers the demand curve for labor. Labor monopolists surely do not in general prefer lower demand curves for covered labor to higher ones, for the lower the demand curve, the lower the labor monopoly returns. Finally, in an economy such as ours in which enterprise monopoly is unlawful, but monopoly unionism is not, the complementarity in costs between labor and product monopolizing will work to the greatest benefit of monopoly unions if they unionize competitive industries and themselves produce product monopoly conditions that employers, because of the law, could not achieve. Even here, however, there is no incentive for an employee-dominated union to product monopolize an industry unless the fall in the demand schedule for labor resulting from the product monopoly is more than offset in its effects on labor monopoly returns by the readiness with which employers made happy by product monopoly rewards grant wage increases. (A strong product monopoly enforced by a union is more likely for a boss-dominated union, having "business connections" in the industry on the product side, than for an employee-dominated union.)

In my judgment, this analysis leads to the expectation of a small rather than a large correlation between product monopoly and labor monopoly with the causation running more from labor to product monopoly than the reverse.

The substitutes for union labor consist not only of labor in nonunion firms producing commodities that are good substitutes for those of union firms, but also of labor and other resources within union firms that are good factor substitutes for union labor. Therefore, a successful monopoly union will tend to organize labor within union firms that is highly substitutable for the union labor. The labor force within a firm, however, generally will consist of several occupational categories within which there is much substitution, but between which the demand interrelations are those of complements rather than substitutes.

The elasticity of demand for the labor in a given occupational category will tend to be greater the greater the ease with which other resources employed (or potentially employed) by the firm may be substituted for the given labor. For which occupational categories will the "elasticity of factor substitution" be lowest? Economists generally agree that substitution possibilities are least great for skilled craftsman, greatest for unskilled labor. Thus monopoly unionism of skilled craftsmen offers greater likelihood of monopoly returns than monopoly unionism of unskilled workers.

It is sometimes argued that successful monopoly unionism of one occupational category or craft will lead to monopoly unionism of complementary crafts. The issues involved here are almost identical to those discussed above regarding the correlation of product and labor monopolizing.

Consider two complementary *skilled* crafts, A and B, employed in the same industry. If the elasticity of demand for A is low, the elasticity of demand for B also is likely to be low. Thus there will be a tendency, quite apart from monopoly unionism in one craft, for both crafts to be monopoly unionized if one is. Furthermore, because there will be some aspects of monopolizing A that will be complementary on the cost side to monopolizing B, monopoly unionism in A will tend to lower the costs of monopolizing B.

On the other hand, successful monopoly unionism in A will reduce the demand for labor in B, making craft B a less attractive monopolizing opportunity. There is clearly a conflict of interest between employees in A and B; monopoly unionism in B will reduce the demand for labor in A and, therefore, would be opposed by the employees in A. In this respect, then, monopoly unionism in A *raises* the costs of monopolizing B. Thus, though I would expect that often both A and B would be unionized if one was, I would expect this not so much because monopoly unionism in one reduced the costs of monopolizing the other, but because both faced low elasticities of demand. Because successful monopoly unionism of craft B will lower the demand for A, the relative wage effect of A will tend to be lower if B is unionized than if it is not.

Will the employees in A and B belong to the same union? If the union is employee-dominated, those from A have no incentive to admit employees from B into the union except to dominate them—

that is, to forestall successful monopoly unionism on behalf of craft B. Conflicts of interest between A and B will tend to reduce the viability of a monopoly union of both A and B. The conflicts will be small, of course, if the potential relative wage impact of monopoly unionism in A and B taken separately also is small. Thus the bringing together into a single union of a variety of occupational categories in an industry—industrial unionism—is an indication of weak rather than strong monopoly unionism. This is quite consistent with the implications of competitive unionism: industrial unionism is more compatible with competitive unionism than is skilled craft unionism.

If the union is boss-dominated, on the other hand, there are no strong conflicts of interest among complementary occupational categories, since the employees receive no part of the monopoly gains. Indeed, in the boss-dominated union the conflict of interest is between the members as a group and the bosses. Thus a boss-dominated union may very well include complementary crafts. The relative wage impact of the boss-dominated union that includes both of two crafts, A and B, will be distributed between A and B. That is, the relative increase of wages for A will be less great than if B were not also monopoly unionized.

I turn now to factors underlying differences among unions in their costs of monopolizing. Return to Fig. 2. The lower are the costs of monopolizing, the more the cost curve $\overline{AP}$ approaches the supply curve $\overline{pS}$, and the closer the equilibrium point F approaches the "ideal" (for the monopolist) point P′. Thus indexes of the costs of monopolizing that fall as the costs of monopolizing rise will tend to be positively correlated with the relative wage effects of monopolizing.

One of the important factors underlying the cost of monopolizing is the ease with which a union is able to enlist state support in its behalf. Different unions are likely to be very differently situated in this respect. First, a union will tend to obtain state support less expensively if it appears that the supporting legislation will protect the health or safety of the public in some way. Thus unions of doctors are more likely to be helped than unions of dentists and both of these more than unions of automobile and steel workers; similarly unions of workers in building construction and in public transportation as well as unions of barbers and beauticians are likely to be particularly favored groups.

Secondly, monopoly unionism will be favored less or penalized more in communities that are politically "conservative" and "individualistic" than in communities that are "liberal" and "laboristic." Thus monopoly unionism as well as competitive unionism will tend to be less common in the South and in rural communities than outside of the South and in metropolitan communities.

Third, the changes in public policy toward unionism, particularly those occurring in the years of the New Deal, that reduced the penalties imposed on unions for their use of boycotts and other sanctions and increased the penalties on employers for their use of anti-union sanctions, reduced the cost of monopolizing and brought into being new would-be monopoly unions. Classifying unions according to whether they were born before or after the beginning of the New Deal hence classifies them at least crudely by their power to affect relative wages: those born before having greater power than those born after.

It seems very reasonable to suppose that the costs of monopolizing per unit of employment will tend to be greater, the greater the size of the union. For assume that this is not so. Then it is difficult to explain why we do not now have one huge union rather than literally hundreds of more or less autonomous unions. Furthermore, since the costs of monopolizing will tend to include transportation and communication costs, the average costs of monopolizing will tend to be greater the more dispersed geographically are the unionized employers. These two cost factors taken together imply that the costs of monopolizing will be lower and monopoly unionism more successful for craft unionism of workers producing "local market" products (such as haircuts, streetcar rides, medical services, and houses) than for industrial unionism of workers in the huge mass production industries whose plants are widely separated geographically and whose products compete on a national market.

Costs of monopolizing, particularly in an employee-dominated union, will also be greater for employees whose turnover among employments is great, than for employees who tend to be attached to a particular trade. This cost difference leads to the expectation that unionism of skilled, male, and full-time workers will be more successful than unionism of unskilled, female, and casual workers.

In connection with the discussion of monopoly unionism of complementary crafts, I stated that conflict of interest among the union membership would increase the costs of monopoly unionism and hence reduce its chances for success. High and rising unemployment among the union members, particularly during periods of general recession, will tend to cause conflict among the members. Thus the poorer the employment outlook, the weaker the union and the less its wage impact. The unemployment factor will operate to produce procyclical variation in the relative wage impact of monopoly unionism.

Monopoly union wages, however, will tend to respond to changes in the general money wage level with a lag. Refer to Fig. 3. The curve

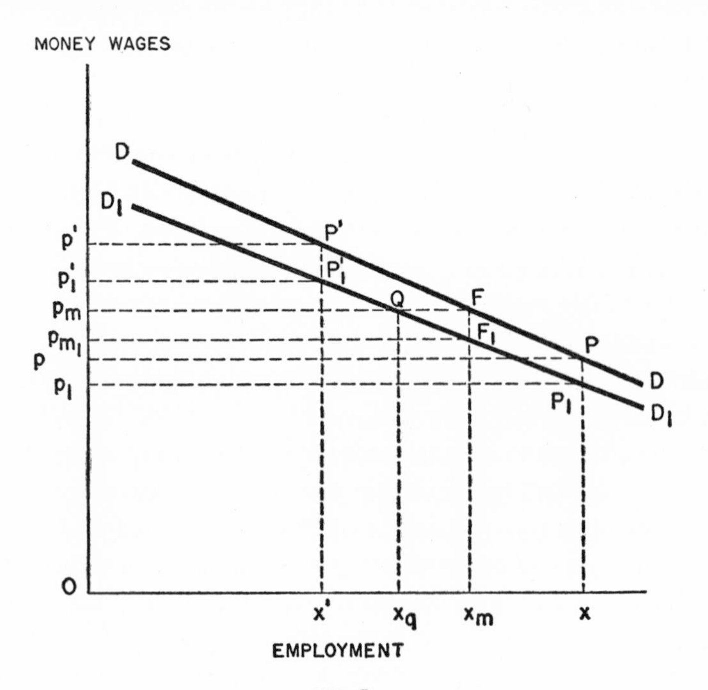

FIG. 3

$\overline{DD}$ is exactly the same as that in Fig. 2 and the points P′, F, and P have the same significance in Fig. 3 as in Fig. 2; that is, P′ is the monopoly equilibrium point assuming no monopolizing costs, F the monopoly equilibrium under monopolizing costs (curve $\overline{AP}$ in Fig. 2), and P is the competitive equilibrium point. Notice that the point F is very substantially below the "ideal" point P′. This reflects my judgment that, in general, monopolizing costs are so substantial that the actual impact of monopoly is only a small fraction of the costless "ideal."

Furthermore, for the present problem, both the demand curve $\overline{DD}$ and the cost curve $\overline{AP}$ in Fig. 2, hence the points P′, F, and P, should be thought of as assuming stable monetary as well as real conditions.

Suppose that money wages and prices generally were to fall by ten per cent under circumstances in which further monetary changes were not expected to take place. Then all of the curves in Fig. 2 would drop by ten per cent along the vertical axis. The curve $\overline{D_1D_1}$ in Fig. 3 is the demand curve $\overline{DD}$ after the ten per cent monetary deflation. In this case the change in monetary conditions produces a ten per cent decline in money wages but no changes in real wages or employment.

Changes in monetary conditions, however, seldom occur under circumstances of such great certainty regarding the future. The kind and degree of uncertainty, however, is not likely to be different for union employees and employers than for nonunion. Therefore, there will be no lag of adjustment of monopoly union wages behind wages in general unless monopoly unionism increases the costs of adjusting money wages.

There is good reason, however, for believing that monopoly unionism will increase such costs. Refer to Fig. 3. Before the ten per cent deflation equilibrium was at point F. Where will it be after the deflation? The union clearly has no incentive to move from this point unless union employers make it expensive for the union to stay there, for the gross *real* monopoly returns to the union at F are much greater after the monetary deflation than before. Thus the union cannot be expected to initiate changes in the collective bargaining agreement.

What can employers do? They can reduce employment from x_m

toward x_q. But notice that unless the reduction of employment substantially increases the costs of monopolizing for the union, the net real monopoly returns to the union may be greater at Q than they were at F before the deflation. The employers can also start cutting wages.

But will union employers do these things? They can expect that if they do, the union will respond by imposing sanctions that will make the reductions in employment or in money wages expensive for the employers. It seems reasonable to suppose that if the deflation occurred after a period of relative monetary stability, employers initially would expect the deflation to be temporary. They would thus tend to hold off doing battle with the union until it became clearer that the costs of changing the wage rates through collective bargaining were less than the costs of continuing with the rates unchanged.

In an unanticipated inflation, the roles of the union and of the union employers—and of the curves $\overline{DD}$ and $\overline{D_1D_1}$—are reversed. The union finds that inflation has wiped out or even more than wiped out its net real monopoly gains and must decide whether the inflation is likely to continue long enough before reversing itself to make the battle with employers worth the cost.

The relative real wage impact of a monopoly union, therefore, will tend to be greatest in the months immediately following a sharp downturn in the general level of money wages and prices, particularly when the downturn follows a period of high level employment and sustained inflation. The 1920–21 downturn is a good example. The relative wage impact will tend to be least at the bottom of a severe, prolonged depression—1933 is such a trough, and during periods of rapid inflation at high levels of employment such as occurred in both World Wars. Even weak unions may look strong if their strength is judged by their relative wage impact in 1921 and 1922, and strong unions may look quite impotent in 1918–20 and in 1943–46.

10

Union Restrictions on Entry*

Gary S. Becker

Economists have long been concerned with the economic power of unions,[1] and in the last twenty years have attempted to determine this power empirically. The principal measure used has been a ratio of the union's wage rate to one that would exist in the union's absence. Most economists would agree that union power has been imperfectly estimated, partly because this measure ignores union effects on nonpecuniary and future income, and partly because it has been difficult to determine wages, especially wages that would exist in the union's absence.[2] The probability of serious error would be reduced if other independent measures were also used. In this chapter, two measures are developed that frequently can be used either to check a relative wage estimate or to measure union power when a relative wage estimate is unavailable. Both incorporate the fact that unions affect the level of employment and the attractiveness of an occupation as well as wages. A union that raises wages attracts people to the union from other occupations, and it becomes necessary to ration entry to the

* I am greatly indebted to Robert Lampman and Philip Nelson for helpful comments and to Eugenia Scandrett for aid in gathering some materials and for very useful criticism of an earlier draft.

[1] Throughout this chapter the word "union" refers to both trade unions and organizations which are in similar economic positions, such as the American Medical Association.

[2] A different criticism is that it may be more important for some problems to measure the effect on the quantity employed than on the income received.

union. One measure of union power is associated with the use of non-price techniques to ration entry, the other with the use of "high" initiation or entrance fees to ration entry.

These two methods of rationing entry not only produce different measures of union power, but also other important differences in admission policies. For example, there is more discrimination against minority groups and more nepotism toward relatives and friends in unions that restrict entry with non-price techniques. The degree of power being the same, unions charging high initiation fees tend to reject fewer applicants. The first section of this chapter relates union power to restrictions on entry and discusses several differences between price and non-price rationing. The second section uses the analysis of the first to understand the actual policies of a few unions.

These two sections seem to demonstrate that union members are better off if initiation fees are used to ration entry, yet it is evident that trade unions rely almost exclusively on non-price rationing. The third and final section tries to reconcile this apparent conflict between actual and rational trade union policy.

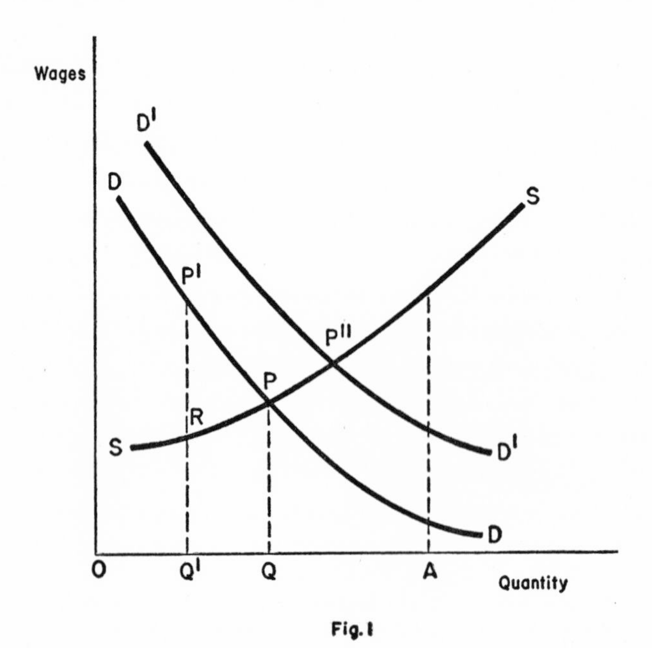

Fig. 1

Consider Fig. 1, where the curves DD and SS represent, respectively, the demand for and supply of a particular factor as a function of its relative wage. In the absence of unions and monopsonists, equilibrium would occur at point P, with PQ the wage rate and OQ the quantity employed. If a union did not change the location of the demand curve it would move along DD to a point like P′ with P′Q′ the new wage rate and OQ′ the new quantity employed. The quantity OA measures the amount that wants to be employed at the union wage rate. The quantity Q′A therefore measures the gap between the quantity available and the quantity demanded. This gap can be closed in three different ways: (a) all applicants could be admitted, but the number of hours worked by the typical union member reduced, (b) some applicants could be arbitrarily excluded, or (c) the number of applicants could be reduced by "high" initiation fees. These three are discussed in turn.

If all applicants were admitted, supply being adjusted entirely through reductions in hours worked, it might be impossible to increase the real income of a typical member. To take an extreme example, let us suppose the supply of persons to a union was infinitely elastic at the income level prevailing under competitive conditions. Then, no matter what the increase in wages, the increase in the number of union members would reduce hours sufficiently to maintain the real incomes prevailing under competitive conditions. In general, the greater the elasticity of supply of persons to a union, the more difficult it is to increase income by reducing hours. Since the long-run supply elasticity to an occupation or industry is probably very high, a reduction in hours would not be a promising way to raise the long-run incomes of union members. The available evidence appears to support this conclusion, for large declines in hours worked by trade union members appear to occur primarily during sharp cyclical or secular declines in demand.[3] Under these conditions a reduction in hours seems like a natural way to ration the limited work available. Reductions in hours to raise long-run incomes appear

[3] I. Sobel, "Collective Bargaining and Decentralization in the Rubber-Tire Industry," *Journal of Political Economy*, Vol. LXII, No. 1 (Feb., 1954), pp. 19–20; S. H. Slichter, *Union Policies and Industrial Management* (Washington, 1941), pp. 269–74.

to be much less common, although it must be admitted that only limited quantitative evidence is available, and I have not systematically examined what is available.[4]

If unions do not reduce long-run supply through a reduction in hours, they must do it through a reduction in numbers. A common way to reduce numbers is to reject arbitrarily some applicants. A strong union—one not faced with much competition from other labor or machinery—would reject many applicants since, over a wide range, income of the average member would be negatively related to the number in the union. There would likewise be an incentive to reduce the number over time by not replacing members who die or retire. On the other hand, a weak union—one faced with intense competition from other labor and machinery—would not reject a large number of applicants, since doing so would cause a reduction in the average member's income. Even a strong union can go too far in the rejection of applicants, for excessive rejections can stimulate the competition from non-union labor.[5] In both strong and weak unions the equilibrium number of members is reached when a further reduction in numbers would reduce the income of the average member.

A diagram is useful in developing some measures of union power. The ratio P′Q′/PQ (in Fig. 1) is the usual relative wage measure of union power. It is tempting to use the ratio OQ/OQ′ as a relative quantity measure of power, for along a given demand curve this quantity measure is directly related to the wage measure. The ranking of the change in quantities, however, could differ considerably from the ranking of the change in wages for unions faced with *different* demand curves.[6]

[4] The building, printing, and a few other unions have negotiated contracts calling for relatively short working days, but white collar workers, most of whom are non-union, have shorter working days than most union members. See S. Brandwein, "Recent Progress Toward Reducing Hours of Work," *Monthly Labor Review*, Vol. 79, No. 11 (Nov., 1956), pp. 1263–65.

[5] For one demonstration of this, see H. G. Lewis, "Competitive and Monopoly Unionism," this volume, pp. 200–201.

[6] Consider two demand curves, the curve DD and a completely inelastic one. A union faced with the inelastic curve could raise its wage rate to infinity without having any effect on the quantity employed. Therefore, the relative wage change would be greater than P′Q′PQ, and the relative quantity change would be less than OQ/OQ′.

If supply were controlled through an arbitrary restriction in the number admitted, the quantity Q′A would measure the number of applicants rejected. An alternative quantity measure, therefore, is $\frac{OA}{OQ'} = 1 + \frac{O'A}{OQ'}$, which measures the number of applicants per union member. This measure equals unity for unions with no economic power, and, more important, it moves in the same direction as the wage measure. A large rise in wages may not greatly decrease the quantity actually employed, but it would (with elastic supply curves) greatly increase the quantity supplied. A large wage increase, therefore, would be associated with a large increase in the number of applicants per union member.

This quantity measure is the ratio of two quantities which in principle are observable at a given time for a given union: actual employment and the quantity seeking employment. This is not true of the relative wage measure, for it is the ratio of two prices that cannot be measured at a given time for a given union. It requires instead measurements either at different times or for different markets at a given time. Whether this is an advantage in fact as well as in principle depends on the ease of measuring the quantity seeking employment (OA).

This relative quantity measure also provides a better estimate of a union's effect on future and non-pecuniary income than does the relative wage measure. The quantity supplied to an occupation is determined by both present and future real income prospects, not by present wages alone. If a union succeeded in improving working conditions, the value of OA/OQ′ would be increased, while the value of P′Q′/PQ may be unchanged. If the future income prospects in an occupation worsened, OA/OQ′ would be reduced, while P′Q′/PQ might again be unchanged.

The quantity supplied is a function of the income prospects of a typical member, which may differ considerably from the income "paid" by employers. This difference is apparent in "racketeering" unions, where part of the income paid by employers is collected by the union "boss" in dues, kickbacks, and bribes. The relative wage measure would often reflect the increase in income paid by employers, while the relative quantity measure would always reflect the increase in income received by a typical member. Since the quantity measure only catches the economic power accruing to a typical member, a union can have appreciable power, yet the relative quantity measure may equal unity.[7]

A union will not move along a given demand curve if it can shift the demand curve, say to D′D′ in Fig. 1. Both employment and income could be raised without raising the value of this relative quantity measure, as illustrated by point P″. This is unlikely, however, because a union has an incentive to move along D′D′ away from P″. A movement away from P″ creates a gap between the quantity of labor demanded and supplied, and thus increases the number of applicants per member. So, even if a union could shift the demand curve for its services, there would still be a positive correlation between the increase in wages and the number of applicants per member.

A union that restricts entry by the "arbitrary" rejection of some applicants does not necessarily select members at random. On the contrary, the union would consider any differences among applicants in choosing among them. For example, if a union did not want colored people in the union, colored applicants would tend to be rejected. If a union preferred sons and nephews of present or former members, they would be admitted more easily than others. Discrimination and nepotism such as this[8] would not cost union members anything as long as the number rejected or accepted because of discrimination or nepotism was less than the number that would be accepted or rejected if new members were chosen at random. This condition is more fully realized in strong unions, since they reject more applicants than do weak unions. When a union can engage in costless discrimination and nepotism, there is every incentive for it to do so. Hence we would

[7] In Fig. 1 let P′Q′ equal the income paid by employers, RQ′ that received by a typical member, and P′R that received by the "boss." The relative quantity measure equals OQ′/OQ′ = 1, although the union has raised the income paid by employers from PQ to P′Q′.

[8] For a general definition of these terms see my *The Economics of Discrimination* (Chicago, 1957), pp. 6–7.

expect discrimination and nepotism to be more prevalent in strong unions.

A union might restrict entry not only by excluding some applicants but also by reducing their number. Suppose a union decided to admit thirty new members from a group of one hundred homogeneous applicants. It could select thirty applicants at random [9] and admit them, or it could substitute an admissions fee for this random mechanism. If the fee were too "low," more than thirty persons would apply and the union would have to select at random thirty persons. If it were too "high," fewer than thirty persons would apply and the union would be unable to secure the desired number. If it were set just "right," exactly thirty persons would apply, and no further rationing would be necessary. Thus an admissions fee could reduce the number of applicants to the desired number. The proceeds, which presumably would be distributed to union members, represent an additional return to the union's economic power.

This equilibrium admissions fee would equal the difference between the present value of the income stream received by a union member and the present value received in the next best occupation. If it were greater, too few people would want to join the union. If it were less, too many people would want to join, with the result that the union could raise the fee and still admit the desired number. Therefore, this fee is an excellent index of a union's economic power, measuring future as well as present income, and implicitly estimating the income expected in comparable occupations. Union economic power would be positively correlated with the size of admissions fees, rather than with the number of applicants per member.

If a union used non-price rationing, rejected applicants might offer bribes to those administering the admissions program. Presumably, the amount offered would be directly related to the union's power. In very strong unions these bribes might be large enough to constitute a major temptation. There is less scope (or perhaps less need) for bribery in a union using price rationing, for if the fee was appropriately set, nothing would be paid sub rosa for admission. Moreover, it

[9] Since the applicants are homogeneous, there is no opportunity to discriminate.

would be difficult to show any favoritism not sanctioned by union members, since this would be relatively easily uncovered by an audit of the books of those in charge.

A union using an admissions fee to ration entry could discriminate against minorities and show favoritism towards relatives, but it would have to pay for this privilege. Consider the union that set an admissions fee high enough to reduce the number of applicants to thirty, the desired number of new members. If the union did not want any colored members and if some of these thirty applicants were colored, it would be necessary to lower the fee in order to secure thirty white applicants. The difference between these two fees would measure the cost of its discrimination against colored people.[10] The amount of discrimination "consumed" is presumably negatively related to its cost or "price." Therefore, the lower the price at which thirty white applicants could be obtained, the greater the incentive to admit colored applicants. Since discrimination is free to unions using non-price rationing, these unions can be expected to discriminate more than other unions.[11]

I have implicitly assumed that the number of persons in a union is independent of admission policies, but I now show that this number varies directly with the degree of price rationing. Under non-price rationing, increased competition from other factors is the only cost of restricting entry. At the margin this cost is balanced against the gain (higher wages) from a reduction in numbers. Under price rationing, foregone admission fees are an additional cost, so that at the margin these two costs must be balanced against the gain from a reduction

[10] Discrimination might take the form of charging colored applicants higher fees as compensation for the disutility of having colored members. The difference between these fees would then measure the cost of discrimination.

[11] In another discussion (*op. cit.*, pp. 54–5) of this subject, I showed that even if discrimination were equally costly in unionized and non-unionized markets, there is apt to be more of it in unionized markets. This conclusion is strengthened when it is recognized that some unions can discriminate at no cost to themselves. I also showed (pp. 35–42) that monopolistic firms would discriminate more than competitive firms, even if discrimination were equally costly to both. The cost of discrimination might be less to monopolistic firms if they were prevented from exploiting fully their monopolistic position. This would be an additional reason why they would discriminate more than competitive firms.

in numbers. If a union converted from non-price to price rationing it would thus increase the marginal cost of a reduction in numbers—approximately by the size of the admissions fee [12]—and this provides an incentive to increase its numbers. It might appear paradoxical that an increase in the entrance fee can result in more, not fewer, admissions. The appearance of a paradox probably stems from an implicit comparison of unions that ration by charging entrance fees with unions that do not ration entry at all. The actual comparison, however, is between unions that use different kinds of rationing. Once this is recognized, the result should not be surprising.

We find, then, that unions using price to ration entry systematically differ from other unions in a few major respects: (1) the present value of their monopoly power can be measured by the size of the admissions fee, while the monopoly power of other unions can be measured by the number of applicants per member; (2) bribery, discrimination, and nepotism would be less important, insofar as admissions are concerned, than in other unions; (3) the relative number rejected would be fewer than in other unions. I now examine several unions and focus my attention on these different effects of price and non-price rationing:

(a). The American Medical Association uses non-price methods to restrict entry, and the extent of the restriction is exhibited by the large number of applicants rejected from medical schools. This has been used as evidence of substantial economic power.[13] Medical schools have been accused, with some justification, I believe, of discrimination against minority groups and of favoritism towards relatives of AMA members. Perhaps this explains why doctors' sons more frequently seem to follow in their fathers' footsteps than do sons of other professional men. Bribes to secure entry to medical schools have also

[12] I say "approximately" because account would be taken of the change in the admissions fee as the number admitted changed.

[13] See M. Friedman and S. Kuznets, *Income from Independent Professional Practice* (New York, 1945), p. 137, and M. Friedman, "Some Comments on the Significance of Labor Unions for Economic Policy," in D. M. Wright (ed.), *The Impact of the Union* (New York, 1951), p. 211.

been reported.[14] It is impossible to determine whether the number admitted to the schools is less than it would be if price were used to ration entry.

(b). The United States uses non-price rationing to restrict the entry of persons from other countries. There is no need to dwell on the large number of persons denied entry, or to spell out the implication that real incomes in the U. S. are considered substantially higher than elsewhere. The discrimination and nepotism in the immigration laws are apparent to all, as exemplified by the almost total exclusion of Asians and the preferential treatment given relatives of United States citizens. It seems likely that immigration restrictions would be weakened if each immigrant were required to pay a "large" entrance fee.

(c). Licenses are required for many activities, such as the sale of liquor, the use of the air waves for radio and television, and the operation of taxicabs. Because new licenses are usually rationed by non-price methods, the economic value of a license can be measured by the relative number of applicants. If old licenses were transferable, the economic value could also be measured by the price of old licenses (see my discussion of taxicabs on pp. 219–20). Recent Congressional hearings uncovered bribery, favoritism and discrimination in the issuance of television licenses by the FCC. Periodic investigations by state and municipal committees disclose similar practices in the issuance of liquor and cab licenses. These practices could be predicted from a knowledge that new licenses are retained by non-price methods.

(d). If, as is generally believed, most trade unions use non-price rationing to restrict entry, their economic power could be measured by the number of applicants per member. Such evidence would indicate that craft unions have more economic power than industrial unions, since it is more difficult to enter craft unions. Direct evidence on the income of industrial and craft unionists tends to support this conclusion. Discrimination against minorities and nepotism towards relatives also appear to be greater in craft unions and greatest in the strongest craft unions. Some exclude minorities (especially Negroes)

[14] See the *New York Times*, Feb. 25, 1958, p. 1.

by constitutional provision,[15] and in some entry is impossible for persons unrelated to a craftsman. "The building trades unions in St. Louis have a very definite policy of keeping the trade in the family and enforce it to such an extent that a boy has as good a chance to get into West Point as into the building trades unless his father or uncle is a building craftsman!"[16]

A trade union may raise wages but have no control over the distribution of new jobs. In a union shop contract this power is nominally[17] controlled by employers. Since a new union member may have no reasonable expectation of finding employment, easy entry would not necessarily indicate that wages have not been raised. The trade union's power would have to be measured by the number of applicants for employment per employed person. The employer, rather than the trade union, would ration entry and could discriminate and show favoritism at no cost to himself. I concluded that craft unions have more power than industrial unions because they reject more applicants and discriminate more. The possibility remains, however, that industrial unions have had the power to raise wages, but have lacked the power to ration jobs.

These four examples are very similar in spite of apparent diversity. Immigration, medicine, television stations and trade unions appear to have little in common, and, indeed, discussions of entry into each usually emphasize unique considerations. Yet unique considerations do not seem so important, as these similarities could be predicted from the knowledge that non-price rationing is used in all four cases.

(e). In New York City a medallion is required to operate a cab,[18] and it is usually transferable from one individual (or company) to another. Since few new medallions are issued[19] the principal way to enter this industry is to buy an old medallion. The price of an old

[15] See H. Northrup, *Organized Labor and the Negro* (New York, 1944).

[16] Bureau of Labor Statistics, *Apprenticeship in Building Construction* (Washington, 1929), p. 9.

[17] I say "nominally" because many contracts are written as union shop contracts to comply with the Taft-Hartley Act, but are in effect closed shop contracts.

[18] This is not the same as the license required to *drive* a cab.

[19] The number of medallions outstanding evidently has declined during the last few years.

medallion, therefore, should approximate the present value of the additional income from operating a cab. In the last few years medallions have sold for about $17,000. At an interest rate of 7% this is equivalent to an annual income of $1,200, implying that the city's reluctance to issue new medallions has raised the income of an owner-operator [20] by about $1,200 per annum. This $1,200 is about 20 per cent of the income he could have earned in another occupation. Although this increase has been gained with but little publicity, it is as large as—and possibly larger than—the increase estimated for a few of the strongest trade unions.[21] There is reason to believe that this simple estimate of the gain to cab operators is more reliable than many estimates of the gains to trade unions. This estimate measures real income and not wages alone, takes account of expected future income as well as present income, and implicitly uses the best estimate of the income that would be received if there were no restrictions on entry.[22]

The sale of medallions seems less affected by discrimination and nepotism than is membership in those trade unions with an equal amount of economic power. Since price is used to ration medallions but not to ration membership in trade unions, this difference is entirely consistent with our earlier analysis.

(f). Although trade unions appear to rely primarily on non-price rationing, initiation fees are also used to ration entry. These fees are greater in craft unions than in industrial ones, thus supporting my earlier conclusion that craft unions have the greater economic power. There is likewise a tendency for stronger craft unions to charge higher fees than others.[23] Some initiation fees amount to several hun-

[20] The number of individual owners is regulated: a medallion owned by an individual can be sold only to another individual.

[21] See S. Sobotka, "Union Influence on Wages: The Construction Industry," *Journal of Political Economy*, Vol. LXI, No. 2 (April, 1953), pp. 127–43; for an estimate of the gain to doctors from restrictions by the AMA, see M. Friedman and S. Kuznets, *op. cit.*, pp. 118–41.

[22] The discussion here also brings out one advantage that price rationing has for policy: it provides a direct and simple measure of economic power. The high price of a medallion informs the city that its restrictions have created a large monopoly income for cab operators.

[23] See, for example, P. Taft, "Dues and Initiation Fees in Labor Unions," *Quarterly Journal of Economics*, Vol. LX, No. 1 (Feb., 1946), pp. 219–32.

dred dollars and one, reported for the Chicago glaziers in the early 1940's, would equal about $3,000 in today's prices.[24]

Even "high" fees, such as the $3,000 reported for the glaziers, seem "low" when compared with the $17,000 price of a taxi medallion or with an estimate of what the fee could be in a strong union. If y equals the yearly income of union members, r the interest rate, and b the ratio of the money value of the gain from being a union member to the income of union members, the equilibrium initiation fee, F, would be approximately by/r.[25] If $b = .2$, and $r = .07$, F would be about 3y. The $3,000 charged by the glaziers is much less than three times a year's income, and is more likely only about ½ a year's income.

Receipts from initiation fees accrue to union members, and an estimate of the present value of the gain to an individual member—call this gain G—is easily obtained. If t is the ratio of newly admitted to old members, G is approximately $\frac{tby}{r^2} = \frac{tF}{r}$.[26] It is directly proportional to union strength and to the turnover of union personnel,[27] while it is inversely proportional to the square of the interest rate used in discounting future values. According to Slichter, t is about .03,[28] and again taking $b = .2$ and $r = .07$, G would be about 1.2y, or about 3/7 F. In a strong union, therefore, the gain from charging high initiation fees may amount to more than a year's income. This only deepens the mystery of why trade unions have not used initiation fees more extensively.

The fact that they do not cannot be explained by difficulties of raising large capital sums, as a trade union is in an excellent position both to "lend" the money and to collect installment payments. Psy-

[24] However, W. Green, former president of the AFL, denied in testimony before Congress that anyone actually paid this fee. See the *New York Times*, March 25, 1941, p. 16.

[25] To be more exact, $F = \frac{by}{r}\,[1 - (1 + r)^{-n}]$, where n equals the number of years an applicant expects to be in the union.

[26] To be more exact, $G = \frac{tby}{r^2}\,[1 - (1 + r)^{-n}]\,[1 - (1 + r)^{-m}]$, where m is the number of years that a member expects to remain in the union.

[27] This is not quite true, since n and m (in the previous footnote) are presumably negatively related to t.

[28] Slichter, *op. cit.*, p. 18.

chic income from nepotism would be a poor substitute for the money income from initiation fees because the number of sons or nephews, as well as the money value placed on this psychic income, would vary widely from member to member. Thus, nepotism would produce a major inequality in the distribution of income among union members. The Taft-Hartley stricture against "excessive" fees cannot explain the low fees since fees were low long before Taft-Hartley was passed.

Likewise, it cannot completely be explained by union weakness, by racketeering in unions, or by any fear that rival unions would be created. The use of non-price rationing by many trade unions tells against these three hypotheses. If a union were controlled by racketeers or had no power, there would not be any rationing (see pp. 213-214). If a union were afraid that applicants would balk at very high fees and create a rival union, it would still charge a fee that equated marginal costs with marginal revenue; marginal costs, however, would include the probability and cost of a rival union. There would again be no place for non-price rationing.

Trade union constitutions are the usual source of data on fees, but the fees in strong locals may be well above the amount specified in national constitutions. Accordingly, available data probably underestimate the fees in strong locals. It is unlikely, however, that this bias is larger than a few thousand dollars.[29]

A trade union often receives substantial government assistance because the occupation of its members is closely related to the health and safety of the public. As government intervention is assumed to be in the public's interest, a union must avoid giving the impression that it greatly benefits from the intervention.[30] A high initiation fee is prima facie evidence of personal gain, while nepotism and discrimination are not easily distinguished from selection by "quality." The control of the AMA over the certification of medical schools would be rapidly revoked if medical schools had to pay the AMA thousands of dollars in order to be certified. Moreover, government assistance is frequently combined with an implicit outlawing of ad-

[29] It would be virtually impossible to conceal extremely large fees, yet I have seen no references to fees above $5,000.

[30] This argument is also made by Lewis, *op. cit.*

missions fees. The AMA controls the licensing of doctors, and in many states the plumbers union controls the licensing of plumbers, but these licenses cannot be sold. This reliance on government assistance is probably a sufficient explanation of the low initiation fees in many trade unions. Others, however, such as the typographical union, seem to be far enough removed from direct government assistance to have less reason to fear government reaction. And although cab operators in New York are entirely dependent on government assistance, for several years they have managed to charge more than $10,000 for a medallion. It would appear, then, that the connection between economic power and government assistance partly, but not entirely, explains the persistence of low initiation fees in strong trade unions.

Initiation fees may be low because trade unions are not interested in pecuniary income alone. For example, fees would be low if union members believed it was "wrong" to require new members to buy their way in, perhaps because many new members would be related to present members.[31] Surely, few Americans want to charge immigrants substantial entrance fees, the reason presumably being that the sale of citizenship is morally repugnant. A similar objection may prevent trade unions from charging high fees. Admittedly, trade unions may have to forfeit more than a year's income, but a substantial amount is also forfeited because entrance fees are not collected from immigrants. It is often asserted, but rarely demonstrated, that trade union decisions are strongly influenced by non-pecuniary motives. If this explanation of low initiation fees is even partly valid, there would be evidence that trade unions *are* willing to forfeit pecuniary income for non-pecuniary income, and it would suggest that the same may also be true of other trade union decisions. It must be emphasized, however, that this discussion of the use of price rationing by trade unions is highly conjectural and tentative. A fuller consideration of the problem may cast doubt on the factors stressed here and uncover others completely ignored.

[31] Since trade unions take collective action, it is not necessary that all members feel this way; only a majority or perhaps only the "important" members need to. Cab operators, on the other hand, take individual action, and a market in medallions would develop unless all operators were against the sale of medallions.

To summarize:

(1) The number of persons trying to enter a union varies directly with its economic power. Since a strong union can only admit some applicants, entry must be rationed. If non-price rationing is used, the union's power can be measured by the number of applicants per member; if price rationing is used, by the admissions fee. These measures are in many ways better than the usual measure of union power, which is the ratio of union wages to the wages that would exist in the union's absence.

(2) If non-price rationing is used, strong unions can discriminate against minorities and show favoritism to relatives and friends at no cost to themselves. This explains why such unions greatly discriminate and show much favoritism. If price rationing is used, unions must pay for discrimination and favoritism, and this discourages such behavior.

If price rationing is used, an admissions fee is received from each new member, and this provides an incentive to admit new members which other unions do not have. It is, therefore, natural to expect unions using price rationing to be less restrictive than other unions with equal power.

(3) An examination of several actual unions clearly showed that the technique used to ration entry not only determined how a union's power could be measured, but also determined the amount of discrimination, favoritism, and exclusiveness in a union.

(4) Price-rationing would seem to be the most "rational" union policy, yet trade unions seldom use it. Two ways to reconcile this apparent conflict between actual and rational policy merit further consideration. One emphasizes that trade union power is often based on government aid, and argues that this aid would be withdrawn if trade unions charged high fees. The other emphasizes that trade union decisions are strongly affected by non-pecuniary factors, and argues that trade unions are unwilling to sell the privilege of membership. There is only limited evidence for either explanation and much further work is needed.

11

Demand Inflation, Cost Inflation, and Collective Bargaining

William Fellner

SINCE the end of the Second World War the countries of the Western world have been living under conditions of inflationary pressure. More recently the conviction has been growing that the price inflation observable in some of the leading Western economies has acquired characteristics different from those of earlier inflationary processes. Earlier inflations were demand inflations, or at least traditional theory interpreted them as such. During World War II there was also demand inflation and in the immediate postwar period this type of inflation continued for some time. Subsequently, in the United States from about 1951 on,[1] a push from the cost side rather than a pull from the demand side has become responsible for the uptrend in the price level, or for part of this uptrend. This is now a widely held view both by advocates and critics of the restrictive monetary policies which were adopted in the United States and in Great Britain in 1955–1957.

[1] As will be seen later, the American general price indexes did not register the inflationary trend from the ending of the first phase of the Korean boom in 1951 to the end of 1955. But this was a consequence of declining agricultural prices. The price index applicable to the value added in the non-agricultural sector did show a rising trend even in those years and this trend accelerated subsequently. After 1955 the general price level also rose (the consumer price index and the over-all GNP deflator with a tendency toward acceleration in the late phases of the expansion period, the wholesale price index with no such tendency).

I feel that this diagnosis points in the right direction for the United States and, in part at least, also for some other Western economies. But the concepts used in forming the diagnosis have not been made clear in the writings concerned with this subject and hence the diagnosis is hazy. An attempt will be made here to give these concepts analytical precision, that is to say, to *formalize their intuitive content.* This attempt will be followed by a discussion of certain analytical conclusions which can be derived with the aid of the concepts here to be developed.

The intuitive content of the distinction between demand inflation and cost inflation is disclosed by the use which has been widely made of it over the past few years. In general, those arguing that we have been witnessing cost inflation have placed the emphasis on the hypothesis that a reduction of aggregate demand would reduce (or has reduced) the degree of resource utilization, and that this consequence would show *not only* temporarily, during a period of adjustment.

More specifically, it has been argued that the coexistence of excess capacity or of the definite easing of a sellers' market situation, with continued and accelerating price inflation, points to a cost-push in contrast to a demand-pull. And it has been argued that in the event of cost inflation, policies of demand limitation may do more harm than good because the price trend may not give way before the degree of employment is greatly reduced.

In the United States, a definite easing of the sellers' market situation was associated with accelerating price inflation in the period preceding the cyclical downturn of 1957. There exists no evidence that getting the price trend under control would require a very substantial reduction of the degree of employment either in the United States or in other countries. But both arguments disclose clearly enough the "intuitive content" of the distinction with which we are concerned. By cost inflation we mean to designate a process which a policy of demand limitation cannot suppress without reducing the degree of employment—indeed, *possibly* without reducing it by an appreciable margin. If inflation is of this kind, cost trends are responsible for the inflation *at the degree of employment at which the inflationary process is observed.* But this, of course, does not imply that demand is a passive factor, because with a lesser aggregate demand the degree of employment would be smaller, and cost inflation does depend on the degree of employment.

To call an inflation demand inflation merely because at a sufficiently reduced level of activity the price level would cease to rise would mean creating a useless concept. On such a definition practically all inflation would be demand inflation. What characterizes demand inflation *in contrast to* cost inflation is that in the event of demand inflation the reduction of aggregate demand flattens the price trend without reducing the level of resource utilization.

It has sometimes been suggested that during a process of demand inflation profits would be rising relative to wages while cost inflation of the wage-push variety would result in a rising share of labor in the national income. This is essentially an extension of a lag hypothesis to a time path of development. If demand pulls up prices and if costs follow with a lag, then profits will squeeze wages along any observable path of the economy; and if wage-costs push up prices with a lag, then the profit share will be squeezed. But the lag hypothesis which is implied here need not always prove realistic. In a continuous process the behavior of employers and of unions in each sector may become adjusted in such a way that the lag disappears and the squeeze does not develop. In each sector price adjustments may take place more or less simultaneously with the "initiating" cost increases, or cost adjustments may be geared to a more or less correctly anticipated pull of demand on prices.

Furthermore, we never know as compared to what distribution of the national income we should be looking for squeezes. There is no reason to assume that aside from these squeezes the relative share of labor would stay constant.

Let me now return to my earlier statement that the concept of cost inflation which is widely implied in the uses to which this concept has been put must be related to the effect of demand limitations on the degree of resource utilization. I shall try to make suggestions as to how far it is possible to get with this concept along these lines, and as to where it is necessary to supplement the distinction between demand inflation and cost inflation with a conceptual distinction of different kind.

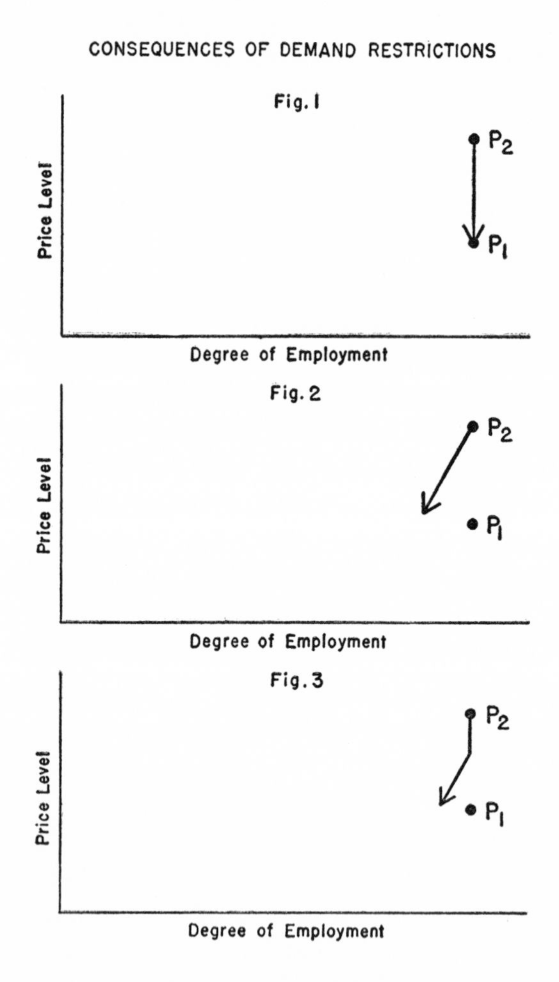

In Figs. 1, 2 and 3 we are looking in period one at the *prospective* price level of period two. The price level of period one is P_1; the prospective price level of period two is P_2. This second (and higher) price level will establish itself if aggregate demand is set at the size required for the inflationary process which we have been observing and which we expect to continue unless our line of policy changes. The process takes place at a degree of employment measured along the abscissa. The degree of employment is defined as one hundred times the number of employed divided by the labor force (possibly with an adjustment for hours performed per week).

We now ask ourselves the question what the consequence would be of restraining aggregate demand for period two by means of monetary-fiscal policy. The line originating in P_2—a vertically downward-moving line in Fig. 1, a leftward-sloping line in Fig. 2, and a line combining these two characteristics with a break in Fig. 3—shows *with what consequences* P_2 is brought down to the P_1 level when aggregate demand is reduced.

There are several reasons why demand restrictions will lower P_2. The lowering of profits and of money wage rates (relative to what is implied in the P_2 level) presumably plays a role in all three cases which are portrayed in these figures. In Figs. 2 and 3 there is also the further possibility that the technological efficiency of the system is greater at lower levels of utilization.

The intricate question arises here as to the time interval after which the consequences of demand restriction are observed in these figures. In a sense this is implicitly decided by the length of the periods to which P_1 and P_2 apply, but to say this settles nothing. I suggest that the best we can do in the present context is to concern ourselves at first with the "long-run" consequences of monetary-fiscal demand restrictions, where the "long-run" will be interpreted, in the Marshallian sense, as the condition to which the system tends if no further disturbances interfere with the adjustments.

However, the fact that the labor force, the capital stock and technological knowledge are gradually increasing—that is, the fact that from period one to period two we "normally" are moving along a growth path—will not be regarded as a "disturbance of equilibrium." We are implying here a concept of dynamic equilibrium. This is why we measure along the abscissa the degree of employment (one hundred minus the percentage of the labor force unemployed), rather than the absolute number of the employed. Also, it will be remembered that absence of monetary-fiscal demand restrictions means *not* unchanging aggregate demand from period one to period two but that trend of demand which results in the rise of prices from the P_1 to the P_2 level.

The situation portrayed in Fig. 1 gives rise to no difficulties of interpretation. The situation is one of demand inflation. Indeed, the traditional theory of inflation is very largely a theory of demand inflation *just because,* with Say's Law (i.e., the Pigou-Patinkin effect) built into one's analytical system, demand restrictions must leave output unchanged, and hence the result must be such as is shown in Fig. 1.

There exist good logical reasons, not merely historical ones, for regarding Fig. 1 as an illustration of demand inflation. For while it is, of course, possible to "object" that in the Fig. 1 situation costs, too, will be pulled up if demand is not restrained, the essential fact here is that for the given degree of employment neither prices nor costs would rise if demand were not inflated. The price trend cannot here be explained by the cost trend.

In the situation portrayed in Fig. 2 we are faced with cost inflation. For a moment we will have to leave the question open whether in some of these Fig. 2 situations we should not say that demand inflation *also* is present. We shall presently decide this question in the negative, but even before explaining this position we may state that in Fig. 2 cost inflation does occur. The fact that the price trend cannot be flattened without a reduction of the level of utilization is a consequence of the *cost trend* at high levels of output.

The only qualification in connection with Fig. 2 arises because of the possibility that a rising trend in "monopoly power" could increase the profits per unit of output at which firms are willing to produce the given outputs. This process *would,* however, be associated with the emergence of a predictable lag favoring profits; in other words, the wage-share in aggregate income would have to become squeezed, even if at each stage the unions were successful in increasing wage rates at the expense of the higher monopoly profits that have become realized.[2] The trends in distributive shares which would be associated

[2] The contrary assumption implies that there has been no increase in the monopoly power of firms in the relevant sense. The argument assumes that there is no appreciable change in the degree of resource-utilization during the inflationary process.

with such a process have been observed neither in the United States nor in the United Kingdom. In the United States the share of corporation profits has diminished since the early part of the present decade; in the United Kingdom the share of company profits seems to have stayed approximately unchanged.[3] This is an essential fact. But in principle "cost inflation," as here defined, includes the case of price increases induced by a rising trend in the monopoly power of firms, and therefore something like "cost or firm-monopoly inflation" would be a better term, at least in principle. However, we shall continue to call the Fig. 2 situation one of cost inflation.

Fig. 3 depicts a blend of demand inflation with cost inflation. In this regard the figure is self-explanatory. By demand restrictions, the price trend could be flattened to some extent at the given degree of employment. But at this degree of employment the cost trend would make it impossible to obtain a horizontal price trend. The vertical stretch of the line originating in P_2 may be longer or shorter, according as demand inflation accounts for more or less in the blend.

At first sight it may seem that the use of these concepts would be made easier if it could be suggested that the situation in Fig. 2 should also be considered a blend of cost inflation with demand inflation, in a sense different from that in which Fig. 3 shows a blend. We could then say that Fig. 2 expresses an inflation which contains more of the demand-inflation constituent and less of the cost-inflation constituent if the line originating in P_2 is steep, and that the figure expresses an inflation containing more of the cost-inflation constituent and less of the demand-inflation constituent if the line is flat. But in reality it would be very confusing to make this particular transition a matter of gradations. Only Fig. 3, not also (in a different sense) Fig. 2, illustrates a *useful* concept of blending.

It is evident that the question whether the line originating in P_2 of Fig. 2 is steep or flat does possess great significance. But this merely

[3] For the United States, see U .S. Congress, Joint Economic Committee, *Prices, Productivity and Incomes* (perhaps particularly Table 11 on page 98); for the United Kingdom see, for example, the materials presented in the "Cohen Council" Report to which more precise reference will be made later.

means that we need further distinctions here, in addition to the distinction between demand and cost inflation. We cannot take care of this further problem by stating that the inflation of Fig. 2 becomes increasingly "demand-like" (less and less "cost-like") as the line becomes increasingly steep.

To be sure, along a steep line, a 10 per cent increase in aggregate demand results in more inflation than does this same increase along a flatter line. But this is because with a steep line *costs* increase more when demand is raised by 10 per cent; with a flat line the same increase in aggregate demand leads to less inflation because *costs* increase less. Consequently, we cannot say that the inflation expressed by the steep line is less "cost-like" than that expressed by a flat line. In Fig. 2 these two types of inflation cannot be said to shade over into one another. Fig. 2 must be interpreted as expressing cost inflation, regardless of the steepness of the line originating in P_2.

What must, of course, be realized is that even in Fig. 2 there is a demand factor behind the cost inflation, because the degree of cost inflation depends on the level of utilization and this in turn depends on demand. In Fig. 2 the demand factor is *behind* the cost inflation in this sense, while in Fig. 1 the demand factor is in the foreground and cost movements on any given level of utilization are merely induced by movements in demand. But *if* we wish to draw a distinction between these two types of inflation, then we cannot qualify the cost-inflation diagnosis for Fig. 2 by pointing out that even here there is a demand factor behind the scene. The existence of a demand factor in the background must simply be taken for granted.

The demand factor does not gain in importance at the expense of the cost factor as the line originating in P_2 becomes steeper, except that when the line becomes vertical the cost factor drops out of the causal mechanism. At that stage the cost trend for a given degree of employment becomes merely an induced trend, a trend induced by demand. Until the line becomes literally vertical we must place the emphasis on the fact that at any given degree of employment the observable inflation is caused by the cost trend, and, therefore, is cost inflation. This is how we must proceed *if the problem at hand makes it pragmatically desirable at all to distinguish between demand inflation and cost inflation.*[4]

Failure of a conceptual distinction to perform well in such a transition is a weakness of the distinction. What was said in explanation of our Figs. 1, 2 and 3 establishes the fact, I think, that the distinction in question is nevertheless useful. However, what was added subsequently suggests that in situations where it is pragmatically desirable to draw a distinction between demand inflation and cost inflation it is necessary to add a further distinction between cost inflation with different slopes. I mean, of course, slopes of the line originating in P_2. The steepness of this line depends on how high the degree of employment is at which the forces of cost-inflation give way.

There exists good reason to expect that if cost inflation is of the wage-push variety, the short-run course of the line originating in P_2 will be flatter than its long-run course. In other words, to stop the inflation requires creating more unemployment for a limited period than in the long run. This is in part a consequence of various delayed effects of the preceding inflationary movement. In particular, it is very likely that inflationary wage demands are partly induced by past price increases. These may generate the expectation of further increases in the cost of living, or they may generate higher wage demands to compensate workers for what may have been an *unexpected* past increase in prices, or they may automatically result in greater wage increases as a consequence of escalator clauses in the wage agreements. Furthermore, past price increases and the expectation of further price increases make employers willing to grant greater raises to workers. Consequently, it very likely takes more unemployment to stop wage-cost inflation if the recent past has been inflationary than if it has not been.

Wage-push inflation stops at some reduced degree of employment because the workers who are not continuously employed exert pressure toward union policies that carry more promise of wider employ-

[4] In other words, one's inclination not to distinguish a Fig. 1 situation from a Fig. 2 situation with a very steep line must be satisfied by not drawing a distinction between demand inflation and cost inflation whenever sufficiently great steepness of the line can be taken for granted.

ment than of a significant yearly rate of increase in money wage rates. And employers get more resistant to high wage claims if they observe that setting high prices for their own product brings *appreciable* losses in sales volume. In the wage bargains both these restraining influences gain in strength if no further increases in the general price level are expected, and if no losses in living standards have arisen to workers (no windfalls to employers) from unexpected price increases in the recent past. It is, therefore, very likely that the restraint will reach the no-inflation point at a higher degree of employment if the recent past has already been non-inflationary than if there has occurred an appreciable inflationary movement. This in itself means that in the short run demand restrictions are very likely to move the P_2 point of Fig. 2 to the P_1 level along a line which is flatter than that applying to the long run.[5]

There exists also another important reason. The lowering of the degree of employment from, say, 97 per cent to 95 per cent will usually lead the economy through a cyclical detour. At first business inventories prove oversized and there develops excess capacity in equipment. The excess capital must become eliminated through obsolescence and/or "depreciation" before the economy can return to its

[5] If, *aside from* a period of adjustment during which price stability is achieved at the cost of temporary contraction and during which price-expectations are made non-inflationary, the degree of employment would not have to be reduced *at all* to keep the price level constant, then the inflation would prove to be "demand inflation," not wage-cost inflation. This would be so even if the preceding periods of rising prices had given the appearance that rising wage claims were generating the process. We have here an advantage of our conceptual framework, since in such circumstances the earlier, rising wage claims would not have expressed efforts of various groups to gain at each other's expense but would merely have reflected the inflationary expectations and the moves of the public to secure compensation for the expected price increases. In this event, it is possible to break the whole process by inducing non-inflationary expectations. At the very beginning of this time sequence, there presumably would have to be a demand-induced rise in the price level and with the aid of our concepts we would diagnose the subsequent process also as demand inflation. Wage-push inflation, on the other hand, is rooted in efforts to make gains in real terms, coupled with efforts to get compensation for *cost-induced* price increases. Since the efforts to make gains in real terms cannot be eliminated at the unchanging degree of employment (regardless of wehther price expectations are or are not inflationary) the degree of employment will here have to be reduced to stop inflation. But it will have to be reduced by a smaller margin after completion of an adjustment during which expectations become non-inflationary.

growth path.[6] For this reason, too, stopping the inflationary movement is very likely to require more unemployment in the short run than in the long run.

The first of these reasons—the further inflationary expectations induced by past cost inflation and the wage demands and wage concessions stemming fom unexpected past price increases—also explain why wage-push inflation is very likely to show an *accelerating* tendency. The process starts by the effort of some groups to gain at the expense of others in real terms. Aggregate income is insufficient to satisfy all claims, but the wage-and-price increases in some sectors catch other sectors unawares. The gains are partly offset by a subsequent wage pull on the other sectors, that is, by price increases. In the subsequent phase, any group attempting to make gains in real terms is almost certain to claim a compensation for price increases as well as to make a bid for a relative improvement in real terms. In such circumstances, after a while one must run fast in order to stand still, and in reality one wants to get ahead rather than merely stand still.

It is possible to maintain that with perfect foresight and full rationality the expectational mechanism would produce no acceleration (and, in general, would not operate in this or any similar fashion). The direct and indirect consequences of next period's wage increases would become clear. Each adjustment in money-income rates would be proportioned in such a way that the results should be a distribution of income acceptable to all, in view of everybody else's money income and in view of the price level which will rule. The objection that no distribution might prove acceptable to all could conceivably be brushed aside with reference to the fact that, as things actually happen, some distribution does become established and *is* accepted for each period. But this is not a convincing set of assumptions. On these assumptions of perfect foresight and rationality, adjustments in the distribution of real income would not have to be made indirectly by

[6] Even in the situation expressed by Fig. 1 there may well be a cyclical detour (i.e., the *short-run* shape of the line originating in P_2 may not be vertical), because an inflationary period may bring types of activity which cease to be profitable when the price level is stabilized. Hence structural rearrangements may be needed.

the cumbersome method of price inflation, but could take place at a constant price level. We could obtain the given degree of employment without inflation. No group would need inflation for achieving its objectives if all objectives were expressible in real terms and if the price-increases took no group by surprise. To explain why the system shows resistance to price-level stabilization at high levels of employment we must *either* substitute money illusion for the rationality assumption *or* must significantly relax the assumption of perfect foresight. Unless we make money illusion the cornerstone of our interpretation, the meaning of wage-push inflation is that it benefits some by catching part of the population unawares (even if employers *within* each individual wage-push sector should adjust their prices promptly). This suggests a subsequent catching-up process and a tendency toward acceleration.

A question already touched upon in our examination of short-run distortions directs attention to an analytical problem which calls for further discussion here. We said that lowering the degree of employment in the long run from, say, 97 per cent to 95 per cent, requires a cyclical detour through a degree of employment which falls short of 95 per cent. This is because of the initial existence of excess capacity at the 95 per cent level of activity. The excess capacity must disappear before the economy can get back on its normal growth path.

Could it not, however, be argued that even after the disappearance of excess capacity it is impossible to get back on the growth path with, say, a 5 per cent rate of permanent unemployment? Could it not be argued that as long as unemployment of this size exists, any investment that is allowed to develop will assume the form of employing more labor along with more capital rather than of using more capital per unit of labor? If this were the case, we would have to conclude that the unemployment rate can be kept at a 5 per cent level only by means of *suppressing all or most of the investment* required for matching savings (so that at the end we arrive at near-static equilibrium with such a low level of employment and with so much "disappearance of excess capacity" that saving corresponds merely to what is absorbable by the needs of employing the additions to the population with an unchanging capital-labor ratio). To put it somewhat crudely, could it not be argued that appreciable growth is incompatible with a permanent slack of labor?

The difficulty with this argument is that the last sentence does indeed put it somewhat crudely, and the refinements bring out decisive qualifications for a whole range of possible unemployment. After all, why is *any* unemployment compatible with vigorous growth and the use of more capital per unit of labor? According to the figures surveyed and discussed by Lord Beveridge, the average level of unemployment among British organized labor seems to have been 5 per cent or more in the decades prior to the First World War, and there occurred, of course, major cyclical swings around the averages. Much of this period showed significant growth rates and the capital stock grew much more rapidly than the employed labor force.

The answer clearly is that what matters here is not the unemployment rate as such but the ease or difficulty with which employers can hire additional labor. For example, if there are fewer suitable unemployed than job vacancies, employers must be prepared to get any additional labor they might need (beyond the equivalent of the gradual increase in the labor force) by bidding workers away from other employers. This cannot be done at the going wage rates. Usually an appreciable wage differential is required for inducing workers to change jobs. Increasing the capital-labor ratio then becomes a superior alternative to horizontal expansion from the individual employer's point of view. Inducements do exist in such circumstances for using more capital per unit of labor and for offsetting or reducing by "innovation" the tendency toward diminishing returns. These required inducements develop not merely if the aggregative vacancies-to-unemployed ratio exceeds one. It is necessary to consider the distribution of the unemployed by regions and specializations (which does, however, become gradually changed through mobility), and it is necessary to consider the quality of the work force in the slack. The second of these two points is frequently disregarded, but it is of very great importance. Ask any employer what compensation he would demand to accept an arrangement by which he will select his workers from the remaining batch of availables, when others have already made *their* choices. The answer will be that he demands significant compensation, except in circumstances when the number of availables is very great, so that even the employer at the end of the queue has a good chance of being faced with a last batch that includes good workers, workers with a distribution of qualities fitting the needs.

What I am saying here implies that the labor force at large includes more inferior workers than the number of jobs that can be filled with such workers at a non-diminishing financial return to employers (given the wage rates). The experience with high levels of activity leaves little doubt in this regard. Consequently, unemployment has got to be large to eliminate a "bottleneck in good workers," and unless this bottleneck is eliminated, there will be a strong inducement to invest in processes requiring a higher capital-labor ratio and to offset or reduce by innovation the tendency toward diminishing returns. If the marginal productivity theory is used, the observable distributive shares may be said to indicate that in the range of yearly changes in the capital-labor ratio the tendency toward diminishing returns works very mildly, even aside from innovations.[7]

The fact remains, nevertheless, that a policy maintaining a large rate of unemployment would have to suppress much if not all of the observable growth. This is because a policy that is confronted with inflation, and hence becomes restrictionist as soon as unemployment declines below a *large* percentage of the labor force, would have to become restrictionist as soon as the capital stock rises more rapidly than does the labor force itself through new additions. The difficulty develops because when unemployment is large, employers can offer employment to the unemployed without running into diminishing returns. They will not raise the capital-labor ratio.

It is impossible to locate the critical point precisely on the basis of the available empirical evidence. To me it seems improbable that *this particular difficulty* should acquire major proportions when, say, 90 per cent to 95 per cent of the labor force is normally employed, although it is conceivable that in such a situation growth would have

[7] On the assumptions underlying this theory, the partial elasticities of the production function can be deduced from the observable distributive shares.

to be somewhat smaller than with a normal employment rate of, say, 97 per cent. The possibility of slower growth exists because, before all the current savings are invested, the diminishing returns from rising capital-labor ratios *might* start getting more costly than the diminishing returns from employing less efficient labor, and improvements could, of course, be used to offset either of these two types of diminishing returns.

Chronic unemployment of major proportions would give rise to this difficulty in a major way, and unemployment of major proportions would, of course, be thoroughly intolerable from a social and political point of view. The growth-rates dampening effect we have been considering in the present section might not yet be of very great significance at degrees of unemployment which are already excluded by social and political considerations. But empirical evidence is lacking in this regard.

The countries facing appreciable wage-push inflation are, therefore, compelled to feel their way through this problem with an experimental attitude. It is quite impossible to arrive at a reasonable judgment concerning the best method of dealing with the problem unless one has at least a tentative estimate of the degree of unemployment at which wage-push inflation would become insignificant. Dissenters from this statement would have to maintain that literally *any* increase in unemployment beyond the degrees observable during strongly inflationary periods is a worse evil than are those of alternative modes of dealing with our difficulties. It seems to me that this would be an extreme position, elevating some arbitrarily defined degree of "just sufficiently 'full' employment" to the status of a quasi-religious dogma.

For example, during the postwar intervals with significant inflationary pressures, the American unemployment ratio was never higher than about 4 per cent.[8] At the end of 1956 this rate of unemployment had prevailed for long enough to show a mature structure. At that

[8] I am disregarding the cyclical recessions of 1948–49 and of 1953–54. During the first of these the unemployment ratio rose to almost 7 per cent (for a very short phase). The second recession was milder. I will return to the *current* recession later in the text.

time the distribution of unemployment by its duration had the following characteristics: about 50 per cent of the unemployed had been unemployed for less than four weeks; only about one-fifth for fifteen weeks or longer; fewer than 10 per cent for twenty-six weeks or longer. When this situation existed, the President of the United States was re-elected by a very great majority. His party did not obtain a majority, but the unemployment problem was hardly a significant national issue during the elections or in general.

Given such a rate of turnover, nevertheless, an appreciable proportion of the labor force must be aware of having an interest in getting new jobs easily, when needed. Furthermore, the proportion showing such awareness and the actual ease of getting new jobs may be quite sensitive to changes in the over-all rate of unemployment.

We do not know what the mature distribution by durations would be of, say, a 5 per cent rate of unemployment. The social consequences of unemployment depend very greatly on its duration. But it would be dogmatic to argue that 4 per cent or 3 per cent (or what not) is the absolute maximum, regardless of what price needs to be paid for achieving this target. In Sweden the observed degree of unemployment in recent inflationary periods has been in the range between 2 per cent and 3 per cent; in Great Britain between 1 per cent and 2 per cent. The "acceptable maximum" is obviously a somewhat flexible concept. Alternatives need to be weighed.

There do, of course, exist several alternatives to somewhat lowering the degree of employment. One of these is "not to be worried too much about inflation." The main difficulty here is that, for reasons explained earlier, wage-push inflation carries a serious threat of acceleration, and accelerating inflation is surely intolerable.

It must be admitted, however, that acceleration cannot be firmly established by methods of empirical analysis. I would say that at least for some countries not only logical reasoning but also the empirical evidence suggests acceleration, but one cannot make a very categoric statement to this effect.

In the United States a significant degree of demand inflation was observable during the first phase of the Korean War. This phase ended in 1951. The over-all price indexes showed no inflationary tendency from the second half of 1951 to about the end of 1955, but this was exclusively a consequence of the fall in agricultural prices during those years. To stop this fall was one of the policy objectives of the United States. The price index applicable to the output produced in the private non-farm sector was rising even during the interval 1951–55. Subsequently, the rise in this implicit price index accelerated, and the general price indexes, too, started registering the inflationary movement to an increasing extent. The easing of sellers' markets and the lowering of the degree of utilization suggests that the inflation of the 'fifties had the characteristics of cost inflation, aside from the early stage of the Korean War. In the twelve-month period just before the current recession the cost-of-living index rose by between 3.5 per cent and 4 per cent; the GNP deflator rose by this percentage even if we compare the calendar year 1956 with the calendar year 1957, part of which already falls in the recession.[9]

In Great Britain retail prices rose at a yearly rate of about 3.5 per cent–4 per cent when in September, 1957, the government greatly increased its effort to cope with the British balance of payments problem and the inflation problem by means of monetary restriction. While price increases were smaller in some of the earlier years, they were greater in others. The interpretation of the previous British trends is particularly difficult because the rise of the prices of imported raw materials was so largely responsible for the price increases up to about 1951. This too must be regarded as cost inflation, although not of the variety which originates in a wage-push. Subsequently, the reduction of food subsidies and further measures of decontrol have influenced the picture.[10]

[9] Toward the end of the cyclical expansion period, acceleration of the movement was observable in the consumer price index (cost of living) and in the GNP deflator, but not in the wholesale price index which rose more in the immediately preceding phase. See *Productivity, Earnings and Prices in the Private Nonagricultural Sector,* a release of the U. S. Department of Labor, May, 1957, and the *Economic Report of the President* (Jan., 1958).

[10] Among the recent British contributions to the analysis of the inflation problem, see J. R. Hicks, "The Instability of Wages," *The Three Banks Review,* No. 31 (Sept., 1956); Ely Devons, "The Wage-Price Spiral," *District Bank Review,* No. 119 (Sept., 1956); J. C. R. Dow, "Analysis of the Generation of Price Inflation," *Oxford Economic Papers,* New Series, Vol. 8, No. 3, and Vol. 9, No. 1 (Oct., 1956 and Feb., 1957); B. C.

As we shall see, in the years just prior to 1957 Great Britain seems to have been faced with a blend of demand inflation and wage-cost inflation such as is expressed by our Fig. 3. Whether these constituents should be said to have accelerated after 1951 depends on our appraisal of how greatly *ceteris paribus* the inflationary movement "should have been" slowed by the change of the import-price trend from unfavorable to favorable in the early 'fifties, and this in turn depends on how great the indirect inflationary effect is which we attribute as a matter of course to rising import prices due to the money-wage claims they generate (that is, on whether this indirect inflationary effect is interpreted as the same kind of inflationary wage-push which is observable when import prices stay unchanged or whether the induced wage-push is merged with the initiating import-price factor and is regarded as part of the import-price-induced inflation).[11] The naked eye sees no acceleration in the British data. What it sees is that inflation proceeded more rapidly in the earlier period of sharply rising import prices. But this does not exclude acceleration of those constituents of the process which do not originate in import prices, directly or indirectly.

In such circumstances, the position that we should experiment with stabilizing a moderate rate of inflation is not a piece of absurdity.

Roberts, "Towards a Rational Wage Structure," *Lloyds Bank Review*, New Series, No. 44 (April, 1957); ——, "National Wage Policy in the Netherlands," *Economica*, New Series, Vol. XXIV, No. 95 (August, 1957); the symposium contained in the *Bulletin of the Oxford University Institute of Statistics*, Vol. 19, No. 4 (Nov., 1957); R. G. D. Allen, *On the Decline of the Value of Money*, The Stamp Memorial Lecture in 1957, University of London; ——, "Movement in Retail Prices Since 1953," *Economica*, New Series, Vol. XXV, No. 97 (February, 1958); F. W. Paish, "Progress, Prices and the Pound," *District Bank Review*, No. 125 (March, 1958); Lionel Robbins, "Thoughts on the Crisis," *Lloyds Bank Review*, New Series, No. 48 (April, 1958); the *First Report of the Council on Prices, Productivity and Incomes* (London, 1958) (the "Cohen Council" report) to be referred to below; also a further contribution by B. C. Roberts to be referred to later.

[11] In a sense, such an induced wage-push, like any other wage-push, is an effort to make gains (avoid losses) at the expense of other groups in the economy. The effort becomes partly or wholly thwarted by money-income adjustments elsewhere in the economy and by further price increases, as is the case with wage-push inflation in general. Still, for some purposes one would like to distinguish an import-price-induced from an initiating push. Something does "accelerate" if the latter gains momentum.

In most countries, prominently including Great Britain, this rate would have to be set with an eye on what the price trends are in other countries, since otherwise balance of payments difficulties would at the end become chronic (unless a system of flexible exchange rates were introduced). But this is another question. As for the threat of acceleration, it could be argued that in the United States the experience with wage-push inflation extends merely over a brief period, and hypotheses concerning the second derivatives of trend-lines require more than a brief period for verification. For Great Britain no more can be said than that there is (at least in my mind) a suspicion of the acceleration of those constituents of the inflationary process originating partly in a pull of demand and partly in a wage-push. Such a suspicion there may exist for other countries too, but an accelerating tendency for wage-push inflation is more indicated by the logical considerations discussed earlier than empirically established (with the United States, perhaps, coming nearest to providing data that actually confirm the hypothesis). Yet even a stable rate of price inflation gives rise to difficulties which could not be overcome quickly.[12] The attitude of trying to let the inflationary process go "within limits" involves substantial risks and these must be set against the costs of experimenting with the no-inflation level of activity.

It is quite possible that the clearer tendency toward acceleration in the United States than elsewhere is a consequence of the fact that in other Western countries that constituent of the process not originating in import prices has *in good part* been demand inflation, while from 1951 on the American process has been wage-push inflation. The argument concerning almost inevitable acceleration relates primarily to wage-push inflation.

The United States has given the most convincing illustration of continuation of the inflationary process after the emergence of excess capacity in equipment and later at growing rates of unemployment. This points to cost inflation. Import prices are of no appreciable importance for the United States. As for trends in distributive shares, after 1951 these have on the whole moved against profits, so that the

[12] See footnote 17.

inflationary movement could hardly have been rooted in rising monopolistic profit margins. The indications here suggest cost inflation of the wage-push variety.

For the United Kingdom, the indications concerning a constituent originating in wage-push are less definite, although most observers would agree that stabilizing the price level by demand restrictions would involve some lowering of the degree of utilization in the long run. This strongly suggests a wage-cost constituent, because it implies that at the former level of utilization the cost trend probably precludes price stabilization (even in periods of favorable trends in import prices).

The mere fact that in Britain in the course of short oscillations the diminution of the monetary demand for labor has tended to be associated with somewhat rising unemployment does not in itself prove the existence of a wage-push constituent in the process, because while *in the short run* this points to a Fig. 2 situation rather than a Fig. 1 situation, we have seen that we must give the system more time than it has in the course of short oscillations to prove whether it conforms to the assumptions of Fig. 1 or of Fig. 2.[13] What matters is that even in the long run there probably will have to be some diminution in the degree of employment if the inflationary process is to be stopped by means of monetary demand-restriction.

But for the United Kingdom there exist very strong indications that an element of demand inflation has also been present (not only in the early postwar phase and in 1950–51, as in the United States, but also in the more recent phases of development). In the first place, in Great Britain the number of unemployed has been kept below the number of unfilled job vacancies most of the time, and this is almost tanta-

[13] The reference here is to the fact that on the occasions on which the vacancies-unemployed ratio turned temporarily from greater than one to smaller than one, this was not only because vacancies declined but also because at the same time the number of the unemployed rose. The vacancies series is notoriously undependable, although it is probably less hazardous to rely on the direction of its movements than on the numbers it indicates at any time. Consequently, the statement in the text may alternatively be said to refer to the following finding: in the course of the British short oscillations, a diminution of unfilled vacancies has tended to be associated with a rise in the degree of unemployment. See, for example, the *First Report of the Council on Prices, Productivity and Incomes* (the "Cohen Council" report), (London, 1958), pp. 68–69.

mount to saying that aggregate demand has exceeded the requirement for producing the given output. While the vacancies series is notoriously undependable, it presumably *understates* the existing number of unfilled vacancies. Furthermore, the hourly earnings of labor have risen appreciably more than wage rates. There may be several reasons for this discrepancy, but we may conclude with confidence that an appreciable part of the discrepancy results from the fact that employers have been granting greater wage increases than those stipulated in the wage agreements with unions.[14] This surely suggests demand inflation, and the general appraisal, therefore, points to the Fig. 3 situation.

I do not know whether this is what the Cohen Council had in mind when diagnosing the British position primarily in terms of a demand-pull rather than a cost-push. To me a reference to Fig. 3, *supra,* would seem to provide the most reasonable interpretation of the Cohen Council's diagnosis. An alternative possibility is that the Council had in mind a Fig. 1 situation in the long run, that is, when the system has adjusted itself to the shift to a restrictive monetary policy of which the Cohen Council approves.[15] Such a diagnosis in terms of Fig. 1 would seem implausible to me. The third possibility is that the Cohen Council had in mind a Fig. 2 situation but meant to call the inflationary process primarily demand inflation rather than cost inflation because of a conviction that the line originating in P_2 of Fig. 2 is very steep. I gave reasons for believing that this way of ranking inflationary situations from "demand-like" to "cost-like" should be avoided. Once we find it pragmatically helpful to draw a distinction between these two types of inflation, we should regard the Fig. 2 situation as cost inflation, and the Fig. 3 situation (which does seem to apply to the United Kingdom) as a blend of the two types. If the vertical stretch of the line originating in P_2 of Fig. 3 is rather long, that is, if the Fig. 1 element rather than the Fig. 2 element predominates in

[14] The wage-rate series is based on the wage agreements.

[15] The Cohen Council did take it for granted that the shift to a more restrictive monetary policy in September, 1957, would lead to some increase of the degree of unemployment beyond the earlier rate of about 1.5%. But it is not quite clear from the report whether according to the Council this increase in the unemployment rate was necessary merely in the short run or also in the long run.

Fig. 3, then the emphasis should be placed primarily on the demand-inflation aspect of the process.

The significance of the demand-inflation aspect in Britain may explain why the chances of avoiding acceleration would have been somewhat greater there than in the United States. The *a priori* expectation of acceleration for wage-push inflation seems justified because of the fact that a compensation for wage-induced price increases is very likely to become added to those wage claims which express bids for relative gains in real terms. It is less convincing to argue that the rate of *demand* inflation could not be stabilized.

But while the threat of acceleration may have been greater in the United States than in Great Britain, this argument does not mean that it would have been reasonable for the British to let inflation go "within limits" rather than to engage in the monetary restrictions which they have recently adopted. In the first place, the United Kingdom has a balance of payments problem that requires careful watching. Unless she adopts a system of flexible exchange rates, she cannot afford to inflate for long at a rate which exceeds that of her customers.[16] Secondly, even if we placed practically all the emphasis on the demand-inflation constituent of the process in Britain and concluded that stabilization of a mild rate of inflation would be possible, this would merely mean that some of the difficulties of the policy of "letting it go within limits" would be smaller. Other difficulties would remain, because in practice even the adjustment to a stable rate of inflation is far from easy.[17] We must remember also that, to the extent

[16] However, the more rapid rate of inflation in Britain than in the United States and in many other countries for the postwar period as a whole was merely in the background of the 1957 situation, since the high degree of devaluation in 1949 gave the British leeway, which does not seem to have been fully used up by 1957. The balance of payments problem of 1957 was a consequence not of current-account deficit, but of the shifting of foreign owners of sterling balances from that currency to others. This presumably was motivated in good part by such factors as the strong position of the German currency, the devaluation of the French, etc. But awareness of the long-run implications of a rapid rate of inflation in Britain must have played a role.

[17] An economy "smoothly geared" to a stable rate of inflation would have to have money rates of interest which are higher by the rate of inflation than what they would be at a stable price level. However, in practice, some liquid assets cannot be made to earn interest (e.g., hand-to-hand currency and probably also the more rapidly circulating check deposits). Also continuous revaluation of payments, based on longer con-

that a country is faced with demand inflation, it can put an end to the process without suffering a loss in the degree of employment in the long run. Therefore, it is not clear at all whether letting the process go within limits compares more or less favorably with alternative attitudes in the event of demand inflation than in that of wage-push inflation.

So far as wage-push inflation—or the wage-push constituent of the process—is concerned, there are two more possibilities in addition to coping with the problem by means of demand restrictions and to letting it go. In the first place, it is possible to introduce governmental wage controls (alone or supplemented by governmental price controls). Since the method necessarily involves controlling individual wage rates, this amounts to excluding the forces of the market from the allocative process at a strategic point. This certainly is a grave disadvantage. It is questionable how much of the market economy would be left after such a reform, even if the administrative decisions were based on an attempt to copy the market forces. What I have said here applies in varying degrees also to such euphemisms for direct controls as "friendly agreements" between governments and national representatives of labor and management. These involve the risk of getting us step by step into an unwanted position.

The objection that, given the degree of monopoly power in Western economies, the market fails to perform its allocative functions properly anyhow, would be unconvincing. What matters mostly in a dynamic economy, from the allocative point of view, is that the allocation of resources should respond properly to changes in relative costs and demands. A constantly rising degree of monopoly would be required to prevent the market from performing satisfactorily in this regard. In reality, the market mechanism brings about these adjustments with much better results than those which could be expected from a complex system of centralized administrative decisions. Also,

---

tracts, would create a significant administrative difficulty, even where revaluation is foreseen in the contract. Last but not least, the difficulties connected with the existence of old contracts stipulating fixed money payments (with no revaluation) would disappear only very gradually.

the market mechanism provides incentives for innovating activity more effectively; and it decentralizes political power with reasonable effectiveness, while comprehensive administrative controls concentrate much additional power in the hands of the central authority.

Most people in the Western economies would agree that (notwithstanding the existing degree of monopoly power) the market mechanism compares favorably with a system of comprehensive direct controls. Still, the degree of monopoly in Western markets creates difficult problems of which the problem of cost inflation is merely one. There remains the possibility of dealing with cost inflation by the extension of anti-trust legislation to the unions, and by increased enforcement efforts against firms possessing monopoly power. The political difficulties would be grave, particularly if I am right in believing that the only reform that would really help here is to reduce the unions by and large to company-size.

It seems to me that in public opinion the conviction *is* gradually gaining ground that complete exemption of labor unions from the anti-trust acts has led to a lopsided situation. After all, unions undoubtedly possess substantial monopoly power, and any wage agreement between employers and unions practices "artificial exclusion" against workers who would be willing to compete with the employed members of the union. Public opinion might well get around to the conviction that it is illogical to exclude significant monopolistic units from certain controls. But reduction of unions to company-size is a specific measure which evidently would create political friction on a very major scale. The risks of this line of action would have to be set against the risks and costs of the alternative lines previously discussed.

My reason for believing that reduction to company-size is at stake here is the following. The essential point is that in a state of very high employment unions should not be a position to get together with employers to raise money wage rates beyond the over-all increase of labor productivity [18] in the economy as a whole. This in turn implies

[18] In precise formulation, this should be "marginal productivity." The somewhat sloppy use of average productivity (man-hour output) in this context assumes constancy of the percentage gap between average and marginal productivity.

that *even when aggregate demand is kept high enough for full employment at a constant general price level,* individual employers in the industries in which labor productivity is rising at a more rapid rate than in the economy as a whole should resist wage claims which would preclude the *lowering* of their prices, and that individual employers in the industries with less rapidly rising productivity should resist wage claims that would result in a steeper increase in their prices than is required for keeping the general price level constant.

A deflationary deviation from this wage-trend norm is *remedied automatically by forces of the free market if aggregate demand is kept at the level here assumed and if employers compete for labor.* An inflationary deviation from the wage-trend norm results in a rising price level and in under-utilization if the monetary authority does not let the aggregate demand increase subsequently, and it leads to a rising price level and full use if aggregate demand is adjusted upward. In the event of an inflationary deviation from the wage-trend norm, the monetary-fiscal authority cannot prevent a rise in the general price level unless it is willing to create the degree of under-utilization at which the inflationary deviation stops. The problem, therefore, is to make inflationary deviations from the wage-trend norm unattractively expensive to the bargaining parties.

As long as the individual employer bargains with the same union which will also be involved in bargaining relations with the other firms of the industry, the firm can obtain a practical guarantee as to the wage rates which will be established in the industry as a whole. The interest of the firm in resisting inflationary wage claims at the risk of labor trouble is greatly reduced, although, perhaps, not reduced to quite the same extent as in the event of industry-wide bargaining. On the other hand, the interest of the employers (and indirectly but obviously also of the workers) in avoiding inflationary wage increases is very significant indeed if there is no reason to assume that the rival producers will be forced into granting the same wage increases, since in this case the risk of being priced out of the market is exceedingly severe. Indeed, in the event of wholly independent bargaining between individual firms and company-sized unions the interest in resisting *any* claim to increased money wage rates becomes very great, because the demand elasticity for the product of the individual firms (the elasticity of E. H. Chamberlin's dd′ curve) is significant. The tendency would be toward deflationary deviations from the wage-trend norm, but we have seen that these deviations would become automatically remedied if aggregate demand were kept at the level required for full utilization at a constant price level.

A reform of this character would constitute a major piece of political surgery which public opinion would hardly accept unless it were convinced of the impossibility of finding easier solutions. There is certainly no good anti-monopolies logic in refusal to regard unions as monopolistic organizations, and, perhaps, there is no good anti-monopolies logic in letting the organized labor of an entire industry be represented by one union while the firms of the same industry are prevented from merging. But most of us would have to witness the failure of other approaches before we would like to consider union-splitting on a major scale.

In terms of basic principles, administrative wage controls (with or without explicit price controls) constitute, of course, a fundamentally different solution from enforcing greater competition in the wage-setting process. But the two have one formal property in common. Of both it could be said that they belong as subheadings under the heading of "coping with inflation by demand restriction." Both types of institutional reform considered in this section aim at assuring full use when demand is restricted to the no-inflation point. Both reforms could be said to aim at changing a wage-push inflation to a demand inflation and at stopping the demand inflation by the restriction of demand. In a formal sense, we might be said to have only two major alternatives, namely, letting the inflation process go or suppressing it by restrictive monetary-fiscal policies; and the two policies considered in the present section, namely, adoption of governmental wage controls or of anti-monopolies measures might be considered subheadings under the second major heading. But it is convenient to regard the last two also as independent headings.

In principle, a fifth possibility should also be considered. This is the alternative of raising investment at the expense of consumption, and of thus reinforcing the productivity trend. This will help, provided that the money-wage increases do not become speeded up at the level of activity which previously was inflationary.

No logical error is involved in this reasoning but the orders of magnitude suggest that the method can make no *major* contribution to solving the problem. If, as is the case, the usual amount of investment in the countries under consideration is normally associated with a yearly growth rate of output in the order of, say, 3 per cent, then even doubling this flow of new investment at the expense of current consumption would yield *appreciably* less than another 3 per cent of growth per year.[19] Minor changes in the investment-consumption ratio could make merely a very minor contribution. After all, where inflation proceeds at a yearly rate of 3 per cent–4 per cent, the output trend would have to speeded up by this percentage to eliminate the inflationary process without a change in the trend in aggregate demand.

We have considered the disadvantages of each alternative at some length, and it is obvious that at the end the choice must depend on individual preferences of an essentially political character. These preferences should, however, be formed in view of empirical observations and analytical results.

So far as my own preferences are concerned, I would first like to see how we come out in the United States and in some other countries with attempts to find the degree of employment at which there exists no appreciable inflationary tendency. To me there seems to be a fairly good chance that this will turn out to be a "socially and politically tolerable level." To be more specific, I would hope that in the United States an average unemployment rate in the general neighborhood of 5 per cent, with some leeway for moderate cyclical swings both ways, would reduce the inflationary forces to relative insignificance. At least for Great Britain and Sweden, the best estimates of the degree of unemployment required for this purpose seem to be appre-

[19] The growth rate of the labor force would, of course, stay unchanged and the rate of technological-organizational progress would not be doubled.

ciably lower. Various factors make the critical level different for different countries.[20] The question whether any given average degree of unemployment is "tolerable" or not is, of course, in part objective, in that at the end political reactions give the answer; the question, however, also has subjective aspects, because those expressing an opinion on such a question are themselves members of a political community. For my part, I would like to say that I attribute great significance to the distribution of unemployment by durations. My own appraisal of just where in the general neighborhood of roughly 5 per cent (with a moderate cyclical leeway in both directions) the limit of the tolerable level lies for the United States would depend to some considerable extent on the duration factor. My appraisal would depend also on the unemployment compensation system and, last but not least, on whether growth rates would or would not keep up well at such degrees of employment.

The fact that at this writing a 7 per cent–8 per cent rate of unemployment,[21] and a 6 per cent shortening of the work-week in manufacturing, have merely slowed the rise in the American price level but have not put an end to it, throws no light on this question. The current recession came after a gradual shift to increasingly tight money. Lags are involved in the workings of the economy, and, in general, it must be expected that in the short run the unemployment required for price stabilization appears to be greater than what it truly is after the adjustments are made.[22] At what stage of such an adjustment process it is desirable to aid cyclical recovery by, say, temporary tax reductions, is a question not concerning us here; yet I will add that I would favor such an aid to recovery at this writing (April, 1958).

[20] The amount of movement between regions and sectors of the economy plays an obvious role here. So does the size of the country. Nor are all the relevant characteristics of the labor organizations the same in the various countries. Not even the definition of "unemployment" is; and the methods of computing the figures are different.

[21] The present unemployment figures are not quite comparable with the figures relating to earlier periods, because of the recent change to a somewhat more comprehensive concept of unemployment. There is reason to believe, however, that numerically the difference is small.

[22] Also, recent rises give the impression of having been induced almost exclusively by an increase in certain agricultural prices, which in turn need to be explained in specific terms rather than in the general terms of aggregate demand-cost relations.

The meaning of an optimistic hypothesis for the long run is that at a "tolerable" level of unemployment (which in the United States nevertheless is very likely to be somewhat higher than 3 per cent–4 per cent) the unions of the industries with high productivity increases will have a much less clear-cut preference for wage increases such as preclude the gradual *lowering* of prices, and that in these same industries the employers will put up a much more determined effort against wage increases of such size; also that consequently in the industries with low productivity increases the rise in wage rates (and here also the *rise* in prices) will be reduced.

For the United Kingdom, the investigations of B. C. Roberts, which were published in the September, 1957, issue of the *London-Cambridge Economic Service,*[23] point to the likelihood that the intensity of the inflationary movement is quite sensitive to changes in the degree of employment. For Sweden, Erik Lundberg has expressed an optimistic view in this regard in his *Business Cycles and Economic Policy.*[24] The American data are inconclusive, but the discussion on page 240 above suggests the possibility of a sensitive relationship here too.

If at the maximum tolerable level of unemployment price inflation should continue or should be resumed, we would then have to see whether this inflation is *and stays* very mild. If the answer should come out in the negative, we will be facing a serious situation.

In this case, my personal preferences would favor increasing the intensity of anti-monopolies policy, and its extension to labor unions with a view to preventing industry-wide wage-setting. The argument that the favorable American trends in real wage rates and in labor's relative share have depended on the strength of unions, or on their size being bigger than that of the firms, seems unconvincing to me.[25]

[23] *London and Cambridge Economic Bulletin,* New Series, No. 23 (Sept., 1957).

[24] This book was published in Swedish in 1953, and the data, therefore, do not extend to recent years. (English translation by James Potter of the London School of Economics, Cambridge, Mass., 1957).

[25] See my *Trends and Cycles in Economic Activity,* Appendix to Part 3 (e.g., pp. 268–270). More specifically, the data indicate the following for the United States: From 1929 to 1950 there was an increase in the relative share of labor (with or without correction for the changing weight of the self-employed), but all of this increase is explained by changes in the composition of output rather than by trends within the

Therefore, I should perhaps say that I would prefer the anti-monopolies line of action not only to a comprehensive system of wage and price controls, but also to experimenting with a tolerable level of unemployment. I do have the first of these two preferences. I do not have the second because, in the ultimately relevant sense, the cost of such an approach might well turn out to be much greater than the cost of the unemployment rate at which inflation ceases to be a significant problem.

I feel moderately optimistic with respect to the degree of employment which would prove compatible in the long run with the insignificance of inflationary tendencies. I feel pessimistic with respect to reforms aiming at a sudden, radical change of the rules applying to unions. A reasonable attitude of balancing full-employment objectives with other objectives has a fair chance of becoming national policy—a common good of otherwise competing political groups—regardless of the give and take that surrounds the shift to such a policy. Furthermore, there does seem to be a gradual change in attitudes to the relationship between the problem of labor unions and the monopoly problem in general.

Why would it then be unwise to give the free-market solution more than a *fair* chance? The reason for this is that some of the observable political forces work step by step in the direction of administrative controls. The road to these would be paved by informal "agreements" which at first would be non-mandatory. Whenever someone suggests that we should set our employment goals without regard to price-stability objectives, and then should take care of the inflation problem "by some other method," he should be required to explain what precisely he has in mind.

---

individual sectors of the economy. For the preceding 50-year period, during which unions were weak, the relative share of labor (with correction for the changing weight of the self-employed) seems to have shown an approximately horizontal trend. But there are indications that during this earlier period, changes in the composition of output, taken in themselves, would have lowered the relative share of labor, so that at least during some sub-periods, trends within the individual sectors are likely to have been more favorable for labor.

12

Wage, Price, and National Income Relationships in Light of Recent Findings on the Behavior of Large Business Corporations

John R. Meyer

RECENT DEVELOPMENTS have seen the emergence of less than fully employed plant capacities in the American economy and at least one consequence has been renewed emphasis by labor unions on the so called "purchasing power" justification or philosophy of higher wages.[1] As presented today the argument does not differ too markedly from earlier statements.[2] The emphasis again is upon promoting increased stability and economic growth through a redistribution of income from corporate profits to labor wages. In the specific context of today's economy, wage increases are emphasized as being necessary if effective consumer demand is to be increased to a point where consumption will be sufficient to utilize fully the increased produc-

[1] "The National Economy in Review: Balanced Economic Growth Needed," as reprinted from the "National Economy" section of the *Report of the Executive Council of the AFL-CIO,* second convention, Atlantic City, New Jersey, December 5th, 1957.

[2] See Robert B. Nathan Associates, Incorporated, *A National Economic Policy for 1949: Analysis Prepared for the Congress of Industrial Organizations,* (Washington, D.C., 1949) and the "Comments on the Steel Report" by Seymour E. Harris, Sumner H. Slichter, and Robert B. Nathan in the *Review of Economics and Statistics,* Vol. XXXI, No. 4 (Nov., 1949). For a more complete historical bibliography on the subject see M. Bronfenbrenner, "A Contribution to the Aggregative Theory of Wages," *Journal of Political Economy,* Vol. LXIV, No. 6 (Dec., 1956), p. 460.

tive capacity put in place during the post-war investment booms.

A certain qualitative difference is discernible, however, between the new and the old statements of the "high-wage case." Greater stress is now placed on the ways in which changing patterns of business behavior will modify the mechanism by which wage changes are translated into changes in the aggregate welfare of the economy. For example, more analysis is made of the ways in which differences in corporate pricing and investment policies will alter the effect upon the economy of collective bargains between union and employer.[3] In the same vein, more attention now is being given to the importance of institutional and market structures in establishing wage-price relationships.[4]

An increased effort has also been directed toward lifting the discussion out of the realm of partial or Marshallian micro-analysis. Properly tracing the demand effects of wage changes virtually requires formulating the problem in terms of a national income model.[5] Such a formulation places the arguments in the broader context needed for public policy discussions and facilitates checking for internal consistency.

The need for such checking seems urgent. For example, it is somewhat confounding and seemingly paradoxical that the unions which advocate wage increases in deflation as a stimulant for the economy commonly will deny that wage increases are inflationary in times of inflation. Conversely, there are those on the other side of the issue who apparently contend that wage increases are inflationary except when there is some unemployment in the economy. It should be

[3] This emphasis upon a behavioral theory of business decisions seems needed since discussions of the implications of wage changes often have floundered in an over-reliance upon normative or marginal theories of business behavior. While the conventional marginal theories are probably quite relevant and pertinent in pointing up long-run tendencies, such tools can be misleading when used to analyze short-period changes. For an example of such a long-run analysis see Milton Friedman, "Some Comments on the Significance of Labor Unions for Economic Policy," in D. M. Wright (ed.), *The Impact of the Union* (New York, 1951).

[4] For example see J. K. Galbraith, "Market Structure and Stabilization Policy," *The Review of Economics and Statistics,* Vol. XXXIX, No. 2 (May, 1957), and "The National Economy in Review," *op. cit.*

[5] The only major alternative, and a rather infeasible one, would be to work with a Walrasian general equilibrium model.

stressed that these positions may only seem to be paradoxical; in reality, there may be very plausible assumptions that will justify such contentions. Evaluation of these possibilities requires, however, a formal analysis that integrates "micro level" behavioral patterns into an aggregate income determination model.

This chapter will attempt a beginning of such a synthesis. Explicitly, an effort will be made to integrate systematically recent findings on the behavior of large corporations into a simple national income model so as better to analyze the possible effects of wage changes on national income. A useful but very primitive income model for this purpose is presented in the following paragraphs; it is stated in terms of comparative statics as a pedagogical convenience —even though a more dynamic statement would clearly be useful. Following that, a simple summary of recent findings on corporation dividend, investment, financial and price policy behavior is presented. An interpretation of some of the more obvious and seemingly plausible implications of these findings for national income determination is then offered; in particular, an effort is made to determine how wage pressures might reshape certain functions in the national income model. The final paragraphs summarize and present some possible implications for public policy; the emphasis in this final discussion is upon determining which policies are consistent and which are inconsistent with the achievement of other economic and social goals.

The essential difference between those who favor and those who oppose wage increases as a method of promoting fuller employment is, when stated in terms of the theory of the firm, that one group emphasizes the cost effects and the other group the demand effects of wage changes. Translated into aggregate terms, the question is whether the effect of wage changes on savings or on investment is emphasized.[6] In simplest essence, the argument at the aggregate

[6] Besides the previously cited pieces by Nathan, Harris, and Slichter, other useful discussions of these questions are to be found in Gottfried Haberler, "Wage Policy, Employment, and Economic Stability," in *The Impact of the Union;* Sumner H. Slichter, "Wage Price Policy and Employment," in *American Economic Review,* Vol. XXXVI, No. 2 (May, 1946); K. E. Boulding, "Collective Bargaining in Fiscal Policy," *Proceedings of Industrial Relations Research Association,* 1949; M. W. Reder, "The Theoretical Prob-

level really involves two elements: (a) differing views about what a wage increase does to the shape of the investment and savings functions; and (b) how much a wage change will shift each of these functions.

The questions involved are analytically similar to those that arose in the late 'thirties about the nature of the Keynesian system and policies. From that discussion a consensus eventually emerged that the major distinction between Keynesian and so-called "classical" models lay in different assumptions about the functional relationship between the money supply and the interest rate.[7] In that case, the explicit mathematical formulation of the different models proved to be a major aid in clarifying the issues and such an exercise would also appear useful here. Following the usual notation, a simple static income determination model can be stated as follows: [8]

---

lems of a National Wage Price Policy," *Canadian Journal of Economics and Political Science*, Vol. 14, No. 1 (February, 1948); W. A. Morton, "Trade Unionism, Full Employment and Inflation," *American Economic Review*, Vol. XL, No. 1 (March, 1950); L. G. Reynolds, "Relations Between Wage Rates, Costs, and Prices," *American Economic Review Supplement* (1942); Sumner H. Slichter, "The Problem of Wage Policy in the Spring of 1947," in the *Review of Economics and Statistics*, Vol. XXIX, No. 3 (Aug., 1947); James Tobin, "Money Wage Rates and Employment," in Seymour E. Harris (ed.), *The New Economics* (New York, 1947); C. E. Lindblom, *Unions and Capitalism* (New Haven, 1949); E. S. Mason, *Economic Concentration and the Monopoly Problem* (Cambridge, Mass., 1957); and James R. Schlesinger, "The Role of the Monetary Environment in Cost-Inflation," *The Southern Economic Journal*, Vol. XXIV, No. 1 (July, 1957).

[7] Taken together with the Keynesian assumption of rigid wages instead of the "classical" marginal productivity model of wage determination, these differences accounted for the major discrepancies in the conclusions and concomitant policy prescriptions of the different models. For example, see J. R. Hicks, "Mr. Keynes and the 'Classics'; a Suggested Interpretation," *Econometrica*, Vol. 5, No. 2 (April, 1937), and Franco Modigliani, "Liquidity Preference and the Theory of Interest and Money," *Econometrica*, Vol. 12, No. 1 (January, 1944).

[8] This model is essentially the same both in statement and notation as the Hicks and Modigliani models, *op. cit.* The analytical approach adopted here is similar, although not identical, to that employed by both J. Tinbergen ("The Significance of Wage Policy for Employment," *International Economic Papers*, [New York, 1951] Vol. I) and M. Bronfenbrenner (*op. cit.*) when analysing similar problems. The principal difference is that Bronfenbrenner, in particular, assumes that the effect of a wage change is the same at all levels of income; in this paper the major emphasis is upon the possibility that the effects are not identical at different income levels. This stress on possible non-linearities in the system explains the heavy reliance in later sections on geometric presentations.

$$(1)\ M_t = M(Y)$$
$$(2)\ M = M_a + M_t$$
$$(3)\ M_a = L\ (Y,r)$$
$$(4)\ I = I\ (Y,r,w)$$
$$(5)\ S = S\ (Y,w)$$
$$(6)\ I = S$$

where M = exogenously determined total money supply;
w = exogenously determined wage rate;
M_t = transactions demand or need for money;
M_a = money held as an asset;
Y = money income;
r = the interest rate;
I = investment;
and S = savings.

The model includes six equations or identities and six unknown or endogenous variables are to be determined. Equation (1) states that the money needed for transaction purposes will be a function of the level of monetary income. (Possible monetary effects of wage rate changes could have been included by putting the wage rate in this equation; since these effects are probably small, and to a certain extent somewhat uncertain, this refinement was foregone.) Equation (2) is an identity stating that the total supply of money equals the supply of money held as an asset plus the supply of money used for transaction purposes. The third equation is a generalized expression of the well-known Keynesian liquidity preference function; it establishes a relationship between the supply of money held as an asset, the level of monetary income, and the interest rate. Equation (4) is the investment function; it differs from the investment functions usually employed in income models (e.g., the Hicks or Modigliani models) in that it includes the wage rate as a determinant of the investment level. Equation (5), the savings function, has been similarly modified. The interest rate also might have been included in the savings equation but it was omitted because of uncertainty about the exact nature of the interest-savings relationship; such an omission also makes the later geometrical presentation of the argument somewhat simpler. Equation (6) is a statement of the usual identity that investment equals savings in equilibrium.

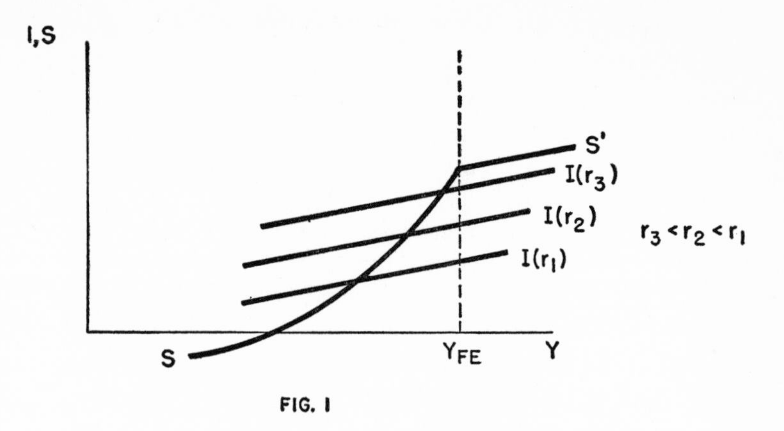

FIG. 1

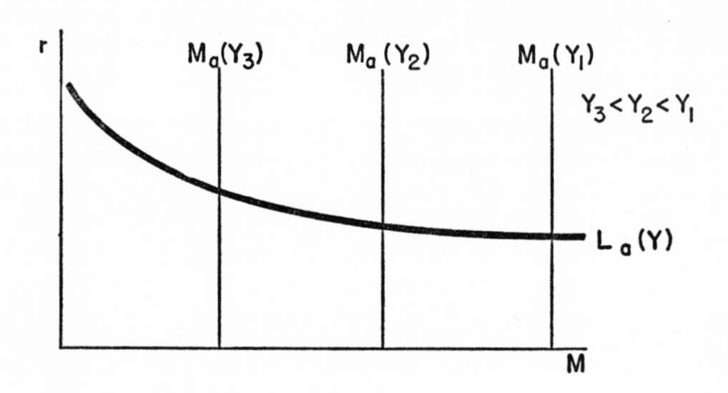

Fig. 2

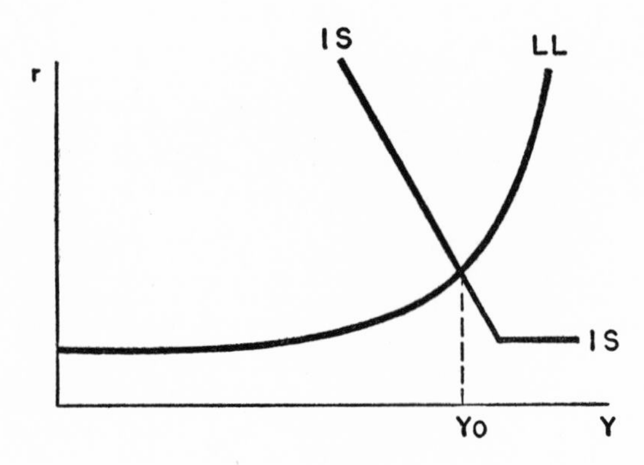

Fig. 3

The above model is incomplete in the sense that it includes only the "monetary" sector. To complete the model one would need additional equations defining the price level, relating physical output to employment, defining the employment level in terms of the monetary wage rate, etc. The argument will be expanded to include these real factors later but for now the omission greatly simplifies the discussion at no serious cost.

A simple geometric representation and solution of the model is shown in Figs. 1, 2 and 3. In Fig. 1 are found the investment and savings functions. Because the investment function has been hypothesized to be sensitive to interest rate changes, several functions have been drawn corresponding to several different interest rates. Thus, as the interest rate falls the investment function shifts upward. A perpendicular dashed line has been inserted on the figure corresponding to what has been designated Y_{FE}, the full employment level of monetary income.

In Fig. 2 the demand and supply situation for monetary assets is represented. The liquidity preference function is a demand function for monetary assets and slopes downward from left to right. As drawn, the liquidity function is Keynesian in the sense that there is a positive interest rate at which an infinite amount of money will be absorbed into the system. This assumption of absolute liquidity preference will be reconsidered (i.e., relaxed) later in the discussion. The vertical lines in Fig. 2, designated $M_a(Y_1)$, represent the supply of money available for asset holding at different levels of income; such functions can be derived from equations (1) and (2) of the model. In drawing the functions it has been assumed that as the level of monetary income increases the supply of money available for asset holding decreases, everything else equal. Fig. 3 brings together the interest rate to income relationships that can be derived from the first two figures. The LL function in Fig. 3 represents all interest rate-income relationships that will equate the demand for money to the supply of money available for asset holding. Similarly, the IS function is the locus of interest and income points that will equate investment and saving. The intersection of these two functions yields the final money income solution to the system; that solution has been designated as

Yo in the diagram. The kink in the IS function occurs at the level of monetary income corresponding to full employment; at higher levels of monetary income, the system inflates symetrically so that consumption and investment maintain their same proportional relationship and the interest rate is unaffected. This is what has been called the "Wicksellian case" of absolute inflation.

In all that precedes the wage rate has been assumed to be set or given. As already noted, the essential problem is determining what a wage increase will do at various levels of income to the savings and investment functions.

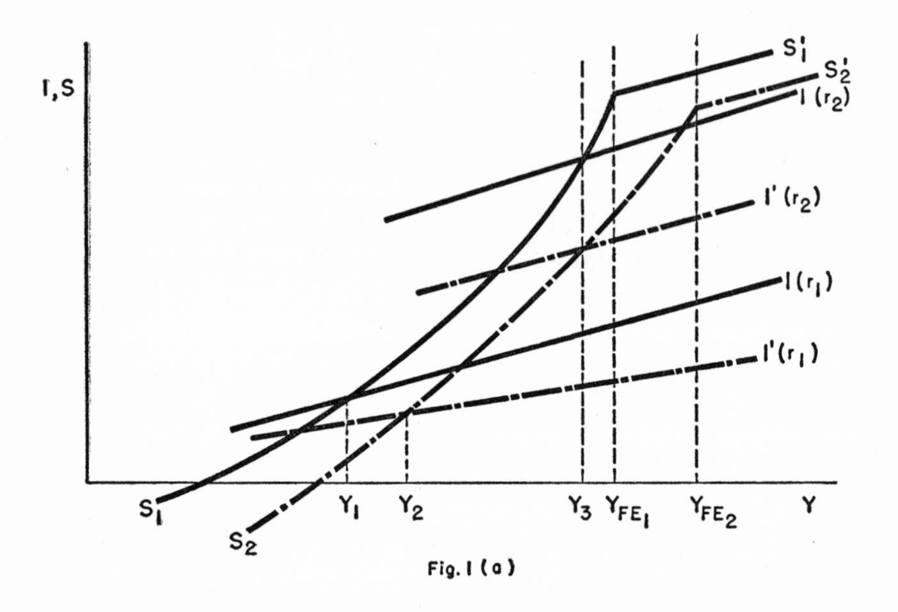

Fig. 1 (a)

One plausible interpretation of the union case for high wages is to be found in Fig. 1(a). There the effect of a wage increase on the investment and savings function has been shown by drawing "before" and "after" functions. The "after" functions are indicated by the interspersed dashed and dotted lines. As drawn, the wage increase has a much larger impact on the savings function at low levels than at high levels of income. Conversely, the wage increase depresses the investment function more at high levels of income than at low levels. As a consequence, the wage increase pushes income up from Y_1 to Y_2

at the low end of the income scale and leaves income unaffected at high levels of activity. Assuming no offsetting changes elsewhere in the economic system, the effect of the wage increase, therefore, would be inflationary at low levels of income and neutral at high levels. (A second full-employment level has been drawn in to indicate that at higher wage levels, a larger monetary income would be needed to sustain full employment.)

This is a simple and primitive version of the high-wage case. Recent developments, mainly the investment boom of 1955–1957, have led to an elaboration of the argument in which the case is made that wage increases would reduce or even eliminate the possibility of price inflation when there is substantial unutilized productive capacity in some sectors of the economy. Also, it is contended that wage increases under such circumstances would lead to fuller use of the available productive facilities. The argument assumes most of the unutilized capacity to be in the consumer goods sector of the economy while the inflationary pressures are generated in the investment goods sector, of which the capital can be hypothesized to be utilized fully.

This elaborated argument obviously involves price effects that cannot be handled within the simplified "monetary-sector-only" model used up to this point. Furthermore, not only must price and physical output relationships be stipulated, but the economy must be broken down into investment and consumer goods sectors. One simple but plausible extension of the model which is compatible with the union argument follows:

$$(7)\quad I = P_i X_i;$$
$$(8)\quad C = P_c X_c;$$
$$(9)\quad Y = C + I;$$
$$(10)\quad N_c = N_c(X_c);$$
$$(11)\quad N_i = N_i(X_i);$$
$$(12)\quad X_i = \overline{X}_i \text{ (given full employment in the investment sector);}$$

and
$$(13)\quad P_c = \overline{P}_c \text{ (given less than full employment in the consumer sector)}$$

where

C = money income spent in the consumer goods sector;
P_i = price of investment goods;

P_c = price of consumer goods;
$\overline{P}_c$ = the fixed, less-than-full-employment price in the consumer goods sector;
X_i = physical output of investment goods;
X_c = physical output of consumer goods;
$\overline{X}_i$ = full employment output in investment sector;
N_i = employment in investment sector;
N_c = employment in consumer sector.

Equations (7), (8), and (9) define the relationship between prices, physical output and money expenditures in the two sectors of the economy and stipulate that the sum of the expenditures in the two sectors must equal total monetary income. Equations (10) and (11) state that employment is a function only of physical output. Equation (12) asserts that there is an upper limit on the physical output of the investment goods sector and that this output is currently being met. By contrast, equation (13) states that the consumer price level is given by exogenous factors as long as the capacity of the sector is less than fully utilized. These last two equations, together with equations (7) and (8), define the investment goods price level and the consumer goods output level, remembering that money income and its composition is defined by equations (1) through (6).

The union case is that wages should be increased to a point that: (a) enough money income is transferred from the investment to the consumer goods sector that the capacity utilization in the investment goods sectors is pulled below full capacity utilization; and (b) capacity utilization in the consumer goods sectors is increased, but not above the point where available capacity is fully used. It should be noted that this assumes that there is more than enough available unused capacity in the consumer goods sector (and also sufficient unemployed labor if consumer goods production is more labor intensive) to carry out this readjustment effectively. Assuming this to be true, no price effects follow from the wage change because it is hypothesized that consumer prices are rigid until full employment of consumer goods' capacity is reached. Furthermore, there should be some downward pressure on investment prices since $P_i = \frac{I}{\overline{X}_i}$ and

I would be reduced by the transfer of money income from profits to wages; meanwhile, $\overline{X}_i$ would be unaffected until investment capacity is less than fully utilized.

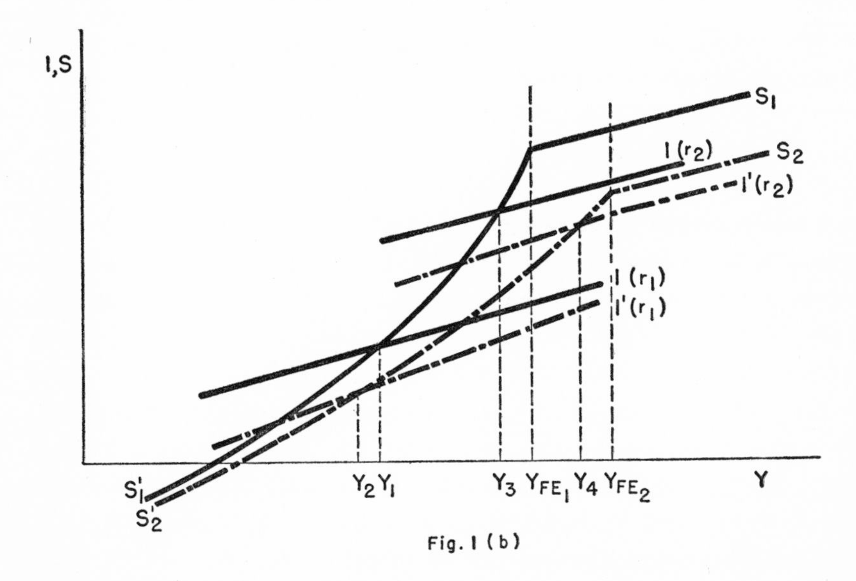

Fig. 1 (b)

This apparently summarizes the essential features of the union argument. The opposed view would interpret the probable outcome of the wage changes quite differently and would also deny the validity of some of the price relationships hypothesized above. In the strongest version of the counter-argument, the contention would be made that the shifts of the investment and savings functions would be such that the effects of a wage increase always would be deflationary at low levels of income and inflationary at high levels. That is, something like the situation diagrammed in Fig. 1(b) would be the outcome of a wage change. At low levels of income the savings function would be little influenced by a wage increase while the investment function would be depressed substantially; conversely, at high levels of income the savings function would be greatly depressed while the investment function would be little depressed. As shown in Fig. 1(b) the total effect of the wage change under these conditions would be to depress the low level of income, Y_1, to an even lower level, Y_2, while the high level of income Y_3 would be pushed up to the level Y_4. The effect of a wage increase, therefore, would be mildly deflationary at low levels of income and, as diagrammed, inflationary at high levels of income.

In a milder and more sophisticated counter-argument, some opponents of the "purchasing power theory" have contended that wage increases are always deflationary, *assuming that the monetary authorities take no offsetting action.* However, they argue, such an assumption about monetary policy seems dubious in a modern democratic society where politicians have learned that small amounts of unemployment can be readily "cured" by simply expanding the money supply.[9] It does not follow, though, in this argument that unemployment induced by wage increases in deflated times, when there is already a good deal of unemployment, can be offset by monetary action. The reasons for this ineffectiveness of monetary policy in really depressed times are usually not explicitly spelled out. One obvious possibility is the existence of a Keynesian liquidity trap. Thus, in the "sophisticated" version of the anti-high-wage argument, wages remain deflationary in really depressed times and inflationary in good times because the deflationary effects of wage increases in good times will be offset by monetary inflation while such an offset is impossible in really depressed periods.

The opponents of the high-wage argument would also contest the price behavior assumptions needed for the labor statement of the case. Prices in their view are likely to respond to wage increases even before full capacity utilization is achieved, at least in many impor-

[9] This more sophisticated argument dominates the discussions cited in footnote 6, but a bit of both arguments can be found in some of the papers. If the assumption that unemployment and expansionary monetary policies are bound to follow wage increases is removed, and the assumption that such an outcome is likely but not certain is inserted in its stead, the above argument becomes very similar to Slichter's presentation of the case. Slichter considers it inevitable and probably desirable that technological gains in our society are going to be realized largely through increased wage payments rather than price reductions. Since he feels that wage increases in deflationary times will heighten the deflation, he advocates that the wage hikes be taken during revival or expansionary periods; while admitting the possibility that this may increase potential inflationary pressures existing during such periods, he does not consider this risk terribly great. In short, Slichter's position is a sort of middle position in which wage increases are considered deflationary during depressed times and only slightly inflationary, at most, during business upswings.

tant sectors of the economy. The net effect, therefore, of wage increase under unbalanced inflationary conditions, such as those recently experienced, would be no real reduction in the demand for investment goods and little reduction in the pressures on investment goods' prices. At the same time, the increased demand for consumer goods brought on by the wage increases would only lead to increased pressures on prices in that sector. The over-all consequence of a wage increase under such conditions thus would be an intensification of the inflationary pressures in the economy.

The crucial question, of course, is: Which of these many assumptions about the economy and the effects of wage increases are correct? Answering such a question means analyzing the consequences of a wage increase upon a whole host of individual decisions. Since many of the most crucial of these decisions are made in or around the modern corporation, it seems particularly imperative to analyse corporation behavior patterns.

Traditional or "marginalist" theories of the firm have concentrated almost exclusively on price-output decisions. Aggregate investment and savings functions, however, will be as much, if not more, a product of corporation financial, dividend, and investment decisions as of price decisions. Therefore, the major categories of corporation decisions—financial, dividend, investment, and price—will each be considered in turn.

The dominant financial characteristic of modern corporations, particularly in the manufacturing sector, has been a fundamental reliance on internal sources of funds.[10] The most plausible explanations of this pattern are a strong aversion on the part of professional man-

[10] In the period between 1947 and 1956, a little over seventy per cent of corporate plant and equipment outlays were financed out of depreciation allowances and retained profits, according to Department of Commerce statistics. Of the remainder, about 20 per cent came from bonds and other long term debts while only an approximate 10 per cent came from new stock issues. The same percentages, remarkably enough, continued to hold through the recent bull market. Furthermore, a very large percentage of the equity and debt issues are accounted for by the regulated public utilities and communication industries. For example, the manufacturing sector financed only about three per cent of its needs from new stock issues during the 1947–56 period and only one per cent in the bull market year of 1956.

agements to the risks involved in utilizing outside sources and a tax structure that treats capital gains more favorably than income. Certain structural changes, like the introduction of the Securities and Exchange Commission, may also have helped by making money raised through public issues more expensive than otherwise would have been the case. It is particularly significant that most of the external financing recently used in the manufacturing sector was confined to a few rapidly growing and relatively competitive industries.[11]

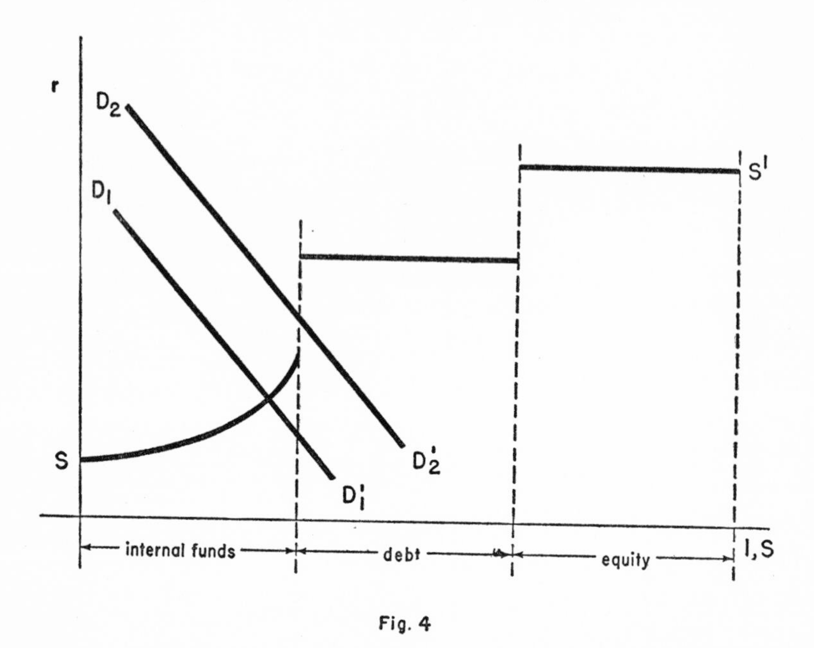

Fig. 4

It would appear therefore that the typical corporation (with the probable exception of those in public utilities and communications) views its supply of funds function as composed of a series of steps, perhaps like the illustrative function shown in Fig. 4.[12] Interpret-

[11] For more detailed statistics and comments on these financial developments see D. H. Brill, "Financing of Capital Formation," in Conference on Research in Income and Wealth, *Problems of Capital Formation Studies in Income and Wealth,* Vol. 19 (Princeton, 1957) and J. Meyer and E. Kuh, *The Investment Decision* (Cambridge, Mass., 1957), Chapter IX.

[12] The function drawn in Fig. 4 is similar, and the underlying rational is also similar, to that developed by E. M. Hoover, "Some Institutional Factors in Business Investment Decisions," *American Economic Review,* Vol. XLIV, No. 2 (May, 1954).

ing the *r* along the vertical axis as a measure of what the firm's management considers the cost of funds to be, the diagram suggests that the typical firm regards internal funds as relatively inexpensive, debt issues as substantially more expensive, and equity issues as quite expensive. The shape of the function implies, moreover, that at given rates the corporation can utilize its various external financial sources up to limits set by the familiar phenomenon of "credit rationing." As illustrated by the two demand curves in Fig. 4, if the demand for investment funds cuts the supply function near the lower end of one of the steps or discontinuities, there can be quite a substantial shift in the demand for investment without a concomitant increase in outlays. On the other hand, growing and competitive firms will use outside funds because their demand for investment outlays is often more than sufficient to exhaust internal sources.

Conservatism has also been observed in the handling of corporate cash balances. It is, for example, fairly well established that corporations, particularly the large ones, tend to increase their relative holdings of liquid funds during recessions and to decrease these holdings during peace-time inflations or expansionary periods.[13] For example, at the end of 1953, a period of mild recession, the ratio of money or near money to total current liabilities for non-financial corporations was approximately .56 while at the end of the second quarter of 1957 it was roughly .43.[14] In large measure the change of the ratio reflects a preference for less liquidity over external borrowing during the recent period of tight money, i.e., for financing inventories by reducing liquidity rather than by borrowing.

Corporation dividend practices are consistent with this basic financial conservatism.[15] If there is to be a heavy reliance on retained

[13] This point was first developed at length by F. A. Lutz, *Corporate Cash Balances 1914–43* (New York, 1945).

[14] Based on Securities and Exchange Commission and *Statistics of Income* data.

[15] The discussion of dividends presented here is heavily dependent on the work of J. Lintner. See his "The Determinants of Corporate Savings," *Savings in the Modern Economy* (Minneapolis, 1953), pp. 230–255, and "Distribution of Income of Corporations Among Dividends, Retained Earnings and Taxes," *American Economic Review* (Proceedings Issue), Vol. XLVI, No. 2 (May, 1956). Also see S. Dobrovalsky, *Corporate Income Retention, 1915–1943* (New York, 1951); F. Modigliani, "Fluctuation in the Savings Income Ratio: A Problem in Economic Forecasting," in Conference on Research in Income and Wealth, *Studies in Income and Wealth,* Part V, Vol. 11; and

earnings as a source for financing corporation expansion, dividend increases must almost necessarily lag behind profit increases. It is also true, however, that dividend cuts seem to lag behind profit reductions. In essence, current dividends seem to be based to a first approximation on previous dividends. The dividend rate will be revised upward only when there is a solid belief that the present profit rates will continue into the future; if there is some uncertainty, the tendency is to call any increase an "extra," until such a time as the increase seems fully justified by the earnings situation. Aversion to letting dividends decline is apparently due to a fear of such an act being interpreted by market analysts, institutional investors, and other investors as a sign of distress or general weakness. Perhaps, too, some of this fear has a sound basis in market psychology in a world in which ownership and control are increasingly divorced and returns on equity have come to be regarded as only slightly less certain than returns on debt.

Partly as a consequence of increased knowledge of financial and dividend behavior, corporation investment decisions are regarded today as substantially too complex to be handled properly within the framework of traditional marginal theories of investment. In the first place, investment decisions—mainly because of the long time horizons and substantial uncertainty usually involved—are believed to be conditioned by a somewhat wider range of motives than that hypothesized by simple profit maximization. Also, the role of constraints in determining investment levels is now widely acknowledged. Finally, an expansion has occurred in the list of physical needs that are considered to be important justifications for or means of implementing investment programs.[16]

F. G. Darling, "The Influence of Expectations and Liquidity on Dividend Policy," *The Journal of Political Economy*, Vol. LXV, No. 3 (June, 1957).

[16] The discussion of investment decisions is based on several sources. A few of them are: W. Heller, "The Anatomy of Investment Decisions," *Harvard Business Review*, Vol. XXIX, No. 2 (March, 1951); A. D. Knox, "The Acceleration Principle and the Theory of Investment; A Survey," *Economica*, New Series, Vol. XIX, No. 75 (Aug., 1952); M. F. Foss and V. Natrella, "The Structure and Realization of Business Investment Anticipations," presented at the National Bureau of Economic Research *Conference on the Quality and Significance of Anticipations Data;* and J. Meyer and E. Kuh, *The Investment Decision, op. cit.*, particularly Chapters II, VIII, and XII.

At the level of psychological motivation, there is a tendency today to speak of sufficient profits being the goal rather than maximum profits. Specifically, if profits are "sufficient," management will entertain and place greater stress on long-run goals. This longer-run perspective may be as much related to maximizing or maintaining the general power position of the corporation as to profit maximization in its pure form. The usual index of achievement in this contest for power has been "market share," which is the corporation's percentage of the industry's total sales. Thus, if profits are sufficient and market share or trade position declines, it is suggested that many modern corporations will undertake expanded investment programs even if it is not clear that such a program will increase the present value of the future stream of corporation profits.

In the necessarily materialistic world of business it could not be expected, however, that psychological motives in and of themselves would be sufficient justification for investment outlays. Obviously, there must be some physical need for making an investment if the outlay is to be justified. The traditional emphasis in economic theory has been upon either the need for greater productive capacity so the firm can expand its output to meet expanded demand (the so-called acceleration theory of investment) or an introduction of cost reducing technology. In recent years, though, there has been an increased emphasis both in the economics literature and statements by businessmen upon the use of investment funds for the introduction and development of new products.[17]

The previous remarks refer mainly to the demand side of the investment picture. On the supply side, emphasis increasingly has been placed on what is termed the financial constraint. In essence, this is just another way of saying that looked at from the standpoint of the firm, there is a large discontinuity appearing in the supply-of-funds function between the point at which internal funds are exhausted and the first external sources are used.

Other constraints have also received increased attention. The most important would appear to be what has been called the "managerial

[17] For some recent quantitative evidence on this point see the McGraw-Hill report on capital spending problems in *Business Week,* No. 1494 (April 19, 1958), pp. 31–36.

constraint." This refers to a lack of sufficient executive talent to expand at any faster rate than that already being undertaken. An anti-trust constraint has also been mentioned; this ostensibly leads a firm to slow its rate of expansion in order not to encourage anti-trust prosecution.

From the behavioral standpoint, the question is how these various psychological motives, physical needs, and constraints act and interact upon one another to influence investment patterns under different cyclical and general economic conditions. We do not have all the knowledge that we need or would like to have on this subject. The best guess would appear to be that in the major industrial and commercial sectors outside public utilities and communications, investment will be undertaken strictly according to the dictates of physical need (that is, straightforward acceleration-type investment will occur) when plant capacity is fully utilized and demand is strong and expanding. Under such circumstances profits and finances are usually so adequate that physical need dominates all other considerations. Only managerial or supply constraints will interfere. Satisfying expanded demands as quickly as possible in such cyclically buoyant times is in keeping, moreover, with trying to maintain long-run market share. By contrast, when capacity is adequate it appears that the liquidity constraint often becomes a dominant, although not singular, concern. At such times, external debt apparently becomes more expensive, at least from the management's viewpoint; this lengthens the step between the cost of internally available funds and the cost of external funds. In short, under these circumstances, the demand for investment will usually involve an expenditure that cuts off at a level approximately equal to the internally available financial sources. There is, moreover, some evidence that the emphasis during these periods will be upon investments aimed at product development and cost reduction. Some have characterized such periods, especially when they occur after years of rapid expansion, as a time for technological catching-up. In recent years this would seem to be the only ready explanation of the phenomenon that led many firms to invest in new capacity at a time when existing capacity was underutilized.

These considerations suggest a close interrelationship between corporate savings and investment patterns and a distinctly different behavioral pattern in corporate than in household savings decisions. Obviously, the previous income model must be modified if it is to handle these more complex behavioral patterns properly. Following the lead of L. R. Klein and A. S. Goldberger,[18] the minimum requirements would appear to be separate savings and liquidity preference equations for the corporate and private sectors, a depreciation equation to explain the generation of investable funds from this source, and the inclusion of corporate profits and depreciation accruals in the investment function as additional explanatory variables. In addition, it would seem useful to distinguish between several different types of investment: at a minimum between plant and equipment, housing, and inventory investment.[19] For the present analysis, however, the more elaborate modifications will be foregone; the only major change will be to define the investment and savings functions—like those in Figs. 1, 1(a) and 1(b)—as being net of internally financed corporation investment and savings.

Still more complex difficulties are faced when a theory of price determination for oligopolistic markets is sought. Fortunately, there recently has been what one reviewer aptly describes as "a welcome major breakthrough on the oligopoly front."[20] Specifically, new theories of oligopoly pricing have been developed that emphasize the concept of entry or potential competition. In these new theories it is the behavior and cost structures of potential entrants into an oligopolistic market that are likely to be crucial determinants of price. Particular emphasis is placed on the entry preventive price. This is

[18] L. R. Klein and A. S. Goldberger, *An Econometric Model of the United States, 1929–52* (Amsterdam, 1955), Chapter II.

[19] It is interesting in this regard that the more recent Klein-Goldberger model does not distinguish between as many kinds of investment behavior as the earlier Klein model in L. R. Klein, *Economic Fluctuations in the United States, 1921–1941* (New York, 1950).

[20] Franco Modigliani, "Much New on the Oligopoly Front," *Journal of Political Economy*, Vol. LXVI, No. 3 (June, 1958). This review presents a concise and thorough summary of recent developments in the theory of oligopoly pricing. For further detail on these developments, see J. Bain, *Barriers to New Competition* (Cambridge, Mass., 1956), P. W. S. Andrews, *Manufacturing Business* (London, 1949), and P. S. Labini, *Oligopolice Progresso Tecnio* (Milan, 1957).

the upper limit price that may be charged by the firms already in an oligopolistic market without making it profitable for a potential entrant to enter the market. That is, prices above the entry preventive price would make it profitable for one or more new firms to enter the industry. By contrast, the lower limit on price will be the competitive price, that is the price at which average total costs, including a normal profit, will be covered. Whether or not a price actually approaches or becomes equal to the upper or entry preventing limit will depend upon a host of considerations which can be lumped under the general heading of "the oligopoly's tightness." Under this heading of tightness would be included such things as the relative size and number of firms already in the market, traditions or lack of traditions of price leadership, strength of customer attachments to the different producers, etc.[21] If a measure of "oligopoly tightness" could be constructed, it normally would be expected that price would be closer to the entry preventive price the tighter the oligopoly.

Such a theory of oligopoly pricing has important implications for determining the range within which unions might increase wages at the expense of profits. Several different possibilities can be discerned. If the corporation price is already at the entry preventive price and if a wage increase is extracted from the firms already in the market (that is, the existing oligopolists), and no wage increases are extracted from or induced for potential competitors, the wage increase will come completely out of profits. If the price is below the entry preventive price, and if again the wage increase is extracted only from those firms already in the industry, the probable effect will be some increase in prices. Whether or not the price increase is sufficient to maintain the before-wage-increase profit levels completely will depend upon how close the previous price was to the entry preventive price and the extent to which the different oligopolists consider a wage increase a "safe" signal for a price increase. This, in turn, will depend upon how "tight" the oligopoly is.

While the two previous situations will unquestionably occur at certain times and places, the most common case would appear to be

[21] For a full discussion of these points see W. Fellner, *Competition Among the Few* (New York, 1949).

one in which a wage increase within one industry either directly or indirectly induces a wage increase for the potential competitors. Such an outcome would be a virtually direct consequence if the potential competitors were, as they often are, organized by the same union as the original oligopolists. Even without such direct links, similar effects might be expected because of the working of competitive forces in the labor market. The fact that the potential entrants are likely to employ very similar kinds of labor as those already in the industry only heightens the probability. At any rate, when the wage increase is shared in this fashion by both the existing and potential oligopolists, the effect will be to make a price increase almost inevitable. This follows even if the oligopoly price is already at the entry preventive level because the wage increase will shift the potential entrants cost function upward and therefore also shift the entry preventive price level upwards.

To a degree, it is a matter of judgment just which one of these three basic situations is considered most likely. It seems reasonably obvious, however, that the second and third cases involve the least restrictive assumptions and in both of these situations the probable result of the wage increase will be a price increase. Put differently, the assumptions necessary for a wage increase not to be followed by a price increase in modern oligopoly markets seem rather highly specialized and unlikely.

It is in the context of these recent findings on corporation behavior that a reappraisal of the effects of wage changes on aggregate investment and savings functions must be carried out. The objective is to determine which assumptions, those favoring or those opposed to the high-wage theory, seem most justifiable in the light of modern corporation practices. A complete evaluation requires, of course, that the impact of wage changes on household decisions to consume and save also be evaluated. These household effects will be discussed in the following analysis but the emphasis will be on corporation savings and investment patterns. As already pointed out, this follows a current emphasis in the policy discussions. Separate consideration will be given to three different cyclical situations: conventional or so-called demand-pull inflation, plain, old-fashioned deflation, and "newfangled" or cost-push inflation (defined here to be a situation like 1955–57 in which excess capacity exists in consumers' goods).

The demand-pull inflation is, by definition, an inflation in which most capacity is near full utilization, e.g., the inflation of 1946 through 1948 and 1950 through 1952. As previously noted, the available evidence indicates that corporation demand for plant and equipment under such circumstances will be little influenced by liquidity or any other constraint. Quite contrarily, the stress is upon expanding capacity to meet unsatisfied demand. Under such circumstances, it seems doubtful—indeed the experience of these two periods almost would seem to prove the point—that wage increases are going to have any serious effects upon the demand for investment goods. However, one probable investment effect of a wage increase during a conventional inflation will be to increase slightly the demand for capital assets in efforts to cut costs by substituting capital for labor. The indirect effects of the wage changes, that is the multiplier-accelerator interaction effects, also would work toward the strengthening of investment demand.

By contrast, savings probably would decline some but not significantly with a wage increase during ordinary inflation. Because of the rigidity of corporate dividend payments, higher wages would come initially, that is in the very short run, out of retained earnings. But this phenomenon would be short-lived as prices could be expected to increase, quickly restoring retained earnings and, later, profits. The price increase seems almost inevitable, unless a very stringent monetary policy is followed, because in conventional inflations with the accompanying tight labor markets, a wage increase should be quickly transmitted through the economy, raising the costs of oligopolist and potential entrants alike. Furthermore, for reasons developed elsewhere,[22] it is in inflationary circumstances that oligopoly prices are likely to be below the entry preventive level. Until profits were fully restored, the effect would be to shift funds in a relative sense from retained earnings and dividend recipients to wage earners, i.e., a higher proportion of national income would temporarily go to wage

[22] Galbraith, *op. cit.*

recipients.[23] The usual assumption, although not fully verified, is that wage earners save less than dividend recipients.[24] Wage earners almost surely save less of their incomes than corporations do of retained earnings. To the extent that these statements are true, the immediate effect of the wage increase would be to decrease total savings, but the phenomenon would be very short-lived.

The preceding effects are clearly inflationary. The net effect, therefore, of a wage increase during a conventional inflation, without a strongly offsetting monetary restriction, almost surely would be more inflation. Consumption would have been strengthened at the expense of saving and there would be little offsetting drop in the demand for investment. Furthermore, with widespread areas of unsatiated demand and tight labor markets, most wage increases should be rather quickly transmitted throughout the economy. Thus even oligopolies already at the entry preventive price would find room within which to increase prices.[25]

The deflation case is somewhat more difficult to analyze. In the first place, the effects on the investment demand function of a wage increase at low levels of income will be quite mixed. The dominant concern in such periods is likely to be with investments that result in cost reduction and product development. A wage increase might stimulate investment for cost reduction purposes. On the other hand, a wage increase probably would cut back on product innovation and development by reducing profit expectations. The net effect of these

[23] It seems doubtful that the effect would be more than temporary. See, for example, H. M. Levinson, *Unionism, Wage Trends, and Income Distribution, 1914–1947* ("Michigan Business Studies," Vol. X, No. 4 [Ann Arbor, 1951]).

[24] Klein and Goldberger, *op. cit.*, pp. 62–64, report short-run marginal propensities to consume of .62 from disposable employee income, .46 from disposable nonwage, nonfarm income, and .39 from disposable farm income. The equivalent long-run propensities were .81, .60, and .51, respectively.

[25] A minor offset to all this might be some tendency for the wage increase to raise the transaction demand for money; this in turn might lower the supply of money available for asset holding, thus increasing the interest rate. However, even this is likely to be offset by a general downward shift in liquidity preference functions in the economy (or alternatively an increase in the velocity of money induced by expectations of price inflation). Furthermore, such a policy assumes that the monetary authorities would hold the money supply reasonably constant; as recent experiences have indicated, this may or may not be the case under inflationary conditions.

two offsetting tendencies is difficult to determine but a slight downward pressure on investment demand seems likely.

A more important effect upon savings and investment during deflation is likely to result, however, from the influence of the wage increase on the availability of internal funds. Unlike the inflationary situation, the probability would be quite high in deflation that any wage increase could not be passed along in a price increase. Therefore, the wage increase almost surely would cut back on internal funds available for investment. This decline in internally available money would result in a shift of firms' supply of funds functions to the left. If the demand for investment had been sufficient almost to exhaust the internally available funds of most firms before the wage increase,[26] the effect of the reduced availability of internal funds effectively would be to cut back investment. On the other hand, the typical firm's investment demand function might intersect the supply of funds function far to the left of the point at which internal funds are exhausted; that is, many firms could be hoarding liquid funds or building up cash balances. A leftward shift of the "funds availability function" then would have no impact on investment planning and demand unless the "hoarding" took precedence over investment.[27] If it is further assumed that investment demands drop more rapidly than profits during deflation, this would imply that the deeper the depression, the more likely it is that a wage increase would not cut into the effective demand for investment outlays. Indeed, a limiting situation might be envisaged in which investment demand functions of firms were typically synonymous with the vertical axis in Fig. 4. Under such circumstances, wage increases could come out of profits, assuming that some still existed, with no deleterious effects upon investment.[28]

The probable effect on savings (net of corporate retentions) of a

[26] Because the liquidity constraint is apparently important under deflationary conditions, we ignore the possibility that the demand functions typically intersect firms' supply functions to the right of the point where internal funds are exhausted.

[27] Such an increase in hoarding seems unlikely but it is difficult to make very positive assertions on this matter since empirical information on this point is scarce.

[28] Gross profits are emphasized because the internally available funds making up the first portion of the supply function in Fig. 4 are composed of both depreciation allowances and retained *accounting* profits.

wage increase during deflation will be to push the function downward. This follows as long as dividend recipients have a lower propensity to consume than wage recipients and some of the increased wages are paid by reducing dividends. The deeper the recession, the more likely these conditions would appear to be.

It is obviously difficult to draw specific conclusions from these many, and often conflicting, considerations. However, a wage increase would appear to be a better anti-recession antidote the deeper the depression. That is, both the savings and the investment effects would appear to be more favorable under really depressed conditions when there would seem to be less chance of the wage increase reducing investment demand and more chance of cutting into hoarded funds.

A wage increase during a cost-push inflation combines certain aspects of both the deflation and conventional inflationary conditions just analyzed. On the investment side the situation would seem similar, though not identical, to the deflation case. A cost-push inflation would appear to be differentiated from a conventional inflation mainly by the existence of substantial amounts of unutilized capacity in at least some sectors of the economy. Therefore, acceleration type demand for investment should not be too strong, or at least not universal. Much investment will be of a less urgent nature, that is for product development and cost reduction. As already noted, product development investment probably would not be helped much by the wage increase while cost reducing investments probably would be. The net effect of these two offsetting tendencies is not apparent.

It should be noted, however, that in these mixed inflation-deflation situations, the investment demand for many firms seems to be tailored to fit the supply of internal funds; that is, the two functions intersect near the first kink in the supply function where internal funds are exhausted. Some firms continue to use outside funds, of course, mainly in the more rapidly growing and trade share competitive sectors. But in either circumstance, a wage increase probably would reduce investment as long as the increase is paid by a reduction in retained earnings. In the first case, investment probably would be actually cut back to fit the curtailed liquidity situation. In the second case, it is doubtful that investment demand as such would be affected but there would be a substantial increase in the demand for investment to be financed by non-corporate savings—and, as will shortly be shown, there is no reason to expect that an increase in such savings will be induced by a wage increase.

The crucial question, obviously, is whether the wage increase can and will be passed along in the form of higher prices. The extent to which the price increases could be controlled or contained would appear to depend: (a) on the degree to which the wage increases were limited to firms that were not marginal or potential entrants into oligopolistic markets; and (b) the existence of trade share rivalry or instability in the oligopolistic market relationships in the economy. Unfortunately, there is little reason to expect that wage increases would be limited to existing oligopolists and would exempt potential competitors. On the other hand, the existence of excess capacity in the economy would probably work toward keeping some oligopoly relationships less than perfectly defined and stable. But there almost surely would be some rather "tight" oligopoly situations even in the under-utilized sectors of the economy. Thus, there probably would be price increases even in the face of under-utilized capacity.

The effect of a wage increase upon non-corporate savings during a cost-push inflation should be similar to the standard inflationary situation. In general, dividends would not be cut in order to pay higher wages, thus the initial effect would be to transfer income from retained earnings to wage earners. Unlike the "pure" inflationary case, however, it is not obvious that prices, though they would probably rise, would necessarily go up enough to restore retained earnings and profits, particularly in the under-utilized sectors of the economy. There would thus be a short-run, and possibly even a longer-run, redistribution of income in favor of wages at the expense of both retained earnings and dividends. Again assuming that dividend recipients have a lower marginal propensity to consume than wage earners, non-corporate savings would be depressed.

If the previous analysis is correct, the general effect of a wage increase would perhaps be desirable in times of a cost-push inflation when investment capacity is fully utilized and consumer goods capacity is under-utilized. In other words, under circumstances like those of the 1955–1957 period, a case could be made that wage increases act as a balancing element in the economy. However, this balance would not be attained at no cost in price increases. It is not apparent, though, that prices would necessarily go up more with the wage increases than without such increases. A cost-push inflation marked by an over-balance of investment demand therefore might not be the worst (nor the best!) time for the economy to absorb a wage increase.

In sum, there would appear to be at least a limited case for the technical feasibility of the high-wage theory. Technical feasibility, however, is only one criterion of a good policy. Obviously, consideration also must be given to practical workability and the compatibility of any policy with other objectives that society might wish to attain.

Thus, in deciding whether wage increases should be used to achieve greater cyclical stability, a decision first must be made on just how productivity increases are to be realized and distributed to different groups in the society. The basic issue is the extent to which greater productivity is to be realized in the form of wage increases instead of price decreases. While the situation is not entirely obvious, it seems highly probable that wage increases will be the dominant form of adjustment in the United States in the near future. Furthermore, there are several good reasons for preferring adjustment through wage increases to price decreases, although it would be unfortunate to have one arrangement occur to the complete exclusion of the other.

Once the probability is granted that wage increases will be the usual means for realizing productivity gains, it is still necessary to determine just which timing of the wage increases will have the best or least harmful effect on the economy. Assuming for the moment that this timing pattern really is a matter of choice, it would appear from the preceding discussion that unbalanced cost-push inflations or really substantial deflations would be the best time to incur wage increases. Conventional demand-pull inflations and minor recessions, on the other hand, would appear to be the worst times.

It is probably unrealistic, however, to assume that the timing of wage increases is really something that can be dictated according to the needs of cyclical stabilization policy. Such timing depends on managements granting wage increases during depressions when resistance to wage demands should be easiest and unions exercising restraint in their wage demands during those periods in which it would be easiest to obtain wage increases; that is, periods in which labor is fully employed, product demand exceeds supply, and wages are rising in the unorganized, competitive sectors of the labor market. It seems safe to say that neither managements nor unions are likely to behave in the required manner. Specifically, in the present context the chances of unions being able or willing to exercise wage restraint during inflationary periods would seem small.

A major reason why such restraint seems unlikely is the present nature of inter-union political rivalries in the United States. Wage increases are as much a measure of the success and potential power of a union leader as increased profits are of professional business managers. We need look no further than the well-known rivalry between the auto and steel union leaderships to realize that the temptation would be very strong during any inflationary period to push up wages to garner the concomitant political gain that is likely to go with such a "display of power." Perhaps some day when the American labor movement has reached a greater maturity, this type of inter-union rivalry will no longer be a major force in shaping wage demands.[29] At present, however, the nature of American labor union politics stands as a very real argument against the possibility of using wage adjustments as a counter-cyclical policy.

There are other substantial arguments, moreover, against relying on wage variations as an antidote to inflation or deflation. As others have stressed, wage increases are not likely to be a very efficient or

[29] For statements of the kind of wage settlement criteria that are needed see S. H. Slichter, *Review of Economics and Statistics,* Vol. XXXI, No. 4 (Nov., 1949) and J. M. Clark, "Criteria for Wage Adjustment, with Emphasis on the Question of Inflationary Effects," in *The Impact of the Union, op. cit.*

flexible way of stabilizing economic activity.[30] The recent cost-push inflation of 1955 through 1957 provides an excellent case in point. The apparent need during this period was to reduce investment. One very simple and obvious aid toward accomplishing this end would have been to tighten up on grants of accelerated amortization for so-called special defense purposes and to have interpreted and administered the rules on depreciation allowances narrowly and rigorously. Clearly, the investment boom of the period was heavily fed by the availability of special amortization and depreciation privileges and reversal of this situation required nothing more difficult than a few administrative acts.[31]

Arguments also might be raised about the relative social desirability and humanitarianism of using wage increases as an anti-deflation policy during periods of depression. For example, if the economy was in a really serious recession, it might be quicker and socially more desirable to halt the recession by increased unemployment benefits than by increasing the wages of those already at work. Similarly, there might be some long-run needs of the economy for roads, schools, and hospitals that properly could be best met during deflationary periods.

In short, the redistribution of income and resources involved in using wage changes as an anti-deflation policy is not obviously optimal when evaluated in terms of a wide range of economic and social objectives.

[30] For example, G. Haberler in *The Impact of the Union, op. cit.*

[31] It should be observed that if a wage increase would decrease investment by reducing retained business earnings, tougher scrutiny of depreciation allowances for tax purposes would have the same effect—and for exactly the same reasons except that the reduction in investment would be effectuated by a redistribution of income from business to government rather than from business to labor.

13

The Limits of Union Power*

G. Warren Nutter

> Labor organization without large powers of coercion and intimidation is an unreal abstraction. Unions now have such powers; they always have had and always will have, so long as they persist in their present form. Where the power is small or insecurely possessed, it must be exercised overtly and extensively; large and unchallenged, it becomes like the power of strong government, confidently held, respectfully regarded, and rarely displayed conspicuously.
>
> *Henry C. Simons*[1]

THERE is much to be said for a periodic scrapping of theory and a thoroughgoing reconstruction from the bottom up. This is what we mean by "getting down to fundamentals," and it could be argued that economists do not do this often enough. I should like to try to get down to fundamentals on one very narrow aspect of the labor union question, namely, the nature and bases of the economic power

* In preparing this chapter, I have relied heavily on the following publications, and many of the ideas expressed here will be found to be developed much more adequately in them: Martin Bronfenbrenner, "Wages in Excess of Marginal Revenue Product," *Southern Economic Journal,* Vol. XVI, No. 3 (Jan., 1950); Edward H. Chamberlin, *The Economic Analysis of Labor Union Power* (Washington, D.C., 1958); Milton Friedman, "Some Comments on the Significance of Labor Unions for Economic Policy," in D. M. Wright (ed.), *The Impact of the Union* (New York, 1951); H. Gregg Lewis, "The Labor-Monopoly Problem: A Positive Program," *Journal of Political Economy,* Vol. LIX, No. 4 (Aug., 1951); and Henry C. Simons, "Some Reflections on Syndicalism," *Journal of Political Economy,* Vol. LII, No. 1 (March, 1944).

[1] "Some Reflections on Syndicalism," *Journal of Political Economy,* Vol. LII, No. 1 (March, 1944), p. 22.

wielded by labor unions. The issues here are complex and puzzling—in many respects paradoxical; and I will not pretend to comprehend the complexities, let alone how they are to be resolved. My function will be as much to raise questions as to answer them, and I issue the special warning that no effort will be made to discuss "solutions" to the "labor problem."

The concept of economic power is perhaps made clear by considering what we mean by its absence. The absence of economic power means, in a word, competition, used in its technical sense: no buyer or seller of a product is able, when acting alone and in his own interest, to affect the terms of exchange. The terms of exchange are, for all practical purposes, set by a market—by all exchanges taken together, under conditions in which no individual exchange has any effect in and of itself on the terms.

Economic power arises through exclusion and collusion. On the selling side, monopoly and oligopoly result from exclusion of other sellers, and cartels from collusion with them. On the buying side, the corresponding forms are monopsony and oligopsony, along with collusive purchasing agreements, which have not yet been honored by economists with a special title. In each of these cases the resulting economic unit is able, when acting alone and in its own interest, to affect terms of exchange. For simplicity, let us limit our discussion to economic power on the selling side.

Economic power may exist on two different levels. At the first level, there is the ability to set prices in the market place as a whole; at the second level, there is the ability to set differing terms of exchange with different purchasers. Power exists at the second level when it is possible to regulate exchanges not only with the market as a whole, but also within the market. That is, it is possible to restrain trade within the market, to limit or eliminate the sellers of a product other than the "producer." This second kind of power, which cannot exist without the first, is usually referred to as discriminatory or exploitative power, and it may exist in varying degrees, from discrimination among submarkets to discrimination among individual purchasers.

It would hardly be possible or of much value to catalog the preconditions of discriminatory power. It can, of course, be exercised when buyers are ignorant of alternatives or when they are few in number, that is, when they also possess economic power. These conditions aside, discrimination would seem to be most favored when the thing being sold is, at least in critical part, non-storable and non-durable—that is, a perishable product or a service of some kind. For, in this case, control over alternative sellers is facilitated: arbitrage cannot be practiced, or can be practiced only indirectly and with great difficulty.

The discussion so far is a belaboring of the commonplace. We are all familiar with discrimination in the selling of such products as electricity, transportation, medical and legal services, and services of patented machines (where discrimination is made possible through the device of compulsory rental), to name only a few examples. The existence of substantial discriminatory power is without doubt an important explanation for the development of special legal principles (as the "public carrier") governing the so-called public utilities. On the other hand, some types of discrimination—as practiced, for instance, by doctors and lawyers—are socially approved.

In any event, this is all incidental to the point I am leading up to, namely, that monopolistic control over any kind of labor service implies discriminatory power as well. This follows directly from the fact that the labor service cannot be separated from the worker, and the worker cannot be bought and sold.[2] Hence there cannot be an intermediate market in labor services in any meaningful sense. Nobody can buy specific labor services from one source and sell them to another. This is merely to say that there are no arbitrageurs in the labor market except workers themselves. If they combine into a union with monopolistic power, they also gain discriminatory power.

A union is essentially a business organization that sells labor services. It is, in the first place, a cartel, an association of workers who act in concert in selling their labor services. To the extent the cartel is effective, it becomes more than a cartel, for its discriminatory power

[2] It is interesting that Alfred Marshall considers this factor only as it acts to the disadvantage of the worker in individual bargaining (*Principles of Economics* [8th ed.; London, 1936], pp. 567 ff.). Of course, discriminatory power is two-sided to the extent that the firm has monopsonistic powers over the individual employee.

allows it to keep the employers it deals with from hiring non-union labor. Hence it is able to exclude rivals to a greater or lesser degree and thereby to take on the form of a partial monopoly. Briefly put, a union is a cartel with the power to regulate entry; hence it may act as a monopolist, in particular as a discriminating monopolist.

Perhaps union power is best thought of as "organic" in nature: successful collusion leads to successful exclusion, and conversely. In a very real sense, "success breeds success," and "power feeds on itself." We must immediately add that this is true only within limits set by relevant economic conditions, the established mores, and law, but for the moment we shall not try to specify these limits. The point being made here is that union power is not derived from a logical sequence of causes, but from the interaction of many factors, reinforcing each other.

If any one factor is to be considered as antecedent, it is the right to organize and collude, which has as its corollary the right to strike. Once this right is granted, the ground is laid for the creation of labor monopolies. The first problem is to organize the workers in a relevant category into a union and to achieve their loyalty to collective decisions. There must be a large enough group with strict loyalty to enforce it in the rest, through such forms of pressure and persuasion as are effective and socially respectable.[3] True loyalty on the part of any member is ultimately founded on anticipated benefits of collusive action, either in the narrowly material sense or in a broader social and political sense. Hence, to the extent that collusive action achieves benefits for union members, the power of a union is strengthened.

Collusive action is expressed through a willingness to strike, or to withhold labor services collectively unless specified terms of employment are met. The strike, if exercised and effective, imposes a penalty on the nonconforming employer by stopping his productive activity or by making it more costly. To be effective at all, a strike must do two things: first, withhold labor services that are "essential" to the

[3] The problem of enforcing discipline without overt terror has been simplified by our laws governing collective bargaining. A union becomes the certified agent for a "bargaining unit" if a majority of the workers qualified and voting choose it. If the union then succeeds in getting the union shop or equivalent, specialized union officers can take over the task of enforcing discipline in all workers.

productive activity of the employer, or at least labor services for which there are no perfect substitutes; and, second, prevent the employer from replacing all strikers with equally efficient workers drawn from non-union sources. Let us suppose that these two things can be done, without inquiring at this stage into the reasons why.

In order to analyze the nature of penalties that may be imposed by a strike, let us suppose further that the union is able to stop production of an employer altogether, or at least to reduce it substantially, through withholding the labor services under its control. The damages such a work stoppage imposes on the employer depend on conditions that are generally ignored by the economic theorist in his study of pricing in a market economy, since he is concerned with how resources are allocated in a system in which production is continuous, though at varying rates. By the very nature of the strike problem, the effects of interruptions in production are obviously of primary concern, and here we get into the theory of "bottlenecks," if we may presume to speak of a "theory."

The damages to the employer are, of course, the losses in net revenue attributable to the stoppage. If the product in question is storable, losses can be ameliorated by raising production rates before and after the stoppage, and by varying inventories correspondingly. Even with "perfect" foresight, losses probably could not be wholly avoided, since unit costs of production would probably be higher with the varying production rate than with the more or less steady rate that would have existed in the absence of a stoppage. This says nothing about the extra costs of inventory management or about special expenses of interrupting production processes. A familiar example of the latter is the considerable expense of closing down and refiring furnaces and mills in the steel industry.

If the product is non-storable, it is much more difficult to ameliorate losses. To some extent consumers might willingly "postpone" consumption during the stoppage; that is, they might consume more afterward than they otherwise would have. But this kind of offset is not likely to be significant. In the main, any "temporary" loss in consumption of perishables is viewed as permanent, not to be compensated for by consuming more later. This is particularly true when the production (and consumption) is "non-recurrent," associated with a specific time and place: if musicians scheduled for a one-night stand refuse to perform after the audience is assembled, the producer must refund the tickets, and that is that. Similarly, the publisher of a newspaper cannot make up for a strike by publishing extra news before and after it. For all practical purposes, the employer must bear in full the direct losses of stoppage in production of a service or non-storable commodity. The same thing holds where production amounts to custom work, as in virtually all construction.

The damages to the public from such a stoppage may be many times the damages to the struck employer, as becomes clear when we consider stoppage of productive activity in fields like transportation and electricity. Through its strike, the union may create a temporary "bottleneck" that curtails productive activity over a very wide area. This point is trite to say the least, but it needs to be made to fill out the picture. The special circumstances surrounding a strike of this sort, together with general public attitudes toward "labor" and "management," will determine which side will be brought to account for the damages and consequently be put under public pressure to come to terms.

The points made so far are all well known, but they are nonetheless often forgotten in discussions of the power of unions. We could go on to enumerate a large number of special circumstances that would enhance the power of unions to inflict damages on employers through strikes, but these are perhaps best treated as special cases. The main point has been sufficiently well developed, namely, that monopolistic unions have coercive power, power to inflict penalties on employers individually and discriminatingly through punitive strikes. In this sense, as H. Gregg Lewis has pointed out,[4] unions act as organizations levying taxes on employers, their levies being enforced through coercive power at their disposal. This is, moreover, not the whole story, for the coercive power may be used to enforce non-pecuniary exactions, that is, to enforce other "laws." For example, the union can bargain for a union shop or its equivalent instead of, say, for higher

[4] *Op. cit.*, pp. 282 ff. This generally excellent article is a penetrating analysis of the nature of labor monopolies.

wages; if successful, the union will strengthen its power to exclude rivals, to raise funds, and to discipline members and thus will indirectly strengthen its coercive power.[5] The "original" coercive power may be magnified through contractual agreements. This is to say nothing of the possibilities of pressuring the community into passing laws that strengthen union power.

It should be made clear that coercive power is inherent to a greater or lesser degree in all economic power, but its exercise is unlawful for all forms except labor monopolies. If allowed to do so, an electric utility company could collect sizable tolls from its customers by threatening disruption of service at the pleasure of the company. The dilemma in the case of the labor unions arises from the fact that the privilege of using the strike for coercive purposes has been granted to enable workers to restrain the exploitative and discriminatory power of the employer. Exploitative power is, to some extent at least, a two-sided coin, as can be seen by reflecting on the element of truth in the phrase "tyranny of the foreman." Having pointed out the dilemma, I shall pass on, for I do not wish in this discussion to judge the merits of existing institutions as much as to analyze their effects.

Economic power is limited, of course, by the cost of exercising it and by the willingness of purchasers to acquiesce, both of which are interrelated to some extent. For the moment, we shall ignore the limits placed by cost. Demand, as traditionally conceived, is frequently described as the condition on the purchasing side that limits economic power of sellers. In the words of Milton Friedman:

> The power of unions, as of any other monopoly, is ultimately limited by the elasticity of the demand curve for the monopolized services. Unions have significant potential power only if this demand curve is fairly inelastic at what would otherwise be the competitive price. Even then, of course, they must be able to control either the supply of workers or the wage rate employers will offer workers.[6]

[5] The union shop is not the only means of enforcing discipline among union members (see n. 3 above). The union may accomplish many of the same results by administering and dispensing benefits granted by employers, such as pension plans and welfare funds. Walter Reuther's recent "profit-sharing" scheme fits in this category. This is to say nothing of the fine art of applying pressure without actually clubbing over the head. On these and related matters, see E. H. Chamberlin, *op. cit.*, pp. 18 ff.

[6] *Op. cit.*, p. 207.

This clear and succinct statement is largely correct, but it leaves out of account the coercive and discriminatory elements of union power, which are not directly limited by the elasticity of demand for the monopolized services. The demand curve rests on the assumption that the purchaser is free to adjust either the wage rate to the quantity of labor services offered or the quantity of services hired to the wage rate offered. Discriminatory power of a seller implies power to control both wage rate and employment simultaneously, to make all-or-none offers instead of more-or-less offers. The limiting factor on the buying side is not the demand curve, but rather what might be called an "acquiescence" curve. To see what this means, we must move on to a more detailed formal analysis.

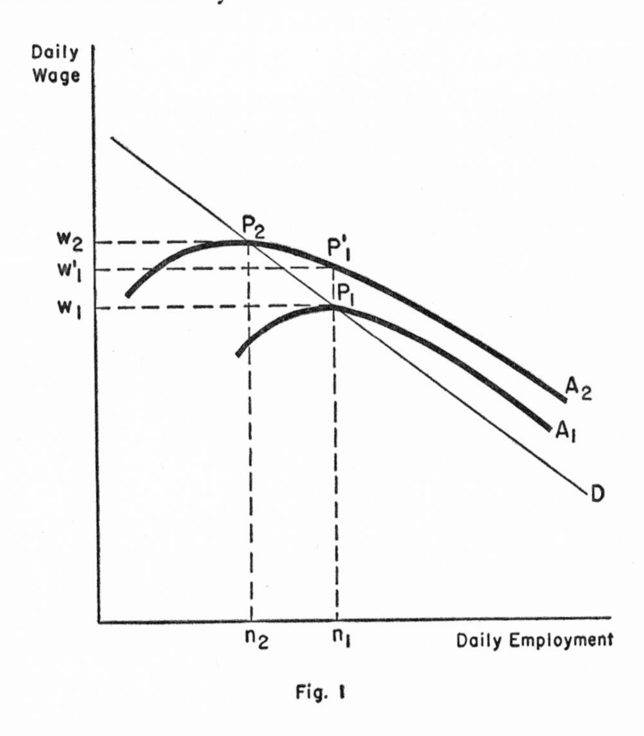

Fig. 1

Let us suppose a labor union controls the entire supply of a particular kind of labor that is "essential" to the productive activity of industries in which it is employed. Let us suppose further that the cost to the union of practicing complete discrimination—of setting terms with each employer separately—is negligible. Under these conditions, the union may bargain with each employer on an all-or-none basis. In order to see what this implies, let us turn our attention to Fig. 1, which pictures for one employer the short-run conditions of demand for his labor (the curve labeled D) and of acquiescence to the terms set by it (the curves labeled A_1 and A_2).

The demand curve is based on the *ceteris paribus* conditions relevant for the short run and on the usual assumption that the firm attempts to maximize net revenue. To each point on the demand curve there corresponds an output and a combination of inputs such that net revenue is maximized. This implies further that the costs of producing the output in question have been minimized. Under ordinary laws of costs and demand for a product, the net revenue becomes smaller as we move upward on the demand curve for labor.

Let us consider the specific point P_1, representing wage rate w_1, employment n_1, and a unique level of net revenue. The conditions underlying the demand curve tell us that, if the wage rate is w_1, any level of employment larger or smaller than n_1 will mean a net revenue lower than for P_1. If net revenue is to remain the same as for P_1, the wage rate must be reduced as employment moves in either direction from n_1. The curve A_1 traces out the combinations of wage rate and employment that lead to the same net revenue as the combination at P_1, on the assumption that other inputs are always adjusted so as to minimize costs of producing the relevant output. The curve A_2 represents the same thing for the lower net revenue corresponding to P_2. In technical language, A_1 and A_2 are isoquants of net revenue, the net revenue varying inversely with the subscript. For reasons to become apparent, I shall refer to these curves as acquiescence curves.

In order to simply the analysis, we may suppose that the labor union has just come into existence and that the labor services now monopolized had been supplied and hired competitively. The competitive wage is w_1 and the firm we are concerned with has been hiring n_1 of the labor services.[7] What may we expect to happen? First,

[7] If the firm had monopsonistic power and if the wage rate actually paid had been w_1, employment would have been less than n_1. But this does not affect the argument as made here. It should be noted that the demand curve traces out the marginal reve-

the union will undoubtedly serve notice of its intention to strike if the firm does not accept its terms. The potential damages of the strike will be assessed by both sides, and we suppose for the moment that these assessments are consistent and that the potential damages to the union are not sufficient to deter it from striking if necessary to get its terms. The potential damages to the firm may be translated into an equivalent reduction in net revenue discounted over the appropriate time horizon. All this done, the common assessment is that a strike would be equivalent to reducing net revenue from the current level to the level represented by acquiescence curve A_2. We suppose the firm is moved solely by economic motives and is willing to accept any terms consistent with the determined acquiescence curve.

The union is now in a position to set a variety of terms. It may ask for a higher wage rate together with decreased, increased, or the same employment. The last set of terms would be wage rate w'_1 and employment n_1. Or it might even ask for a lower wage rate and considerably increased employment, though this is most improbable. The only terms that will not be set are those beneath the demand curve. In any case, the union is in a position to specify wage rate and employment simultaneously. Under quite common circumstances, it will choose to specify only the wage rate—in this case, w_2—and allow the employer to hire whatever number of workers he wishes. But this is only one of a very large number of possible terms open to the union, at least in principle. Moreover, there is no obvious criterion for an "optimum" set of terms; the nature of an "optimum" depends on whose wage rate the union is trying to maximize—or, more realistically, whose wage rate it is compelled to maximize by the ultimate

---

nue products associated with alternative rates of employment, other relevant things remaining the same. The marginal revenue product will be equal to the value of the marginal product if the firm sells its product competitively; otherwise, it will not be equal. This matter is also not relevant to the discussion as presented here.

It might seem at first glance that each acquiescence curve is directly related to the schedule for the average product of labor. In particular, it might be thought that the wage bill at each point on a given acquiescence curve is simply the difference between the corresponding total revenue and the given net revenue of the firm. This is, of course, not so, since we have supposed that the firm is free to arrange its expenditures on (variable) inputs other than labor in any way it desires. There is no reason to presume a fixed relation between wage bill and total revenue unless the union manages the firm completely.

factors limiting its monopolistic power. One possible "optimum" is the set of terms that leads to the largest total wage bill, which will depend ultimately on the elasticities of the employer's demand and acquiescence. Maximizing the wage bill will not be of any particular concern, however, to the union that is able to regulate membership very strictly.

As noted before, the union may be viewed as a fiscal agent levying taxes on the employer and disbursing the proceeds to its members—or, with racketeering, to its officers. Setting the terms of constant employment and a higher wage is equivalent to levying a tax on the employer's net revenue, as in the case of Reuther's "profit-sharing" plan. A higher wage rate with a reduction in employment not as great as if the wage rate alone were fixed is equivalent to some excise tax on the product, as the United Mine Worker's royalties on coal output for its welfare fund. A higher wage rate with increased employment is equivalent to some combined excise tax and payroll subsidy. And so on.

Our abstract theorizing has obviously greatly oversimplified the analysis, and much of what has been said must be modified if it is to be relevant. To give a complete picture, one would have to get into the complexities of "bargaining theory," something far beyond my competence. The following observations are, however, in order.

First, if the union and employer differ in their assessments of strike damages and the conditions of acquiescence, then there will be a strike. The parties will consequently adjust terms as seems appropriate and a settlement of some kind will be reached, if only capitulation by one side or the other. Second, the firm may decide that positions can be reversed, that the union can be made to acquiesce, in which case the pressure will be by the firm on the union. The aim would be to "break" effective unionization, as in the Kohler Company case. Such cases are rare, to say the least, but this probably reflects the discriminatory nature of laws as much as general absence of conditions otherwise favorable to such practices. The ability to "break" unionization depends primarily on how easy it is to recruit non-union labor and on how heavy strike costs are to the union, which depends in turn on how large the union is relative to the members involved in the strike. Third, the resistance of a firm will usually vary with the nature of the terms laid down as well as with the effect on net revenue alone. That is to say, some terms—as direct regulation of employment—will be viewed as encroaching more severely than others on established managerial prerogatives, and the willingness to withstand a strike will consequently be stronger than otherwise. This point also brings to light the fact that unions may have control over the shapes of acquiescence curves to the extent they are allowed to regulate hiring of resources other than the unionized labor.

These factors all modify the details of our analysis and some of the conclusions, but they do not affect the fundamentals. It is perhaps more important to allow for the effects of time, to consider the longer-run consequences of a union's exercise of power.

The essentials are best revealed by supposing that the firm in question sells its product competitively. Then, to the extent its productive services other than labor have not been earning rents of any kind, it must in the long run go out of business. If the union has imposed comparable terms on all firms in the industry, some must go out of business in order to make it possible for others to remain, that is, for others to earn a normal rate of return on investment. Hence, employment will tend to be smaller in the long than in the short run regardless of the terms originally set by the union.[8] The union can, of course, keep up this process indefinitely if it can retain effective control over the relevant workers, eventually turning the industry into an oligopoly or a monopoly. Non-union firms will probably increase in number as unionized employment declines, and this may impose limits on the process if nothing else does. It should be noted on the other side that the substitution by firms of other productive services for the unionized labor may have the paradoxical effect of strengthening the union if the substitution is not total. The essential point is

[8] The tendency for unionized employment to decline (other relevant things the same) could be counteracted at least in part by renegotiating wage-employment terms to raise employment in the remaining firms. If employing firms are tending to expand by virtue of increasing demand or improving technology, unionized employment could actually increase historically, whether the union renegotiated or not. In this respect, a union's power is enhanced when it deals with expanding industries.

that the union's power tends to be stronger, the smaller the share of wages in the total costs of a firm, a point to be developed in greater detail below.

Once an oligopoly or monopoly is established, the union can gain further in a long-run sense only to the extent that the firm being dealt with is making true profits. There might be conditions in which short-run exploitation would pay off for union members even though the firm were driven out of business, but these conditions will not be general and may be ignored. The question remains whether a union would prefer to deal with an oligopoly or with a monopoly, and the answer is far from clear to me. It would seem that all one can say is that "it all depends." The obvious advantage in dealing with an oligopoly is that the firms may be played off against each other, some being "allowed" to operate while others are struck; the union can in effect combine bribes with penalties, as has been the usual practice in the automobile and steel industries. The advantage in dealing with a monopoly is that, if profits are being made in an industry, it probably would have more profits to share. The primary disadvantage is the greater monopsony power in the hands of the employer, though this may not be significant if the union is organized on craft rather than industrial lines. If the syndicalist solution were feasible and acceptable, the union would almost certainly prefer to eliminate all firms but one from an industry. Though this day may well come in our country, it is not quite here yet.

What, then, are the limits of union power? In the first place, there are the established mores. We cannot begin to discuss union power without knowing which practices the public condones and which it prohibits. If unions are, for instance, allowed to enforce their terms through terror, then any other limits that there might be to their power are greatly attenuated. The same holds true if they are allowed to use non-violent practices such as secondary strikes and boycotts, or if they are empowered to control supply through various forms of licensure. We shall take the current state of law and law enforcement as representing public attitude, which means, incidentally, that some forms of terror on the part of the unions are condoned.

The limits of union power that operate within this framework of mores may be divided roughly into two categories: those that affect the costs of organizing, maintaining, and utilizing the union; and those that affect the benefits from union action. The difficulty here is that these two groups of factors are not independent; in particular, the costs depend heavily and directly on the benefits. For instance, the larger the benefits from unionization, the less costly it is likely to be to organize and control a union. Nevertheless, there is something to be gained in clarity in our analysis by separating the limiting factors.

The cost of organizing and controlling a union depends in the first instance on its size; the cost of exercising power, particularly of a discriminatory nature, depends on the number of employers and such factors as turn-over of labor. This is simply to say that these costs will tend to be lowest where, other relevant things the same, a relatively small number of workers and employers are involved and where workers tend to remain attached to the same employers. The matter is, however, by no means so simple as these sweeping remarks would suggest. For one thing, the cost of strikes, viewed as disciplinary measures to enforce conformity of employers, is to some extent minimized if (other relevant things the same) the union membership is large relative to the number of members that have to engage in the strikes. A full-scale discussion of these matters would require far more knowledge of labor markets and collective bargaining than I possess, and the definitive analysis must be left to somebody else. The few tentative generalizations made here will perhaps serve to focus attention on some important considerations.

On the benefit side, everything hinges on the power of the union to inflict damages on the employer—and the community—through strikes. As already pointed out, this power rests on the "essentiality" of the labor service and the non-durability and uniqueness of the product, among other "bottleneck-type" features. For any given potential strike damage, the short-run percentage gain in wage rate per employed worker, to consider the relevant variable under union control, will depend most directly on what share of total costs is accounted for by the wage bill of the unionized labor. The smaller the share, the larger the potential percentage gain in wage rate.[9] The short-run elasticity of demand for the unionized labor, taken together with the elasticity of acquiescence, will affect the nature of terms set by the union insofar as declines in unionized employment are believed to raise the costs of unionization. In the longer run, the decline in unionized employment associated with any given short-run union gain will depend primarily on the elasticity of demand for the product and on the freedom allowed the employer in substituting other productive services for the unionized labor.

One thing is clear from the foregoing discussion: jurisdictional disputes between unions are an inevitable consequence of unionization as we know it. These are nothing more or less than fights over who is to get the spoils of unionization, or who is to exploit whom. The conflict between craft and industrial unions is particularly unavoidable, since the former are virtually always in a superior exploitative

[9] Marshall argued that the smaller this share, the lower the employer's elasticity of demand for the given labor (*op. cit.*, p. 385), an argument reaffirmed by Milton Friedman (*op. cit.*, pp. 207 f.). I doubt that this proposition has a broad application. Though they do not help much in a decision of this sort, the formal conditions needed to make the proposition valid are stated in detail by J. R. Hicks (*The Theory of Wages* [New York, 1948], pp. 241 ff.). To illustrate the difficulties with the proposition, let us suppose that the unionized labor has a perfect substitute, that is, that the marginal rate of substitution of it for some other productive service is constant for all possible combinations of the two that might be hired. Then, if the other productive service may be hired competitively, demand for the unionized labor is completely elastic no matter what share of total costs it accounts for.

From context, one might argue that Marshall had in mind conditions of acquiescence as described here but mistakenly attributed them to demand. He speaks of wages of plasterers, presumably organized into a union, and notes that "a rise of even 50 per cent in them would add but a very small percentage to the expenses of production of a house and would check demand but a little" (*op. cit.*, p. 385). This might simply mean what I have argued in the text, namely, that a given amount of potential strike damage makes possible a higher percentage wage increase for this type of labor than for another type accounting for a larger fraction of expenses. If this is what Marshall meant, he was guilty only of faulty language.

Alternatively, he may have wished to argue that a firm will be moved to economize only in proportion to the saving gained through each economizing action taken by itself. If this is what he meant, his error is more fundamental: a firm consistently following such practices would soon be bankrupt. On this matter see George J. Stigler, *The Theory of Price* (rev. ed.; New York, 1952), pp. 190 ff.

Finally, he may have been stating an empirical generalization taking full account of the formal conditions later pointed out by Hicks. This interpretation seems to have the most tenuous foundation of those mentioned here.

position, while the actual or potential members of the latter must bear a major part of the burden of exploitation through reduced employment in affected industries and so on.

A few words of summary are now in order, though it will hardly be possible to derive a succinct list of conclusions from this analysis. The first thing that may be said is that the economic power of labor unions is truly different in kind from the economic power of enterprise monopolies and cartels. Unions have been granted the unique privilege of coercing others into accepting the terms they lay down; that is, they have been granted the privilege of inflicting penalties and dispensing rewards in accord with whether they disapprove or approve of behavior in others. Such powers are inherent in economic power, especially when it is discriminatory, but their exercise has been specifically denied to all monopolistic organizations except those involving "labor."

We should expect the strongest unions to arise from the following conditions: (1) the labor service is "essential"—cannot be done without under existing technology; (2) the wage bill for this labor generally accounts for a small fraction of cost among its employers; (3) the product is non-storable or otherwise unique and is sold in large part to other firms; (4) interruptions in production are expensive to the employers for technological reasons; and (5) the relevant supply of this labor can be closely regulated by the union through one means or another. These conditions would seem to hold in varying degrees for many of the groups we normally think of as having been organized into strong unions: teamsters, bakers, musicians, stagehands, locomotive engineers, typesetters, and so on.

Unions should be expected to utilize their discriminatory powers to the full extent consistent with public opinion, except insofar as such behavior is prohibitively expensive. The latter is likely to be the case where the workforce is mobile and fluid and the number of employers is very large. Exploitative conditions appear in greater or lesser degree in virtually every contract accomplished through collective bargaining, in the form of "featherbedding," work rules of various kinds, employment guarantees, output royalties for union benefit, penalty rates of various types (e.g., overtime pay), and so on. The so-called "guaranteed annual wage" and union-controlled "profit-sharing" schemes are outright exploitative devices, and their offerance as union terms in recent years may be viewed as the launching of trial balloons to test the limits of employer and public tolerance to this type of practice. As far as industrial unions are concerned, all exploitation tends toward the ultimate "optimum": syndicalism. Therein lies a basic source of conflict between craft unionism and industrial unionism.

I have not tried in this discussion to assess the importance of the economic power of unions or to suggest policies to regulate that power. The objective has been much more modest, namely, to explore the nature and bases of that power, with particular concern for the "limiting" factors. As stated at the beginning, I am not at all satisfied with the present state of my thinking on this problem, and I look forward to continuing enlightenment through the growing discussion that is bound to take place on the labor union issue. As of the moment, I am impressed by the peculiar importance of two generalizations. First, the power of unions in a strictly economic sense will almost certainly be underestimated if we pay attention to their effect on wage rates alone. Second, public opinion is the decisive factor that will determine whether labor unions are to be limited to the degree and extent of economic power enjoyed by ordinary enterprise monopolies. The trend of public opinion has been steadily in the other direction, and it would be rash to predict a sudden reversal.

14

Wage Theory in an Age of Organized Labor

J. M. Clark

What should be said concerning wages
Would run to several hundred pages.
One difficulty bars the way:
We can't agree on what to say.

K. E. Boulding, comment in a CED staff conference.

THIS CHAPTER deals with the problem whether, when widespread and powerful collective bargaining comes in the door, "economic laws" governing wages, and useful theorizing about them, fly out the window. The case is difficult, but I am not prepared to admit that it is hopeless. As to the setting in which this problem will be discussed, it starts with recognition that some kind of collective bargaining is a necessity to redress inequalities of power that would result without it, both as to wages and as to human rights on the job. This recognition does not carry with it any judgment as to how much power is healthy, in either area. It leaves open the question whether protection of workers' rights on the job may encroach on the employer's needed scope for managing the business, and whether economically unsound wage adjustments may be reached. Tough borderline problems remain, such as compulsory union membership versus freedom not to join, the use of various degrees of coercion, or the conditions under which the filling of strikers' places may be justified.

The approach to modern wage theory has been handicapped by an inherited one-sided view of the task of price theory in general. This task properly includes both the processes of bargaining and the economic forces that govern the result, or at least set limits on it. Theory has traditionally neglected the first half of this task, disparaging it as the "higgling of the market," about which there was supposedly nothing important to be said. The job of theory was conceived as defining the conditions of a precisely-determinate equilibrium which was supposed to come about when the higgling was over. There was occasional recognition—notably by Alfred Marshall—that the level of equilibrium was itself modified by the route followed in reaching it. But in general, theory has neglected the ways in which equilibria are approached in a free market—to the extent that they are approached. If theory had all along done justice to both halves of its task, it might have been less unprepared to deal with the problems of wages under collective bargaining, though one must admit that these present harder problems than the bargainings of commodity markets.[1] Such

[1] There is a terminological question here, arising from the need for a general term to designate the whole group of price-making processes, which I have charged price-theory with negelecting. For this purpose, "bargaining" appears to be the most available generic term. Its character and scope differ widely in different forms of marketing. One may distinguish the "bourse" or supply-and-demand type prevailing on organized exchanges; the "quoted-price" type prevalent in industry and trade, auctions, selling by sealed bids and; finally, the "negotiated price" in which single exchanges are matters of active negotiation between buyer and seller, each trying to induce the other to improve the terms of his offer. (See Neil W. Chamberlain, *A General Theory of Economic Process* [New York, 1955], pp. 85–99.) Wages under collective bargaining constitute one of three major varieties of negotiated price.

In the quoted-price type, bargaining is reduced to the setting of the price on one side, and accepting or rejecting it on the other. If the price-setter has a monopoly, rejecting his offer means going without the product; if there is competition, it means looking for better offers from rival sellers. The pure quoted-price system is often modified by what may be called "fringe negotiation," in which the party faced by a quoted price (who may be buyer or seller) tries to negotiate special concessions which do not automatically apply to the others.

Where negotiation is the regular method, two main types may be illustrated by the real-estate market, and collective bargaining by organized labor. In the real-estate market, each party has the chance to resort to alternative offers from different buyers and sellers, making the situation one of differentiated competition. In collective bargaining, there is ordinarily no resort to competing offers from third parties; the almost-inevitable outcome is an ultimate settlement between the two negotiating parties. Only in rare and extreme cases will the union members look *en masse* for other work, or the employer try to replace his whole work-force from other sources ("scabs"). The

a two-sided theory might be less insistent on assuming impossibly precise knowledge, and readier to treat supply and demand functions as zones or ranges, rather than precise lines, and as setting limits on the scope of discretionary action of bargainers, rather than extinguishing it.[2]

At present there is no comprehensive theory of wages that commands general acceptance.[3] The 1954 conference of the International Economic Association, the proceedings of which were published in 1957, brought together a wide variety of attitudes and approaches, plus evidence of important international differences in some of the determining factors; but if there was notable progress toward agreement on a theory, it was not clearly manifest.[4] The only serious attempt at the kind of theory that analyses determining economic forces under conditions of collective bargaining appears to be that of John Dunlop, who very ably applies to labor unions the kind of analytical tools already employed in the theory of the business firm.[5] He assumes that the union tries to maximize the total wages of its members, with higher wage-rates tending to reduce total employment but increase union membership, resulting in an equilibrium model. This model does not seem to have won wide acceptance, and critics find Dunlop's inductive observations more enlightening.

In the field of the processes and maneuvers of negotiation, the least abstruse theory is Sumner H. Slichter's.[6] He starts with a simple

four-year-long Kohler strike, now under investigation, is the exception that illustrates the rule. Collective bargaining thus approaches the model of "bilateral monopoly," though it may not quite reach it. The sanction back of non-agreement is the infliction of mutual loss through an interruption (strike or lockout) which is normally regarded as temporary and through which each side hopes to induce the other to change its latest offer into one that may be accepted. After a collective bargain has been reached, the hiring of individual workers takes place at the quoted price and other terms fixed in the collective agreement.

[2] See R. A. Lester, "A Range Theory of Wage Differentials," *Industrial and Labor Relations Review*, Vol. 5, No. 4 (July, 1952), pp. 483–500. Lester begins with observation of actual ranges of differentials, and goes on to analyse the forms in which competitive forces work, and other factors which impede or actively oppose them.

[3] See A. M. Ross, *Trade Union Wage Policy* (Berkeley, 1948), p. 1.

[4] These proceedings are published under the title of *The Theory of Wage Determination*, John T. Dunlop (ed.), (New York and London, 1957).

[5] See Dunlop, *Wage Determination Under Trade Unions* (New York and London, 1944; 2nd ed., 1950).

[6] See Slichter, *The Challenge of Industrial Relations* (New York, 1947), pp. 127–137.

model based on the idea that if each side knew accurately the other's willingness to fight, there would never be a strike or lockout. He uses an arithmetic example in which the union would stand an eight-week strike to gain 10 cents an hour, or a six-week strike to gain 5 cents, while the employer would stand a ten-week strike to defeat a 10 cent gain, or a five-week strike to defeat a 5-cent gain. This implies that the union's willingness to fight for a second 5-cent gain is less than for a first 5 cents, while the employer's resistance to the second 5 cents is greater than to the first. In this example, a settlement would be reached between five and ten cents. With this model as a point of departure, Slichter goes on to make room for different attitudes, co-operative and combative, and for change and uncertainty as to the sticking-points in a given situation.

A group of more abstract theorists have produced an incipient body of theory of a more esoteric sort, choosing their assumptions with a view to producing a determinate equilibrium.[7] For this purpose they carry assumptions like those of Slichter's initial model to greater lengths of rational precision in the calculus of expected gains and costs, while some assume predictable reactions to deception, uncertainty and face-saving. So far, they do not seem to have made room for such things as a strike that costs far more than the amount of wages at issue, which Ross cites as an example of a different kind of logic, in the contest for survival.[8] One fears that the penalty of investing so much intellectual ingenuity in a model may be paid in the shape of inability to get away from its artificial conditions when this becomes necessary, if complex reality is to be dealt with.

The majority of labor students examine bargaining processes more concretely and without formal theorizing. They generally recognize that bargaining is limited by economic forces, but differ as to whether the limits are narrow or wide, and pay little attention to defining how

[7] See G. L. S. Shackle, "The Nature of the Bargaining Process," in *The Theory of Wage Determination, op. cit.*, pp. 292–316. Shackle reviews the theories of Zeuthen, Hicks, Pen and his own, briefly but with references to works in which fuller treatments can be found. See also K. W. Rothschild, "Approaches to the Theory of Bargaining," *ibid.*, pp. 281, 286–288.

[8] See Ross, "Wage Determination under Collective Bargaining," *American Economic Review*, Vol. XXXVII, No. 5 (Dec., 1947), p. 822.

they are set. They appear to unite in rejecting the marginal productivity theory, which makes it a trifle ironic that one of their most widely-held principles is a limited version of marginal productivity, approached from an unfamiliar direction which apparently makes its identity unrecognizable. Of this more later.

It may be worthwhile to review very briefly some of the high spots in past wage theories. Starting with theories of differential rewards, the Middle Ages invoked a traditional form of equity based on the requirements of the individual's station in life. Adam Smith analyzed competitive forces tending to equalize the attractiveness of different occupations and also forces tending to maintain differences. J. E. Cairnes used a theory of "non-competing groups" to explain persistent differentials. Now, via widespread unionism, a modernized sense of equity is once more a potent force.

As to general levels of wages, late eighteenth-century thinking was overshadowed by the pressure of population, driving wages down to a subsistence minimum. Adam Smith softened this theory by the idea that continued progress could keep the level of wages above bare subsistence in a race in which, like the Red Queen, the economy had to keep running to hold wages in the same place, if that place was above the subsistence-minimum. John Stuart Mill went further, leaving room for a rising level, on condition that large gains were made, in which case the workers might incorporate them into the standard of living which they would protect by limiting the birth rate. He also held, at least at one time, that while it would be desirable if labor unions could raise wages, this was impossible under the limits imposed by the "wages-fund."

Later came the marginal productivity theory, adapted to an economy emancipated from Malthusian limitations. It is at least not inconsistent with the observed tendency for wages to maintain a roughly uniform percentage share in an increasing total. Under the Cobb-Douglas formula, the share of wages on a marginal-productivity basis would always be two-thirds of the total, so that labor's imputed product would get a majority of the gains for which technical progress and increased capital per worker might be historically responsible.[9] Finally, the growing power of organized labor has led to the present period, in which theories and descriptive appraisals of bargaining power hold the field. Such theories cannot hope to be universally valid, since conditions differ so much from country to country, notably in the degree of centralization of bargaining strategy and of governmental participation or control. What one might still expect is that in all the industrially developed countries of the free world there may be some common limiting principles, indicating either what results are inevitable or what the necessary consequences of given behavior are. I shall be looking for such common principles. Meanwhile, for the majority of the world's people, the pressure of population remains the dominant fact, keeping levels of living below what we in this country would consider a minimum of subsistence.

What must a modern theory of wages include? In the first place, it must deal with both money and real wages: with money wages because that is what unions and employers bargain about, and with real wages because that is the substance that results from the bargaining. This means that the forces governing prices of consumer goods are part of the picture. In the second place, it must be dynamic, since the crux of the problem is the division of an annually increasing total made up of parts that increase at different rates, in size and in productivity. These differential rates of increase give rise to some of the toughest nuts which wage adjustment has to crack. In the third place, it must have some conception of the motives of the parties—not a complete picture since, like all theories, it must do some simplifying, but sufficient to explain their characteristic actions. These include things that cannot be explained by the method so common in economic theories of assuming that each party has some single objective which he undertakes to maximize with mechanical single-mindedness and

[9] C. W. Cobb and Paul H. Douglas, "A Theory of Production," *American Economic Review Supplement,* Vol. XVIII, No. 1 (March, 1928), pp. 139–165; and Paul H. Douglas, "Are There Laws of Production?", *American Economic Review,* Vol. XXXVIII, No. 1 (March, 1948), pp. 1–41. The statistical evidence for the formula, though massive, appears inconclusive. The simplest form of the formula is: $P = L^{2/3} C^{1/3}$, the symbols standing for product, labor and fixed capital. It is a standard feature of our system that the gains of progress do not remain long the property of those who created them, but are diffused as the new methods become standard practice.

impossibly perfect knowledge. Such a method can produce determinate models, but only at the expense of unreality when dealing with anything as complex as collective bargaining. The examination of motives brings in the various strategic situations which call forth different motives on the part of the bargainers. The task is simplified if one focuses on the limits set on bargaining by economic forces, but even here the various motives back of these economic forces need to be recognized. In the fourth place, a modern theory cannot possibly escape the need of formulating standards of judgment by which to appraise the desirability of the behavior of the markets. These standards need to be clearly independent of the analysis of the forces that determine what actually happens. It is no longer possible to accept a freely-competitive adjustment as both a simplified picture of what actually happens and of the result that is economically correct. Some writers still attach some normative weight to the differential wage structure that presumably *would* be brought about in a freely competitive market, but the specifications become so conjectural that few positive conclusions can be drawn from them. They appear to serve mainly to support a verdict of "not proven" to the charge that collective bargaining operates consistently to distort the structure of wage differentials that would result from competition.[10] It seems more likely that its effect is mixed, distorting the structure in some cases and in others bringing it closer to the competitive ideal than actual imperfect markets would do.

Lastly, wage theory needs to deal both with differential wage structures and with wage levels. The differential structures include differences between persons, between plants or firms, between industries, between workers' occupations (which cross industry lines) and between areas. Differences between men and women doing the same work have largely disappeared, and remaining differences due to sex are probably merged in the occupational differentials between occupations predominantly male and those predominantly female. Differences due to race are similarly merged with occupational differentials, fortified by obstacles to admission into various occupations.

[10] See papers by Clark Kerr and Lloyd G. Reynolds, in *The Theory of Wage Determination, op. cit.*, pp. 173–221.

Some racial differentials are also presumably merged with differentials between areas. In studying wage-differentials plenty of complexities arise. To what extent are existing differentials merely an allowance for differences in skill, consistent with the idea of an equal efficiency-wage? To what extent do they offset differences in cost of living, in harmony with the idea of equality of "real income?" And how should one treat differentials between plants which show different productivity per man-hour on account of different degrees of mechanization with different amounts of capital per worker?

Any study of the general levels of wages presupposes some kind of a structure of differentials. It may assume the existing structure or some conjectural structure in which differentials would be in equilibrium. If it examines changes in general levels, it may assume that they have no effect on the assumed structure, but if it is to get close enough to reality to interpret the way in which such changes actually work, it must allow for the fact that their effect is not evenly distributed through the system, but creates dynamic movements in the differential-structure.

The level of wages may mean a number of things. It may mean an average money wage or an average real wage. Or it may mean the aggregate amount that goes to wages, generally figured as a fraction of either the gross national product or the net national income. It would need to take some kind of account of the growing total of "fringe benefits," and this presents a problem in view of the different forms these take and the different sources from which they come. It seems that different items would need to be included and perhaps differently estimated, according as the investigator is concerned with the effect on the employer's costs, on the total of savings in the economy, or on the wage-earner's total real income, or his level of consumption.

The wage bill of a single enterprise may be a relatively minor part of its total costs, simply because a large part goes for materials and supplies. The small size of this fraction may be an important fact in figuring the effect of a single wage increase on a single employer's costs and the amount of the price increase that would be needed to offset it. But such figuring would be quite misleading as an indication of the effect of widespread wage increases on the structure of costs in the economy at large. The expenditures for materials and supplies and the work of distributing the product all contain their own quotas of labor costs. For this purpose the important fact is that wages in this country have consistently absorbed sixty-odd per cent of total income. Since profits fluctuate more than wages in business fluctuations, wages form a larger share in depressions than in booms. At the depth of the 1932 depression, industry as a whole was operating in the red.

Wage theory may be able to base its main findings on a fairly limited range of motives. But if it is to make a useful judgment as to what motives it needs to take into account, it needs to do this in the setting of an awareness of a much wider range, from which it may select the ones that are important for its limited purposes, and on which it should be prepared to draw at any time when its original simplified scheme of motives proves insufficient to explain important facts. In the first place, this calls for identifying the bargaining agents on behalf of union and employer and the pressures which each must satisfy in order to hold his job securely. Mutual survival, stressed by Bakke, means on the employer's side chiefly solvency. On the union side it means both survival of the union and that of its leader in the union's internal politics—he must hold the support of his constituents. His attitude toward them ranges from crusading for their rights to exploiting or betraying them, in cases in which he has gained the kind of power that corrupts and uses it in the predatory fashion which he may wrongly conceive to be typical among business executives. In any case, he is a salaried executive with functions and rewards that put him in that class.

To describe the objectives in the case, simple terms are bound to be used and are bound to be insufficiently specific. "Power versus equity" has meaning, but how much power and what standards of equity? "Political versus economic" also wants explaining—does it refer to internal union politics, to lobbying, to action through party organizations or merely to the pursuit of ends that are not measured in money? "Survival," "security" and "responsibility" are all meaningful, and all want defining, especially as any reduction in an existing degree of power is almost sure to be viewed with alarm as a threat to security, if not to survival. Even the distinction between defending what one has and gaining more tends to become blurred, when one is defending something one regards as a right but has never actually possessed. One of the most meaningful distinctions is between gaining (or defending) some degree of power and using it to gain (or to defend) specific ends. The ends at stake in the employment relation include real and money wages; physical conditions in the work-place including recreation facilities, hours and vacation provisions; and human relations and rights on the job, including protections against arbitrary disciplinary action. In this field the mid-nineteenth-century employer held an arbitrary power that would be intolerable by modern standards. Whether the balance is swinging in the other direction is a question we cannot afford to forget. In any case, it seems hardly profitable to spend time trying to decide whether some of these ends are "economic" and others something else.

As Ross points out very enlighteningly, union attitudes differ with the different stage the union may be in as to the struggle for security or power. Where the minimum basis of union status is at stake, immediate economic gains and costs will not be figured closely. On a more tactical level, the union's aggressiveness may be affected by the state of its strike fund or the amount of unemployment, while the employer's ruggedness in bargaining may be influenced by whether he has important orders he must fill, or whether he has an extra-large inventory on hand. Such factors come into play at different phases of business cycles, but here the chief effect of union strength is to strengthen the resistance to wage-deflation during depressions so that wages move with a ratchet action instead of fluctuating freely up and down.

What are the standards in terms of which we should judge whether the forces determining wages tend to bring about results that are economically sound or desirable? One of the most disturbing standards actually employed is that of inevitability. This began to be used in the days of Malthus: we don't like the "iron law of wages," but unless the masses will control their biological tendency to multiply beyond the means of support, there is nothing useful we can do about it. (Malthus himself did not go quite this far.) A few modern economists approximate Mill's idea of the inability of unions to raise wages. But a larger number apply the standard of inevitability in a very different way: if organized labor—given its present degree of power—inevitably brings about unsound economic results, there is nothing we can do about it, short of resorting to direct controls of wages and prices and thus—in this view—abandoning the basic condition of a free economy. This conclusion is so unwelcome that either the unsoundness or the inevitability is bound to be called in question.

Another set of criteria goes under the name of "equity." Here one trouble is that ideas of equity are so conveniently various that it is a weak claim that cannot find some ground of "equity" to support it, and claimants select the criterion that best supports their particular case.[11] A. M. Ross calls ideas of equity "the strongest equalizing tendencies in wage determination."[12] But this is presumably not to be construed to mean that one group's ideas of what is equitably due to other groups cause that group to forego advantages that are within its reach; it means rather that other groups' ideas of what is equitably due to them decide whether they will acquiesce in the first group's gain or make a determined fight to restore previous relationships. The standards of equity which actually prevail include approval of differentials based on contribution or performance, or judgments as to the skill involved in different jobs, or their worth and proper standing. Seniority plays a part. The workers' ideas on these matters have to reach an adjustment with the employer's sense of the internal structure of rewards which is necessary to the effective organization of a plant. On this account the employer is bound to struggle, if necessary, for a wage system that will contain adequate incentives to efficient

[11] See S. H. Slichter, *The Challenge of Industrial Relations, op. cit.,* p. 137; See also A. M. Ross, *Trade Union Wage Policy, op. cit.,* p. 9. For example, different results might be indicated by the employer's capacity to pay and by uniformity between places, or by changes in cost of living and in productivity.

[12] See his *Trade Union Wage Policy, op. cit.*, p. 74. For the theoretical case for absolute equality of incomes, see A. P. Lerner, *The Economics of Control* (New York, 1944), pp. 24–32.

performance. The workers, on their side, have ways of resisting anything they consider an unwarranted "speed-up."

In terms of the proportions in which the product of industry and trade is divided between the rewards of labor and those of capital and enterprise, it seems fair to say that the prevalent attitude in this country approves of the highest wages consistent with the smallest return to capital and enterprise that would afford them capacity and incentive to do their job efficiently. This standard should not be confined to the wages of organized labor. This attitude regards the return to capital and enterprise as justified, so long as it is a payment for service rendered, and it wants to buy the service as cheaply as it can. Increased real wages, on the other hand, are regarded as desirable in their own right. And this attitude toward wages is shared by the typical progressive and enlightened American employer, though one could hardly expect him to enter fully into the view that profits are a payment to be minimized. In practice, the minimum return that has to be allowed to capital and enterprise may be about the same in size, whether it is regarded as the end and aim of business or as a grudging payment which society allows to the functionaries whom it allows to serve as its hired men to organize and direct an efficient economy.

Another criterion for a wage structure is its effect on the allocation of workers between industries, occupations and areas, including the relative use of labor and capital. Another is its effect in putting economically handicapped employers out of business or enabling some of them to survive. Another is the effect on employment, if such an effect can be identified. There are particular situations in which higher wages mean fewer jobs; and there appears to be a possibility of "wage-distortion unemployment," either of the sort Slichter describes, or merely because overpriced categories of labor become unprofitable to employ, relatively or absolutely.[13] However, the chief use made of the employment effect in wage theory is based on the

[13] See S. H. Slichter, *The Challenge of Industrial Relations, op. cit.*, pp. 73, 76–77, and *The American Economy* (New York, 1948), pp. 40–42. Slichter concludes that if wages are extra-high relative to quality of work in particular plants, industries, occupations or places, this tends to attract an oversupply of labor, resulting in partial unemployment. As between this and Reynolds' view that labor moves in response to job openings more than to higher wage rates, Slichter's view seems more applicable to employments that are casual or irregular, while Reynolds' appears more appropriate

general assumption that a higher level of wages means a lower level of employment. This may be true of single industries; as to the economy as a whole it is opposed by the doctrine of labor economists that higher wages mean a higher level of employment. These contradictory theories cannot both be true—certainly not under all conditions—and this leaves us with a problem which will be examined later.[14]

Last, but not least, since wage increases are charged with pushing up the price level in a special kind of price-inflation, any effect they may have of this sort is one of the important criteria by which the behavior of wages can properly be judged. It is also one of the most controversial. So much for standards of appraisal. They admit of a good deal of give and take, but they can serve as useful guides if we can only decide what effects the operation of the wage system has on the values which these standards embody.

A full discussion of the large and complicated subject of wage-differentials is out of the question, but the observations of students point toward a few generalizations that appear tenable. One is a general tendency toward a narrowing of the proportional differentials in the structure. Such a narrowing, of course, takes place every time there is an over-all wage increase of a flat amount in dollars and cents, so that the differentials in dollars and cents remain the same while the total wage-scale rises. Workers at the upper end of the wage-scale naturally exert their pressure in favor of maintaining proportionate differentials, and the result is a balance of some sort between opposing pressures. The dissatisfaction of a skilled group who felt that their interests were not fairly taken care of in mass bargaining was illustrated by the 1957 motormen's strike on the New York subway. A minimum wage, if it is effective in raising the lowest wage rates, naturally reduces the range of differentials, and this may result in pressures from the higher-paid occupations toward restoring what they consider a normal proportionate range.

---

to industries in which job turnover is low. Tendencies to lay off less profitable workers are restricted by the cost of labor turnover and by bargaining rules, such as those giving preferred tenure based on seniority, or limiting disciplinary discharge.

[14] If workers, low-paid, seek to better their lot | By grabbing some dough from the rich, | It makes jobs for more workers—or else it does not: | I cannot be positive which. (With apologies to Hilaire Belloc for borrowing from his piece on The Yak.)

The relative standing of white-collar occupations has become less favorable and their prestige-value has declined, and this could probably be rationalized without reference to stronger organized bargaining power on the part of the manual trades, as a result of the increased number of workers who have the kind of education needed to qualify for the white-collar occupations. But a great deal happens in the differential wage-structure for which the forces of supply and demand are clearly not the active causes. Perhaps the most spectacular single change is the one that has raised bituminous coal mining from one of the lowest-paid occupations to one of the highest, in the teeth of competition and the obvious forces of supply and demand, involving a drastic shrinkage of employment in the industry. Differentials between areas and industries have been thought to play some part in the mobility of the labor supply, helping to attract labor from sectors where its productivity is less to others where it is greater. On this matter, it seems necessary to distinguish between conditions of a normal or more-than-normal amount of unemployment and conditions of high-level employment with special features appearing when extra-strong expansion is called for in some sector of the economy. And one of the superficially paradoxical conclusions to which the findings of the experts point is that, if added labor is to be attracted into a given area or industry under conditions of high employment, it may be necessary to offer workers a higher wage than they are getting where they are; but under conditions of substantial unemployment, a given sector of the economy may be helped to expand its volume of employment by paying a lower wage than prevails elsewhere for similar labor. This paradox calls for some examination.

In the first place, if an area or an industry is to increase its share of the total employment in the country, the increase may come from three principal sources: new additions to the country's labor force, looking for their first regular job; workers who have been laid off; and workers who have jobs, but can be induced to change them if the prospects look brighter elsewhere.[15] It appears that the first two groups

[15] Lloyd G. Reynolds notes that normally "interplant movement" of labor is mostly the employment of workers who have been discharged or laid off, or have quit their jobs because of dissatisfaction. See Reynolds, *The Structure of Labor Markets* (New Haven, 1951), p. 241.

are the principal source of mobile labor supply in normal or subnormal times, and that at such times the thing that will attract them is the existence of job-openings without close comparison of relative wage-rates. But job openings tend to be plentiful where employers can make good profits rather than where wages are high. In fact, if wages are lower than elsewhere for the same grade of labor or in proportion to the grade available, that helps to enable employers there to offer more jobs. It is obvious that a firm has an advantage if it can get labor cheaper than its competitors, and the tendency of industries to migrate to areas of low wages is too familiar to need proof. It is obvious why labor unions aim to iron out such differentials by raising the lower rates to protect the higher-wage areas against the competition of the lower wages. But such ironing-out often has to proceed gradually. The mobility of labor does not in itself appear to be effective in ironing-out differentials of these sorts.[16]

On the other hand, when jobs are plentiful, an industry wanting to expand may find difficulty in getting all the labor it wants, and may offer wages above the market level as a way of attracting more workers, some of whom might have to be lured away from other jobs. In special conditions, like a defense emergency, an expanding industry might draw into the labor force workers who are not normally members—married women or workers who have retired. This is mainly a temporary matter, and often dependent on non-economic motives; since the normal long-term effect of a sustained increase in the real earnings of employed workers is not to attract extra numbers into the working force, but the reverse: if the husband is well-paid, the wife is under less pressure to take a job; and a well-paid worker may be in a position to retire from the working force earlier than he otherwise would. One study of labor mobility in six cities, directed by Gladys L. Palmer and covering the period 1940–1950, found evidence that the pull of differential wage-rates had an effect on labor mobility.[17] This finding should be interpreted in the light of the fact that the period covered included World War II, the defense drive

[16] Charles A. Meyers has noted that a study at the Massachusetts Institute of Technology showed little equalization of wages through labor movement in a period of unemployment. See *The Theory of Wage Determination, op. cit.*, p. 375.

[17] See C. A. Myers, in *The Theory of Wage Determination, op. cit.*, p. 319.

immediately preceding and the "catching-up" period that immediately followed. It was a period of insistent economic mobilization, with demand for labor increasing until it exceeded supply, while wages rose in response. The pulling power of differential wage-rates was abnormally active in this period.

When it is a question of attracting workers away from the jobs they hold, the ones most ready to respond are mostly young, unmarried workers with short service and little in the way of seniority or pension rights to sacrifice by moving. If it is a question of mobilizing a larger number than will be furnished from this most footloose part of the working force, the resistance to movement increases rapidly, and moderate wage-differentials cannot be expected to overcome it.

When mobilization is of the sort that brings wage-differentials strongly into play, and especially if the time factor is urgent, the result often is that the wage-differential that is needed for a rapid build-up is more than is necessary to maintain the resulting supply after the build-up period is over. Then it leaves the wage structure out of equilibrium. In extreme cases, this may be adjusted by reducing the extra-high rates, but since wage-reductions face such stubborn resistance, the more normal way of restoring equilibrium is to leave the high rates unchanged while the rest of the market catches up.

The aggregate share of the national income that goes to wages is subject to economic limits that are more cogent and definite than those bearing on wage differentials. I will take up the problem of price inflation of the pushed-up variety, the grounds for a residual theory of wages, and the action of the principle of substitution between factors of production—in other words, the modern version of the principle of marginal productivity, which is basically quite an old version. The analysis will build on two main premises. First, the differential structure of wages, while far from frozen, shows considerable tenacity in restoring accepted and approved relationships if they are disturbed, and something similar applies to the long-term proportion between wages and the rewards of capital and enterprise. Second, the sum of the shares into which the national real income is divided cannot exceed the whole, and the whole depends on physical productivity. Accepting an over-all long-term yearly increase of close to two per cent a year in real productivity, no one group's share can increase at more than this two per cent rate without encroaching on the relative shares of other groups, and if one major group absorbs more than the whole national increase, it encroaches on the absolute shares of other groups.

These truisms are obscured by the fact that the total of money claims to income can, and often does, increase more than physical product does. For our purposes, the problem takes the shape of wage rates increasing faster than the economy-wide average increase of man-hour productivity. The excess spells an increase in unit labor costs in money terms, and it may merely be dissipated in increased prices, provided that the total flow of money spending and money income expands enough to cover the increase in physical product plus price increases to cover the increased costs, and perhaps restore what employers regard as a normal proportion between costs and profits. If this expanded money-flow is not forthcoming, two things may happen. Prices may fail to rise, causing profits to shrink absolutely. Profits may contain some slack out of which a shrinkage could be absorbed, but the important thing is not the effect on the most profitable firms, but on the less profitable ones which are needed to keep competition healthy.[18] In any case, if the process of absorbing increased costs out of profits goes on continuously, it will use up whatever expendable slack there may be. Then prices may be forced up to cover the increased costs in the face of insufficient spending, at the expense of output and employment. This, given the conditions, would happen in either a competitive or a monopoloidal industry, though there would be more discretion as to the timing and amount of the price increase if competition were not powerfully active. Aside from this, there is no clear proof for the widespread impression that it implies monopoly pricing if the industry can pass increased costs on to the customer.

[18] Competition will not be healthy if these less profitable firms are really inefficient. If prices are governed by the costs of such firms, this points toward something wrong in the structure of the industry which prevents efficiency from spreading as readily as it should.

The conclusion is sometimes drawn that it takes some unemployment, brought about if necessary by a squeeze on credit, to keep the increase in wage-costs within non-inflationary bounds by reducing labor's bargaining power. Apparently, in the light of the first quarter of 1958, unemployment of over five million has not been enough to stop a creeping price-rise, and we are warned against the obvious anti-unemployment measures on the ground that they might lead to further inflation. This potential dilemma is worth examination in the light of the conditions and forces actually at work.

A major difficulty arises from the fact that the two per cent annual increase in nation-wide real productivity, out of which all increases in real incomes must come, is a composite of sectors where the increase is greater and others where it is less. Then if the price-level is to remain stable, if the structure of wage-differentials does not change greatly and if the proportionate share going to labor remains approximately stable, money costs and prices must be reduced in the most rapidly progressing industries and must rise in the least progressive ones. Real wages would keep pace with money wages and both would rise at the nation-wide average rate of increase in productivity, not the rate of increase in the particular industry where the workers are employed. But in the most rapidly progressing industries, neither organized workers nor employers are likely voluntarily to follow this rule. Employers will make profits and try to hold onto them, and workers will try to get their share based on their better-than-average rise in productivity in their particular industries. In fact, they may succeed in getting more than this. Then wages elsewhere tend to rise in excess of productivity in the other industries, bringing about the now-familiar dilemma.

How likely is union bargaining to stay within the indicated limits? Here a frankly oversimplified picture may have some meaning. The leaders of the great federation, which covers many industries, have an understanding of this limiting principle—but they do not do the bargaining. This is largely controlled by the heads of national (and international) unions. They have a realistic understanding of what can be got from a single industry, and they tend to moderate the unattainable demands for which rank-and-file and locals may press. But these pressures have some effect. Progress seems to rest on an increase in the influence of the great federation over bargaining policy.[19] Some such progress seems to be under way, but one must expect it to be gradual. In the meantime, if creeping inflation stays between one per cent and two per cent a year as an average trend, that may be regarded as tolerable, though not desirable.[20] It is only since, let us say, 1952, that this "pushed-up" variety of inflation has been clearly distinguishable, operating in the absence of excessive demand such as results from defense drives and war production, and gives rise to the usual, "pulled-up" variety of inflation. But it seems clear that the "push-up" process has been a part of the economic picture for a longer period.

Turning to another aspect of the theory of distribution, let us inquire into the over-all demand and supply schedules of labor, and of capital and enterprise. The first stage of this analysis lends a rather surprising amount of support to a highly unorthodox theory of wages, namely, that over the long run and in the aggregate, capital and enterprise get a return governed by what is needed to induce the existing supply of these factors, and labor gets what is left—in short, a residual theory of wages. This has an appearance of reversing the obvious and accepted convention that wages are a cost and profits are the residual share. That is true, of course, for the financial operations of a single firm, but there is no reason why the reverse might not be true of the over-all distribution of the social income. A residual theory is unlikely to be adequate or final, but a study of the evidence will be enlightening.

If we look for a share that constitutes the minimum reward necessary to call forth the services of the factor that receives it, that share cannot be wages, increasing as they have been. As for capital and enterprise, while their rewards may contain a good deal that is supramarginal, there is at least a presumption that a reduced return tends to reduce the amount offered and increase the amount demanded, and *vice versa*—in short, that the supply and demand schedules have

[19] See Slichter, *The Challenge of Industrial Relations, op. cit.*, pp. 175–6; and *The American Economy*, p. 63.

[20] A 2 per cent annual increase would cut in half the purchasing power of a fixed dollar income in 35 years.

normal slopes and intersect in the normal way, pointing to an equilibrium adjustment.

As for the long-run effect of higher or lower wages on the over-all supply of labor, this includes the percentage of the population in the working force, but this percentage responds to various other things than wages, such as education, life expectancy and mechanized housekeeping. For our purposes, perhaps the best single index is the shortening of the work-week as real wages rise, indicating that American labor has, over a long period, taken more than half its gains in increased consumption and less than half—say roughly four-tenths—in shorter hours, indicating a steeply-sloping supply-schedule with an inverse elasticity in the neighborhood of four-tenths. That is, higher wages result in fewer hours of labor supplied.

As to the over-all demand function for labor, we have seen that contradictory theories are held, indicating that the answer is not known. Some light may be thrown on it by visualizing the effects of paying labor different percentages of the national income. It seems clear that a very low percentage—say fifty per cent or less—would reduce employment, directly by reducing the flow of consumer spending, and indirectly because reduced consumer spending would reduce the field for investment. It also seems clear that a very high percentage—say above seventy per cent—would reduce employment by reducing the returns that constitute the incentive to investment outlays. In that case, the optimum range must lie between. At the precise point of maximum employment, if there is one and wherever it is, the over-all demand function for labor would be completely inelastic; limited changes in wages would have no effect on the volume of employment.

With labor's bargaining power as strong as it is, the inherent probability is that labor's actual share has been pushed above this optimum point, but not much above it. This would mean that higher wages probably reduce employment, but only slightly—the demand schedule would have an elasticity considerably less than one. In other words, its slope would be very similar to what we have inferred as the slope of the supply schedule. Then, on a supply-and-demand basis, wages would be determined by the intersection of two curves, each of which is best conceived as a zone of some width, and which may be very nearly parallel to one another. To the extent that this reasoning may accord with the facts, wages would be indeterminate within rather wide limits, and within these limits there would be room for them to be determined residually.

I have purposely left to the last a final factor in the demand function for labor, which tends toward an elasticity sufficient to redeem wages from complete indeterminacy. It is generally recognized that if rising wages make labor more expensive, this puts pressure on employers to introduce innovations, especially mechanization, by which increased capital per worker is used to increase product per worker, until the worker becomes worth his increased wage. American labor leaders at the top levels recognize this principle and instead of blindly opposing mechanization they have accepted it as a necessary means to high wages, seeking to control the manner and rate of introduction so that it may not bring unemployment. The present uneasiness about the phase of mechanization known as "automation" is due to the fear that the impact of this change may be too large and too sudden to be assimilated as the previous progress of mechanization has been. The principle involved is the principle of altering the proportions in which productive factors are combined so as to economize factors that have become more expensive by combining larger proportions of other factors with them. In this fashion, labor and capital are substitutable for one another.

This, be it noted, is a form of the supposedly-discarded marginal productivity theory, resurrected without using the name. The form that has been thus revived is the form first presented to the American Economic Association over sixty-nine years ago by Stuart Wood at the time that John Bates Clark presented his formulation of a marginal productivity theory.[21] Clark held that Wood's theory and his

[21] "Contributions to the Wages Question," *Publications of the American Economic Association,* Vol. IV, No. 2 (March, 1889). It has been objected that a general increase in wages could not stimulate the use of larger proportions of capital, since it would increase the cost of capital instruments as much as that of direct labor, so that only a reduction of interest rates could really make capital relatively cheaper. As against this, the fact is that, owing to economies in production, the cost of capital instruments has not risen in the same proportion as wages of direct labor, so that capital has become relatively cheaper, aside from a decline in interest rates.

own were not different principles but different versions of the same principle.

The arithmetic of this proposition is basically simple though its ramifications are involved. If the employer finds that a given amount of capital can be substituted for a given amount of labor in making a given amount of product, he is comparing a plus increment of capital with a minus increment of labor and finds their incremental productivities equal in this particular situation. But if he can make this substitution, he can also use more capital with the same amount of labor to produce a larger product, thus gauging the incremental productivity of capital. In an expanding economy such as ours, this is the direction in which the adjustment generally works. When the new proportions have become standard practice, the incremental productivity of labor has been raised by giving it more capital to work with, while if the expansion of the economy is sufficient, it can prevent the substitution from leading to added unemployment.

As to how this principle operates, a few further propositions may need to be stated. First, the relevant adjustment is of the long-run sort involving a reconstruction of capital equipment, not the short-run effect of adding or laying off workers in a plant with a given capacity. Second, in any particular case these adjustments are often—not always—likely to go by large, discontinuous steps. Third, they generally involve some technical innovation and the uncertainty that goes with it. Fourth, in this version of the principle, wages appear as the active factor, not a passive result. A wage increase stimulates action by employers which raises labor's productivity. Whether this productivity is increased as much as wages have risen cannot be guaranteed; if not, real wages, being limited by real productivity, will not rise as much as money wages. Here wage bargaining is subject to limiting forces, but these do not appear likely to be closely or precisely determinate.

A final word as to the way in which changing proportions of factors are being worked out. In recent years it appears that the increase in product per worker in manufacturing has roughly kept pace with the increase of capital per worker, indicating that technical progress has offset what would otherwise be a tendency to diminishing returns to added capital. On this basis, if the relative shares going to labor and to capital-and-enterprise remained unchanged, capital-and-enterprise could get their share in the shape of an unchanged rate of return on an increased investment, while labor gets its share in the shape of an increased rate of return per worker. If this relationship persists, there is no necessary prospect of a long-run shrinkage of profits, such as the British classical economists envisaged, not as long as technical progress remains vigorous.

15

Regulated Wages in Under-developed Countries*

P. T. Bauer

In an unregulated market, the available supplies or numbers determine the wage, but, under regulated conditions, wages determine the numbers.
Report of the South African Industrial Legislation Commission, 1935.

I SHALL DISCUSS some major implications and results of wage regulation [1] in under-developed countries. Besides examining the factors behind its introduction, I shall consider such economic effects of wage regulation as its influence on economic development, on the structure and location of industry, and on the occupational distribution of the population. I shall consider these economic issues partly in terms of general economic analysis and partly by means of specific examples from various parts of the under-developed world. Beyond the more

* Both the substance and the presentation of this paper owe much to suggestions from B. S. Yamey of the University of London.

[1] The term "regulated wages" is used in this chapter to refer to wages determined by government, statutory authorities, and trade unions, in contrast to those emerging from the play of market forces. Even without such organised prescription of wages, the institutions of society affect wages, as they do all other prices. But such general influences act by affecting the conditions of supply and demand, and not by setting rates with given conditions of supply and demand, or by monopolistic measures restricting the supply reaching the market.

Monopsonists, that is employers or employers' associations with some power of monopoly in the hiring of labour, can depress wages below the rates which measure what labour is worth to them (the marginal value product). They can do this by diminishing the amount of employment they offer, which in these conditions reduces the wage rate. The special problems raised by monopsony are examined below.

narrowly economic implications, the establishment of regulated wages has far-reaching and pervasive social and political results which I shall also discuss, albeit briefly.

In most under-developed countries wages are regulated in important sectors of the economy. The principal instruments of regulation are: minimum wage legislation; promotion of binding wage arbitration; official insistence on, or promotion of, payment of wages above the supply price of labour, as for instance by fair wages clauses in government contracts and in protected industries; and also trade union action, often sponsored or facilitated by government, notably by the granting of special legal rights and immunities. Regulated wages, when they are effective, are instruments of restriction, irrespective of the agency which has established them; their introduction implies the withholding from employment of part of the labour supply available at the regulated wage or at lower rates. By thus curtailing supplies which can be offered compared to the total available supply, regulated wages create, and indeed are often designed to create, a situation which may be conveniently called a contrived scarcity.[2]

Wage regulation in under-developed countries dates from the inter-war period, and has become very widespread since the second world war. It is neither possible nor necessary to estimate its extent quantitatively. There are several reasons why specific quantification is not possible. These include the presence of much subsistence activity in most under-developed countries, frequent shifts between activities, and imperfect occupational specialisation. Moreover, it is often difficult to discover whether a particular wage is above the supply price of labour (i.e., whether it is a regulated wage), and also the extent and effectiveness of its enforcement. However, these difficulties do not vitiate the general discussion or the confident general conclu-

[2] Unavoidable scarcity, sometimes termed natural scarcity, reflects the limitation of the total available supply, while a contrived scarcity results from the withholding from the market of part of the total supply. A contrived scarcity is often superimposed on a natural scarcity. But the two concepts are logically distinct and have very different implications for policy. The distinction corresponds to the traditional distinction between rents on the one hand and monopoly earnings or prices on the other. The convenient terms of natural and contrived scarcity have been proposed by W. H. Hutt of the University of Cape Town.

sion that regulated wages affect economic activity over a wide area of the under-developed world.[3]

Industry-wide collective bargaining by trade unions is officially encouraged throughout the under-developed world, notably in Latin America, Asia, and the British Commonwealth.[4] In important and controllable sectors where collective bargaining is not yet effective, the government generally regulates wages either by statute or by the other measures already mentioned. Thus there is wage regulation either by official action or by industry-wide collective bargaining. This is the pattern officially and explicitly promoted by the I.L.O., the British Colonial Office, and the Indian government. In most under-developed countries, official action is as yet more important than the activities of trade unions. There are statutory minimum wages in important sectors of practically every Latin American and Caribbean country, coupled generally with maximum hours and frequently with fines for discharging workers.[5] In Asia statutory minimum wages are in force in several countries, including India, where they are supplemented by maximum hours, binding arbitration and at times by compulsory bonuses varying with company profits. In many African territories there are statutory minimum wages as well as compulsory arbitration, and their establishment elsewhere is proposed or foreshadowed. There are fair wages clauses in government contracts in practically all British dependencies; their adoption is a condition for receiving Colonial Development and Welfare funds.

[3] For instance, according to a recent report by the International Labour Office (I.L.O.) on *Minimum Wages in Latin America* (Geneva, 1954), p. 22: "Brazil, Chile, Costa Rica, Cuba, Haiti, Mexico, Paraguay and Uruguay have had considerable experience in the fixing and enforcement of minimum wage rates. In each of these countries it may be said that, taken together, the rates fixed have had a substantial influence on wages as a whole."

[4] Throughout this chapter the discussion refers to industry-wide bargaining and wage determination. It does not bear on collective negotiation by workers of a single enterprise, which raises issues quite different from those here considered. The relevance of this distinction has been noted by writers as different as Henry C. Simons and Sumner H. Slichter.

[5] The I.LO. report on *Labour Policies in the West Indies* (Geneva, 1952), says (p. 173), "The regulation of hours of work, whether by collective agreement, by administrative order or by general legislation, has developed during the period 1939–1949 as part of the general process of the introduction and strengthening of modern labour legislation in the area, and of the development of collective bargaining."

The comprehensive labour legislation in India which, as just noted, provides, among other matters, for minimum wages, maximum hours, and compulsory and binding arbitration, and compulsory profit sharing, affects the interests and prospects of vast numbers. Some of this legislation dates from the inter-war period or very exceptionally from before 1919, but the bulk, including the most important items, has been introduced since 1948.[6] The industries covered include, among others, agriculture, cotton manufacturing, motor transport, tanning, vegetable oil milling, rice milling, and tobacco manufacture. The legislation applies to the whole of India, and the rates are prescribed for entire states with populations up to sixty million. The areas covered include a large part of the poorest regions of this poverty-stricken country. In many of the areas there is ample evidence of much lower incomes earned in unregulated activities compared to the statutory minimum wages.

Regulated wages are not always effectively applied and observed; there are in this respect differences between countries and between different sectors within a single country. They apply widely to the larger enterprises and are usually observed by them. The same applies generally to enterprises owned by foreigners or by members of distinct ethnic, linguistic, or religious minorities, an important category in most under-developed countries. The smaller local enterprises are often legally exempt. In other instances the legislation is enforced only on foreigners or minorities. In yet other circumstances it applies nominally to all employers, even to those operating in tribal conditions, but is unenforced or even unenforceable over large sectors. Such a situation presents opportunities for corruption and extortion, as many people are always technically in breach of the law.

Many of the reasons behind the spread of restrictionism in the labour market are familiar from experience elsewhere. They include

[6] India ratified in 1921 the Convention for a 48-hour week which was adopted in principle by the Washington Labor Conference of 1919. It was not, however, generally introduced in India until 1948.

That Convention was ratified in the 1920's by a number of under-developed countries which were then, or are even now, at very early stages of economic development. Yet in British industry the 48-hour week was not adopted generally until after the first World War.

the influence of the organised employee beneficiaries of such policies; the influence of established employers, especially the largest employers, who benefit from such measures when they impede actual or potential competitors much more than themselves, as is often the case; the influence of those who favor a more closely controlled economy; the influence of vested interests in the organisation and administration of wage regulation; and humanitarian sentiment, which habitually ignores the serious adverse effects of these measures on the poorest people. Moreover, these influences are rarely counteracted effectively, partly because those who are most adversely affected are usually not aware of the causal sequence, and they are in any case unorganised and politically impotent.

But there is a further major factor in this particular sphere of restrictionism. This factor is an international emulation effect which suggests to politicians, administrators and others that their country is backward unless it has labour legislation and organisation modelled on those of the most advanced industrial countries; that is, that the introduction and extension of wage regulation and other labour controls (for instance, of hours and conditions of work) are evidence of development.

This influence operates pervasively in the under-developed world. It can be conveniently illustrated by quoting some statements of prominent Indian spokesmen. Thus, according to N. M. Joshi, a prominent Indian labour leader, "India's desire to prevent being classed at the International Labour Conference as a backward country in matters of social policy has led to the initiation of labour measures which might not otherwise have come up for consideration at all." [7]
And according to Sir Atul Chatterjee, "The eyes of the world, of the democracies of every country in the world, are at the moment on us. I am confident that the Council has a full sense of its responsibility for the good name and dignity of India in international councils. We do not want to be considered a backward nation always and for ever." [8]

[7] Preparatory Asiatic Regional Conference of the International Labour Organisation, New Delhi, 1947.

[8] Quoted by P. P. Pillai, "India and the I.L.O.," in *Indian Labour Problems* (London, 1947).

This emulation effect is both recognised and magnified by the I.L.O. According to one of its publications, "Every State . . . now knows that the measures by which it applies the Convention's provisions will be closely scrutinised by authorised bodies at Geneva, and that any serious discrepancy will in all probability be discussed in public debate."[9]

And a commentator has concluded justifiably, "It may not then be far-fetched to attribute to the I.L.O. a decisive role in accelerating Indian labour legislation if one realises that, in the days immediately after the first world war, the I.L.O. possessed the incomparable prestige of the international organisations in Geneva."[10]

Thus there are powerful political, social, intellectual, economic and administrative forces behind the imposition and extension of wage regulation. A recent, and in some ways illuminating, example of this influence is mentioned in another I.L.O. publication:

> As a sequel to technical assistance provided to Burma by the International Labour Office, the first wage council, for the cigar and cheroot manufacturing industry, was established by the Government in 1953. This council has prepared proposals for fixing minimum rates of wages . . . . . . the Government of Burma plans to extend the system progressively to other industries and other parts of the country.[11]

The relative abundance of manual labour compared to capital, developed natural resources, and administrative and technical skills, is a general characteristic of under-developed countries. Indeed, the possession of—or access to—comparatively cheap labour is among their few economic advantages compared to more developed and richer countries. Wage regulation raises the price of labour and endows it with some element of contrived scarcity, and it thus reduces this advantage and injures these countries' prospects of economic

---

The text of these and a number of similar passages are reproduced in Robert L. Aronson and John P. Windmuller (eds.), *Labor, Management, and Economic Growth*, Institute of International Industrial and Labor Relations, Cornell University (Ithaca, N.Y., 1954), p. 175 *et seq.*

[9] *The International Labour Organisation, the First Decade* (Geneva, 1931), p. 314.

[10] Subbiah Kannappan, "The Impact of the I.L.O. on Labor Legislation and Policy in India," in *Labor, Management, and Economic Growth*, p. 188.

[11] I.L.O., *Problems of Wage Policy in Asian Countries* (Geneva, 1956), p. 64.

progress. This applies whenever labour costs affect the establishment of economic activities and their scale of operation, and this is practically always the case. The presence of costs and their relevance to the establishment, location, and scale of economic activities, ultimately flow from the limitation of resources and of incomes, and are thus general; only the extent and readiness of the responses vary with different conditions and activities.[12] A few illustrations will demonstrate the relevance of this obvious consideration to the under-developed world.

The history of the rubber growing industry and of its impact on Southeast Asia is an outstanding example of the attractive power of cheap labour and of the profound economic and social transformation brought about with its aid.

The rapid and massive development of rubber production in Southeast Asia is comparatively recent. There were no exports of rubber from Southeast Asia in 1900; they are now about 1.8 million tons annually, worth over one billion dollars. Rubber is the most important North American import from the eastern hemisphere. Its rise has transformed the economic life of Southeast Asia. For instance, around 1900 Malaya was a sparsely populated country, largely of Malays living in hamlets and engaged in subsistence cultivation, where tribal warfare and endemic and epidemic disease were widespread. It is now a thriving country with populous cities linked by excellent communications. Since the 1890's the population has increased by natural growth and by immigration from about two million people to over seven million people, living longer and at a far higher standard of living. National income is about $300 per head annually, by far the highest in Southeast Asia. Rubber is the basis of the cash economy, of government revenues, and of further progress throughout the area.

[12] The relevance of the level of labour costs is often denied implicitly and at times explicitly. For instance, Gunnar Myrdal in a recent book (*Economic Theory and Under-developed Regions* [London, 1957], p. 31) expresses a widely held view, "All history shows that the cheap and often docile labour of under-developed regions does not usually attract industry."

If this suggests simply that industrial production requires more than one factor of production, it is truistic but not interesting. If it suggests that labour costs are irrelevant, it is untrue.

Cheap labour was the principal attractive force which brought the industry to Southeast Asia; this has been widely and explicitly recognised throughout its history.[13] The rubber tree (*Hevea brasiliensis*) was not indigenous in Southeast Asia. Until the beginning of the century the small quantity of exports came from South America. The hardy rubber tree thrives practically anywhere in the tropical rain forest. Cheap labour is important in this industry, the main phases of which are labour intensive (labour costs are about two-thirds of production costs), and even on American-owned estates have not yet been mechanised. Most of the labour supply which attracted the industry to Southeast Asia was not in the principal producing territories but in other countries, which themselves were not so suitable for rubber cultivation, but from which labour could be obtained. Cheap labour in turn attracted to Southeast Asia large amounts of capital and specialized administrative and technical skills. Rapid economic development and pervasive social changes resulted from the interplay of these forces. Had cheap labour not been available this development would have been obstructed or prevented altogether. The relevance of cost is indisputable.

The very high profits of the few rubber companies in the early years of the century, especially from 1908 to 1912, greatly stimulated expansion. The total planted area, which was about 8000 acres in 1900 (almost all of which was still immature), increased to about 250,000 acres in 1906 and to about 2¼ million acres in 1914. The high profits were secured by a small volume of capital on a small output, about two per cent of present production. If wages had been raised greatly, whether directly or by compulsory profit sharing systems, such as are now operated in many Indian industries, the incentive for rapid expansion would have been greatly reduced. This experience bears on the proposals and measures in under-developed countries

[13] The first issue, in 1906, of *Rubber Producing Companies*, an annual reference book of the rubber industry, designed in part to attract capital into the industry contained the following passage (p. v): "It may therefore be well for intending investors to consider what advantages the cultivated rubber of the East may have over the wild and uncultivated rubber of the West.

"The first consideration is that of labour. This is in favor of the Malay Peninsula and Ceylon, both countries being conveniently situated for the supplies of cheap coolie labour to be drawn from Southern India."

designed to raise regulated wages and incomes in specific activities, whether by direct wage increases or by bonuses, when these activities are specially profitable. Such measures obstruct the flow of capital into industries the expansion of which would be economic, and which would raise labour incomes generally.

In India, although the comprehensive labour legislation is recent, the merits of maximum hours and minimum wages have been discussed for about a century. Factory production of textiles in India began in the 1850's, and it developed rapidly. From the 1870's the establishment of minimum wages and particularly of maximum hours for Indian industry (especially textiles and jute) was frequently proposed by manufacturing interests in Britain. These proposals were resisted in India, where it was often pointed out that they were designed to reduce the effectiveness of Indian competition by inflating industrial costs. Indian manufacturers and effective public opinion at the time were well aware of the relevance of costs for attracting capital, securing markets and providing employment.[14] It is ironic that under the influence of the international emulation effect the measures which were resisted fifty years ago, and the implications of which were then so clearly realised, are now vigorously espoused. These effects and implications remain the same. The deliberate inflation of industrial costs is paradoxical in view of the insistence in

[14] The *Report of the Indian Factory Labour Commission of 1908* (London, 1908), refers explicitly to the adverse effects on industrialisation of restrictive measures. The Commission was especially concerned with working hours, but its remarks apply equally to other restrictive measures: ". . . We are strongly opposed to the imposition of any unnecessary restriction on the employment of labour in factories, especially at a time when the further industrial development of the country is of such vital importance . . . the strongest practical objections exist to the general enforcement in India of any law rigidly restricting the working hours of adult males . . . the imposition of a direct restriction on the hours of adult labour would be repugnant to the great majority of capitalists, both in India and abroad, who have invested, or are considering the question of investing money in India. . . . the opinion is widely and strongly held that, if interference with adult labour be permitted, pressure will be brought to bear in order to utilise that power of interference in a manner calculated to promote the interests of Lancashire and Dundee, rather than of India . . . [and this] would undoubtedly adversely affect India's industrial development . . . we are strongly opposed to any direct limitation of adult working hours, because we consider there is no necessity for the adoption of this drastic course, because we are convinced that it would cause the gravest inconvenience to existing industries." (Pp. 32–33.)

Indian economic planning on accelerated industrialisation.[15] And there is probably no country where contrived barriers to industrialisation are more seriously damaging than in India, because of the severe population pressure, the poor quality of the soil, the abject rural poverty, the social obstacles to economic mobility and to the raising of agricultural productivity, and the barriers to emigration.[16]

There are many other specific examples in under-developed countries of the relevance and importance of labour costs. A large and elastic supply of cheap and efficient labour has been a major factor, probably the major factor, in the emergence and growth of Hong Kong as a producer and exporter of manufactures. This tiny country has practically no raw materials, fuel, hydro-electric power, and only a very restricted domestic market. In spite of these limitations, often said to be crippling to development of manufacturing in under-developed countries, unsubsidised manufacturing industry has advanced rapidly in Hong Kong. The annual output of manufactures is now about 300 million U.S. dollars, about half of which is exported. Hong Kong is now a major textile exporter to the United Kingdom, and, indeed, these textile imports have become a major issue in British home politics. Cheap labour has also been important in the growth of the cotton textile industries of India and Pakistan.

Low labour costs have also played a major part in Japanese industrialisation. For instance, the textile industry relied extensively on young girls from rural areas who accepted industrial employment at very low wages for a few years before marriage. Such activities are now obstructed or even prevented by wage regulation.

[15] The importance of labour costs in Indian manufacturing is shown by the share of wages in the net product (value added), which for manufacturing industry as a whole in India was 44 per cent in 1950. In cotton textiles, a major industry affected by minimum wages, it was 64 per cent; in tanning it was 64 per cent; in jute manufacture 51 per cent; and in rice milling 45 per cent. These are all regulated activities. These are official figures quoted by S. A. Palekar, "Real Wages and Profits in India, 1939–50," *Indian Economic Review,* Vol. III, No. 4 (Aug., 1957).

[16] These simple considerations are no new discoveries: "Whatever, besides, tends to diminish in any country the number of artificers and manufacturers, tends to diminish the home market, the most important of all markets for the rude produce of the land, and thereby still further to discourage agriculture." Adam Smith, *Wealth of Nations,* Book IV, Chapter viii.

Conversely, there are many examples of the inhibiting effects of high labour costs on the establishment and expansion of enterprises. For instance, the British Colonial Development Corporation has recently (in 1957 and 1958) contemplated the establishment of various industrial projects in Fiji. But these proved uneconomic in view of the high rates of wages (about $1.50 a day) prescribed by powerful trade unions of Indian labourers.

Indeed, the relevance of labour costs to the establishment and operation of overseas enterprises is a commonplace of British and American business literature.[17]

The essential economic analysis of the results of regulated wages is straightforward, and it can be found in easily accessible publications.

Unless it is either redundant or unobserved, wage regulation raises wage rates in the industries in which it is introduced. This reduces the volume of employment in the regulated industry compared to what it would be otherwise. This decrease[18] of employment will vary directly with three factors: the readiness of the consumers of the product to turn to alternatives (elasticity of demand); the readiness of the other productive resources employed in the regulated activity to withdraw from that activity if their rewards are reduced (elasticity of supply); and the ease of substitution of other productive resources for labour when its cost is raised (elasticity of substitution). The influence of these factors is often accentuated when labour costs are a large proportion of total costs. The cost of wage regulation, that is the excess of the wage over the supply price of labour to the regulated activity, falls on those consumers and owners of factors of production who cannot turn easily to alternative commodities or activities. In under-developed economies the effect on employment is usually considerable, and, further, a large share of the cost is borne by very poor people.

[17] For instance, E. R. Barlow, *Management of Foreign Manufacturing Subsidiaries* (Cambridge, Mass., 1953), especially Chapter 2.

[18] It seems necessary to say explicitly that this refers to the curtailment in the volume of employment compared to what it would be otherwise, that is, it refers to a functional relationship and not to an observed change in employment during the relevant period.

The elasticity of demand for the products of the regulated industries is often very high, as in export industries, such as mines, plantations, and simple manufactures. In under-developed countries these export industries, especially mining and plantation industries, are the most prominent and easily controllable activities, and are likely to attract wage regulation. The elasticity of demand for the product is often likely to be high also in the domestic market for local industries, though not so high as in the export markets. These products have to compete for the low cash incomes of consumers with products of unregulated activities, often including cottage industry, handicrafts, and even imports.[19] When the elasticity of demand for the product is high, the effect on the volume of employment will be substantial. In practice this generally takes the form of the retardation of the growth of employment in that industry (or possibly a decline in a subsequent recession) rather than an immediate reduction in the number of those already employed, which is one reason why the effect is so often overlooked. On the other hand, when the elasticity of demand is low, the main burden falls on consumers in the form of higher prices. In under-developed countries most of the consumers of local industrial products are themselves very poor.

The supply of capital, enterprise, and skills, whether domestic or foreign, but more particularly when foreign, is likely to be elastic to the regulated industry. This response may not operate immediately. For example, capital invested in specific assets cannot be withdrawn promptly when returns are reduced, even to levels below those which would induce initial investment. But after a while investment com-

[19] Even the products of subsistence agriculture can be at times substitutes for the output of the regulated industries. This is obvious when agriculture is among the regulated activities, as in India. Moreover, where production for the market is only slightly more profitable than subsistence production, as often happens in small-scale agriculture, higher prices of consumer goods in the exchange sector reduce the attractiveness of agricultural production for sale compared to subsistence production, which may discourage agriculturalists from producing for sale. This may at times affect the elasticity of demand and thus the incidence of higher labour costs. This effect of regulated wages is analogous to that of a tax on production which is likely to retard the development of the exchange economy. A fuller treatment of this type of problem will be found in P. T. Bauer and B. S. Yamey, *The Economics of Under-developed Countries* (London and Chicago, 1957), Chapter 7.

mitments and employment contracts will not be renewed, and fresh resources will not be directed to the regulated industry, at least not in the volume in which they would have been in the absence of the regulation. Moreover, even if much of production remains profitable, part of the output is normally marginal, and it is thus affected adversely by higher costs. For instance, the large variations in the amount of payable ore with variations in cost is a well documented theme of the literature of gold mining. This reasoning applies even when the employers have a substantial measure of selling monopoly, as part of the output will still be marginal in terms of the maximisation of monopoly profits.[20]

The extent of factor substitution is less easy to assess. It depends on technical and economic factors as well as on legal and social influences. It is often likely to be important, as is shown by differences in methods of production in different firms or in similar industries in different countries.[21] Of course, such substitution may be prevented by further restrictive measures limiting the replacement of the regulated labour by unregulated categories of labour or by machinery. Examples of such measures, which are familiar also in highly industrialised countries, range from the prescription of ratios between European and non-European labour in some branches of South African mining and manufacturing industry to the regulation of the ratio of machinery to labour in the Mexican textile industry.

Even if the extent of factor substitution is small, the other responses (the elasticities of consumer demand and of the supply of other factors) ensure a high elasticity of demand to labour. Thus wage regulation generally affects employment appreciably. As already noted, in practice this expresses itself in a retardation of growth rather than in an actual contraction. The effect on employment is increased further by the fact that those responsible for wage regulation, especially when wages are regulated by government rather than by trade

[20] This argument does not apply when there is monopoly in the hiring of labour. This problem is considered below.

[21] Differences in factor availability are often reflected in differences in methods of production even when at first sight there seems to be little scope for such variations. Differences in planting density in rubber production on estates and small-holdings are an example discussed in some detail in Bauer and Yamey, *op. cit.*, Chapter 4.

unions, do not take into account the relevant factors influencing the growth of employment opportunities, so that the adverse effects on employment are not minimised by selecting for regulation those industries in which the elasticity of demand for labour is relatively small. Indeed, in the under-developed countries regulated wages are especially likely to be introduced in activities in which the elasticity of demand for labour is likely to be high. I have already noted the liability of export industries to wage regulation. For different reasons, to be noted in the next section, competitive industries in which wage rates are relatively low and labour costs a comparatively large part of total cost are also likely to attract wage regulation, and the elasticity of demand for labour in such industries is usually comparatively high.

The decrease in employment opportunities in the regulated activity implies that much or most of the cost of its introduction falls on those who have to accept less preferred employment, either in another grade of the same industry or, more likely, in some other activity.

At this point it is necessary to take cognizance of a category of situations in which wage regulation need not, in principle, contract employment, and in which the cost will fall entirely on employers. This is the case of monopsony, that is monopoly in the purchase of labour, whether exercised by a single dominant firm or by a group of firms acting in concert. Where a monopsonist is confronted by a rising supply curve of labour, the wage rate can be reduced by decreasing the amount of labour employed, and up to a point the advantage of this exceeds the disadvantage of the smaller gross proceeds resulting from the reduction of output.[22] The imposition of minimum wages may then raise wages without increasing the marginal cost of labour (because the employment of additional labour no longer raises wage rates) and thereby secure more employment and higher wages.

Such conditions are not unknown. The arrangements in the recruitment, wage determination, and allocation of labour in the South African mining industry are an example. However, regulated wages

[22] If the monopsonist is a group of employers acting in concert, the labour has to be rationed among them formally or informally.

are unlikely to be the most effective remedy for monopsony. For instance, there is the difficulty of setting and adjusting the dose, that is of determining the wage which transfers monopsony profits without affecting employment adversely. Moreover, it does not affect the source of monopsony, which is the absence of accessible employment alternatives for the workers. Development of a wider range of such alternatives is likely to be the more appropriate policy. Lastly, even if monopsony did call for wage regulation, it would do so generally on a plant or local level and not on an industry-wide or national level, since monopsony, even where it exists, is essentially a local phenomenon.

Monopsony, though not unknown, is exceptional in under-developed countries, as elsewhere. The high degree of concentration in an industry or trade often encountered in under-developed countries does not imply even effective monopoly power, since such power is also affected by ease of entry and access of customers to alternatives, and these are not measured by the degree of concentration. And even monopoly in the product market does not indicate monopsony in the labour market, since industries producing widely different commodities compete for the same factor of production, so that a monopolistic industry may have no monopsony power whatever. Again, even wide disparities in wealth, knowledge, literacy or commercial sophistication between employers and workers are not evidence of monopsony, or of differences in bargaining power which would result in exploitation. Liability to exploitation results from lack of independent competing alternatives, and not from differences in wealth or commercial sophistication. Even illiterate poor workers will be paid what they are worth to their employers if these employers can obtain their services only by competing for them, that is attracting them from other employers.

Monopsony is clearly absent in most of the sectors in under-developed countries in which wages are regulated. Throughout the under-developed world wages have been regulated in many highly competitive industries into which entry is easy and in which producers act independently, both in the purchase of labour, which is relatively undifferentiated and occupationally mobile, and in the sale of the products. They have also been introduced in areas in which there are many alternative forms of employment. Minimum wages have been established in India in agriculture, cotton manufacture, leather manufacture, simple food processing; and in Burma in the manufacture of cigars and cheroots; and in Latin America in many small-scale industries, including handicrafts. In these activities there is no monopoly, still less monopsony. Thus, wage regulation in under-developed countries is neither required to counteract the effects of monopsony, nor is it designed for this purpose. And, as already noted, industry or nation-wide wage regulation (as distinct from regulation on a plant or local basis) is in any event especially irrelevant to action designed to counter monopsony or its effects.

The irrelevance of monopsony to wage regulation as practised in under-developed countries is evident from the absence in the literature of the I.L.O., the British Colonial Office, and the Indian government, of references to this phenomenon as a condition or requirement or argument for the establishment of regulated wages. On the contrary, this literature often deplores the absence of employers' organisations on the ground that the multiplicity of independent employers obstructs the introduction of industry-wide collective bargaining and even the establishment of statutory wage determination. Indeed such measures often issue in the formation of employers' associations, the influence of which may extend beyond the labour market.[23]

Indeed, wage regulation is especially likely to be introduced in competitive industries. For instance, in Great Britain statutory minimum wages were first introduced in the so-called sweated trades, which were highly competitive. This is not accidental. Industries in which labour costs are relatively large are likely to be highly competitive because of the comparative unimportance of fixed capital.

[23] According to a multigraphed memorandum by the Information Department of the British Colonial Office, *Notes on the Development of Trade Unionism and Labour Relations in the Colonies* (London 1953), p. 5: "The degree of employer organisation varies considerably between territories, but in general it can be said that the greatest degree of organisation is to be found where either the formation of workers' associations has demonstrated the need for combination on the part of the employers, or the common problems of an industry, . . . have brought about co-operation."

Moreover, wage rates in these industries are likely to be low compared to less competitive industries. The firms in competitive activities cannot afford to pay more than the market rate. On the other hand, firms with some measure of monopoly are often anxious to placate public opinion by paying wages higher than are necessary, and they are often well placed to do so by virtue of monopoly profits and scarcity rents. The lower wages in the competitive activities lend plausibility to the demands for official intervention.

Thus, although in principle a case might be made out for wage regulation to counter the presence and effects of monopsony, it is essentially irrelevant to the actual establishment and operation of wage regulation in under-developed countries.

Regulated wages and other restrictions on the supply of labour reaching the market raise the wage above the supply price of labour which measures its highest contribution to output in alternative uses, which in turn reflects its economic scarcity.[24] The regulated wage creates a contrived scarcity which overstates its unavoidable or natural scarcity, and which induces economy in the use of labour in the regulated activity, both through curtailment of production and by the substitution of other factors. The economy in the use of labour in this activity increases its availability elsewhere, where its contribution to output is less because the supply price which measures its highest contribution elsewhere is less than the prescribed wage. The contrived scarcity results in uneconomic allocation of resources and thus diminishes aggregate output. Besides this effect on current production, regulated wages and similar measures retard the growth of output by reducing the national income and thus the volume of investible resources, and also by reducing the flexibility and adaptability of the economy.

In under-developed countries special factors reinforce the usual wasteful results of regulated wages. The diversity of supply and de-

[24] The supply price itself may exceed this productivity. Thus members of agricultural families often share in the family or group income even though their contribution to output is very small. Their supply price to industry may be governed by the average productivity of the group, which may much exceed their marginal productivity.

mand conditions of labour is one of these. Such diversity does not reflect generally, or even primarily, institutional barriers to movement, but rather differences in aptitudes, resources and customs, and also the undeveloped state of transport facilities. Even within apparently undifferentiated unskilled labour there are wide differences in attitudes, adaptability, skill and productivity. They are reflected in wide differences in earnings of workers on piece rates in particular enterprises as, for instance, the earnings of rubber tappers on Malayan estates. These differ widely even within the same ethnic group, and much more so between workers of different ethnic groups, such as Chinese, Indian, and Malay tappers. Again, the efficiency of newcomers to town and industry from rural and tribal areas is usually far lower than that of more experienced workers.

The supply price of different types of unskilled labour also differs widely. For instance, the supply price of migrant labour from rural to urban areas varies with distance, family circumstances, the length of stay envisaged, agricultural prosperity, employment opportunities of dependants, and other factors.

In these conditions the compulsory standardisation implied in regulated wages is very wasteful in terms both of the allocation and the growth of resources. For instance, it prevents the migration of prospective newcomers to industry and the acquisition of skill by them, because in view of their inexperience they are not worth the prescribed wage. Thus the incomes of the would-be migrants are depressed, and they are also disqualified from improving their condition. Not only is there an uneconomic allocation of resources, but their growth is manifestly inhibited.

Thus in under-developed countries the adverse economic results of regulated wages are likely to be specially pronounced. Moreover, this affects the factor of which the relatively ample supply is among the few economic assets of these countries. And they can least afford wasteful policies.

The gap between prescribed wages and the incomes and earnings of those excluded from the regulated trades is generally wide in under-developed countries, proportionately much wider than in developed countries. The gap cannot be attributed to differences in skills and aptitudes: if this were the reason, the wage regulation would be redundant. Those who cannot secure employment in the regulated industries are forced to accept other employment on less attractive terms.[25] The most important of these overflow activities are agriculture, petty trading, domestic service and casual labour, and participation in them takes the form of self-employment, full-time or part-time employment, under-employment or virtual unemployment. Unless they are either redundant or flouted, regulated wages and other restrictive devices curtail employment in these activities and thus enhance the over-crowding in the over-flow occupations. Further depression of the very low incomes in these occupations is the general result of the overcrowding of the lowest level of the labour market.[26]

The very low incomes in the overflow activities have often been reported in widely different conditions, and they have been noted in various publications of the I.L.O. For instance, the I.L.O. study on *Problems of Wage Policy in Asian Countries* quotes several official Indian and Indonesian reports which show regulated unskilled wages exceeding, by a factor of over three, wages and earnings of similar labour in unregulated activities in the same area. The extremely low incomes in unregulated activities are usually attributed in this literature to the absence of regulation, and its extension is urged accordingly. The legislation of several Latin American countries, including

[25] Without seniority rules or other barriers to entry, the inflow of labour attracted by the prescribed wage rate tends to reduce earnings by the sharing of employment, since by definition the rate is above the level at which supply and demand balance. It could even reduce earnings over a period to the level prevailing in the absence of prescribed rates if entry is easy and labour is hired entirely indiscriminately. In practice, however, differences in efficiency between established and outside labour, together with preference for those already employed, maintain at least part of the privileged or monopoly incomes. Inflow of labour does not affect the adverse effects of minimum wages on the volume of employment, but only the distribution of the privileged earnings among employees.

[26] There may be exceptions to this proposition which are unimportant, especially in under-developed countries. There may be a number of distinct types of unregulated labour. An increase in the supply of one type brought about by the establishment of regulated wages for another type may increase the demand for a third type which is complementary to the first.

the Argentine and Uruguay, specifically provides for the extension of minimum wages to cottage industry at rates comparable to those in the corresponding factory trades. Such measures, if they could be carried to their logical conclusion, would deny all sources of earned income to those who fail to secure employment at the regulated wages; they would be reduced to the cold comfort of public relief or private charity, or would have to face starvation.

The burden of wage regulation on the poorest people is a noteworthy but not accidental outcome of measures promoted by social reformers motivated by an allegedly sensitive and rational social conscience. In part it reflects the popular failure to perceive effects which are inevitable but do not occur immediately; nor are these effects or their cause immediately obvious when they do occur. It probably also reflects differences in political effectiveness between the beneficiaries of these measures and those harmed by them. The former include, besides the protected workers, influential employers (whom such measures protect from competition by firms relying on cheap labour, and who also gain prestige from paying comparatively high wages), and also those who benefit politically and personally from the administration of such measures. Those who are harmed are the consumers of the products of the regulated activity, and, more substantially, those who are forced into the overflow activities or compelled to remain there. The difference in effectiveness is obvious.

It is sometimes urged that the adverse effects of regulated wages on development are offset by benefits resulting from the adoption of more capital-intensive methods induced by raising the money cost of labour, notably by the impetus this provides to technical change. Among other relevant factors, this reasoning ignores the retardation of technical change in the activities where wages are depressed as a result of overcrowding brought about by the curtailment of employment opportunities in the regulated activities, the effect on investment resulting from the reduction in the current national income, and the reduced flexibility and mobility resulting from institutional wage determination. Although criteria based on the allocation of resources may conceivably be inadequate guides for policy designed to promote their growth (especially in the field of public finance), it does not follow that indiscriminate inflation of the money cost of labour somehow conduces to growth to offset the wasteful allocation of resources to which it gives rise.[27]

There are some arguments in support of wage regulation which may be noted in passing because of their popularity. One is that such measures maintain or increase purchasing power. But they only transfer purchasing power from some individuals and groups to others without increasing it. In fact they necessarily diminish aggregate demand because they affect adversely the total national income, the ultimate source of real purchasing power. The unemployment of unskilled labour in these countries, which reflects the lack of co-operant factors of production, is also aggravated by the wasteful results of these measures. The further suggestion that prescribed higher wages increase the productivity of under-nourished workers ignores the effect of wage regulation on the incomes of those excluded from the regulated activity. These are people poorer than those protected by the regulated wages, and their low incomes are depressed still further by them. As such measures both tend to diminish the total national income, and especially the incomes of the poorest people (that is, those excluded from the regulated activities), they are unlikely to improve nutritional standards. The suggestion also implies that the incidental results of the activities of outside bodies are re-

[27] W. Galenson and H. Leibenstein have ingeniously suggested in an important article, "Investment Criteria, Productivity, and Economic Development," *Quarterly Journal of Economics*, Vol. LXIX, No. 3 (Aug., 1955), that higher capital intensity in certain activities brought about by higher wage costs may promote development even when there is surplus labour. The suggestion is that although the current national income may be reduced, the difference between production and consumption, that is the volume of investible resources, may be increased. The formal validity of this argument depends in part on an assumed equivalence of future and present output, and on specific assumptions on factor productivities and consumption habits in different sectors, and on the irrelevance of consumer preferences. Acceptance of these assumptions and premises raises large questions of political judgment as well as matters of empirical fact. However, even if these are accepted, the policy appropriate to the promotion of development would be a tax proportionate to the wage bill, rather than the indiscriminate imposition of minimum wages and conditions, since such taxation would conduce to the most efficient deployment of different types of labour, and possibly of other resources, within individual enterprises.

quired to correct the misjudgment of those personally and constantly engaged in conducting industry or in managing their own private lives.

It is sometimes urged that restrictions such as the imposition of regulated wages are required to protect the welfare of poor, illiterate workers in under-developed countries, as they cannot perceive their own interests, much less protect them. As already mentioned, this line of argument is irrelevant to exploitation which reflects monopsony power of employers, since the possibility of this depends on the absence of alternative employment opportunities and not on the ignorance or poverty of workers; and, again, wage regulation is not generally the appropriate instrument to counteract monopsony, nor is it generally introduced for that purpose. Further, wage regulation is generally calculated to harm rather than benefit the poorest sections of the community whose employment opportunities it restricts. Nor is the assumption of the workers' ignorance of suitable alternatives and of their lack of response to opportunities generally valid. Throughout the under-developed world there is much detailed evidence of the awareness of poor and illiterate people of differences in economic conditions and in net advantages of different occupations and of their readiness to respond to these differences within the opportunities open to them. For instance, in the early decades of this century hundreds of thousands of South Indian labourers migrated from the rural areas of Madras to Malaya and Ceylon. The volume and direction of this migration responded promptly and markedly to changes in economic conditions in these countries; the illiterate rural population was remarkably well informed of working conditions and employment opportunities in these countries.

The restrictive effects of minimum wage regulation are thrown into exceptionally clear relief by the arrangements in the labour market in South Africa. They help to identify remarkably clearly the operation and effects of forces at work elsewhere, more especially to show that the cost falls primarily on those excluded from the regulated activities.

The rapid expansion of South African gold and diamond mining in the closing decades of the nineteenth century created a great scarcity of skilled white labour with correspondingly high wages. The scarcity value was subsequently threatened by various factors, notably by immigration from Europe, by exodus of South African Europeans from rural areas, and by the acquisition of some industrial experience and settled habits by Africans. To replace the lost natural scarcity by contrived scarcity, and scarcity rents by monopoly earnings, the skilled European workers, especially miners, promoted and enforced severe restrictions, among them minimum wages, and an industrial color bar enforced by custom and trade unions. These measures aggravated the overcrowding of the unskilled labour market and depressed unskilled wages, at that time earned chiefly by Africans. But many Europeans were unable to secure skilled employment because they lacked the qualifications, and, moreover, high wages restricted the demand for labour. The excess supply in the labour market depressed the unskilled wages of Europeans to levels which alarmed public opinion. This led to the establishment of minimum wages in a number of trades in the hope of securing employment to Europeans at so-called civilized rates. But each stage of this process restricted further the opportunities and depressed the wages of those who could not find employment at the prescribed rates. Employment was then specifically created for poor whites in government enterprises, especially the railway, and in private industry by official pressure on employers by various means, including threats of the removal of protection from industries not employing a sufficient proportion of Europeans. Moreover, non-Europeans came to be excluded from an ever-widening range of activities by various devices, including prescription of minimum wages above unskilled rates, which in effect excluded non-Europeans. This, however, again also barred many Europeans who were not worth the prescribed minimum wages for various reasons, such as their inadequate education or rural background.

The imposition of statutory minimum wages was among the restrictive measures adopted. Not only has this restrictive device been employed widely, but its effects have been publicly discussed and understood. For instance, a section in an important report, that of the Economic and Wage Commission of 1925, is headed "The minimum wage as an instrument of the colour bar."

In several instances statutory minimum wages were at first confined to Europeans. But this sometimes led to the substitution of non-Europeans at unregulated wages for white labour at regulated wages, and the wage fixing machinery was deliberately extended to cover non-European labour. This measure effectively barred non-Europeans because it removed the incentive to employ them. The effect is well documented on both the volume of employment and on the racial composition of the labour force of the prescription of minimum wages at equal rates for European and non-European labour. For instance, a survey of poor relief in Cape Town found that in the district surveyed the majority of those unemployed and on relief were people insufficiently qualified to earn the prescribed minimum wage, though they were worth employing at a lower wage. A survey of the confectionery trade in Pietermaritzburg found that the prescription of minimum wages in 1931 both decreased total employment and reduced the proportion of non-Europeans. The establishment of minimum wages for non-Europeans in truck driving led to their dismissal and replacement by Europeans over a wide area in the 1930's.

Gold mining has been the most important single industry affected by these measures. As the price of gold is fixed, no part of the cost falls on the user. Part of the cost of the inflated wages of European miners falls on capital. But there is always a grade of ore which is only just payable. Many detailed surveys have shown the wide variations in the amount of payable ore with variations in costs. It is much easier for capital to find alternative employment at comparable returns than it is for labour excluded from the mines, so that the greater part of the burden is clearly borne by those Europeans and Africans who fail to secure employment. The same principle applies throughout the scale. The overcrowding of the labour market has, however, also depressed the wages in employments specially created for Europeans. The large proportion of the cost of such measures borne by those excluded from the regulated activities stands out exceptionally clearly in South Africa.

The repercussions of this process, outlined here only very briefly, have extended far beyond the economic life of the country and also well beyond its frontiers. The process has been a major factor in the political development of the country. A leading historian of the British Commonwealth has written on this subject:

> The colour bar in industry originated among British workers under the Union Jack. "It was at the diamond fields that the gate to all but low paid and unskilled labour was slammed against the native in industry." (C. W. de Kiewiet, *The Imperial Factor in South Africa*). From the Kimberley diggings the colour bar was carried by English-speaking workers into the mining areas of the South African Republic . . .
> South Africa's national historian, if ever he should arise to tell with pride the story of how his country rejected a liberal doctrine which was foreign to her blood and soil, will not, if he is just, give all the glory to the descendants of the Voortrekkers. The triumph, if ever it be completely won, will belong in part to those sturdy British workmen who made themselves at home on South African soil. The historian will not forget their vindication of the colour bar. Nor will he omit to record that it was their labour party which first appealed to the white voters of South Africa with a full-blooded programme of racial segregation.[28]

This is only one pertinent and striking instance of the far-reaching political repercussions of restrictionism in the labour market of under-developed countries, including wage regulation. These implications and results of restrictionism cannot be discussed here. But it is important to remember that the effects of such policies pervade social life well beyond what is usually regarded as the sphere of economics.

The basic analysis of the implications of regulated wages is not complicated. Yet it is largely ignored in the influential literature on under-developed countries. This is perhaps strange in view of the concern in this literature with enterprise monopoly and with imperfections in product markets. The neglect is certainly unwarranted in view of the wide scope and pervasive influence of restrictions in the labour markets in under-developed countries. Both the intellectual interest and the practical importance of the subject would justify and reward sustained and disinterested enquiry in this sphere.

[28] W. K. Hancock, *Survey of British Commonwealth Affairs* (London, 1941), Vol. II, Part 2, pp. 40 and 42.

The investigator who will turn his attention to the field of restrictionism in the labour markets of under-developed countries will have to reckon with the ingrained neglect of the basic analysis. Moreover, he must be prepared to face intense hostility directed from entrenched intellectual, political and economic interests and influences. He will do well to remember certain pertinent remarks by Adam Smith:

This monopoly has so much increased the number of some particular tribes of them, that, like an overgrown standing army, they have become formidable to the government, and upon many occasions intimidate the legislature . . . If he opposes them . . . and still more if he has authority enough to be able to thwart them, neither the most acknowledged probity, nor the highest rank, nor the greatest public services, can protect him from the most infamous abuse and detraction, from personal insults, nor sometimes from real danger, arising from the insolent outrage of furious and disappointed monopolists.[29]

Academic economists are exceptionally well placed to appreciate the truth of these observations—and also to ignore the warning they imply.

[29] *Wealth of Nations,* Book IV, Chapter ii.

16

Private Property and the Relative Cost of Tenure

Armen A. Alchian

PRIVATE PROPERTY and consumer sovereignty have effects that can be more vividly revealed by case studies than by a statement of principles. I should like, therefore, to examine a special labor market whose product is regarded as unique, so that special employment relations are necessary to preserve the quality of that product. I am speaking of the collegiate market for professors. The special employment relations in the professors' market is tenure, whereby the professor has job security except for immoral acts, loss of mental competence, or financial disability by the college. The professor is assured of his job security so long as his teaching reflects his search for the truth. I shall pass over the questions of how one determines dishonest expounding of the search for the truth and how incompetence and immorality are established. And I shall not dispute the meaning of financial inability. But assuming they are answerable questions, we can concentrate on the question of why tenure is desirable and viable.

Why is this kind of security deemed necessary for the professor? That is, for what is it necessary? Let me quote some of the arguments. I quote first from the Statement of Principles of the American Association of University Professors, a statement endorsed by many other academic professional associations.

Institutions of higher education are conducted for the common good and not to further the interest of either the individual teacher or the institution as a whole. The common good depends upon the free search for truth and its free exposition. Academic freedom is essential to these purposes and applies to both teaching and research.

Tenure is a means to certain ends; specifically: (1) Freedom of teaching and research and of extramural activities, and (2) A sufficient degree of economic security to make the profession attractive to men and women of ability. Freedom and economic security, hence tenure, are indispensable to the success of an institution in fulfilling its obligations to its students and to society.[1]

I give another quotation.

The modern university . . . is a unique type of organization. For many reasons it must differ from a corporation created for the purpose of producing a salable article for profit. Its internal structure, procedures, and discipline are properly quite different from those of business organizations. It is not so closely integrated and there is no such hierarchy of authority as is appropriate to a business concern; the permanent members of a university are essentially equals. . . .

Free enterprise is as essential to intellectual as to economic progress. *A* university [my italics] must therefore be hospitable to an infinite variety of skills and viewpoints, relying upon open competition among them as the surest safeguard of truth. *Its* [my italics] whole spirit requires investigation, criticism, and presentation of ideas in an atmosphere of freedom and mutual confidence. This is the real meaning of 'academic' freedom. It is essential to the achievement of its ends that the faculty be guaranteed this freedom by its governing board, and that the reasons for the guarantee be understood by the public.

When the [scholar's] opinions challenge existing orthodox points of view, his freedom may be more in need of defense than that of men in other professions. The guarantee of tenure of professors of mature and proven scholarship is one such defense. As in the case of judges, tenure protects the scholar against undue economic or political pressure and ensures the continuity of the scholarly process.[2]

What are the reasons for tenure? Apparently it is necessary to insure efficient searching for the truth because of the special nature

[1] American Association of University Professors, "Academic Freedom and Tenure," *AAUP Bulletin*, Vol. XLII, No. 1 (Spring, 1956), p. 42.

[2] Association of American Universities, *The Right and Responsibilities of Universities and Their Faculties* (March, 1953); reprinted in the *University Bulletin* of the University of California, Vol. 1, No. 33 (April 20, 1953), p. 162–4.

of the product, truth, and because the university is different from ordinary business entities. However, my conclusion is that the reason for the general acceptance of tenure is not that the search for truth has some special characteristics which distinguish it from other products, but that instead its acceptance springs from the special ownership arrangement and financial structures of our colleges. Economic analysis has driven me to this conclusion, that it arises from an absence of the ordinary kind of property rights that exist in profit-seeking businesses.

What is the economic analysis or what are the theorems that yield this conclusion? The simplest and most fundamental postulates and theorems of economics are sufficient. The first theorem says individuals act so as to further their own interest, even when acting as members of a group. The second fundamental theorem of economics says the lower the relative price of any good or source of satisfaction the more will be purchased. These are called the first and second fundamental theorems of economics to suggest that their power is comparable to that of the first and second fundamental theorems of physics.

A person can further his interest—or as we say in the jargon of economics, he can increase his utility—in many different ways. He can increase his pecuniary wealth and personal consumption expenditures. He can further his interests or satisfaction by having more pleasant working conditions, a bigger and plushier office, a more beautiful and cooperative secretary, a jovial, friendly and lenient employer, cleaner and more elaborate wash rooms, more convenient and automatic equipment with which to work, music in the factory, or if he is the employer he might have more responsible employees with desirable personal and cultural characteristics. The lower the costs that must be paid for any of these the more he will buy them, in exactly the same way that a person revises his purchases of types of food in response to their prices. A person will always spend some of his personal wealth on his job environment, but every dollar so spent means a dollar less for expenditure at home. If the costs of things bought for home consumption were to rise relative to costs of business connected sources of personal satisfaction he would buy more of the latter.[3]

What this all says is that a person has at least two ways to spend money. He can take it out of the business, if he owns it, and spend it at home and wherever he pleases. Or he can spend it in the business not merely for the sake of increasing the net profits or income of the business but for the personal benefits he gets in the course of his income earning activity. He can always take a smaller salary or profits in exchange for better working conditions or for greater job security. The less of any one of these things he must sacrifice to get the other, the more of the other he will take. The more the personal, take-home wealth he must sacrifice to get pleasanter working conditions, the poorer will be his working conditions. For example, if he sacrificed no profits or salary he would indulge in job choices exclusively on the basis of security and working conditions.

People differ in their preferences for various ways to spend their personal wealth at home and they differ in their business-connected expenditures. Some will be willing to buy more in the way of attractive working surroundings than will other people in the same wealth position. Some will want their business-connected sources of personal satisfaction more in the form of congenial employees and others will place a greater emphasis on physical surroundings. It all depends upon their personal preference patterns. But if the cost of beautiful secretaries should rise, everyone will be induced to cut down somewhat on the amount of beautiful secretarial services, regardless of his relative preferences for beauty and efficient secretarial work. Of course it is possible that some employers may attach no significance to degree of beauty, but as long as some do, the effect will be noted. Only if employers attached no value whatsoever to beauty—perhaps such as might happen if the employer's wife were in some way to be in control of secretarial hiring—would it not follow that more would be bought at a lower price.

To be more explicit, suppose that a certain secretary was capable of

[3] For an excellent illustration of this see G. S. Becker, *The Economics of Discrimination* (Chicago, 1957).

producing $ .80 of pecuniary income per hour. At $1.00 an hour the employer would have to sacrifice $ .20 of personal profits which he could have used in any way he saw fit in or out of the business. Let us suppose that he decided the extra attractions of the secretary were not worth the $ .20 per hour sacrifice of profits that he could have taken home and devoted to, say, his wife's beauty. Now, modify the system so that he is not allowed to take home all the profits. As an extreme, suppose that he can take home only one fourth, $ .05 per hour. Now the attraction of the secretary, formerly not worth $ .20 per hour, need be compared only with $ .05 of sacrificed domestic expenditures. The cost to him of business-connected satisfaction has fallen from $ .20 per hour to $ .05 per hour. The employer will find his satisfaction enhanced if he spends more in the business, getting a larger portion of this personal satisfaction through business connected expenditures or costs. Not only will he hire a prettier secretary but he will enlarge all business costs that in any way provide personal satisfaction.

A word of caution: it has not been said that he would have spent nothing for secretarial beauty before a tax or confiscation of profits. All that is implied is that he would have bought *less* of it before, not none of it. Everyone always is willing to buy some pleasantness of working environment depending upon the costs of domestic consumption. What is being said here is that more will be bought as the domestic consumption sacrifice or price is made lower. And not only will secretarial beauty be more extensively purchased, but *every* source of personal satisfaction obtainable through business-connected costs will be increased. And the increase will be greater, the greater is the cost of taking profits home.

Significant also is that there is inefficiency when his profits are taxed. The business is using up $1.00 worth of resources to provide a benefit worth less than $1.00. The business owner is spending a dollar to get $ .80 worth of pecuniary service via typing and $ .05 worth of extra pleasure of beauty. Formerly he got $1.00 worth of typing services, whereas now he gets a total satisfaction worth only $ .85, a loss of $ .15. But that loss is not imposed on him. Instead it is borne by the whole of society as a consequence of not using resources in their most valuable ways as judged by consumers. It is possible to have provided just as much typing services and beauty and still have other things too. This, of course, is merely the well-known efficiency aspect of the competitive, free price system under private property.

The task to which we turn now is to see what affects the relative prices of these various sources of satisfaction, some of which are domestic, business-free expenditures and others of which are business-connected cost-covered expenditures. In particular, we shall consider the effects of profit-seeking privately owned institutions as compared to non-profit organizations on the cost ratios of various forms of business-connected sources of satisfaction, and the particular form of business-connected source of satisfaction to which we shall devote most of our attention is tenure.

An ordinary privately owned profit-seeking business, whether it sells shoes or news, whether it be proprietorship or a corporation, is operated for the sake of increasing the wealth of the owners and not for the common good. That the business will survive only if it benefits other people as a consequence of its owner's search for personal profits does not deny this latter objective. In other words, the test of survival of such a business is not that it intend to serve the public interest or common good, but instead that it produce profits—which the owner can take out of the business if he wishes. To make profits the business must be taking resources from less useful alternative activities and putting them to work in more valuable channels. From this difference in usefulness, as judged by the consumers, arise the profits. If the owner fails to satisfy this condition, he will suffer a loss in his personal wealth which will compensate other people for the reduction in the value of output which he has caused. Thus the owner is forced to bear through smaller profits or through losses the true economic costs of his actions. Losses of personal wealth are a powerful dissuader, while profits are a powerful persuader to pay heed to other people's preferences.

Any employer who may be induced by an employee to produce a service inefficiently will find that consumers punish him by making him bear the costs through losses. And this dissuades the employer from supporting inefficient behavior. But no one employer can prevent the employee from continuing his inefficient activities elsewhere if any other member of the community will agree to bear the costs out of his personal wealth. In summary, the profit-seeking owner who satisfies the consumer best makes profits and he can use the profit in any way he likes, at home or in the business. His range of choice of places and ways in which he can spend the income of the business is not confined to business avenues or working conditions only.

This kind of private ownership or private property right, common as it is, is not universal. A non-profit-seeking business is the name usually given to an entity or institution administered by individuals acting in the capacity of trustees and who *cannot* appropriate the net wealth gains directly to themselves as profits nor completely as higher salaries. Nor can anyone else take the wealth out of the business as an owner could and spend it on as wide a range of alternatives as he could with his own personal wealth. The administrator is a trustee and not for any particular person's private wealth. There is no owner in the conventional sense; there are merely managers, administrators and operators. This does *not* mean that no one can further his own interest through the ways the wealth of the organization is spent. But what it does mean is that since there is no residual owner who can spend the net profits more efficiently at home and in the business than in the narrower range of business associated sources of personal benefits, the inducement to increase profits is reduced. In fact, it is turned into an inducement to reduce them to zero, but not into losses. Avoidance of losses is still a binding, effective constraint on the activities of a non-profit-seeking institution that relies upon sales to consumers for its income.

In a non-profit-seeking enterprise, the administrator must spend all the income in the business for salaries, materials, building, etc. Some of the expenditures will contribute to future income and some will be spent in ways to enhance the working environment or to acquire personal satisfaction through business cost expenditures. This all is merely an application of the earlier stated principle about buying more of these things that are cheaper and less of those that become more expensive. It is more expensive in a non-profit organization to take the profits home, and the ruse of raising the administrator's salary to equal the profits is not completely available. If it were, then the non-profit organization would be the same as a profit-seeking institution. But the fact which we have to accept is that the profits cannot all be taken out in this way as cheaply as in a privately owned profit seeking organization. And so in conformity with the second fundamental theorem of economics, a greater portion of the business expenditures will be spent for business-connected sources of personal satisfaction than in a profit-making organization. Of course, the particular kinds of business associated or business cost activities that will in any case be *most* increased depends upon the particular tastes and preference patterns of the administrators. But whatever ones are increased most, all will be increased.

It is easy to cite many examples. Medical insurance in the business, especially if it is proportional to salaries or status, becomes more attractive since this substitutes for domestic, personally purchased medical aid. Life insurance for all the employees is now a cheaper way of getting it for the administrator—without sacrificing so much profits. And if the key officials like coffee, the coffee break is longer and more elaborate. If they like baseball, the company will have a box at the ball park for its employees, with you-know-who going most often. Company cars will be newer. Athletic facilities in the plant will be more common because their cost via the business has fallen relative to take-home profits. The administrator can devote more of his time to community affairs and act more like a statesman and less like a grubbing profit seeker. Some, or even all of these things, will be found in a profit-seeking business, but since their cost is even less in a non-profit organization relative to profits, these things will be more common and on a larger scale.

For example, an administrator of an automobile company, if non-profit-seeking, would find it more in his interest (than in a profit-seeking business) to lower prices and sacrifice some revenue and profits, in order to create a backlog of orders, or as they say—a waiting list. His production scheduling and inventory problems would be eased. Prestige and personal benefits could be gained by his being able to favor and obtain various acceptable favors from certain customers by special priorities. He would be willing also to increase costs and lower profits if in that way he could reduce internal management nuisances and employee relations problems. Unproductive but congenial workers who would be fired in a profit-seeking business will be more readily kept. Firing a person is an unpleasant task, but in a profit-seeking business it is even more unpleasant not to fire them.

His employment policy will be *less* closely related to productivity in a pecuniary sense and more oriented toward satisfying his own welfare through non-pecuniary forms, e.g., employees who agree with his point of view, or employee cultural characteristics, or special employment arrangements which are conducive to administrative ease. But insofar as employment policies reflect considerations other than productivity in the business, some employees without these side characteristics will feel unjustly discriminated against if they are not promoted or are fired when doing what they think is consistent with the avowed purposes of the enterprise. They will demand less "arbitrary" hiring, firing and employment policies and will seek to protect themselves from the inefficient practices of the employer. But the policies they seek will reduce efficiency. Weakened as the consumer controls are on the employer because of the elimination or reduction of the available profits, they are even weaker on the employees. The less such policy costs the administrator-employer the more he will be induced to accept it. He will be more ready to accept employment policies that mean a quieter, more peaceful, even if less profitable life. And one of the forms of employment policy that will be pressed on him and more willingly brought now is greater job security for the employees.

At any given wage rate, the greater the job security an employee can get, the better for him and the worse for the employer. An employer who grants a long term contract must bear the consequences of changes in the employee's productivity. If the employee proves to be less productive than anticipated, the employer suffers and the employee is the gainer. If the employee proves to be better than anticipated, the employee can quit his job and go elsewhere and get a higher pay. The risks are not symmetrical. Hence at the same wage rate an employer prefers shorter term to longer-term contracts. And since the employer cannot revise wages downward, else the whole objective of security would be negated, he will offer a lower wage guarantee than he expects the employee's productivity to be.

If we look at our private colleges and universities we find that they are typically non-profit-seeking institutions. Whatever the attitude of the administrator of the college toward academic freedom and exposition of the truth, his ability to impose his own standards of acceptable employee behavior are enhanced above those in a profit-seeking enterprise. His actions do, of course, affect the status of the college and the attraction it has for students or for donors. Yet since he does not have a right to keep the profits for personal expenditures he is not so severely affected by the loss of profits caused by the unpopularity of his decisions. Of all the forces that can be brought to bear on him, one is now weakened and this one is the personal wealth effect. Students and their parents are less able to punish him so severely for behavior not in conformity with their desires, since the profits incentive is attenuated, as it is *not* in a profit-seeking owned institution. As said earlier, it is in just such situations that the administrator will more frequently evidence arbitrariness in hiring and firing people. And similarly, in just such institutions would we expect employees to react most strongly and seek protection from this apparently capricious behavior by the college administrator who seems to be paying even less attention to the criterion of truthful teaching. It is perfectly true, however, that those administrators who already stand for the truth are even more willing to retain teachers of the truth who present the unpleasant truth. But what all this means is that those who would defend such teachers from discharge by keeping them despite their statements are more easily able—that is, at lower cost to themselves—to grant tenure. Those who do not want such teaching are more insulated from the pressure of their customers' withdrawal of purchases since the losses of profits are not all imposed on him as his costs. But whatever his degree of opposition and whatever his attitude toward the truth, the cost imposed on him for granting tenure is lower in a non-profit organization. Therefore, because the demand for it is larger and because the gains to the employer from opposing it get smaller, the probability of tenure is increased in non-profit organizations.

It is not necessarily the college president or board of governors whose capricious behavior is made cheaper as a source of personal satisfaction. Many college staffs have attempted to protect themselves from this by having fellow faculty members decide on new appointments, retentions and promotions. This is called democracy, but it is not clear that this makes any difference. Who is to protect the individual faculty member from the equally-cheap-to-exercise personal preferences of his colleagues when they assume the administrative powers?

Everyone wants security, if the cost is zero. And the higher the cost the less they will want. But there is a particular set of employees who will most desire tenure. These are older people, whose productivity is nearing or past its peak. By securing tenure at existing current wages they will be assured of continuing employment, despite declining productivity, at a high wage rate. At the same time all current employees on short-term contracts will be happy to switch to a tenure contract if no cut in pay is involved, for then it would appear as though they had obtained job security without any cost to themselves with all the cost being dumped on the employer. An employer will, of course, resist this, but the extent will depend upon the cost, and in a non-profit institution the costs imposed on the administrator are lower than the same person would bear in the same kind of business if it were a profit-seeking enterprise. Hence the extent to which employers are induced to resist this demand is reduced and tenure is more likely to exist, as are other forms of inefficiency.

But it should not be assumed that all the costs of tenure will be shifted by the employer to society at large. Actually they have also been shifted onto *some* of the employees. Nothing is guaranteed in a tenure contract as to the rate of advance of pay. The employer, once he has granted tenure, may subsequently resist pay increases until the margin between pay and productivity reflects the risk-bearing aspect mentioned earlier. As a partial defense the employees insist on provisions about the rate at which pay will advance. But the beginning rate under tenure will be lower than under non-tenure as a result of the risks of long term contracts. In such arrangements, who proves to be gainers and losers—since this is essentially a vast insurance-type gamble? Individuals who live longest and turn out to be below average in productivity growth gain at the expense of the short-lived in this profession and whose productivity increases the most. Those who had short lives received less of their total productivity. The risk the employer bore was that they, later in life, would be less productive and at that time their wages would not be decreasing. Hence in the earlier part of his career the employee is underpaid in the gamble that later he will over-collect.

Another gamble also occurs. Those who prove to be most productive will have received less than they would have received without tenure, even though they earn more than the average worker. And those who turn out to be below average in productivity growth will earn more than they would have got without tenure, but still they earn less than the average of better workers.

Mobility is penalized because every new job means the task of resolving some doubt in the new employer's mind. This implies that older and less able people, who are now getting a reward more than they are worth, will find very few new job offers elsewhere at equivalent or better wages since no new employer is likely to induce a person to leave a job at which he is currently being overpaid. On the other hand, the better men will be paid less than they are worth and so should be receiving offers from other employers who will offer to narrow the gap.

This does not mean that new employers want to hire only the best people, rather it means that they will find the better people are more willing to move because of the discrepancy of their wages and productivity. Tenure benefits the older, less able people at the expense of the younger, more able and shorter-lived individuals.

If one goes one step farther and assumes that in such a non-profit organization the older people are in authority, as seems likely by virtue of the weaker pecuniary productivity rewards because "profits" are less efficiently used, one would expect the interests of older people to be given greater consideration than that of younger people.

This would be evident in the way facilities and privileges were rationed among the many employees.

The drive for tenure involves compelling most, but not all, employees to accept the tenure system. In many colleges all staff members must acquire tenure—as it is euphemistically stated—at the end of a fixed number of years outside the tenure system. Any member who wants to continue without tenure at a higher wage for a non-tenure appointment is not allowed to do so. To permit this would undermine the position of those in the tenure situation exactly in the same way that a non-member of a cartel is able to undermine the cartel.

Furthermore, if wages are tied to rank, and rank to tenure, it becomes impossible for the younger, more able men to bargain for higher pay without tenure. They are prevented from foregoing tenure in the interests of a higher current wage. In this way tenure is harder to break. If this is so, why should anyone be allowed to teach without tenure? For two reasons: in the first place, a trial period gives the administrator and his colleagues a better idea of what a person's productivity will be—or was. Also, they can get a better idea of whether he will be a compatible, docile, agreeable colleague, or will be obstreperous and overly competitive in what he seeks to do. And if one's colleagues are involved in determining appointment and promotion these questions become even more pertinent. This system has been called democratic. Indeed it is democratic, along the same lines of democracy that would prevail if auto manufacturers were to be the democratic deciders as to who could make cars, or as in fact the medical profession does in deciding who can be a doctor. The question of democracy is a red herring. The correct question is whose tastes and preferences are to be satisfied and who is to bear the gains and the costs, the consumer or one's fellow employees? The second reason for not insisting on tenure for every member is that a non-profit institution may become a "loss" institution and will then have to curtail expenditures. This will mean cutting the staff. But who is to go if all have tenure? To protect those who do have tenure, a buffer, non-permanent group is created to absorb the possible shock.

There is one more institutional factor that also enhances tenure's viability. In addition to student fees, colleges get income from current gifts and from current income from past gifts—the endowment. Consider the extreme of endowed income, where the income is dependent upon how well the endowment is invested and not upon current activities of teaching and research, which do affect student fees and current gifts. Colleges with endowments can and do sell their services at prices less than the cost of the education received by the student. No longer is the old constraint of no losses binding on the administrator. It will be recalled that under a profit-seeking owned institution increments in profits are sought, but under a non-profit institution costs are magnified until they equal income. In each of those cases the extent to which profit or income was sought depended upon their costs relative to other sources of satisfaction that could be obtained with the money available to the institution. Now as we introduce another feature, that of a source of income independent of how well one uses the money to enhance current income, it will be even more in the administrator's interest to devote some more of the income of the institution to sources of satisfaction that do not bring in pecuniary income. In addition, he can more cheaply devote more of his own time to non-pecuniary income-obtaining activities and more to leisure or statesmanship. He can be consciously or unconsciously less efficient in the way he spends the organization's money. Of course, he is still efficiently pursuing his own interests at the new relative costs of various activities. He can use more assistants; he can delegate out to assistants tasks that he would have performed himself; he can also delegate to less able persons and committees. The faculty can be brought more and more into administrative work if they complain about the way he is doing things. He can let them do it, and even if it is more inefficient in the usual sense it will give him a quieter, more placid life among more friendly fellows. And tenure will again be still less costly and the demand for it will be still greater, exactly as outlined earlier. Activities which would not be tolerated by consumers are now more viable, hence more common.

How can the validity of the preceding analysis be established? That it follows directly from the simplest and most powerful economic theorems is subject to a logical test. But more pertinent, for present purposes, is the question, "Is it empirically valid?" What empirically observable results, if observed, would refute the analysis and what would be consistent with it? First, non-profit-seeking schools will be observed to have a higher incidence of tenure than will private profit-seeking schools. And there are both types, so this can be checked. There are hundreds, if not thousands, of privately owned profit-seeking schools. Some survive entirely from student fees. Some of our best accounting and engineering schools are profit-seeking, financed entirely from student fees, as are some girls' colleges. Schools of advertising, art, music, theatre, television, design, secretarial work, foreign languages, law, nursing, beauty shop work, barbering are straight profit-seeking institutions. Here student consumer sovereignty exists jointly with the explictly imposed costs of inefficient behavior. If tenure is not more frequent in non-profit educational institutions the analysis is refuted.

Second, the preceding analysis implies that the incidence of tenure is correlated with the ratio of total income that is covered by endowed income. If such a test were made and the evidence refuted this empirical proposition, the immediately preceding analysis would be conceded to be wrong. However, nothing is implied to the effect that teaching or research will be better or worse as a larger fraction of the income is endowed nor is anything said about the quality of teaching between private profit-seeking and non-profit organizations. The relationship in that respect may be positive, negative or zero and still be consistent with the preceding analysis, even if there were agreement on a measure of good teaching and good research.

It is implied also that tenure should be observed more frequently where rank and pay are tied to tenure than where rank and pay are not tied to tenure. I have not gathered these observable pieces of evidence, but I can illustrate the idea by noting that the extension service at my university teaches much the same courses as the regular university and in it we find full cost pricing for the student and no tenure, nor is pay related to age. The summer session which operates on the same basis also operates with no tenure. Furthermore, it does not invite full professors to teach because they don't earn their way compared with the younger, lower-salaried men. The truth is sometimes concealed by asserting that the young men "need" the jobs.

Purposely excluded from this discussion have been the state-owned schools, not because I teach at one and presented this analysis at another one. Rather, I can't decide whether the taxpayers should be regarded as customers or as endowers. I *conjecture* that they are close to endowers and so would predict that tenure would be more common than in profit-seeking private and in non-profit private schools that are wholly supported by tuition fees, and I would expect tenure to be less frequent than in the most heavily endowed private schools.

Another, and possibly humorous, implication is that the eagerness with which the administrators devote themselves to seeking new sources of revenue, as distinct from gifts, should be inversely related to the fraction of the total income that is endowed. Although less eager, because less rewarding than in a private profit-seeking institution, it will still pay the non-profit-seeking institution to spend some of its money so as to enhance its total revenue. Recall that this was not denied earlier, instead it was merely stated that the rewards obtained from it were less captureable, hence less valuable, than in a private profit-seeking institution. Now, if I may indulge in a bit of by-play, I would predict that football would be more avidly used as a source of income, the smaller the fraction of income covered by endowment. But I shall not pursue that further here.

Other lines of reasoning have been advanced for tenure. It is not entirely clear whether these other reasons attempt to explain why tenure ought to exist, or why it does exist. The analysis presented so far sought to explain why it developed and why it continues to persist. It did not seek to justify tenure. Essentially the analysis said that it developed because it was one way to further the interests of people working for non-profit institutions. However, some proponents of tenure argue that it ensures a higher probability of the truth being taught, or that it gets more of it taught. And some argue that it is necessary if the truth is to be sought and taught. With respect to the first argument, more truth may in fact be taught, but the reason is that if tenure is granted more resources are devoted to teachers than would otherwise be diverted to them. But by what criterion is this judged desirable—except that of inducing a greater demand for one's services?

Or maybe the argument is that greater job security enhances the teaching of the truth. It certainly does, but it also induces one to take his job less carefully and to devote more time to one's politics or social ambitions. The net effect is by no means necessarily, nor even more probably, favorable to greater truth. Neither theoretical analysis nor empirical evidence suggests that result, nor is there anything in economics to imply that compulsory lifetime contracts are more efficient than shorter-term voluntary contracts. In truth quite the contrary is implied.

Could it not be argued alternatively that it is indeed fortunate that colleges are not privately owned, profit-seeking, enterprises, for then tenure would not have survived and without it the search for the truth would have been dissuaded? Therefore these arrangements have grown up in order that the inefficiencies of tenure can be borne in order to preserve the exposition of truth. This would make a virtue of a necessity, if tenure were necessary. To argue that it is, is to ignore the relevance and effect of competition. If there were but one employer of teachers from whose decision there could be no escape, then suppression of the truth would be cheap. With alternative available employers, suppression by one would not prevent other employers from hiring the intimidated individual and paying him to speak his piece. It would pay another employer to hire him if what he had to say were wanted by other people. A new employer may pay less than the former employer. However much this may be distressing to the employee, there is no cause for anyone else to be concerned. No one has any right to compel another person to support him in the style he would like to have, merely because he is, or believes he is, seeking the truth. And yet that is exactly the position taken when one argues that no person ought to be discharged for teaching the truth.

The news industry is an excellent example of the effect of competition. Any newspaper or radio station owner who prints or broadcasts false news will be hurt by other competitors who reveal the truth—not just the polite superficial truth, but all the truth in its most lurid details. While the *New York Times* may be justly proud of its wide coverage, it is debatable as to whether it prints as much truth in depth as some of the more sensational papers, which are sensational primarily because they print more of the facts of some events. Competition among newspapers for profits by catering to the customers' pocketbooks brings out the truth. A news agency could suppress honesty and truth only if it were a protected monopoly, but it would not succeed in the face of competitors who would seek profits by appealing to the consumer's desire for the truth. The truth in news reporting is not the result of tenure for reporters or editors, nor of a code of ethics, and by no stretch of my imagination can I understand why reporters are not just as much in search of the truth as are teachers.

Competition does exist among our schools. Schools that do not satisfy students desires will lose their students; the repute of the school will decline among those people who want honesty in teaching. People who do have different ideas about the truth or who care more for indoctrination in some other ideal will support schools that satisfy their demands, as they are entitled to do. We must acknowledge that such schools have a valid place in our society unless we were to seek to impose our tastes on everyone—a position somewhat incompatible with voluntaristic, individualistic principles.

A criticism of this substitution of competition for tenure is that students and parents can't tell good from bad teaching. I do believe they have ways of discerning good from bad: they can also tell the difference between hard and easy, interesting and dull. And they reveal their choices unmercifully, but in accord with the rules of success that are imposed on them by the colleges that ask of them only grade points unweighted by difficulty or severity or importance of material. As long as we weigh grades only by hours of class work, we should hesitate to say that students cannot discern good from bad or truth from falsity. Furthermore, to the extent that students pay less in fees or tuition than the course is worth, to that extent will they sensibly tolerate inefficiency and bad teaching. Would one say that students who go to Massachusetts Institute of Technology or California Institute of Technology do so without knowledge of the best engineering schools? If the students can't tell good from bad teaching, one has to wonder how they manage to choose among colleges?

It may be true that some students can't tell a true theorem from a false one. But so long as some students can detect the difference, they will challenge the teacher. And, furthermore, a teacher will challenge his colleague's teaching when he thinks he detects error in it. The ethic of not criticizing one's colleagues, or competitors, in the fashion of the medical profession, is a very dangerous one to the discernment of the truth. Of course, some of the ideas taught are incapable of being proven true or false. They are recital of doctrines and preferences, and economists certainly are not free of this fault. We shouldn't be alarmed if we then find students unable to detect truth from falsity; there may be none to detect. There may be just accuracy of note taking.

What if consumers do not want the truth and instead want romance and illusion? The theatre and the movies are much more efficient at that than the teachers are. Fiction writers may have outclassed teachers for many centuries. And in any event, so much the worse for tenure, for then those who want tenure to foster the truth, if such it did, would be trying to impose their preference on other people. To assert that some college officials do not always want the truth and that some alumni or outsiders criticise the teacher and seek to get him fired is certainly true—and commendable. If the truth harms or offends some people, in a free society why should they not have the right to use their resources to combat it? Others may desire the truth even more, and be willing to pay for it. When I buy a house, the fact that I outbid the other bidders means that someone else did not get what he otherwise would have got. And so it is with the bidding for the truth. If someone prefers to buy up the time of teachers to induce them not to speak the truth he is entitled to do so. And if he tries to buy up a college president in order to persuade him not to continue to hire a certain teacher he is entitled to do so. Teachers have no claim on the resources of society or of any person. The crucible of the truth is open competition among ideas, although ideas are costly.

A question still hangs over my head. Why do non-profit-seeking subsidized schools exist if they are less efficient, as revealed by the willingness to make inefficient labor contracts. The answer, I think, lies in two places. One is our state school system, in which the state, through its taxing power, not only subsidizes education but also administers the state schools on a non-full-cost tuition basis. Even the most efficient private profit-seeking business would have a difficult time surviving, if survival is possible, in any endeavor where the taxing power is used to support a competitor. The non-state, non-owned private schools, can survive only if they too are given subsidies. If the tax-supported education were instead given to students as tuition grants in the fashion of the G.I. educational benefits, there would be a chance for the private profit-seeking school to provide us with a test of efficient education and truth seeking.[4] But barring that change in our educational structure there seems little hope for avoiding the inefficiencies of the non-profit-seeking non-owned educational system. The efforts of many people to help education will take the form of grants to institutions if they are non-profit, whereas such grants would not occur if they were profit-making. If they were profit-seeking, the grant would merely go into the owners' pockets. Under a private profit-seeking school arrangement, givers would be induced to give to students or to set up charities for students rather than for schools, much on the lines of the Guggenheim and Carnegie grants. But if non-profit institutions exist, it will be possible to aid education via grants to schools, although such grants will be less efficient than direct grants to students.

The answer lies, second, in that special and legal advantages given to a non-profit institution have enabled it to grow and survive, and with it the particular feature developed in this analysis. The persistence of the non-profit college arises, not from its ability to support tenure and the search for the truth, but rather from legal and tax advantages given it, and the granting of gifts to the college rather than to students. And even with these aids it is highly doubtful that it will be able to survive against the tax-subsidized support of the state

[4] M. Friedman, "The Role of Government in Education," in R. Solo (ed.), *Economics and the Public Interest* (New Brunswick, N.J., 1955).

schools. Admittedly, these last remarks about the reasons for the existence of non-profit schools are based on personal conjecture.

In sum, the conclusion suggested is that tenure is neither necessary nor efficient. Its survival depends upon the absence of private ownership and also is encouraged by subsidization of education by non-customer income sources. Without a private profit-seeking system and without full cost tuition, the demand for tenure increases and the cost of granting it appears to be cheaper because the full costs are not imposed on those granting it. Competition among schools, teachers, and students provides protection to the search for the truth without tenure. Just as in the dissemination of news, the exposition of the search for the truth is tested in the open market for ideas and empirical verification. Truth is not something given the stamp of authority or validity by appointed persons. Authority cannot establish what people will believe is the truth. The individual must do that. Truth then is no higher an objective than that of voluntary individualism. The two are not incompatible. Indeed, what does one mean in the absence of the other?

As a test of whether or not my exposition has been even moderately successful, let me quote a passage from a far better than average defense of tenure. If the passage now appears humorous or transparent I will have passed the test.

> The demand we of the academic world make for academic freedom is not made primarily for our own benefit. We enjoy the exercise of freedom; but the purposes of liberty lie, in a democracy, in the common welfare. It has recently been said, "With regard to some occupations, it is eminently in the interest of society that the men concerned speak their minds without fear of retribution. . . . The occupational work of the vast majority of people is largely independent of their thought and speech. The professor's work consists of his thought and speech. If he loses his position for what he writes or says, he will, as a rule, have to leave his profession, and may no longer be able effectively to question and challenge accepted doctrines or effectively to defend challenged doctrines. And if *some* professors lose their positions for what they write or say, the effect on many other professors will be such that their usefulness to their students and to society will be gravely reduced."

We ask then for the maintenance of academic freedom and of the civil liberties of scholars, not as a special right, but as a means whereby we may make our appointed contributions to the life of the commonwealth and share equitably, but not more than equitably, in the American heritage.[5]

[5] American Association of University Professors, "Academic Freedom and Tenure in the Quest for National Security, Report of a Special Committee," *AAUP Bulletin*, Vol. XLII, No. 1 (Spring, 1956), pp. 54–55.

Index